Advance Praise for *A Thicker Jesus*

"Has anybody worried about the Sermon on the Mount in Bonhoeffer's theology as much as Glen Stassen? His grappling with that issue in this book—as much witness and advocacy as theological and ethical monograph—will provoke debate. So will his 'incarnational theology of the cross' as describing Bonhoeffer's treatment of atonement. But nobody will contest his focus on the powerful incarnational Christology as the key in Bonhoeffer's theology to 'transcending the bifurcation between the ideal and the real.'"

—Clifford Green, Executive Director of Dietrich Bonhoeffer Works
and professor emeritus at Hartford Seminary

"Glen Stassen has contributed steadily and constructively to Christian ethics for decades. *A Thicker Jesus* is, however, clearly his magnum opus. All that has gone before comes together here as 'incarnational discipleship.' But it also goes beyond, to give us solid ground in a very uncertain time. This was worth the wait!"

—Larry Rasmussen, Reinhold Niebuhr Professor Emeritus
of Social Ethics at Union Theological Seminary, New York City;
author of *Dietrich Bonhoeffer: Reality and Resistance*

"Stassen offers a relevant, concrete, and theologically rich method for doing Christian ethics in 'a secular age.' Discerning common characteristics shaping the ethics of historical figures we admire, he invites readers into this 'tradition of incarnational discipleship' based on a realistic Jesus, the lordship of Christ, and the need for continuous repentance from ideologies that hold Christians captive. This is Stassen's legacy to the field of Christian ethics."

—Jennifer McBride, Wartburg College, author of
The Church for the World: A Theology of Public Witness

"Stassen has accomplished in this book, a solid argument that helps to provide concrete ethical guidance from the life and teachings of Jesus. . . . Stassen's method advocates real-life discipleship in the church, and in the larger society, that moves us beyond a Christianity of thin principles that wind up slipping into harmful ideologies and turning Jesus into a representative of injustice. What we need is a thicker Jesus!"

—Reggie Williams, Assistant Professor of Christian Ethics,
McCormick Theological Seminary

"This broad-ranging conversation about the meaning of Christian faith in a secular age sets forth a vital Christian ethics for the twenty-first century, a masterpiece of empathetic encounter and engagement."

—Cheryl J. Sanders, Professor of Christian Ethics,
Howard University School of Divinity and author of *Ministry
at the Margins* and *Empowerment Ethics for a Liberated People*

D1036559

A Thicker Jesus

Incarnational Discipleship in a Secular Age

GLEN HAROLD STASSEN

WESTMINSTER
JOHN KNOX PRESS
LOUISVILLE · KENTUCKY

First edition
Published by Westminster John Knox Press
Louisville, Kentucky

12 13 14 15 16 17 18 19 20 21—10 9 8 7 6 5 4 3 2 1

Book design by Sharon Adams
Cover design by Eric Walljasper, Minneapolis, MN
Cover illustration: © Tina Lorien/istockphoto.com

Library of Congress Cataloging-in-Publication Data

Stassen, Glen Harold, 1936–
   A thicker Jesus : incarnational discipleship in a secular age / by Glen H. Stassen.
   p. cm.
   Includes index.
   ISBN 978-0-664-23817-9 (alk. paper)
   1. Christianity and culture. 2. Secularism. 3. Jesus Christ—Example. 4. Christian ethics. 5. Bonhoeffer, Dietrich, 1906–1945. 6. Taylor, Charles, 1931– Secular age. I. Title.
   BR115.C8S725 2012
   261—dc23

                          2012013170

Most Westminster John Knox Press books are available at special quantity discounts when purchased in bulk by corporations, organizations, and special-interest groups. For more information, please e-mail SpecialSales@wjkbooks.com.

To my father, Harold E. Stassen

I pray for his integrity, and for one-tenth of his wisdom.

Contents

List of Illustrations

Preface

We are all influenced by our culture. I come from a humble German-immigrant family in Minnesota, the North Star State. My father grew up on a small farm with twenty acres of tomatoes, and was the only one of my parents and fifteen aunts and uncles to earn a college education. But he became the youngest governor in the history of the United States, was a founder of the United Nations, and had a promising political future, which he sacrificed in order to try to warn the nation and his party against what he saw as an immoral, Machiavellian future of unrestrained greed if it would choose Richard Nixon as its leader. He had prophetic insight and wisdom, and he was committed to human rights for all, including racial minorities. He was also a committed Christian, with never a scandal, and became president of the American Baptist Convention. He greatly influenced my own decision to become a Christian ethicist.

But the worst thing to do in Minnesota culture would be to "put on airs." So I have never written of my father, Harold E. Stassen, thinking I might seem to be claiming something about myself because of the historical accident that I did nothing to deserve—having him as my dad. I did not realize how much this book testifies to his integrity and formative influence until now, as I am finishing it and looking back. Partly that comes from just having read the manuscript for a biography of Dad by Alec Kirby, David Dalin, and John Rothman, *Harold E. Stassen: The Life and Perennial Candidacy of the Progressive Republican* (Jefferson, NC: McFarland Press, 2012). Now it is time finally to say a public, deeply felt thank-you to Dad. But this book is not about him. For that you need the book the three others have written. Except now I see that it *is* about him, indirectly and subconsciously—by formative influence.

Minnesota culture values humility, and also integrity. And populism. It believes in government of the people, by the people, and for the people, and in funding public education well. This is one explanation for its low unemployment rate, even in the time of the Great Recession of 2008. Companies want to hire Minnesotans, because they are well educated and have integrity and humility. So I write plain English, aiming my books to be readable by ordinary people. Students often tell me that they can understand what I have written more readily than other books they read. I hope you agree—even though I am arguing for a way of doing Christian ethics that I think offers more solid ground than the way you may be used to doing ethics.

I deeply believe churches need renewal. Mainline churches need a clearer and deeper theology and ethics, and theology needs to focus on a thicker Jesus. To paraphrase Bonhoeffer, people don't want to know what some church leaders want; they want to know what Jesus wants.[1] Evangelical churches and seeker-friendly churches need a thicker Jesus to guard their members against being coopted by political ideologies that are leading both churches and nation to judgment for unfaithfulness to the way of Jesus, by which I do not mean unfaithfulness to a particular political ideology. Because I deeply believe churches and church members need renewal, I do try to write clearly so people can understand what I mean. As our former pastor, Wyatt Tee Walker often said, "I just want to make it plain."

I am also significantly influenced by intentionally choosing to go to school in the border-South of Virginia, Kentucky, and North Carolina, and by my friendly acquaintance with William Faulkner many afternoons at the University of Virginia. My wife and all three sons are native Southerners. So sometimes I write a little more openly, personally, and narratively rather than pretending to be totally "objective." I am hoping that my confessional narrative style, or historical drama style, will stimulate some new thinking—and new doing. I am hoping not merely to make you comfortable in old ways of thinking, but to stretch you a little. I am counting on you to be personally open to some new exploration here and there.

I appreciate what my students say—that I am readily understandable. But the downside is that scholars may not notice that I am making what I hope is a sophisticated, scholarly, even, in a sense, scientific argument for method in Christian ethics: I am too readable, so I must not be scholarly. I am too concerned about church people, some sophisticated scholars might think. True; I am; and I write hoping for church renewal. As the teenage Dietrich Bonhoeffer said, reminded of some deep problems in the church, "In that case, I will reform the church."[2]

Despite all this, I have nevertheless experienced more affirmation from fellow scholars than I probably deserve. So I am counting on scholars, too, to notice what is happening here. I am arguing for a change, maybe even a reformation, based on enough openness to assess the evidence of the data of history. It is a constructive argument, not merely a history; but it pays attention to history as the laboratory in which our faith is tested, as H. Richard Niebuhr advocated, and in which our faith is challenged, as Charles Taylor argues.

I begin with an assessment of which ethicists actually stood the test in difficult historical times. For example, I believe that Dietrich Bonhoeffer came through in astoundingly threatening times. He will show up fairly often, because he saw the vision that we desperately need. But this is not a study of Bonhoeffer. It is an effort to carry forward what he pointed to. He was executed in one of Hitler's last dastardly acts before Hitler committed suicide. We need to continue to carry on Bonhoeffer's work, to develop what he was hoping for. I wrote a readers' theatre on Bonhoeffer that you can access on the Web and perhaps perform.[3]

I ask whether some features of Bonhoeffer's ethics and of those others who came through in other testing times help explain their integrity, courage, and perspicacity. The answer is incarnational discipleship. I hope to show how this kind of ethic has been validated as solid ground. We surely need some solid ground in these shifting times.

Then I take Charles Taylor's *A Secular Age* as an insightful and perceptive diagnosis of the causes of secularism. These causes of secularism are challenges for Christian faith. How can we develop a faith and an ethics that suggest helpful answers for the challenges of secularism? Can incarnational discipleship provide strong answers? If it can, then it is doubly validated.

My way of thinking is incurably curious and integrative: I can't do theology and ethics without attention to numerous related disciplines, and Charles Taylor's challenges give me more than an excuse to do so. So get ready for a ride through several different kinds of territory.

I thank Susan Wood, David Gushee, Ron Sanders, Hak Joon Lee, Oliver Crisp, Ray Anderson, Marc Gopin, Sameer Yadav, Jonathan Rothchild, Patrick Coleman, Brant Himes, Norman Kraus, Joel Green, Andrew Wright, and Jim Purves—and thank those present for the International Bonhoeffer Society meeting in Prague, those attending the Nordenhaug Lectures at the International Baptist Theological Seminary, and those who participated in the National Association of Baptist Professors of Religion's annual meeting at Baylor University—for reading or hearing all or parts of these chapters and helping to make this a book readers can like. Jana Riess is simply the best editor I have ever worked with; you will be grateful to her without even knowing where you should be feeling that gratitude.

PART 1
INCARNATIONAL
DISCIPLESHIP

Chapter 1

Who Stands the Test of History?

The Ground Is Shifting

Ours is an age of interaction, mobility, and change. Unlike most of our grandparents, many of us have moved several times in our lifetimes and have seen our neighbors move in and out. We are more intensely aware, even in our own neighborhoods, that our kind of faith is not the only kind. We see how others have been shaped by very different histories than our own. It becomes clear to us that we, too, have been shaped—and continue to be shaped—by our own history.

Fuller Theological Seminary, where I teach, is in California. Every now and then we feel the ground shifting. The chandelier in our dining room swings or the bed on which we are lying begins to rock. The whole world may not be experiencing little earthquakes as we are, but people are surely experiencing change and variety in faiths and ideologies. This change and diversity can rock a person's faith. We ask, How do we validate the truth of what we perceive and what we believe? In our time of pluralistic encounter with multiple ideologies and religions and with rapid social, economic, and political change, people search for what Dietrich Bonhoeffer called solid ground to stand on.[1]

Philip Clayton teaches at Claremont Theological Seminary in California. He attended the mainline Presbyterian church that had been his church home since elementary school, plus an evangelical Bible study group, a charismatic prayer meeting once a week in a Pentecostal church, the Assemblies of God church, and a community of "Jesus People." He writes,

> Most of us know friends, colleagues, or acquaintances who are Christian, Jewish, Muslim; Buddhist, Hindu, Taoist; atheist, agnostic, "doubting believers"; pantheist, panentheist, neo-pagan; Mormon, Jehovah's Witness, Church of God; Baha'i, Zoroastrian, perennialist—the list goes on and on. Faced with such a confusing array of options, more and more Americans are choosing not to choose. . . . You have to admit, pretty much everything these days is up for grabs. We are in the midst of the most rapid social and technological change that our species has ever undergone.[2]

Not all of us have had as diverse experiences as Philip. Ever since my own conversion experience and baptism at age eleven, I have been a loyal Baptist—though six different kinds of Baptist. Yet all of us at least have religious diversity in our sphere of awareness. We can identify with Bonhoeffer when he asks, "have there ever been people in history who in their time, like us, had so little ground under their feet . . . ?"[3]

In a book on leadership for the missional church, Alan Roxburgh writes,

> People are losing their orientation. The political, social, and economic systems that brought prosperity over the past fifty years no longer function and people see no alternatives. They feel caught in a web of change they neither understand nor control. The result is a high level of anxiety, insecurity, and confusion. At the same time, most people have no words to explain these experiences nor names for the forces shaping their lives and creating insecurity.[4]

Not only do we need a sense of having our feet on the ground, a clear sense of our own identity; we need to know how that identity helps us navigate the multiple shifting changes around us. It feels as if other cultures are changing our rapidly globalizing world, and we wish we understood them more thoughtfully. In *A Thicker Jesus*, I am asking two questions: (1) how to find a faithful and solid identity for faith and ethics; and (2) how that identity can be a compass in our rapidly changing and interactive age. Specifically, here I seek orientation in relation to the secularizing forces in our age. Charles Taylor's important book *A Secular Age* argues that

> we have undergone a change in our condition, involving both an alteration of the structures we live within, and our way of imagining these structures. . . . The developments of Western modernity have destabilized and rendered virtually unsustainable earlier forms of religious life, but new forms have sprung up. . . . As a result the religious life of Western societies is much more fragmented than ever before, and also much more unstable, as people change their positions during a lifetime, or between generations, to a greater degree than ever before.[5]

Fearing we are losing our solid basis and our orientation amongst the surrounding changes can lead some to reactionary authoritarianism. Presently we see many Muslims reacting against the influence of Western Enlightenment in their societies, as some seek certainty in a reactionary kind of Islam. Fundamentalists in the United States a century ago might have understood such a response against Enlightenment modernism. Fritz Stern's study, *The Politics of Cultural Despair,* shows that in Germany during the early twentieth century—another time of unsettling change—three popular German philosophers (Paul de Lagarde, Julius Langbehn, and Moeller van den Bruck) wrote in reaction against the Enlightenment.[6] The Enlightenment reduced truth to allegedly universal principles, and swept the wisdom of particular communities and particular faiths aside. It influenced churches as well as public ethics to thin down their teaching to generic maxims that lost the particular sense of identity and the confrontational power of biblical narrative. In their reaction, the three German philosophers lusted for homogeneous community—which in a world of diversity requires authoritarianism to maintain. That homogeneous community became German nationalism of blood and soil. Thus they prepared the way for fascism. Their authoritarianism supported policies to exclude diversity—Jews especially, but also Poles, communists, homosexuals, and even the disabled. It supported a militaristic reaction against the punitive and degrading Versailles Treaty forced on Germany when it lost World War I. This facilitated Hitler's forceful takeover of Czechoslovakia and Poland and then World War II against France, Belgium, Holland, Russia, and England, and eventually the United States. The drive toward nationalistic homogeneity became exclusionary, militaristic, and war-supporting.

My father resigned as governor of Minnesota to enlist in the Navy and fight in World War II against such authoritarianism, and for a painful time of deep grief we thought he had been killed in that war. I have experienced the backlash of authoritarianism myself in the civil rights struggle and in the aftereffects from unresolved issues in that struggle. I was formed by three generations of family who shared a deep commitment to helping people find ground to stand on that gives normative guidance—but not an authoritarian mandate that excludes everyone different from us. It combined a thick understanding of identity in Jesus with commitment to human rights for all. Although I, too, have been developing my own theological ethics all my life as a criticism of the Enlightenment rationalism that has so thinned out the basis of Christian ethics, I hope that from Fritz Stern's account of the dangers of reaction we can learn to do ethics another way than authoritarian reaction.

Yet alongside authoritarian reactions to the fear and uncertainty of shaky ground, another response has led to secularism. Charles Taylor shows that in a society where state authority is closely connected with church authority, or where authoritarian fundamentalism co-opts the claim to speak for Christianity, many react against authoritarianism and become secularists. Or they dissolve faith into subjectivism, privatistic normlessness, situationism, freedom as individualistic autonomy, avant-gardism, or an inward emigration out of covenant responsibility for the common good. Then we get a society of disconnected or cynical individuals who are more concerned with self-seeking than civic responsibility.[7] We hear subjectivistic assertions of "my rights" that oppose civic responsibility. We see opposition to social safety nets for the vulnerable and the poor—an attitude that says, in effect, "Let them fend for themselves." We spawn interest groups that seek only their own interests and not the common good. We get self-centered consumerism that erodes neighborhoods, churches, and cooperative action for the common good.[8]

Some churches seek to avoid offending any members, and so steer clear of controversial issues and confrontations. This is "Enlightenment lite": it reduces the gospel to private matters or general principles that do not clash with interests and ideologies. These churches fail to confront members in ways that provide the guidance we need in our lives, and they avoid addressing injustices and problems that threaten us. They offer something far removed from the Jesus in the gospels who challenges the religious and social complacency of his generation. Sociological studies show that church members feel they need more specific instruction, even confrontation that calls us to grow in discipleship. Lacking this, "Enlightenment lite" churches lack the depth of commitment and the vigor they need to avoid the decline and decay that constitute a growing crisis.[9]

Our question is this: How do we find the solid ground for an ethic that is neither authoritarian nor merely privatistic? How can we validate an ethic that can provide theologically sound and practically relevant footing in our secular age? How can we discover solid ground? And from that solid ground, how can we find orientation in a changing, confusing, and secular age?

TESTING TRADITION

Alasdair MacIntyre argues for doing ethics within a tradition, defined as "an historically extended, socially embodied argument."[10] Life is too complicated for any one of us to work out all the questions alone. We need to participate in an ongoing discussion in which others are also working out answers. We need a community, friends with whom we can parse the meaning of things. But which tradition? Whose ongoing argument? As Michael Walzer says, most of us are embedded in a number of traditions and have "Divided Selves."[11] We may make philosophical arguments for one tradition, but in our age of awareness when we know that our perspectives are strongly influenced by our own social, philosophical, ideological, and theological location and history, arguments for our own tradition may not be convincing for others—or even for ourselves. Additionally, the equally important question is, How does a tradition engage in self-correction, or continuous repentance? Awareness that traditions are shaped by theological, social, and historical interactions tells us we need humility and a commitment to change. Any tradition needs a process of continuous repentance—learning and self-correction.

MacIntyre also argues for learning from "epistemological crises," when a tradition is not finding adequate answers to challenges it faces. Charles Taylor's *A Secular Age* can help us do this. Taylor insightfully identifies major challenges that Christianity faces. Both MacIntyre and Taylor are saying, in their somewhat different ways, that we cannot simply insist on the rightness of our tradition as if it were the absolute and unchangeable authority. A degenerate tradition that can't adjust but stays rigid and authoritarian—or a reactionary tradition that won't adjust but becomes defensively fundamentalist—refuses Jesus' call to continuous repentance.

Every tradition has some truth and some error in it: "For all alike have sinned" (Rom. 3:23 NEB)—and that "all" includes traditions. Jesus replied to the scribes and Pharisees, "Why do you break the commandment of God for the sake of your tradition?" (Matt. 15:3). Most of us want to find solid ground in a way that tests what is right and wrong in our traditions. Furthermore, any tradition is an ongoing discussion; it includes different voices, and it is always growing—or maybe stultifying. We can't work without a tradition, but we also need ways of being called to continuous repentance within that tradition or traditions. Most Christians seek deeper grounding in the bedrock that Jesus Christ is Lord. "On Christ the Solid Rock I Stand." That is different from insisting that everything I think, or my tradition thinks, is always right. Jesus says, "repent, for the kingdom of God has come near" (Matt. 3:2). The Christian life is continuous repenting, continuous learning.

HUMILITY

In fact, humility may be a major part of learning now as we experience many different perspectives, different loyalties, different faiths or convictions, and different kinds of ethics. We may be learning a little humility about our own knowing. But then how do we still hold our faith with conviction?

In the time of the Enlightenment, Immanuel Kant, who had a prodigious mind, concluded that logic dictated two principles: always treat others as ends, and not only as means to our ends; and only affirm principles that we could resolve that everyone would affirm, universally. Utilitarians argue for a different principle: do whatever is for the greatest happiness (or greatest or highest good) for the largest number of people. John Rawls argues for two principles: the priority of basic liberties and the distribution of social and economic inequalities so that they maximize benefit to the least advantaged and are open to all with fair equality of opportunity.

But what is becoming clear to us is that people's ethics in actual practice is not determined merely by these thin principles of reasoning. Our ethics is strongly formed by the historical influences that shape the various dimensions of our loyalties, perceptions, and convictions. These historically formed loyalties shape our actions more powerfully than a thin rational principle that lacks historical and emotional context.[12] Therefore, trying to validate an ethic by an allegedly universal principle is no longer convincing. No one has a universal perspective. What people actually do is strongly shaped by what they see happening, by how they perceive the actual context in which they are acting. Their thin principles take on very different meanings depending on their basic convictions, the faith-narratives that give their lives meaning. This is why David Gushee and I advocate a *holistic* character ethics: ethical character depends on basic loyalties and passions, on ways of perceiving, and on basic convictions as well as on ways of reasoning.[13] And these are shaped by traditions as well as ideologies. To understand our own ethics and the ethics of others we relate to, we need awareness of the various dimensions that shape us and them.

For example, in 1914, at the beginning of World War I, Karl Barth wrote that loyalties and ideologies were manipulating and corrupting faith: "For me, the saddest thing in these sad times is to see how in all of Germany now, love for the Fatherland, delight in war, and Christian faith are brought together in hopeless confusion." Barth scholar Bruce McCormack comments that Barth's primary concern was "what he saw as a manipulation of religious experience to legitimate the most sinful and catastrophic of human actions."[14]

And during World War II, Dietrich Bonhoeffer saw that ethical ideals based on our autonomous reason cannot face the reality of evil that manipulates and undermines those very ideals. Followers of these idealistic ethical theories piously deceive themselves when they view themselves as good and true. By refusing to face their own sin and complicity in the sin of society, they may fail to identify enormous evil, such as that of the Third Reich.[15]

Barth and Bonhoeffer were calling for a deeper understanding of solidarity in sin and for an ethic of profound repentance for manipulation by ideologies, loyalties, and interests. With historical hindsight, we can learn from both of them.

HISTORY AS THE LABORATORY
IN WHICH FAITH IS TESTED

So we are aware of being shaped by history. We interact with others who see things differently because of their own peculiar historical backgrounds. We know that we see what we see from our own place in history. We recognize that we cannot stand in a universal rational location above history in order to test an ethic. We understand that we are moved by diverse historical influences in ways deeper than we can identify. In that case, what kind of validation of an ethic can work?

The logical step must be to adopt a method that acknowledges the reality of historical perspective. Awareness of our and others' historicity suggests that validation works best from within our historical limits—by historical testing. We can assess how a particular ethic has worked out in its history—whether it has supported faithfulness or unfaithful behavior. We can examine historical times when, with hindsight, we agree widely, despite our different ethical perspectives, on who passed and who failed, who was faithful and who was unfaithful. For example, Bonhoeffer was faithful in recognizing the injustice of Hitler from the start and speaking out for Jews earlier and more clearly than others. By contrast, theologians Gerhard Kittel, Paul Althaus, Emmanuel Hirsch, Walter Grundmann, and others failed to see rightly and gave their support to Hitler and to his anti-Semitism. We can ask what in Bonhoeffer's ethics enabled him to see so truly while others failed.

When we test an ethic by its historical fruits, we are part of a long Hebraic tradition. Israel emerged from mythopoeic thinking by searching for a realistic understanding of what goes wrong in history and how it can be corrected. God was revealed not somewhere above history, but in actual history—in the Exodus and in the actual historical life of the people and their rulers. This means history itself had become "a revelation of the dynamic will of God. . . . The doctrine of a single, unconditioned, transcendent God rejected time-honored values, proclaimed new ones, and postulated a metaphysical significance for history."[16]

This engendered the biblical expectation of an order to history, since God is faithful. Like Leo Tolstoy, Mahatma Gandhi, Martin Luther King, and John Howard Yoder closer to our time, they had cosmic faith that God is working patiently and sometimes surprisingly through history to bring deliverance and community. As King famously said, "there is something in the universe that unfolds for justice."[17] So the biblical prophets studied history to learn God's will, and to learn where Israel had made errors and should seek correction.

But the Israelites did not assume they knew the pattern merely by rational thinking. God says "my ways are higher than your ways" (Isa. 55:9). Therefore, discerning the pattern required attention to the actual data of history. God wills justice and faithfulness and interacts with specific human actions. The Israelites paid attention to empirical data about their own actions and to historical patterns and historical outcomes. God called people and nations to repentance for unfaithfulness and injustice, threatened judgment, and promised deliverance—in real history. So the Chroniclers and the Prophets pointed out the unfaithfulness and injustice, and the disasters, exiles, and judgments that resulted within real history.

At the same time that Greece emerged from mythopoeic thinking by a philosophical search for rational order and consistency, Hebraic thinking emerged by paying attention to faithfulness and unfaithfulness in actual history, and to the peace and justice that resulted or the injustice, war, and judgment that took place.

We can notice the significance of Hebraic attention to historical data by contrast with its neighbors when we notice Henrik Frankfort's observation that the literature of Egypt and Babylonia lacks the historical realism of Israel's description of its leaders, "astonishingly real in their mixture of ugliness and beauty, pride and contrition, achievement and failure."[18] The literature of

Israel's neighbors before the sixth century BCE was mythopoeic thinking about gods above history, beyond our knowing, beyond our ability to test the truths of the stories. "A cosmogonic myth is beyond discussion. It describes a sequence of sacred events, which one can either accept or reject. But no cosmogony can become part of a progressive and cumulative increase of knowledge."[19] The pharaohs of Egypt were considered to be gods; the literature of Egypt never told of their errors or their need for correction. If anyone was blamed for what went wrong, it was underlings or foreigners. Mythopoeic thinking tends to keep people subservient to the dominating myths and authorities, without checking and balancing their injustices and their powers by realistic historical testing.

Hebraic thinking does realistic historical testing with the actual data of history. Why would that not be a good procedure for us in our time of awareness of the influence of historical differences?

TESTING BY HISTORICAL DRAMA AS A SPECIFIC GENRE OF NARRATIVE

Many ethicists and theologians are adopting narrative methods as a corrective for the thinness of Enlightenment thinking. When we use a method of testing how an ethic works out in actual history, we are adopting a specific variety of narrative method: *historical drama*.

I want to pick up the trail blazed by my beloved former colleague, James Wm. McClendon, who pioneered narrative theology with his *Biography as Theology* in 1974 and his "Three Strands of Christian Ethics" in 1978, and then his *Ethics* in 1986 and 2002, [20] with their attention to embodied historicity. McClendon saw that he was pioneering a resumption of Hebraic method. He wrote that Martin Luther King Jr. got his activism from the importance for African American tradition of the Exodus and Moses. King "enabled his followers to see that the lesson of the Old Testament, the lesson that God was doing things in history, was true of Black folk in America now. . . . What this shows us is that we must press behind the New Testament to the Old in order to understand the religion of Martin King. King's use of the image of oppressive Pharaohs, Hebrews longing for freedom from Egypt, the threatening wilderness, and the Promised Land in his writing [often] took the form of incisive metaphors" that made sense of the struggle of the civil rights movement.[21] Particularly in the Old Testament King discovered "two elements of his faith, man's own role and the role of the God of history, held together in productive tension."[22]

McClendon's subjects played a public role in the history that we have participated in, that we can validate, and that shapes our "character-in-community."[23] In addition to Martin Luther King Jr., he writes of Clarence Jordan, Dag Hammarskjöld, Charles Ives, Ludwig Wittgenstein, Jonathan and Sarah Edwards,

Dietrich Bonhoeffer, and Dorothy Day. McClendon sees in all of these figures: "a oneness, a wholeness, a holiness not otherwise available to them or to us. Their lives witness to their vision, even as they challenge the depth of our own. So there comes the question, not so much of the suitability of their vision to their own circumstances, but of the justification of our present way of life when held against theirs."[24]

If we pay attention to McClendon's theological ethics, we realize that by "our," he means not only single individuals but also our communities. He wrote biography not only to witness to the validity of others' vision but also to challenge our own vision. He said this character-forming function plus attention to historical accuracy and validation makes biography a form of story well suited to Christian faith.[25]

Because of this attention to historical accuracy, to character formation, and to community rather than only to individual readers, I prefer to speak not only of "story" but also of "historical drama" as the most helpful form of narrative theology and ethics.[26] Many think of "story" as fiction merely to be read for entertainment by individuals sitting in an easy chair. And often the "narrative" that a nation or corporation, or even a church, tells of itself is fashioned, intentionally or unintentionally, to gloss over unfaithful parts of its history and to defend its own interests. It resembles ideology designed to defend interest and power. Or it resembles mythopoeic thinking. This is why James McClendon points to corrections by the realism of Augustine and Sigmund Freud.[27]

Because I intend to test kinds of ethics by their faithfulness in actual history, and actual history includes important dimensions of community and power that are often overlooked in our individualistic culture, I want to explain briefly what I mean by "historical drama" as the genre of narrative that I advocate. Here are twelve characteristics of historical drama as I understand them:

1. Historical drama is written with historical realism and attention to accuracy, even though it is condensed in order to make a witness, like the Gospels of the New Testament and the accounts of the Old Testament. As fits John Howard Yoder's argument in *Politics of Jesus*, it corrects a docetic, or spiritualizing interpretation of Jesus.
2. It is not only read like a novel, but enacted, embodied, incarnated, as in a drama performed in community. For Christians, it is originally enacted by Israel and by Jesus and the disciples, and then read or performed in community with shared response, and meant to be enacted, embodied, by the drama's "audience"—communities of disciples in their own ways of living.[28] A secular audience in the performance of a drama, and certainly a church congregation in worship, is not merely learning abstract information or abstract doctrine (modernist), and not merely being entertained for the moment (romantic), but is having their lives and selfhood shaped by experiencing the drama.

3. Therefore, historical drama is contextual; the actors or worship leaders take account of the community experiencing the drama, and they interpret the text in differing ways according to their understanding of the meaning of the text for the community's context.

4. The community is not merely passive, but participates in the enactment and in the drama's reshaping of their own ways of perceiving and acting.[29] Furthermore, the actors or worship leaders interact with the community's response.[30]

5. The actors do not simply make up the play as they proceed; they have a responsibility to the written text that they are enacting and to its central dramatic thrust.[31] For Christians, the central dramatic thrust is Jesus' embodiment of the reign of God as fulfillment of the Old Testament and his confronting the powers and authorities who resist repenting and instead have Jesus crucified, and Jesus' nonviolent victory over them.[32]

6. Therefore, as Richard Hays says, the actors need to do respectful exegesis of the written text; they need to study the subtleties intended in the text—respectfully and not irresponsibly—not merely imposing their own ideologies on the text; and they also need to consider how they can convey the drama in the text in the social context of the gathered audience.[33]

7. And therefore, as James McClendon and Heinz Eduard Tödt say, ethics is in the theology at its very base.[34] We do not only write theological doctrines and then derive ethics from the doctrines; the written text has ethics embedded in it throughout.

8. Historical drama displays the reality of social conflict with powers and authorities. If we think of "story" and "narrative" in our individualistic and power-manipulated suppressive culture, then we risk a romanticism that paints over the power conflicts and clashes of interests that realism sees.

9. Society provides roles that the actors both embody and struggle with, or against, since they and the roles may not fit each other. Did Jesus fit the role of Messiah, Suffering Servant, prophet, Rabbi-teacher, Son of David, Son of God?[35] Yes, but he also redefined the roles.

10. Like a historical drama, biblical narrative has specific basis in real history of sinful people—not just Platonic ideals or romantic fantasies.

11. Historical drama is not merely the inner subjective life of one person; it is about interactions and relationships, the struggle for and against faithfully fulfilling covenants with one another.

12. Historical drama enacts time as events that participate in the next events, time as continuous action in participative duration, not discrete moments that are separated from each other as one street is a block away from another. This is how we regularly sense the meaning of our own lives and the lives of our communities

and congregations—as participants in a true, historical drama, not merely fiction.

As you can see, I contend that "historical drama" is a more accurate understanding of a biblically influenced way of thinking than the generic term "narrative." And actually, when we quietly think of our lives, we don't think of them in a fairy tale, but in the historical drama in which we are actually living. At least that is true if we are being halfway realistic. And surely that is true of the lives we are about to assess, in the midst of their real historical dramas.

HISTORICAL TIMES OF TESTING

I propose that we scrutinize historical times for which almost all of us are now clear about who was faithful and who was unfaithful. History is complicated; each of us reads history differently. So is ethics; each of us approaches ethics differently. But almost all of us, from our varying perspectives, agree that the Third Reich separated the sheep from the goats. Dietrich Bonhoeffer saw from the first how wrong Hitler was, and he spoke and acted with courage.[36] Similarly, Karl Barth drafted the Barmen Declaration and led the Confessing Church in opposing Hitler's takeover of churches. And André Trocmé led the small village of Le Chambon to rescue 3,500 Jews from the grasp of the Nazis. In *Righteous Gentiles of the Holocaust,* David Gushee studied those who rescued Jews, asking what kind of ethics motivated them. Parush Parushev's forthcoming book studies the faith of those who led Bulgaria to rescue all its Jews. At that time, many disagreed on what was faithful action. But by now, with hindsight, almost all of us, regardless of differences in our ethical perspectives, agree that these persons met the historical test more faithfully than many others. By contrast, theologians Kittel, Althaus, Hirsch, and Grundmann, who gave their support to Hitler, did not come through faithfully.

Another such time of testing is the Revolution of the Candles in East Germany in 1989. People overcame the violent dictator, Erich Honecker, and the Berlin Wall, completely nonviolently. Johannes Hamel, Albrecht Schönherr, Heino Falcke, Wolfgang Ullmann, Richard Schröder, Wolf Krötke, and the movement *Aktion Sühnezeichen,* and others came through during that time. The leaders of that movement were disciples of Bonhoeffer and Barth, and they saw Jürgen Moltmann as a key supporter. Moltmann was also a major national figure in the protests against nuclear armaments in Germany when most theologians failed to stand up, and he also was much influenced by Dietrich Bonhoeffer.

Still another such time of testing is the U.S. civil rights movement. Many white church leaders sat on the sidelines or even opposed the movement for civil rights. Some black church leaders had an otherworldly faith or were too beholden to the power structures to support the movement. Clarence Jordan and Martin Luther King Jr. passed the test. Others did as well, but we have the writings of King and Jordan, so we can study their ethics readily. Charles Marsh has written especially insightfully about the sort of historical test of their ethics and contrasted it with the decay that occurred when the leaders of SNCC—the Student Nonviolent Coordinating Committee—dropped King's theological/ethical vision.[37]

Similarly, Dorothy Day, Muriel Lester, Ronald Sider, and Jim Wallis came through faithfully in the struggle for economic justice and for the poor in the face of ideologies that support economic injustice. We can think of others at other times of historical testing: Desmond Tutu, the Catholic bishops in Chile who stood against torture by the Pinochet regime, and George Hunsinger for his wisdom on nuclear weapons and on leading us to speak conscientiously against torture of defenseless prisoners.

Our agreement that these have passed the historical test does not depend on first defining one common ethical perspective from which to evaluate: Regardless of our different ethical perspectives, who among us would argue that William Wilberforce was wrong in opposing slavery? Who of us would argue that Grundmann saw rightly in supporting Hitler, and Bonhoeffer was wrong in declaring him evil?

I am pointing to witnesses who were faithful in historical times of testing. I am not asking about *effectiveness or success*, but about *faithfulness*. Dietrich Bonhoeffer incisively criticizes the worship of success; even Hitler had initial success.[38] John Howard Yoder argues that since God is the Lord, the focus on faithfulness actually goes with the grain of the universe, and often does turn out to be more effective. But the key is to focus on faithfulness.[39]

With Ernst Troeltsch, H. Richard Niebuhr, H. Shelton Smith, James McClendon, John Howard Yoder, Charles Marsh, David Gushee, Scott Becker, Parush Parushev, and others, I am arguing for testing traditions in Christian ethics based on their performance in actual history.[40] Jesus said it: "By their fruits you will know them." Bonhoeffer, Barth, Trocmé, King, Jordan, Hamel, Schönherr, Falcke, *Aktion Sühnezeichen,* Day, Lester, and the rescuers in the Holocaust passed the historical test when others failed.

That conclusion comes not only by interpreting our favorite logic, which is inevitably influenced by our social locations, interests, and ideologies, but by checking the data of historical outcomes. Bonhoeffer saw Hitler this way, while Grundmann and Althaus saw Hitler that other way. On that the data are clear. And almost all of us are clear who was more faithful. I am not arguing that we can achieve a value-free perspective. I am arguing for a method based on enough humility to seek data and agreement that partially transcend or even correct our own perspectives. Nor am I arguing for only one tradition as having all truth; all traditions need continuous correction.

This kind of historical test could also be applied to other Christian traditions and to traditions in other religions. Charles Kimball does this in his highly instructive *When Religion Becomes Evil* and *When Religion Becomes Lethal,* asking what it is in actual history that sometimes leads Buddhism, Islam, Hinduism,

Judaism, and Christianity to turn to violence, and how to correct that turn.[41] I propose that such correction can come from an ethics tested in the crucible of actual history.

I have learned significantly from empathetic and mutually respectful listening and dialogue with persons of other religions and advocate such dialogue.[42] But my humble goal in this book is to work on the log in our own eye—my eye and the eye of fellow Christians—not to try to take a speck out of the eyes of persons of other faiths. I hope that what I work on here could be useful to others as well, but that is a bigger task than I could take on here, and I'm not the best person to try to do it. Here I am arguing for a specifically Christian ethics that passes that test—what several of us call the ethics of incarnational discipleship.

Chapter 2

The Three Dimensions
of Incarnational Discipleship

We have seen that Christian ethics must be grounded in concrete, actual tests of history, and that some historical figures more than others have been able to stand up for justice in difficult times. The next logical step is to ask whether these moral exemplars, these heroes of the faith identified in chapter 1, share some common features in their ethics. Is it possible that Dietrich Bonhoeffer, Karl Barth, André Trocmé, Martin Luther King, Clarence Jordan, Dorothy Day, Muriel Lester, and others agreed in key features that help explain why they came through in historical tests while others failed?

The answer is remarkably striking and dramatic. They *all* did ethics as *incarnational discipleship*, in three senses: (1) They all wrote with a *thick, historically-embodied, realistic understanding of Jesus Christ* as revealing God's character and thus providing norms for guiding our lives. They did not reduce Jesus to a thin principle or high ideal or only doctrinal affirmation without solid grounding in his actual history. (2) They all wrote with a holistic understanding of the Lordship of Christ or sovereignty of God *throughout all of life and all of creation.* They opposed a two-kingdoms or body-soul or temporal-eternal dualism that blocks God's guidance in Christ from applying to a secular realm. (3) They all wrote with a strong call for *repentance from captivity to ideologies* such as nationalism,

Figure 2.1   Incarnational Discipleship

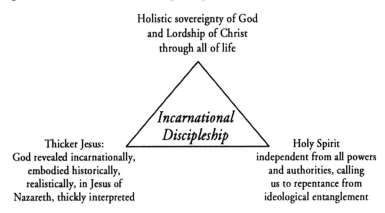

racism, and greed. And their actions, their actual practices, fit their written theological ethics.

Our goal now is to look at their writings and develop some of the specific content of these three dimensions. We can picture the dimensions of incarnational discipleship with the diagram shown in Figure 2.1. (Note that I have also placed this diagram in an appendix for easy access if you should wish to consult it later.)

I propose that these heroes and heroines whose faith has been tested in history point us to solid ground. They enable us to identify a tradition that gives us a basis to stand on—the tradition of incarnational discipleship. This is not a denominational tradition; they come from different denominations. Nor do I mean we should all be strictly Barthians or Bonhoefferians or Martin Luther Kingians or Catholic Workers. Rather we can trace three key dimensions of an ongoing tradition through these faithful witnesses that gives us a solid establishment on which we can stand our ground.

Each of these three dimensions of incarnational discipleship needs continuous development. This is a living tradition. In the following chapters and in other writing, I flesh out the meaning of the dimensions and their implications for us. Other scholars are doing so as well. I invite—I urge—your participation and your contribution.

THE BARMEN DECLARATION
AND INCARNATIONAL DISCIPLESHIP

We can begin to see the three dimensions of incarnational discipleship by examining the Barmen Declaration of 1934.[1] Barmen was the courageous statement of those leaders of the Confessing Church who declared their Christian opposition to Hitler's takeover of Germany's churches. It is the basic theological testimonial of those who gave faithful witness from the first year of the Third Reich, when its authoritarian, nationalistic, militaristic, and racist policies were already beginning to reveal themselves. One of those faithful witnesses was theologian Karl Barth, who drafted the declaration and led the pastors of the Confessing Church.[2] But Barth was just one among many who recognized the rising tide of evil and resisted it with the three themes of incarnational discipleship.

Our first theme is God revealed in the incarnate Jesus of Galilee, thickly interpreted. The Barmen Declaration states,

> The inviolable foundation of the German Evangelical Church is the gospel of Jesus Christ as it is attested for us in Holy Scripture and brought to light again in the Confessions of the Reformation. . . .
>
> "I am the way, and the truth, and the life; no one comes to the Father, but by me" (John 14.6). "Truly, truly, I say to you, he who does not enter the sheepfold by the door, but climbs in by another way, is a thief and a robber. . . . I am the door; if anyone enters by me, he will be saved" (John 10:1, 9).
>
> Jesus Christ, as he is attested for us in Holy Scripture, is the one Word of God which we have to hear and which we have to trust and obey in life and in death.
>
> We reject the false doctrine, as though the Church could and would have to acknowledge as a source of its proclamation, apart from and besides this one Word of God, still other events and powers, figures and truths, as God's revelation.[3]

Barmen was saying that churches must hear, trust, and obey Jesus Christ, as testified to in the Bible, and not Adolf Hitler. For that message to give us solid ground, we must not reduce Jesus to a principle so thin it can fit into the cracks of powerful ideologies; we need a thicker Jesus who can confront ideological manipulations.

By "ideological" I mean a belief system invented in order to defend special privilege for an in-group and provide justification for excluding other groups while covering up what the belief system is doing. It becomes a rival to God's truth, which is higher and more inclusive than our special privileges. The prophets called it idolatry, and Jesus called it hypocrisy. It distorts people's understanding and blinds them from seeing the truth. Hitler justified war and genocide by demagoguery that claimed it would enable Germany to rise from shame to superiority, but led it into far greater national shame.

We too—all nations, corporations, and even churches—can be deceived by falsely self-serving ideology. We need to exegete Jesus concretely so Jesus can give us specific guidance and help us see the truth about our own unintentional hypocrisy. Or, as Ernst Käsemann has famously argued in a more concretely historical key, we need to research the historical Jesus, because "theology about Jesus must be thoroughly grounded in a historical reality or else Jesus can be used to support anything," including Nazism.[4] Narrative about Jesus is realistic historical drama, not just an idealistic story.

David Gushee writes that although Adolf Hitler lied regularly when working to advance his strategic goals, "there is no evidence that he was lying, that is, saying something he did not believe," when he advocated his perverse form of Christianity that contended that the Creator fashioned races and the Aryan race was God's chosen ethnic group for dominating others. Strikingly, for all "the numerous times that he spoke of God, the Lord, the Creator, and the Founder of Christianity he never once uses the name 'Jesus' in *Mein Kampf*."[5]

Our second theme is the sovereignty of God or Lordship of Christ throughout all of life. As the Barmen Declaration says, "Christ Jesus, whom God made our wisdom, our righteousness and sanctification and redemption" (1 Cor. 1:30). . . . We reject the false doctrine, as though there were areas of our life in which we would not belong to Jesus Christ, but to other lords. . . ."[6]

W. A. Visser 't Hooft named the problem that Barmen was confronting. He wrote that, prior to the Third Reich,

> The general tendency of Protestantism becomes . . . more and more to describe the reign of Christ as an invisible, spiritual and heavenly reality located in the souls of men. This shift of emphasis from the universal, all-embracing sovereignty of Christ over the whole world to a purely inward sovereignty leads inevitably to the pietistic conception that the affairs of this world are the sole concern of the secular powers and that the church has no word for the world but only for individuals who are to be saved out of this world. . . . Christianity becomes more and more introspective and the church knows less and less what to do with the world-embracing and world-shaking affirmations of the Bible.[7]

The result was that most churches acquiesced or were confused in their response to Hitler's takeover of churches as well as the nation. By contrast, argues Visser 't Hooft, "Over against this attack upon its very substance the real church . . . could only answer by a radical affirmation of the unique and exclusive Lordship of Christ. The significance of the Barmen Declaration of 1934, the decisive utterance of the Confessing Church, was precisely that it affirmed this Lordship in unmistakably clear and incisive language."[8]

In addition to Barmen, Visser 't Hooft identifies four other declarations of church councils in which the Lordship of Christ over the state breaks through. There were clear church declarations against Nazism in Norway and the Netherlands and also in the Berlin synod and Stuttgart declarations after the war. It was easier to perceive and name the evil being perpetrated by the Nazis in countries they were occupying than in Germany. In Germany it took more perceptiveness and courage because of nationalism, the pervasive Nazi propaganda, and the fear of reprisal. Yet in all four declarations it was their affirmation of the Lordship of Christ over the state and not only over the church that gave them the clarity to speak pointedly and firmly.[9]

The third theme is *the Holy Spirit's evocation of continuous repentance*. The whole Barmen Declaration is a call for repentance from false loyalty to prevailing ideological and political convictions. From the start, it declares, "In opposition to attempts to establish the unity of the German Evangelical Church by means of false doctrine, by the use of force and insincere practices, the Confessional Synod insists that the unity of the Evangelical Churches in Germany can come only from the Word of God in faith through the Holy Spirit. Thus alone is the Church renewed."[10]

Barmen connects God's call for repentance with the Holy Spirit, and it warns against false ideologies:

> The Christian Church is the congregation . . . in which Jesus Christ acts presently as the Lord in Word and sacrament through the Holy Spirit. As the Church of pardoned sinners, it has to testify in the midst of a sinful world, with its faith as with its obedience, with its message as with its order, that it is solely his property . . . . We reject the false doctrine, as though the Church were permitted to abandon the form of its message and order to its own pleasure or to changes in prevailing ideological and political convictions.[11]

Connecting God's call for repentance with the Holy Spirit has biblical precedent. At Pentecost, Peter called on people to "*repent, and be baptized every one of you* in the name of Jesus Christ *so that your sins may be forgiven*; and you will receive the gift of the Holy Spirit. For the promise is for you, for your children, and *for all who are far away, everyone* whom the Lord our God calls to him" (Acts 2:38–39). The book of Acts is the narrative of the Holy Spirit's calling the early church to repent for a narrow and nationalistic faith and to recognize the Spirit's presence *both for you and your children* (Jews) and *for all who are far off* (Samaritans), an Ethiopian eunuch, and even Gentiles ignorant of the faith of Israel, so the gospel would be unhindered by narrow loyalties. The Holy Spirit required repentance by Jews and Gentiles who were excluding the other from the covenant. In the Old Testament, the Spirit is especially associated with the prophets, and in the infancy narratives in Luke, and in John the Baptist and in Jesus, the Spirit is present in prophetic contexts—which regularly include a call to repentance.[12]

THICK INTERPRETATION OF JESUS' TEACHINGS AND ACTIONS

The first striking similarity shared by all these who passed the historical tests is their extensive attention to the teachings and actions of Jesus (or in Barmen, the Lordship of Christ). Those who failed the tests often claimed to be Christians and praised Jesus, but they interpreted Jesus in terms of a vague ideal or principle; or as teaching ideals too high to actually be put into practice; or they limited Jesus' teaching to internal church relations among individuals but not applicable in the rest of life. By contrast, those who came through in these historical times of testing unequivocally interpreted Jesus' way as concrete and specific guidance to be followed. The Barmen Declaration was based on Jesus Christ as Lord over all of life. Bonhoeffer wrote *Discipleship* (1937), a concrete exegesis of the Sermon on the Mount, and contrasted cheap grace with costly grace that repents and actually follows Jesus' way. Trocmé, who led the small French village of Le Chambon to rescue about 3,500 Jews, wrote *Jesus and the Nonviolent Revolution* (1961), again with thick exegesis of Jesus' way, setting Jesus in specific historical context in ways that provide more definite guidance for nonviolence and for economic justice. Martin Luther King Jr. wrote *Strength to Love* (1963), and testified that Jesus' way provided the guidance that held the civil rights movement together and gave it its remarkable discipline and unity. Clarence Jordan wrote *The Sermon on the Mount* (1952)—again with concrete and specific exegesis that states explicitly that this is the way of Christian life, and other ways that do not follow Jesus' way are not Christian. By contrast with many who claim allegiance to Jesus Christ but fail to develop much specific guidance from Jesus, they *all* wrote books on Jesus that present concrete and specific interpretation for actual obedience. Although Dorothy Day and Muriel Lester did not write books, what they did write, and what they did in caring for people in need and advocating policies of justice for the powerless, clearly and explicitly treated Jesus' teachings and actions not as ideals, but as the true guidance for life and practice.

In addition, each of these "heroes of the faith" rejected a two-realms dualism in which Christ's Lordship is effective only for an inner spirituality, whether an inner dimension of selfhood, or only individual relations, or only internal to the church. All emphasized that Christ is Lord for all of life, as does the Barmen Declaration. All found a dimension of their culture in which they saw implications of Christ's Lordship for public life—whether human rights, as in Barth, Bonhoeffer, Trocmé, King, and Day; Gandhian practices of nonviolent direct action, as in King; or economic justice, as especially in King, Day, and Lester. They all spoke a specifically Christian language, and they also spoke a public language. As John Howard Yoder advocates, they were multilingual or polyglossic in their witness.[13] Their selection of a public language for expressing implications of their Christian commitments in public, pluralistic discussion enabled them to witness to Christ as Lord for all of life—public and private. We will see examples of this translation process as we move forward.

Furthermore, they all called for repentance from letting some other lord, ideology, or nationalism take over their ethics and their loyalties.

DIETRICH BONHOEFFER'S EARLY RESISTANCE IN THE PERIOD OF THE SERMON ON THE MOUNT

Much discussion of Dietrich Bonhoeffer focuses on his participation in the conspiracy that may have had its beginning in 1939[14] to organize a coup to depose Hitler, because that provides sensational drama. But the conspiracy's failed attempt came late, when Hitler had already done unspeakable evil and when Bonhoeffer was no longer alone in seeing how evil Hitler was. Discussion of Bonhoeffer should focus much more on his early perspicacity and courage in speaking against Hitler's war spirit and injustice to Jews. At that earlier time Bonhoeffer's faithfulness was dramatically demonstrated against the backdrop of most other theologians who caved in to Hitler's power, or even gave it active support. Hitler needed to have been stopped before he had killed six million Jews and caused fifty million to die in World War II. Bonhoeffer not only spoke out early, but organized others to gather a church leadership that would be faithful to the way of Jesus rather than to the way of militaristic nationalism. If history is the laboratory in which Christian ethics is tested, then Bonhoeffer's ethics passed the test in the early years of Hitler's rule, when so many others failed. His opposition to discrimination against Jews in 1933 was the real test for Bonhoeffer's ethics (and for the ethics of other theologians as well).

Heidelberg theological ethicist H. E. Tödt wrote, "All experts have shown their astonishment at the clear-sightedness and decisiveness with which the twenty-seven-year-old theologian Dietrich Bonhoeffer judged the political situation and the tasks of the church at the beginning of 1933."[15] Bonhoeffer spoke out not only for church members of Jewish descent, but also for Jews in the larger society. When Karl Barth read Eberhard Bethge's biography of Bonhoeffer, he wrote:

> What was most especially new to me was the fact that from 1933 on Bonhoeffer was the first, indeed almost the only one, who focused so centrally and energetically on the Jewish question and attacked it directly. I have felt for a long time that I was guilty of not having made it of decisive importance in the church struggle, at least publicly (for example in both of my drafts of the Barmen Declaration of 1934).[16]

Bonhoeffer was the first, from 1933 on. This means he was focusing energetically, acting decisively, and clearly setting his course of opposition to Hitler during the period when he was so strongly influenced by his deep engagement with the Sermon on the Mount, writing *Discipleship*, and teaching the Sermon on the Mount to his students. I contend that Bonhoeffer's deep engagement with the Sermon on the Mount—and his determination to interpret it concretely, thickly, as God's will for us in all of life—was crucial for his clarity about Hitler's evil. Additionally, as Reggie Williams shows, Bonhoeffer had just been converted by experience with racially oppressed and Christ-following African American Baptists in Harlem to enter empathetically into the experience of racially oppressed Jews in Germany.[17]

In *Discipleship*,[18] he was interpreting the Sermon on the Mount not as high ideals that were impractical in daily life, as many others were doing. He did not reduce the Sermon to a vague principle or two, as many theologians were doing, emphasizing a romantic theme like love, righteousness, nonviolence, renunciation, or reversal. Instead he interpreted each unit, each teaching, for specific and concrete guidance. He wrote with a concrete hermeneutic yielding a thick ethic with specific guidance meant to be followed.

Bonhoeffer's *Discipleship* is also distinctive in connecting the themes of the Sermon on the Mount with the Book of Acts and the writings of Paul. For example, his interpretation of "The Visible Church-Community" emphasizes that the way of life of the visible church's community is "held together by none other than Jesus Christ, the incarnate one himself . . . the Word made flesh." It "fully extends to all areas of life." "There is no area of life" not included, "the whole breadth of human relationships, . . . life as a whole is taken up 'into Christ.'" This resounds with the second theme of incarnational discipleship: that Christian belief not be compartmentalized into one area, but reign over every aspect of life. This included politics. Bonhoeffer rejected an orders-of-creation ethic that gets its norms from interpretation of the present powers rather than from Christ. Christ is Lord over public life as well as over private life. The powers and authorities were created in and through Christ (Col. 1:15) and have their mandate to rule *under* Christ.[19] By contrast, the German theologians and churches that succumbed to Hitler's pressures had previously adopted a pseudo-Lutheran two-realm dualism, relegating human rights and the democracy of the Weimar Republic to a sphere outside Christian concern—and then actually opposed human rights and democracy.[20]

Bonhoeffer also worked on implications of the Lordship of Christ for public ethics. In his *Ethics*, he employed various languages for communicating implications of Christ's independence from self-serving authorities and Christ's defense of the vulnerable: human rights—the language of the right to bodily life, grounded theologically; a theological ethics of mandates, with Christ as Lord over state, family, economic life, and church; a historical account of European heritage; and a discussion of democracy in the United States with checks and balances.

Bonhoeffer's *Discipleship* also exhibits the third theme of incarnational discipleship by repeatedly referring to the Holy Spirit and calling disciples to repentance. "When the Holy Spirit has spoken, but we still continue to listen to the voice of our race, our nature, or our sympathies and antipathies, we are profaning the sacrament," he writes. "Baptism into the body of Christ changes not only a person's personal status with regard to salvation, but also their relationships throughout all of life."[21] He put this ethic into practice by working on his own continuing repentance, involving himself in an African American Baptist church in Harlem,[22] in dialogues with French pacifist Jean Lassere, and in the world church, in order to learn from them. He was brought to his own repentance and conversion by those encounters. He learned to distinguish Christian loyalty sharply from nationalism, as does the Barmen Declaration. He developed a spiritual discipline of mutual confession and called for repentance during a time when many were adopting fascist ideology. Throughout Bonhoeffer's writings after 1933, calls ring out for repentance for solidarity in the guilt that is exemplified by

Hitler's policies and by people's silence, and for looking away from injustice or accommodating to the ideology of the Nazis. David Gushee writes,

> It was Dietrich Bonhoeffer who offered the most penetrating theological and ethical reflection in Germany both on the radical perversity of Nazism and on the necessity for Christians to aid the Jews. His writings on Nazism ranged widely from 1933 to 1945; indeed, one can see all of his theological work as, in a way, a response to the sickness of Nazi ideology and its penetration of Germany. But it was his discussion of the Church's moral responsibility in the Jewish crisis that was unique in his context. No other theological voice in his context called for the Church to confront and resist the state for its gross political injustices against the Jewish people of Germany [as Bonhoeffer did].[23]

Bonhoeffer here is confronting anti-Semitism in German and Western culture. Carrying this further, J. Kameron Carter has argued incisively that modernity's racism "has its genesis in the theological problem of Christianity's quest to sever itself from its Jewish roots."[24] He shows that Immanuel Kant's project of seeking a universal, rationalist ethic included such an amputation, with "Christ overthrowing Judaism" and Christ's wisdom being "continuous not with the Jewish people, [but] the wisdom of the Greek philosophers."[25] The result was a claim that truth is universal and rational rather than historical and a colonialism that identified European with the universal and denigrated all non-European people.

Incarnational discipleship joins Carter in working to correct the timeless idealism of Plato that has much influenced and weakened European Christianity. It seeks a thicker Jesus, rooted in Jesus' own Hebraic tradition. Carter quotes Howard Thurman: "How different might have been the story of the last two thousand years on this planet grown old from suffering if the link between Jesus and Israel had never been severed. . . . [For] the Christian Church has tended to overlook its Judaic origins, . . . the fact that Jesus of Nazareth was a Jew of Palestine." Incarnational discipleship strives to correct that severing and contribute to a better, less secularized history for the coming years.

ANDRÉ TROCMÉ

As pastor, André Trocmé led the 2,500 inhabitants of the village of Le Chambon in France to hide approximately 3,500 Jews and rescue them from the Nazis' determination to transport them to the concentration camps of German-occupied Poland and their death. This required not only a few church members but the whole village to refuse to tell the authorities where the Jews were. One person disloyal to the project could have revealed their location. Trocmé confronted the fascist authorities directly, calling on them to repent. He spent months in prison and was threatened with loss of his own life.

The Trocmé archive at Swarthmore College has his notes for fifty-nine sermons he preached during the seven and a half years of his pastorates at Mauberge and Sin-Le-Noble, before he became pastor at Le Chambon. Examining these sermons reveals the kind of faith and theology that he had and that he proclaimed *before* going to Le Chambon—the kind of faith that guided him in the prophetic witness and courageous stand that he led the whole village to take. Remarkably for a Huguenot pastor in the Reformed tradition, Trocmé preached forty-one of the fifty-nine sermons from the four Gospels. Of the remaining sermons, four texts came from the book of Acts, six from Paul's two letters to the Corinthians, one from Romans, and seven from other books in the Bible, mostly the Old Testament. Trocmé was clearly committed to a thicker Jesus.

He preached a pair of sermons on successive Sundays on the double love command in Matthew 22:39. He has four sets of notes for these two sermons, each longer than the one before, one probably a full manuscript. Both the pairing of sermons and the full-manuscript preparation are unique among these fifty-nine sermons; he must have cared especially for this theme—that the command to love your neighbor is integrally united with the command to love God. Reading his extensive writings in the archive, one is struck that he was especially committed to obeying God's will, that he saw God's will particularly revealed in Jesus, that he endeavored to love all of humankind, and that he practiced this love in his ministry in all three of his pastorates. When his church was mostly working-class members, he was known for the close relations he formed with them. He declined financial enticements from their employers to soften justice themes in his messages.[26] When he was a pastor in Le Chambon, he was known for his frequent walking tours to visit residents in their homes, despite his bad back. On one series of visits, his back became so painful that he could not walk another step. All he could do was to sit down on the road. Someone had to come in an automobile to get him. The church then got him his own car.

The clear conclusion is that Trocmé endeavored to develop among his congregations a richer and thicker understanding of Jesus' teachings as portrayed in the Gospels. Not all of his sermons focused on obeying the way of Jesus; there are sermons on the resurrection and eternal life, who Christ is, the characteristics of the reign of God, overcoming doubt, God's existence, Pentecost, the fruits of the Spirit, thanksgiving, pardon for sin, evangelization, and the historically foundational text for Mennonites "no one can lay any foundation other than the one that has been laid; that foundation is Jesus Christ" (1 Cor. 3:11). In many of the sermons he analyzes the church and calls the church to faithfulness. He has a strong ecclesial focus. And he strongly emphasizes that we are to go the whole way in following Jesus.

Trocmé survived the war and in 1961 published the French version of *Jesus and the Nonviolent Revolution.*[27] By contrast with the work of many New Testament scholars of the time, Trocmé roots Jesus deeply in his Jewish context and develops thick ethical guidance from historical research into Jesus' way. He situates Jesus among the various parties in Judaism in the first century, and rightly emphasizes Jesus' roots in the prophet Isaiah, with more references to Isaiah than to any other book in the Hebrew Scriptures. Jesus' God is "the God of the Jewish prophets."[28] Trocmé argues that "Jesus proclaimed a unique revolution," with Jubilee justice through means of nonviolence—a guide for contemporary Christian witness and practice of economic justice. Jesus was called to the House of Israel, but he included the Syrophoenician woman, Samaritans, and Romans in his ministry. As *go'el*, redeemer, he healed outcasts and restored them to community. "He welcomed women who followed him in his travels, received him in their homes, and accompanied him to his execution. Some of these women even provided financial assistance," writes Trocmé. "There was a whole group of women who entered the narrow door to the kingdom who were scorned by everyone else: the sick one who touched his robe, abandoned widows, and even prostitutes. . . ." Furthermore, "Jesus actually engaged in a kind of civil disobedience, whereby he and his disciples systematically violated those traditions that only helped to oppress the people. . . . He totally transformed the concept of holiness."[29] According to Trocmé, Jesus rejected both the Zealot strategy of war and the Essene strategy of withdrawal from the corrupted world, and instead "chose a third path—the nonviolent entry as Messiah into Jerusalem, his capital city. More than a 'triumphal entry,' Jesus' nonviolent option was packed with redemptive significance. His sacrifice would be the supreme mark of divine compassion."[30]

Trocmé also exemplifies the second dimension of incarnational discipleship. As a Huguenot, he had a central commitment to the sovereignty of God over all of life. His father instructed him and his siblings "that if we did our duty (in all of life), we would never be mistaken. . . . Our days were regulated like a convent." He describes the rule for every hour of the day, every day of the week. Only two hours of free time each week, on Sunday from 5:00 to 7:00, were free and unplanned.[31] Even that free time is structured in obedience to the Ten Commandments, which command some free time on the Sabbath!

He grew up during World War I in a French town near Germany that had been conquered by the Germans. He was seeing German soldiers trudging back toward Germany from the front, horribly wounded. One day he encountered three severely wounded soldiers limping to the hospital: "The one in the middle had an enormous bandage in place of a head. He could not see and was held by his comrades. I saw with horror that his lower jaw was missing. In its place, a mess of linen, from which dangled clots of blood. My heart stopped beating." [32] From then on, that was André's picture of war as contrasted with the teachings of Jesus Christ.

His commitment to justice for the working-class members of his church prior to coming to Le Chambon led him to reject the pressure of wealthy laissez-faire advocates and to support policies of economic justice. His sense of loyalty to God rather than to the government led him to reject patriotic appeals to obey the demands of Marshal Pétain, the fascist Vichy ruler, even prior to the need to shelter Jews. Later, during the Algerian War (1954–1962)—French colonialists versus indigenous Algerians—he wrote incisive analyses of the crucial issues of injustice for Algerians and the urgent need for the French to give up their colonial domination. He argued for a French identity committed to human rights, communicating his Christian commitment to justice for oppressed Algerians and against nationalistic French colonialism:

> There is still time for the French people to wake up from this bad dream, and become again for the African peoples, and for all those who wish to gain their independence . . . the true friend, the champion of the rights of man, freed from racial prejudice, who accord to other peoples equal to themselves in rights and in hopes, the right to lead their own lives.[33]

On war, on economic justice for ordinary people, on human rights for Algerians oppressed by colonialism, and on rescuing Jews from the Nazis, Trocmé clearly saw, and lived, the Lordship of Christ through all of life. Careful reading of his unpublished as well as published writings discloses no private-public split, no partition between his strong loyalty to his church and his public witness. The theme in his preaching is love for God with *all* of our heart, mind, and strength, not just a part. Trocmé embodies Jesus' teaching of purity of heart, in its true biblical meaning of seeking God's will holistically, with integrity, in all of life.[34]

The third theme of incarnational discipleship—the call for repentance from entanglement in loyalties and ideologies that are unfaithful to the Lordship of Christ—could not be clearer throughout Trocmé's writings and life. His loyalty to God in every dimension of life, combined with his thick interpretation of the way of Jesus, naturally led him to call for repentance from seduction by nationalism, financial greed, or militaristic hate in wonderfully dramatic ways. He wrote that Christians hesitate to put Jesus' love command into practice "because they participate in the power structure. Their ethic is one of 'realism.' It is one of compromise with honors, power, money, and war, and they cannot free themselves from it."[35] The church, he taught, "must never give its allegiance to the state, even if the state protects it, but must constantly call the state to a more perfect justice."[36] Trocmé's essays and autobiographical writings are intensely concerned about the integrity and the renewal of churches. For example, in "Message d'André Trocmé 6 October 1958," he pleads three times for the churches to call for conversion; otherwise the churches become insipid. He also published *The Politics of Repentance*, focusing explicitly on the theme of repentance for being misled by ideologies.[37]

THE RIGHTEOUS GENTILES OF THE HOLOCAUST

David Gushee's study of those individual citizens who rescued Jews from the German killing machine at peril to their own lives finds a common theme among them. Many rescuers had "a certain kind of Christianity" that focused extensively on Jesus' teachings, such as the parable of the compassionate Samaritan, the double love command, the Sermon on the Mount, "You shall love your neighbor as yourself" (Lev. 19:17; Matt. 19:19; 22:39), the Great Judgment (Matt. 25:31–46), the Golden Rule (Matt. 7:12), the sacredness of human life

(Gen. 1:28; Gal. 3:28), and My Brother's Keeper (Gen. 4:8–10).[38] This gave them ethical standards that were not merely high ideals, but realistic imperatives grounded in the realism of the Old Testament. Many of them also had high respect for the Old Testament and therefore for Jews. This confirms the incarnational discipleship theme of "a thicker Jesus," with attention to Jesus' affirmation of the Old Testament.

But Gushee also adds another dimension to incarnational discipleship: "Perhaps the religious resource most remarked upon in rescuer literature is *a strong sense of religious kinship with Jews as a people.*"[39] Several Christian traditions, especially Reformed traditions, emphasize the entire Bible, the Old as well as the New Testament. For example, the Dutch Reformed rescuer Corrie ten Boom "makes it clear that the Old Testament was deeply cherished in their home and that immersion in it contributed to the family's profound sense of religious kinship with Jews. . . . Anticipating the need to help Jews, [she] prays: 'Lord Jesus, I offer myself for *Your* people. In any way. Any place. Any time.'" These Christians thus developed a strong sense that Jews are God's chosen people.[40] Likewise, Catholic Eva Fleischner was taught "respect for the Jewish people and gratitude that they had given us the prophets, the Virgin Mary, Christ, and the apostles. Jews were for me people of the Covenant, of God's promises."[41] Gushee points to Catholics, Baptists, Plymouth Brethren, and Lutherans who believed similarly and became rescuers.

Another source of kinship or solidarity was personal friendships. One study found that 59 percent of rescuers had personal friendships with Jews before the war, and only 34 percent of nonrescuers did. An important factor was association with Jews in mixed marriages, in groups like Scouts, shared memberships as fellow townsmen, or in class groups or political parties. Furthermore, research indicates that "the combination of a sense of personal responsibility for others and high empathy for pain," as measured by two psychological scales, "was reflected in the rescuers' greater tendency to get involved in activities on behalf of others in need."[42]

This coheres exactly with what we know of Magda and André Trocmé. They were unusually empathetic toward various others, not only Jews. This is outstandingly true of Magda, as many who knew them observed. It is interesting to read their travel diaries: André is more likely to describe architecture and scenery or ideas; Magda regularly portrays people she meets or observes and discusses their lives and struggles with profound empathy. And indeed, it was Magda who welcomed the first Jew into their home and then resolved, regardless of opposition, to take supportive action for Jews who would come in the future. Much of the praise that is rightly given to André for his remarkable leadership of that whole village is owed to Magda for her remarkable caring and her practical-mindedness in meeting the concrete needs of everyone she encountered, gentile and Jew. Hers was strikingly an ethic of concrete practices, not only abstract ideals.

Similarly, Dietrich Bonhoeffer traveled to Rome to experience Catholic sensibility from within, visited monasteries in England to learn their spiritual practices, and identified with African Americans in Harlem. The centrality of the incarnation in his theological ethics guided him: As God entered history incarnationally in Jesus, and as Jesus entered compassionately into the midst of the lives of outcasts, so we are called to enter incarnationally into the lives of others. Bonhoeffer often uses the German word *eintreten*, "to enter in," to write of this compassionate entering into the concerns and experiences of others. His special emphasis on the word *Stellvertreten* connotes "stepping into the place" of another, or walking in the shoes of another, and acting on behalf of that other. It is often translated "vicarious representation" or "deputyship," but this is too thin to represent its deep meaning in Bonhoeffer's theology. Thus "incarnational" discipleship also has the meaning of "empathetically entering into the pain of others and taking personal responsibility for acting on their behalf." This fits Bonhoeffer's well-known theme that Jesus was a man for others and the church is called to be a church for others. We'll see more on this theme in chapter 9.

Gushee's research shows that the Reformed tradition produced many rescuers. Calvinists emphasize the sovereignty of God over all of life—the second dimension of incarnational discipleship. They are less likely to limit responsibility to God in Christ only to the individualistic dimension of life or only to internal relations within the church.

In addition, many Christian and non-Christian rescuers were often motivated by beliefs in democratic pluralism and in "an inclusive, principled moral commitment to justice and human rights"; they were motivated by beliefs in the sacredness of human life, or by loyalties to Bulgarian or Danish patriotism, or to socialism or even communism, or to opposition to fascism. Gushee concludes,

> An implication of these findings is that those who are tempted to consider patriotism and political ideology outside the boundaries of morality must rethink their stance. An inclusive, democratic, life-affirming and justice-advancing patriotism and political orientation should instead be viewed as a potentially powerful force for sound personal behavior as well as crucial for national character and conduct. Rather than withdraw from debate over the shape of national values and the responsibilities of citizens, people of faith should weigh in for a particular kind of values and citizenship, beginning with their own membership.[43]

In our time, advocates of unrestrained greed and freedom from accountability seek to decapitate the American tradition of human rights as the endowment of all persons, given by our Creator. Gushee is arguing that "Christians in America, so many of whom are wedded to a passive and unquestioning patriotism," need to be called to come to the aid of the human rights part of American tradition influenced by the Pilgrims. This commitment is evident throughout our history: in the preamble of the Constitution promising liberty and justice for all, in the Declaration of Independence with its unalienable human rights, in the Bill of Rights, in the Statue of Liberty's famous inscription ("Give me your tired, your poor, your huddled masses yearning to breathe free; the wretched refuse of your teeming shore, send these, the homeless, tempest-tossed to me"), in

Abraham Lincoln and Martin Luther King. The rescuers during the Holocaust demonstrated "the practice of *solidarity*, the kind of resistance in which those with relatively more power and freedom stand with those who are most threatened, working in partnership with them for survival and ultimately liberation." This is true witnessing to Jesus, who gave himself for those most threatened, and confronted their oppressors, at cost to his own life. This is also "genuine patriotism even if it is out of step with the majority culture or opinion at the time."[44]

Gushee's insight coheres with the sad truth that German churches had been taught the historical error that human rights originated in the secular French Enlightenment, and therefore they rejected human rights. Hence they failed to support Germany's effort to establish democracy during the Weimar Republic (1919–1933), meaning that the task of creating stability was ripe for Hitler's picking. German Christians lacked the strong standard of justice for minorities that should have led them to oppose Hitler's practices of killing Jews, Poles, communists, homosexuals, and disabled people. The exceptions were Bonhoeffer and Barth, both of whom affirmed human rights, and both of whom led the opposition to Hitler's dictatorial practices. Only after the end of the Third Reich did Germans learn that human rights had originated a century prior to the Enlightenment, on Christian grounds, in the struggle for religious liberty among free-church Puritans in England.[45]

Since then, Germans have ingrained the lesson that we all could embrace more decisively; they have published numerous books on human rights and have written human rights into Germany's basic constitutional law. In order for a Christian ethic to make an effective witness to the sovereignty of God or the Lordship of Christ through all of life, it needs this kind of critical assessment of ideologies in the public arena. This requires clear criteria from Christ-centered or biblical teachings of churches—criteria with which to assess which kinds of public ethics, political philosophy, justice, and peacemaking best accord with a truly Christian ethic. And it needs the help of what John Howard Yoder calls "tactical alliances" with languages spoken in public discourse in the society where a truly Christian ethic makes its witness.[46] As Yoder points out, Jews in Babylon spoke their own language, but they also learned Babylonian and other languages and became "expert translators, scribes, diplomats, sages, merchants, astronomers." They thus fulfilled God's command to "seek the welfare of the city where I have sent you into exile, and pray to the LORD on its behalf, for in its welfare you will find your welfare" (Jer. 29:7).[47] Jews were not to spend their time homesick for Jerusalem; they were to be faithful to God in the cities where they were resident aliens, working for the common good there. Likewise, we are to learn to speak the language of public discourse where we are, as well as our internal Christian language, in order to make our public witness. Only in that way can we discern how to be faithful to the Lordship of Christ through all of life in the midst of multiple ideologies that vie for our loyalties.

David Gushee also illustrates the third dimension of incarnational discipleship: *repentance for letting oneself be swayed by ideologies* that violate the way of

Jesus Christ. Before he writes of the rescuers, Gushee presents three chapters of repentance for the horrendous evils of the Holocaust and for those who did nothing to save Jews or even cooperated in their destruction. He also records the repugnance of rescuers at ideologies that led to the disastrous evil that happened to so many:

> Some rescuers objected most profoundly to governmental prosecution of those who had done nothing wrong. . . . This indignation was especially powerful with regard to Jewish children. Other rescuers pointed to the repugnance of Nazi racial doctrine that posited Aryan racial superiority and Jewish inferiority, and its embodiment in laws denying basic human rights to Jews. . . . Some rescuers acted to help Jews because Nazi actions were seen as a fundamental violation of justice, which was understood as the basic right of every human being to a decent and free existence as an equal member of the human community.[48]

Gushee's research is not based on the theological ethicists whose extensive writings enable us to examine their ethics extensively, but it has the advantage of studying a much broader base of all the rescuers recognized by the Jewish memorial to the victims of the Holocaust and to "the righteous Gentiles of the Holocaust," at Yad Vashem in Israel. His results confirm what we have already seen. First, their "certain kind of Christianity" emphasized specific teachings of Jesus, and many of them paid more attention to the Hebrew Scriptures, Jesus' Jewish roots; this is the incarnational discipleship theme of the thicker Jesus. Second, the Calvinists did better because they emphasized the sovereignty of God over all of life, which is the second theme. And many of them had a public ethic like human rights, pluralistic democracy, or antifascism, which gave them guidance against Nazi ideology; they were not limited to an ethic that applied only to private life or inner-churchly concerns. Third, David Gushee himself, as a person profoundly committed to human rights and the sacredness of life for all persons, shares with many rescuers a deep repugnance against Nazi ideology and Nazi treatment of Jews; this gives him more than independence from seduction by that ideology. His book begins by calling on all of us to share in the solidarity of repentance for the unspeakable evil of the Holocaust, including for those Christians who allowed themselves to be mesmerized into supporting Hitler. His broader base of research further confirms the three key themes of incarnational discipleship.

MARTIN LUTHER KING AND CLARENCE JORDAN

Martin Luther King Jr. exemplifies these same truths. He wrote that his African American Baptist tradition had taught him "the Christian doctrine of love," and "the Sermon on the Mount." But he had not seen how love could overcome the structures of racism. To do this, he had to transcend the two-kingdoms split that compartmentalizes Jesus' way and limits it to individual relations.

He came to realize that "the Christian doctrine of love, operating through the Gandhian method of nonviolence, is one of the most potent weapons available to an oppressed people in their struggle for freedom." He wrote that he "was driven back to the Sermon on the Mount. . . . Christ furnished the spirit and motivation and Gandhi furnished the method."[49] I want to add that King's lived experience of nonviolent direct action in the Montgomery bus boycott, begun by Rosa Parks, transformed what his previous reading of Gandhi had left somewhat cerebral into practical and personal commitment. Nonviolent direct action became "a commitment to a way of life," not only expediency, and not only an abstract principle.

The discipline of the civil rights movement—never retaliating violently when faced with violence and indignity—was based deeply on Jesus' way. "It was the Sermon on the Mount . . . that initially inspired the Negroes of Montgomery to dignified action. It was Jesus of Nazareth that stirred the Negroes to protest with the creative weapon of love."[50]

The emphasis on a holistic ethic in which the Lordship of Christ applies to all of life is demonstrated dramatically by King's own experience. His faith grew from seeing a passive, individualistic Jesus whose teachings apply only to individual relationships, to Jesus' way in nonviolent direct action. But then it became clear that passing civil rights laws and changing attitudes was not enough; blacks were still left in poverty. Jesus cared deeply about economic justice and feeding the hungry, over against greed and hoarding treasures for oneself. So in his last book, *Where Do We Go from Here?*,[51] King was probing how to persuade American society to act on Jesus' and his own concerns for economic justice.

Through this he knew he must speak out against the Vietnam War, which was killing many Vietnamese as well as American service people. The way of Jesus applied not only to overcoming racism and economic justice, but also to global human rights and peacemaking.[52] In his Riverside Church address on April 4, 1967, he said that once there was a real promise of hope for America's poor, both black and white, through the antipoverty program. But the huge expenditure of money and national attention to the Vietnam War had eviscerated that struggle for justice "as if it were some idle plaything of a society gone mad on war; and I knew that America would never invest the necessary funds or energies in rehabilitation of its poor so long as adventures like Vietnam continued to draw men and skills and money like some demonic destructive suction tube."[53] He was tragically right. The Vietnam War caused the nation to defund the war on poverty, so an initiative that had begun reducing poverty significantly lost critical momentum.

Of those who questioned his extending his message to include opposing the Vietnam War, King asked, "Could it be that they do not know that the good news was meant for all men—for Communist and capitalist, for their children and ours, for black and for white, for revolutionary and conservative? Have they forgotten that my ministry is in obedience to the one who loved his enemies so fully that he died for them?"[54] So King saw the implications of the way of Jesus extending ever more widely from racial justice to economic justice to peacemaking to global community—demonstrating the first and second dimensions of incarnational discipleship.

And it was a holistic call for repentance, the third dimension. "The black revolution is much more than a struggle for the rights of Negroes," King said. "It is forcing America to face all its interrelated flaws—racism, poverty, militarism and materialism. It is exposing the evils that are rooted deeply in the whole structure of our society."[55] In fact, it was his concerns for the implications of Jesus for economic justice that drove him to go to Memphis to participate in the campaign of garbage workers for a fair wage, against the advice of some of his team members. There he was shot to death on April 4, 1968, one year to the day after his Riverside Church address.

That famous address, as well as his whole leadership, was a call for national repentance. And indeed, he led the nation to a degree of repentance and change that was indispensable for the United States to confront racism. Yet he and John Kennedy and Robert Kennedy were assassinated, and the forces of reactionism have suppressed important dimensions of the needed repentance beneath ideologies of defensiveness.

Clarence Jordan was a white Southern Baptist from south Georgia who was driven by a thick understanding of the way of Jesus to take action to overcome racism. He wrote a book interpreting the Sermon on the Mount with dramatic concreteness, and he lived the sermon's teachings. He published *The Cotton Patch Translation of the New Testament*, in which Galilee becomes his native South Georgia, Jerusalem becomes Atlanta, and the language is homespun. He truly paid attention to a thick understanding of Jesus' teachings and their particular implications for Georgia and the South.

He was deeply concerned about the trying economic conditions for poor farmers in south Georgia in the 1930s and 40s and the sad state of racial prejudice, segregation, and discrimination there. So, instead of teaching New Testament in a comfortable college or seminary, in 1942 he began a cooperative farm near Americus and Plains, Georgia—where President Jimmy Carter is from. I believe he influenced President Carter's Christian commitment to human rights. Jordan enlisted whites and blacks to share in the cooperative farm, experimenting with crops and farming methods, and developing a successful pecan-growing business. Those who farmed became co-owners, sharing work and proceeds as the early Christians had in the book of Acts, and they called the biracial farm Koinonia, the Greek word in Acts for community and participation (Acts 2:43–47; 4:32–37). Through their work they began sharing the gospel of Jesus Christ, in which there is repentance for racism and healing for the heritage of slavery and discrimination, and love for all neighbors.

Jordan's early resistance against racial segregation and his transforming initiative in developing Koinonia Farm in 1942, twelve years before the *Brown v. Board of Education* Supreme Court decision against segregation in the schools, and twenty years before the height of the civil rights movement, is truly remarkable. He and Koinonia were boycotted, shot at, and excluded. But today he is a hero for Southern Baptists who have not succumbed to defensive reactionary ideology.[56] The specificity of his exegesis of each of the teachings of the Sermon on the Mount—and his complete clarity that each teaching is for real living—resemble Dietrich Bonhoeffer's concreteness. Jordan's living the Sermon on the Mount with great courage in the most segregated part of Georgia parallels Bonhoeffer's courage in Germany. His clarity about the sermon's guidance for all of life—not only a part of life—and his direct calls for repentance from ideologies that defend discrimination based on "race, class, caste, color, nationality, education, or wealth,"[57] could not be more direct.

THE REVOLUTION OF THE CANDLES

In 1989 the Berlin Wall, as well as the violent East German dictator Erich Honecker, were both toppled. It was a nonviolent revolution in which not one person died. Jörg Swoboda writes:

> Instead of carrying a stone like David, they carried candles in their hands and marched against the giant Goliath (the East German regime). The government officials threatened and slandered them, and ordered the State Security Forces, Special forces, Emergency Police, State Police, and army against their own people. The cruel game of fear had worked for years. But now the game was up. Gorbachev's perestroika and glasnost had given the people courage. God had blessed them with unyielding patience and unconquerable nonviolence. They had overcome their fear and recovered their voice and self-respect.[58]

I was there as it happened, speaking in churches and discussing the strategies with people in towns in all four corners of East Germany. My experience fully confirms the insightful account by John Burgess in his *The East German Church and the End of Communism*. Burgess shows that the movement for this remarkable nonviolent revolution was based in groups meeting in the churches, and its leaders had their "theological roots in Barth, Bonhoeffer, and Barmen."[59]

Fittingly for followers of Bonhoeffer and Barth, the movement was Christ-centered. "The Sermon on the Mount became an especially important expression of the East German church's hope in history. . . . Their theologians . . . were generally able to agree that the Sermon on the Mount helped define a democratic imperative" with openness, participation, and solidarity.[60] Their writings emphasize a theological exegesis of the Sermon on the Mount and Jesus' other teachings based in God's grace and Christ's eschatology, rather than in legalism. They wanted to show how their exegesis incorporated Martin Luther's themes of grace as well as Dietrich Bonhoeffer's emphasis on discipleship that follows Jesus, and to make such discipleship significantly more prominent than in traditional Lutheran teaching.

Independence from the dominating ideologies was crucial: "The church's standard was the kingdom of God, not any particular political ideology or program. Appealing to Bonhoeffer's notion of 'empathetic incarnational action' (*stellvertretendes Handeln*), the church spoke on behalf of the suffering and marginalized."[61] In many churches where I lectured, I saw pictures of Martin Luther King on the walls and translations of King's writings on the tables. On Sunday a week and a half after the Wall was opened, I preached in Bitterfeld, in the morning in a Baptist church full to overflowing, and then in the main cathedral at 2:00 p.m., where thousands of people had gathered as was usual in their regular strategy for change. Then, as usual, they went out to the town square, where they had an open mike for anyone who wanted to express his or her concerns and celebrations. When that was finished, they sang "We Shall Overcome" in English. They had learned not only the nonviolent strategies of the civil rights movement, but even the music of the movement in English!

I was so moved. Almost as if the Holy Spirit had picked me up by the scruff of my neck, I moved up to the microphone, and said three sentences: "I was deeply involved in the U. S. civil rights movement, and you have done exactly what we were trying to do. I am deeply moved. And I am deeply grateful!" They gave me the biggest applause I have ever received. Clearly what they had done was to follow Martin Luther King, but they had felt isolated, closed in by the Wall. My words had affirmed the connection with the civil rights movement that they had been seeking throughout their struggle.

The churches had developed an ecumenical process for drafting, then a decentralized discussion and feedback process, an ecumenical gathering to redraft, and then again decentralized adoption of a book on the demands that East Germany needed to meet in order to become a nation that stood for justice, peace, and the preservation[62] of creation. They published *Frieden, Gerechtigkeit, und Bewahrung der Schöpfung* (Peace, Justice, and Preservation of Creation) in the face of threats from the dictatorial government. I was riding down the Autobahn in an East German Trabi automobile when the radio broadcast the address by the new interim Chancellor, Hans Modrow, to the East German parliament. We stopped so we could hear every word. Modrow announced the list of reforms that he was beginning to implement that very day—the same reforms that the churches had demanded in their book's section "More Justice in the German Democratic Republic." Against huge odds, the churches had developed the consensus that the new interim government was now seeking to implement, and the movement had brought this about by completely nonviolent direct action, modeled on Martin Luther King and César Chávez—all this nonviolently, against the second-worst dictatorship in the Soviet bloc! I sat and wept, overwhelmed with the breakthrough of this giant mustard seed of the kingdom in our midst, from underneath an enormously repressive and violent dictatorship. I knew leaders of *Aktion Sühnezeichen* had been teaching the strategies of King and Chávez in the churches, modeled on the Sermon on the Mount and emerging strategies of just peacemaking.

Burgess gives two reasons why religion exerted the influence it did: "First, the church developed a theology with democratic political impulses that allowed it to challenge the state and offer alternative groups a free space. Second, Christianity offered alternative groups powerful symbols and themes that helped them articulate and organize their democratic concerns."[63]

And they repented from subversion by ideologies that contradict the ways of the gospel. "The church, and especially Aktion Sühnezeichen, addressed the guilt question clearly and directly. . . . The church spoke of the failure of the majority of Germans, including the church itself. . . . Fascism was not the work of a mere few who had to force themselves on the majority."[64] They pointed to the need to repent of destructive economic interests as well as anti-Judaism and the ideological suppression of democratic movements. They saw the present problems as requiring repentance, requiring commitments to peace and justice, and defending the environment—in inner attitudes, lifestyle changes, and public policies.[65]

DOROTHY DAY AND MURIEL LESTER

Other twentieth-century activists also incorporated the three dimensions of incarnational discipleship into their ministries. Dorothy Day is well known as the founder of the Catholic Worker movement, dedicated to "works of mercy" for the poor and to producing the newspaper she began, edited, and wrote articles for—telling narratives of the poor and calling for living by Jesus' teachings. The Catholic Worker movement is committed to the value of every person, the teaching of Matthew 25, voluntary poverty, pacifism, support of workers, cooperative agricultural practices, "distributism" of resources to people widely, clarification of thought, the spiritual retreat, and the centrality of the Eucharist and church liturgy.[66] Reading Dorothy Day's writings makes it perfectly clear that she interpreted Jesus' writings directly and concretely, and surely believed in living them. Her tangible performance of Jesus' teachings extended to the point of living in poverty so the money could go to caring for the poor and so she wouldn't need to pay income tax that supports wars. She refused to do violence, supported peacemaking, and advocated human rights for all persons based on the human dignity of being created in the image of God and being loved by God in Christ. She practiced a deep prayer discipline and spread the gospel among the poor and among thousands of readers of her newspaper. Many expect her to be declared a Catholic saint.

The teachings of Jesus, including a strong emphasis on the Sermon on the Mount, reverberate throughout Day's writings, and she was absolutely clear that they are not merely ideals but charges to obey and live.[67] She often quoted or referred to Matthew 25—whatever we have done for the least of persons, we have done for Christ—as "a central tenet of the New Testament and the Catholic Worker movement."[68] When you read her journals and her articles, you can't help but be moved by her compassion for human beings. Her contribution to a "thicker Jesus" comes not so much in her pioneering an exegetical method as in her relating it directly to how we embody Jesus' way—in her action, in her community's action, and in her call for our action.

In many different ways she writes that "Love and ever more love is the only solution to every problem that comes up. . . ."[69]

> It is no use saying that we are born two thousand years too late to give room to Christ. Nor will those who live at the end of the world have been born too late. Christ is always with us, always asking for room in our hearts.
>
> But now it is with the voice of our contemporaries that He speaks, with the eyes of store clerks, factory workers, and children that He gazes; with the hands of office workers, slum dwellers, and suburban housewives that He gives. It is with the feet of soldiers and tramps that He walks, and with the heart of anyone in need that He longs for shelter. And giving shelter or food to anyone who asks for it, or needs it, is giving to Christ.[70]

She saw *Christ as Lord over all of life.* She championed justice for workers and support for unions. Beyond that she advocated changing the social order to promote solidarity with immigrant workers and criminal justice.[71] Like Martin Luther King, she made use of American principles that apply to struggles for justice,[72] and in addition, drew principles selectively from socialism, anarchism, and democratic theory. But she kept Jesus' way in the foreground: "Christ is our King."

She wrote that the poor "come to us in droves." Eight hundred would come every morning for coffee and bread with marmalade; one hundred and twenty-five for lunch and again for supper: "Many days the soup runs short and then there is only coffee and cake (thanks to Macy's, which gives us their leftovers every morning)." She said the need was so great that people had to line up out in the street, and the workers served them as quickly as they could. There weren't jobs for these people. Many came even in the winter with no socks and holes in their shoes—woefully inadequate clothing for the cold of New York. "Many days go by with no money coming in at all. Right now our telephone is shut off. . . . Today we expect the gas and electricity to go. . . . As long as we are trusted the bills continue to mount. Even the printer is letting us go to press with $995 owing this summer."[73] Yet the cost of war at that time—in the 1942 U.S. budget—was $17,485,528,049.[74] The contrast between what, by comparison, an infinitesimally small amount would do for the poor and hungry is truly depressing. To cope with it we have to live in prayer and thanks to God for God's love.

Throughout Day's writing, God's love for the poor and her own praying leads to *personal repentance* as well as *to calls for repentance* from uncaring ideologies that defend unneeded acquisitiveness. When she was still a child, perhaps ten years old, her family had moved to Chicago. She had not yet experienced her conversion to Catholicism, which occurred later, and in fact was not yet much of a Christian of any kind. She happened on her first encounter with a Catholic:

> It was Mrs. Barrett who gave me my first impulse toward Catholicism. . . . In the front bedroom Mrs. Barrett was on her knees, saying her prayers. . . . And I felt a warm burst of love toward Mrs. Barrett that I have never forgotten, a feeling of gratitude and happiness that still warms my heart when I remember her. She had God, and there was beauty and joy in her life. . . . I, too, wanted to do penance for my own sins and for the sins of the whole world, for I had a keen sense of sin, of natural imperfection and earthliness.[75]

This awareness of her own status as a sinner followed Day into adulthood. Coming home from a meeting once in Brooklyn, she was seated opposite "a downcast, ragged man," along with several other poor people. He

> epitomized for me the desolation, the hopelessness of the destitute, and I began to weep. . . . It was my own condition that I was weeping about—my own hardness of heart, my own sinfulness. . . . I think that ever since then I have prayed sincerely those scriptural verses, "Take away my heart of stone and give me a heart of flesh," . . . so that I may learn how to truly love my brother because in him, in his meanest guise, I am encountering Christ.[76]

She wrote of her sense of the need for repentance when she spoke to an elite club in Palm Beach. "They told me, when I had finished, 'You know we never pay speakers,' and another woman said, with a tremor, 'Miss Day, I hope you can convey to your readers . . . that we would give our very souls to help the poor, if we saw any constructive way of doing it.'" Another woman spoke to her of her opposition to unions. "They all were deeply moved, they told me, by the picture of conditions in Arkansas and the steel districts and the coal-mining districts, but: 'You can't do anything with them, you know, these poor people. It seems to me the best remedy is birth control and sterilization.'" [77] These women had blocked their own need for repentance by an ideology that defended their own wealth and insensitivity to the compassion that Day's speech had begun to arouse in them.

Her writings are calls for repentance from ideologies that block people from hearing the words of Jesus' love. "As I thought of our breakfast line, our crowded house with people sleeping on the floor, when I thought of cold tenement apartments around us, and the lean gaunt faces of the men who come to us for help, desperation in their eyes, it was impossible not to hate, with a hearty hatred and with a strong anger, the injustices of this world."[78]

Muriel Lester was the Baptist Dorothy Day. When Dorothy Day visited London on her way to the 1963 Pax Conference, she was asked what she would like to do in London. "The one thing I want to do is see Muriel Lester," was her reply. [79] Both were revolutionary women—historian Eileen Eagan calls them prophets—who fought consistently against racism, injustice, poverty, and war.[80] Lester began with family wealth, but she was converted by her own church-influenced experience with poor people, by reading Tolstoy, and by understanding Jesus' way as a practical guide to action. "Practical" may be the key to her way of interpreting Jesus. Lester moved into the London slum of Bow, and there developed effective ways to implement Jesus' teachings, and into effective advocacy for just governmental policies. She eventually became Traveling Secretary for the International Fellowship of Reconciliation.

In the slum of Bow, she started a men's study group, suggesting a practical focus.[81] "We had all heard many speeches from different ideological perspectives on what is wrong, but they lack practical action," she explained. "So let us make up our own minds what was the most needed thing in our neighbourhood. . . . What could a group of individuals do to change the quality of life . . . ? Let us work out a practical plan." But the men weren't initially interested in her suggestion to do Bible study:

> What relevance had it for them? I proposed we should study the words of Jesus for half an hour each Sunday morning. His own words, not what someone said about Him. He Himself, the workman. . . . His teaching was far in advance of our labour leaders. In it there was to be found the solution of every one of our problems, economic, social, personal, and international. I suggested that if, after ten weeks of study, we could not find in His teaching the answer to our local problems . . . , we ought to start a campaign there and then encouraging people to shut up the churches. . . . At this the men brightened considerably. The momentary glimpse they had of themselves touring the country with me on a 'shut the churches' crusade proved titillating.[82]

They did not succumb to the temptation of some Bible study groups, leaving the biblical study hermetically sealed in the first century while avoiding its connections with our lives this week in this century. They regularly discussed what practical action they could take that would be in line with Jesus' prophetic words. I call this "analogous contextualization": first study the meaning of Jesus' teaching in its original Jewish context, and then discuss how it can function in an analogous way in our context. It took Lester's study group months to get through the teachings of the Sermon on the Mount, "so modern and revolutionary did they prove to be. One man was in the middle of reading when he looked up, surprised. 'Upon my word, Miss,' he said, 'it do seem interesting, don't it, when you put your mind to it?'"[83]

The first practical action they decided on was "to set up a teetotal public house" where the people who lived crowded into one or two rooms could come for an evening of socialization and fun. This became "Kingsley Hall" and was the center from which developed an extensive ministry with the poor, the rough equivalent of a "Baptist Worker House."

Muriel Lester and the town of Bow then developed extensive ministries with the people of the slums. She worked not only on "charity," but on organizing shared initiatives by the people. She arranged church groups, with faithfulness to the teachings of Jesus as well as a strong emphasis on the discipline of prayer and character formation. Together these Christians got governmental policies changed for health clinics for the poor and especially for children, as well as food aid for children, and tenants' rights in slum housing.

Then she developed a close friendship with Gandhi, who stayed in Kingsley Hall during his visits to London. In turn she spent weeks in India in his ashram. As Traveling Secretary for the International Fellowship of Reconciliation, she made nine world-speaking tours—in the days of travel by ship rather than plane. She pushed the Japanese government to change its policy of "Extra-Territorial Rights," by which Japanese and Korean drug dealers were destroying the lives of many Chinese with heroin and cocaine dens shielded from Chinese law. In sum, her practical implementation of Jesus' teachings was oriented toward local service, evangelism, and justice in governmental policy. Jesus is Lord through all of life, including over public policies.

CONCLUSION

We have seen that all these "heroes of the faith" embodied the three dimensions of incarnational discipleship and that this was formative for their actions. They all interpreted the way of Jesus with concreteness for our living and acting. They all saw Christ as Lord for all of life, not merely for an internal, private, or segregated portion. Guided by their concrete interpretation of Jesus Christ as Lord, they were able to make tactical use of widely understood themes in the public ethics of their societies, while calling for repentance from ideologies that subvert faithfulness to the way of Jesus.

For these heroes of the faith, the ethic of incarnational discipleship was not merely a theoretical ideal; it was regular practice. They lived it. They practiced it. Churches in our time are in deep need of renewal. They need a vision and an ethic of regular practices of the way of a thicker Jesus. Many see churches as proclaiming ideals that they do not practice. It is as if churches were proclaiming Platonic ideals while practicing the same secular ideologies that the society practices.

But let us recognize some challenges that preclude many from catching the point: The residue of a nineteenth-century individualistic idealism blocks us from seeing Jesus' historical realism in his own time and for our time. How can we put a realistic ethic for all of life, including struggles with power and injustice, together with "a thicker Jesus"? How can we overcome dualistic assumptions that segregate Jesus' way inside churches hermetically sealed from the real, public world? And in a culture influenced by well-financed, shrill media voices that advocate authoritarian ideologies lacking in compassion while claiming to speak in the name of Jesus, how can we recover a more authentic voice? In a world of diverse religions and secularism, how can we claim solid ground in Christ while showing respect for diverse viewpoints?

Significant New Testament scholarship is producing a more historically located and realistic understanding of Jesus and Jesus' way. This understanding is far deeper and more historically engaged than the idealist nineteenth-century understanding of Jesus. Churches in crisis—both mainline churches and evangelical churches, each in their own kinds of crises—need this thicker Jesus. Yet our hangover from nineteenth-century idealism leads many to think that talk of Jesus means either wishful idealism or advocacy of sectarian withdrawal from the real world. Only by showing how a more historically located and realistic understanding of Jesus opposes some ideologies and affirms connecting with some other strands in public ethics, such as covenant, community, common good, and human rights, can we articulate the Lordship of Christ through all of life. But the challenge is to get free from unholy alliances with ideologies of greed and domination.

Chapter 3

Incarnational Discipleship Needs to Resolve the Tension from Platonic Idealism

We have a tradition already available to us for thinking and living theological ethics on solid ground. Incarnational discipleship has come down to us through a stream that flows from the prophetic tradition of Israel, through Jesus of Galilee, through centuries of church history—though in some centuries it has been occluded or entangled with other distorting streams—then through the heroes of the faith I have named, and through numerous current ethicists and through far more faithful ordinary Christians. Its representatives from Dietrich Bonhoeffer through Dorothy Day have passed the test of faithfulness in times of testing when most others were failing the test.

But a tension in our culture subtly blocks us from getting the three themes of incarnational discipleship together. Something like Platonic idealism has influenced us to think "the good" (the ethical truth that makes life right and worthwhile) is a high ideal, eternal and unchanging—high above the struggles, contentions, and contradictions of this real history where we have our lives. Although in theory we ought to strive toward the ideal, we know that "realistically" we have to live in this daily struggle in our present history. So life gets split between high ideals and real struggles. Even Reinhold Niebuhr, whose Christian influence on public life is unmatched in recent history, makes this split.

In this brief chapter, we look for a way out of this divide between Christian ideals and world realities—and find a path in the teachings of Dietrich Bonhoeffer. Bonhoeffer's specific writings and example become even more important in the later chapters of this book, but for now let's look to him as a model of someone who was able to transcend the bifurcation between the ideal and the real. Incarnational discipleship requires shared practices within church communities and in actions within society, not merely ideals. This is the way of renewal and faithfulness for churches in our time. And these practices need to be theologically based in a clear vision of the way of Jesus Christ as Lord—the solid rock, guiding actual life.

IDEALISM VERSUS REALISM

In real life you have to change diapers; compete for a job; figure out how to relate to coworkers, bosses, and rivals; put up with family conflicts about who will decide how we do things; support or oppose wars against terrorism—all with subtle power struggles that we can't quite figure out. That seems beneath God's dignity, if God is the eternal ideal. We then hold the ideal at a distance, far above us or far off in the future, and focus on doing what "realism" dictates.

Or we think that in real life God has given us the unchanging rules for how things should go in the daily struggles, and it is our job to get people to bow down to those rules and obey them. And some human authority—the president, or the champion of my ideology, or the boss, or the pastor, or the man in the house—defines the rules and we should all obey him (it is usually a "him"). But that kind of authoritarianism disempowers us from correcting errors and injustices by the authority. It also leads to resentment and reaction by those who have to bow down to the rules but don't want to. If that is how Christian faith is characterized, it leads to secularism as a negative reaction.

If Jesus is caught in the same problems of idealism versus realism, or authoritarianism, then we think of his teachings either as high and impossible ideals above the struggles of real life or as the authoritarian rules for how life should go. And if only Christians understand Jesus as the revelation of God, then how do we develop a public ethic that can be persuasive in our pluralistic society, with its secularism and its varieties of faiths?

In another way of operating, with this split between eternal ideals and real struggles, God may be thought of not as the ideal, but as the power that determines what happens in real life. Then practical ethics is about how to be effective in real life. As we've seen, Jesus is then understood as the giver of high ideals that aren't very useful in real power struggles. We praise Jesus for his high ideals, but puzzle over how we could actually follow Jesus in the real life, with its daily struggles, that God has given us.

All of these dualisms, these dichotomizing approaches, loosen our connection with conscientious repentance and with the presence of the living God,

God's Holy Spirit, because they locate the "idealistic" in an unchanging, eternal realm that is not active in the present, changing, "real" realm.

Think of Plato's allegory of the cave.[1] Plato describes the human condition as people sitting in a deep cave who can only see shadowy images on the wall of the cave cast by puppets behind us, with a fire behind the puppets. Our heads and legs are chained so we cannot turn and see where the shadowy images come from. Therefore, we wrongly think the shadows we see are the real thing. (If Plato lived today, he might say we think the images on television are the real thing.[2]) We talk about what we see, thinking the shadows we see are reality.

According to Plato's allegory, the real light (the real good) is the sun outside the cave. To see it, we have to be dragged up a steep and rugged ascent into the presence of the sun and then slowly get accustomed to the brightness until we can look up at the actual sun. Then we can see "the good." It is the universal source of everything that is beautiful and right, and of reason and truth. "The good," which is the source of everything rational, is not in the world of history and becoming, where things change, but in the realm of being, which is eternal and unchanging.

BONHOEFFER UNITES THE SOVEREIGNTY OF GOD AND THE WAY OF JESUS

Bonhoeffer diagnoses the problem incisively: The good is not an unchanging ideal high above the cave of actual life; the good is the living God. God has become present in the cave, in the actual history where we live, in the incarnation in Jesus Christ.[3] Here God is present "in the relation between Jesus Christ and the Holy Spirit. The question of the good becomes the question of participating in God's reality revealed in Christ," in compassion toward actual human beings with our conflicts and injustice, with our power struggles and sufferings, with our responsibilities to others, and with our sin. "Since God . . . as ultimate reality is no other than the self-announcing, self-witnessing, self-revealing God in Jesus Christ, the question of good can find its answer only in Christ."[4] "Because in Jesus Christ God and humanity became one, so through Christ what is 'Christian' and what is 'worldly' become one in the action of the Christian. They are not opposed to each other like two eternally hostile principles. . . . In Christ life regains its unity."[5]

Setting God and ordinary human life over against one another destroys the unity of life. It leads to theories that the Sermon on the Mount, for example, has no relevance to some areas of life like politics.[6] The approach of Platonic idealism misses the reality of life as it is revealed in the actual life of Jesus Christ. It is thoroughly unbiblical. The life of Christians is participation in the joy of the reconciliation of the world with God that we see in Jesus Christ, in real history.

Bonhoeffer says that an idealistic view of *the good* as eternal and unchanging splits the good apart from life in actual *human history*, which is temporary and changing. In our real history, we ask the question about the good not under some imaginary circumstances contemplating an abstraction from life, but as creatures who are actually living in relations of responsibility "to people, things, institutions, and powers, that is, in the midst of our historical existence. The question about the good can no longer be separated from the question of life, of history. . . . Our question is not what is good as such, but what is good given life as it actually is, and what is good for us who are living. We ask about the good not in abstraction from life, but precisely by immersing ourselves in it." Even if we could conceive of the absolute criterion of what is good in and of itself, this would turn the good into "a metaphysical entity that exists in and of itself without being essentially related to life," and would sacrifice all life and freedom to some ideological concept. By contrast with such absolute idealism, "as incarnationally empathetic life and action, responsibility is essentially a relation from one human being to another."[7]

So Bonhoeffer writes that the love of God in the God-man Jesus Christ

> embraces even the most abysmal godlessness of the world. . . . God takes on the punishment and suffering that guilt has brought on us. God loves human beings. God loves the world. Not an ideal human, but human beings as they are; not an ideal world, but the real world. . . . God establishes a most intimate unity with this. God becomes human, a real human being. . . . God stands beside the real human being and the real world against all their accusers. So God becomes accused along with human beings and the world. . . . The name of Jesus embraces in itself the whole of humanity and the whole of God.[8]

Bonhoeffer makes the same point in another way, by quoting the apostle Paul: "Christ is my life," and "Christ, our life" (Phil. 1:21; Col. 3:4). He quotes Jesus according to the Gospel of John (11:27; 14:6): "I am the life." Life is what we see in Christ, which includes the No of judgment and death on our life that has fallen away from its origin and the Yes of creation, reconciliation, and redemption. "From now on it is no longer possible to conceive and understand humanity other than in Jesus Christ, nor God other than in the human form of Jesus Christ. In Christ we see humanity as a humanity that is accepted, borne, loved, and reconciled with God. In Christ we see God in the form of the poorest of our brothers and sisters."[9]

Incarnational discipleship affirms what Bonhoeffer is here saying: the incarnation of God in Jesus Christ is reality. But it is insufficient only to affirm the fact of the incarnation. Incarnational discipleship wants a "thicker Jesus." It insists that we also pay attention to what the incarnate Jesus Christ did and said, how he accepted responsibility with compassion toward others, performed particular deeds of deliverance, taught particular ways of faithfulness, and confronted the injustice of the political authorities in Jerusalem in fulfillment of the prophetic tradition of Israel. Without this concept of the thicker Jesus, without the ethical norms that it provides, the incarnation becomes merely divine sanction of the status quo. Bonhoeffer says it exactly:

> Two grave misunderstandings of [the incarnation] are found throughout
> the entire history of Christendom and continue into the present. The first
> misunderstanding considers Jesus Christ to be the founder of a new ethical
> ideology that must be applied to the historical reality. The second misunder-
> standing considers Jesus Christ only as the divine sanction of everything that
> exists. The first case gives rise to an external conflict between the necessities
> of historical action and the "ethic of Jesus." In the second case, everything
> that exists is addressed without any conflict as though it were Christian.[10]

Jesus Christ needs to be understood more realistically than as a high ideal that
we try to apply to historical reality. Jesus Christ was deeply engaged in historical struggle. Jesus is the revelation of God's engagement in historical struggle.[11]

INTERPRETING JESUS NOT IDEALISTICALLY
BUT IN HIS ACTUAL HISTORY

In "Heritage and Decay," a section in *Ethics*, Bonhoeffer writes that the understanding of heritage becomes truly historical rather than mythological when our
thinking is shaped by "the entry of God into history at a definite place and time,
in which God becomes human in Jesus Christ."[12] He is criticizing Platonic idealism, with its sense of the good as timeless and unchanging, and instead advocating the importance of the incarnation.

He is correcting the anti-Semitism that ignores Hebraic emphasis on the
dynamism of God's action in real history and pays attention only to allegedly
timeless principles of Greek philosophy. Hebraic thought moved out of mythological thinking and instead focused on God's action in history, beginning
especially with the historical event of the Exodus from Egypt and hitting a high
point with the prophets of the eighth and subsequent centuries, who interpreted
reality as learning from history, guided by a sense of God's faithfulness and
judgment in relation to people's faithfulness or unfaithfulness. Moreover, Jesus
explicitly identified with the prophets of Israel, with a special affinity for the
prophet Isaiah. Thus, not only the fact of the incarnation but also Jesus' own
teachings participated in the Hebraic and prophetic sense of historical thinking.[13] As Bonhoeffer adds immediately after criticizing Platonic idealism,

> Because Jesus Christ was the promised Messiah of the Israelite-Jewish peo-
> ple the line of our forebears reaches back before the appearance of Jesus
> Christ into the people of Israel. Western history is by God's will inextrica-
> bly bound up with the people of Israel, not just genetically but in an hon-
> est, unceasing encounter. The Jews keep open the question of Christ. . . .
> Driving out the Jews from the West must result in driving out Christ with
> them, for Jesus Christ was a Jew.[14]

Here Bonhoeffer is directly opposing the Nazi ideology that claimed German history arose from mythological origins in pre-Christian Germanic tribes

that had no connection with Hebraic influence, and that even minimized Greek and Roman influences on German and Western history. Bonhoeffer dates this manuscript 1941. On September 19, 1941, the decree took effect that Jews had to wear a yellow Star of David on their clothing, and on October 16, Jews began to be deported from Berlin.

Bonhoeffer criticizes Greek philosophical idealism, and advocates historical thinking, in two senses: He analyzes the problem of decay in Germany in terms of its misunderstanding of its own historical heritage. He also advocates practical realism with its awareness of history as in Hebraic and Roman tradition—pointing out, for example, that the apostle Paul was a Roman citizen who appealed to his Roman citizenship to save his life. Bonhoeffer says Roman heritage is more practically minded and historically focused than Greek and Platonic tradition. Emphasizing the incarnation connects us more with historical reality and connects grace more with nature as does Roman Catholic tradition. French, Dutch, and English humanists emphasized the incarnation and saw ways that Christians could make use of the wisdom of Roman and Greek philosophy. Protestant German theology, by contrast, focused more on the cross and downplayed nature, the Creator, and the incarnation. Therefore, German humanism tended to oppose classical philosophy to Christian faith. Nietzsche's pre-Nazi atheism, setting his philosophy against Christian faith, "could have arisen only from the soil of the German Reformation."[15]

So one challenge for the ethics of incarnational discipleship is to show how a thicker, more Jewishly and prophetically grounded understanding of the way of Jesus can overcome idealistic distortions of Jesus. An idealistic Jesus and an interpretation of the cross as renunciation of selfhood, life, and power make it difficult to develop a public ethic that can communicate in a pluralistic culture. Only if we can see how Jesus actually does give guidance for realistic problems in life can we see how to follow Jesus in power struggles and exercise self-assertion over against the injustice of a Hitler. Only if we free Jesus from the distortions that come from nineteenth-century idealism can we see how to advocate the sovereignty of God through all of life in a way that takes seriously the revelation of God in Jesus Christ. We need a realistic Jesus, not an idealistic one. Only a realistic Jesus who is solidly rooted in history can offer realistic guidance for the public ethics we need in a pluralistic world, without losing our Christian identity in secularism. Meeting that challenge, resolving that tension, will be a running theme throughout the rest of *A Thicker Jesus*.

Chapter 4

The Challenge of *A Secular Age* to Christian Faith

We have already seen that the tradition of incarnational discipleship is solid ground. It has passed the historical test in some very tough times. We have seen it in action in the lives of various twentieth-century heroes from Dietrich Bonhoeffer through Dorothy Day who acted faithfully when most others failed. So their ethic and this tradition are already validated; this is solid ground. But can incarnational discipleship be further validated? Can it help us meet the challenges of what philosopher Charles Taylor calls "a secular age"?[1]

HOLISTIC VALIDATION AND INTERNAL CHALLENGES

Philosopher Nancey Murphy's *Theology in the Age of Scientific Reasoning* develops a holistic method for validating a theological ethic.[2] It is highly respected; it won the American Academy of Religion award for best book of the year in the constructive/reflective category. In what follows I am drawing from her insights, as I will do in two other chapters. Murphy has developed a philosophically and scientifically sophisticated way that helps us test the truth of incarnational discipleship.

Murphy begins by pointing out that after long years of struggle, diverse philosophers are concluding that the meaning of truth claims makes sense not as bits and pieces, but as part of a holistic framework, whether that framework is called a tradition, a narrative, an interpretive scheme, a language, or a research program (163–64). The web of meaning that we use to make sense of life has some core beliefs that we are less likely to give up at the center, connected with peripheral beliefs that we adjust when we recognize the need (7). Therefore, validation needs to focus on the entire belief system that gives facts their meaning, not only on individual facts. I remember H. Richard Niebuhr arguing similarly and insightfully, ahead of his time, and have long agreed. If we see incarnational discipleship as a holistic tradition, then focusing the question of validation not only on one or another isolated proposition, but on its holistic fruitfulness, makes good sense philosophically.

Murphy argues that Imre Lakatos's analysis of how scientific research programs are validated also makes sense for theological research programs: We must first show that a theological program has a coherent series of theories that preserve the unrefuted content of their predecessors and guide further research; second, we must establish that the research program generates new content, predicting some novel, hitherto unexpected discoveries; and third, we have to demonstrate that some of these predicted discoveries are corroborated by others (85–86). Based on her own analysis of the Reformed Jonathan Edwards, the Catholic Ignatius of Loyola, the Anabaptist Pilgram Marpeck, and the early church, Murphy concludes that they each adopt a process of validation like this (150–52, 158).

Subsequently, Murphy has also advocated a parallel contribution of Alasdair MacIntyre. He and Lakatos overlapped as professors of philosophy at Syracuse University, and Lakatos's method may have influenced what MacIntyre later proposed. The similarities are striking; it makes good sense for Murphy to present both.

MacIntyre conceives of traditions as "historically extended and socially embodied," similar to Lakatos's ongoing research programs. Traditions "begin with an authority of some sort, usually a text or set of texts. This is as true of scientific traditions and secular traditions of moral enquiry as it is of Christian ethics."[3] (This is the first step above, identifying a coherent tradition agreeing with predecessors, especially the apostolic witness.) Texts need to be handled with critical care, and this requires being formed and informed by the mutual corrections shared in community.[4] (This is the third step above, corroboration in community, as scientists also engage in mutual correction with one another.)

MacIntyre's book *After Virtue* argues that our ethical discussion has lost any sense of tradition and thus is simply scattered fragments that persuade no one and get nowhere. Jeffrey Stout has countered that even though different persons are shaped by different traditions, nevertheless dialogical discussion works effectively because we learn to understand others even though we come from various backgrounds. The proof is that our moral debates are not as interminable as

MacIntyre makes out: we have reached agreement on slavery, women's suffrage, prohibition, and segregation. These debates are settled, and without massive bloodshed.[5]

MacIntyre was criticized for seeming to argue that we should work within a single tradition and that we cannot fairly understand or assess other traditions than our own. This means we all become relativists and even sectarians, unable to understand how others think, and unable to argue for the cogency of our tradition in a way that can persuade people outside it. Since everyone sees things from the perspective of her or his own tradition, this seems to lock us into relativism or perspectivism.[6]

He responded in a way that moves toward Stout's point: to engage in debate with a rival tradition "requires a work of the imagination whereby the individual is able to place him or herself imaginatively within the scheme of belief inhabited by those whose allegiance is to the rival tradition, so as to perceive and conceive the natural and social worlds as they perceive and conceive them." We have "to become involved in the conversation between traditions, learning to use the idiom of each in order to describe and evaluate the other."[7]

Furthermore, traditions all develop *internal challenges* or incoherences. They need to "supply an account of how these incoherences are best to be characterized, explained, and transcended . . . [and supply] a systematic investigation and elaboration of what is most problematic and poses most difficulty for that particular moral standpoint."[8] Persons from one tradition can learn to understand someone else's tradition and its internal challenges. Their own tradition may enable them to see the other's tradition from a different perspective and to supply a more satisfactory analysis and solution for the challenges in the other person's tradition. This then demonstrates the superiority of their own tradition. Or a person working within the first tradition can learn to understand a rival moral position, acquiring "an ability to understand her or his own tradition in the perspective afforded by that rival."[9] Thus we began to see in the previous chapter how Bonhoeffer diagnosed the challenge and tension caused by Platonic idealism and proposed the solution from within the tradition of incarnational discipleship. That theme will be developed further as we proceed in the book.

Interestingly, MacIntyre speaks of one's "method of inquiry," which parallels Lakatos's "research program." I propose we follow Nancey Murphy's wisdom in learning both from MacIntyre and Lakatos. We can accept MacIntyre's suggestion to try to identify a few internal challenges or incoherences within the broader Christian tradition and inquire whether incarnational discipleship can suggest some cogent solutions.

Murphy's analysis of Lakatos's method of validation says we can ask whether it is possible

1. To show that a coherent series of theories in incarnational discipleship exists in agreement with the apostolic witness to Jesus Christ that functions as a research program, guiding further research. I will *begin*

to show this in this book, especially with a focus here and there on insights from Dietrich Bonhoeffer.

2. To show that incarnational discipleship generates new content, resolving some challenges within Christian faith or producing some hitherto unexpected discoveries. This will be my main focus for the remaining chapters, seeking to show how dimensions of incarnational discipleship as I understand them generate answers or remedies for causes of secularism within Christian tradition.

3. To demonstrate that some of these discoveries are corroborated within the community. I can begin to hint at this; some corroboration from other scholars has come already, but much of the answer will come subsequently.

4. To show that an ethic of incarnational discipleship produces Christlike character and action, fruits of the Spirit. We have already seen this in Bonhoeffer, Trocmé, King, Day, and others. The question is whether, in this and the following chapters, I can begin to show (1) through (3). Even partial success in this brief space for such an extensive task can suggest intriguing validation.

CHARLES TAYLOR DIAGNOSES SEVEN CHALLENGES OF OUR SECULAR AGE

So the task is to show that incarnational discipleship generates new content, resolving some challenges within Christian faith or producing some hitherto unexpected discoveries. The challenges that I want to take up are the various causes of the secularism of our age. These are major challenges in our time that, in MacIntyre's sense, suggest incoherences. They will provide the topics for the remaining chapters. Can incarnational discipleship suggest some answers for the challenges presented by secularism?

To identify those challenges, we will be guided in the following chapters by Charles Taylor's influential book *A Secular Age*. Taylor makes careful distinctions and models the kind of multidisciplinary approach to Christian ethics that I argued for in chapter 1. He provides effectual guidance in identifying major historical causes of secularism. I adopt Taylor as guide for three reasons:

1. *Taylor's method is historical and inductive.* We are shaped by our history in ways we are not aware of, and Taylor helps us understand how we have gotten to where we are. He combs through the history that has shaped our present context, seeking to discern challenges that cause secularism and that need correcting if we are to respond to secularism more adequately. Two other books by Taylor in addition to *A Secular Age* also argue historically. *The Age of Authenticity* seeks to understand contemporary advocacy of authenticity inductively and historically, arguing against flatly rejecting this contemporary historical development, or adopting it without identifying some problems, but suggesting how it can be

partly affirmed with some critical awareness. His *Sources of the Self* similarly studies how our culture has been developing its understanding of selfhood so that we might understand ourselves and what it means to be human more adequately, and then prodding this understanding in a somewhat more fruitful direction. We will focus mostly, however, on his study of secularism, *A Secular Age.*

Taylor is a philosopher, not a theologian. He is not arguing that one particular tradition provides the answers; he is identifying the historical causes of secularism and welcoming others to argue for answers to the challenges. In effect, his diagnosis is an invitation to various traditions, such as incarnational discipleship, to see whether resources of our tradition can provide helpful answers.

We are all influenced by the perspective from which we see. Taylor is a Canadian Catholic with broad sympathies for diverse traditions. He is enormously well-read in the history of Western thought and philosophy, and he works with great erudition to diagnose the problems that come from diverse directions.

Thus Taylor's inductive, historical method fits the historical method that I have argued for, in our time of plural perspectives. It fits a recovery of Hebraic attention to realistic, historical reasoning rather than idealistic claims to possess universal, timeless ideals that we can persuade all rational persons to agree with. It also corresponds with the understanding of heritage that Bonhoeffer advocates in "Heritage and Decay."

2. *A Secular Age is rightly making a major impact on thoughtful analysts of our time.* I have read perhaps forty reviews of the book in scholarly journals—remarkable attention for one book to receive from fellow scholars. It won the *Christianity Today* book award in the history/biography category and the 2007 Templeton Prize and was named one of *Publishers Weekly*'s top ten religion books for that year. Scholarly reviews have praised the book's erudition and intellectual achievement. The third step in validation is to demonstrate that some of the discoveries or claims are corroborated, which is clearly the case for *A Secular Age.*

3. *Every complex outcome has multiple causes,* and the causes become part of the outcome. Taylor's diagnosing multiple causes is an important contribution, because if we assume there is only one major cause of secularism, we may be led to a reactionary response—in reaction against that one cause. Reactionary ethics tends to be resentful, authoritarian, and oversimplified. Focusing on a monolithic diagnosis is a defense mechanism. It defends against paying attention to other causes of the problem and thus against having to change actions and arguments to take those other causes into account.

Taylor's more complex diagnosis suggests a superior response. He argues against a "subtraction theory" of the origin of secularism, as if secularism were merely the subtraction of faith, and the result is simply obvious. Collin May's review summarizes it well:

> Taylor contests this [subtraction] story and what he views as a version of negative liberation, of something "sloughed off." Rather, he argues for a

conception of secularism that brings something new into the mix, with its "newly constructed self-understandings and related practices." Taylor does not accept the . . . view that modern secularism is simply letting loose what was suppressed. Instead, it is an active labor that produces, or at least attempts to produce, a wholly new situation with new possibilities.[10]

The secularism that we experience in our society is not merely a neutral thing, a subtraction of faith. It is complex, and the appropriate answer needs to be aware of its complexity. Specifically, Taylor defines secularism as the shift from earlier ages when belief in God was so widely shared that it was almost automatic to "a condition where we cannot help but be aware that there are a number of different construals, views which intelligent, reasonably undeluded people, of good will, can and do disagree on."[11]

He does not mean that official public spaces do not refer to God. Establishment of religion is unconstitutional in the United States, and he notes that the United States has a larger percentage of believers than most other Northern Hemisphere countries. Aligning religion with governmental authority causes people who resent the government or authority also to resent religion. Nor does he mean that people are turning away from God. Rather, he means we have moved "from a society where belief in God is unchallenged and indeed, unproblematic, to one in which it is understood to be one option among others, and frequently not the easiest to embrace."[12]

Taylor diagnoses seven or more diverse causes of secularism. These qualify as major epistemological challenges in MacIntyre's sense, and they each require a response.[13] But they are indeed diverse: responding to them will require pulling together several explorations that I have been pursuing in my own research program in dialogue with others, as I have been seeking to develop clearer orientation in the midst of our age of interaction. I am grateful to Taylor for this opportunity to show the unity in those explorations and to put that research program to the test of Murphy and Lakatos's four criteria of validation. Putting all this together in one place may help us begin to assess how well the tradition of incarnational discipleship, which is far bigger and broader than my own limited efforts, can begin to meet the Murphy-Lakatos tests.

Taylor's analysis of each challenge is more complex than the following introductory paragraphs can indicate. Here I simply want to identify the seven challenges that the following seven chapters need to respond to. If incarnational discipleship can generate a significant re-narration for each of the challenges that I am here naming, and perhaps suggest a discovery, an innovation, an insight in the process, this will be an important validation of the tradition of incarnational discipleship.

1. *Democracy.* The origin of democracy and human rights is complex; depending on how these are understood, democracy can lead either to secularism or to gratitude for Christian contributions to religious liberty and human rights. Taylor contends that the first Puritan churches formed around the idea of a "Covenant" in the sixteenth and seventeenth centuries, and this gradually

transmutes the social imaginary to form the sense of society as based in constitutions, natural law, and human rights.[14] The people-tradition that had been developing for centuries in opposition to Platonic hierarchy grew strong in seventeenth-century Puritanism. It advocated a society of mutual benefit, not anticommunal individualism. But the reaction both against the Puritan emphasis on order, and then against the Restoration with its hierarchy and state-church establishment, led to the secularism of the Enlightenment, in which democracy was perceived as based on people subjectively constructing social norms, not needing a basis in God.[15]

2. *Modern science.* Western science also had its origin in geniuses with strong Puritan faith commitments in the sixteenth and seventeenth centuries. But it led to a view of the universe as governed by efficient mechanistic causation rather than *telos*-oriented final causation. This mechanistic universe seemed closed to God's present involvement. The result was providential Deism, in which God has arranged the universe for human benefit, but is no longer actively involved.[16] The resulting Closed World System narratives block us from the littler narratives of God's breakthroughs in our lives, transformative experiences, moments of experienced joy and fulfillment, and epiphanies.[17] This worldview thus contributes to the secularism we face in our time.

3. *Individualism.* Detached individualism, the "buffered self" who is isolated from close relations with others, withdrawn from modes of intimacy and covenant, contributed to secularism. "The mistake of moderns is to take this understanding of the individual so much for granted, that it is taken to be our first-off self-understanding 'naturally,'" says Taylor. On the contrary, "our first understanding was *deeply embedded in society.* Our essential identity was as father, son, etc., and member of a particular tribe. Only later did we come to conceive ourselves as free individuals first." On the one hand, we understand ourselves to be living in a democratic age that imagines us—the public sphere and the self-ruling people—as collective agencies. "But the account of economic life in terms of an invisible hand is quite different. . . . It is a spontaneous order arising among *corrupt*, that is, purely self-regarding actors."[18] Such self-regarding individualists pursuing their own interests have little room for God who advocates the double love command—to God and to our neighbors—making individualism another challenge of secularism.

4. *Sin.* Deism and optimistic liberal Christianity leave out the dark side of creation, nuclear war, the climate crisis, entropy—the world and universe running down and trending toward chaos—and massive unjust suffering. The neo-Nietzschean, tragic view attacks religion as too optimistic. Freud, Foucault, Tocqueville, Sorel, Jünger, and in a way Bernard Williams and Isaiah Berlin also attack this optimism.[19] What does a Christian ethic offer in the face of both sin and secularism?

5. *The Cross.* Christianity has failed to articulate the way the suffering of the cross brings redemption. Taylor argues that the hegemony of the judicial-penal model of the atonement "plays an important role in the later rise of unbelief,

both in repelling people from the faith, and in modifying it in the direction of deism."[20] I will not argue against the classic models of atonement but will suggest that incarnational discipleship can point toward a persuasive incarnational theory of the cross that supplements them and articulates what they now seem to be reaching for. Taylor writes,

> The joy of God has gone through the poverty of the manger and the agony of the cross; that is why it is invincible, irrefutable. It does not deny the anguish, when it is there, but finds God in the midst of it, in fact precisely there; it does not deny grave sin but finds forgiveness precisely in this way; it looks death straight in the eye, but it finds life precisely within it. . . . It alone is credible; it alone helps and heals.[21]

We need more work on the cross's meaning.

6. *Love.* A perennial tension has existed between loving God even to the cross and *renouncing* everything versus affirming ordinary human life and flourishing. Platonic idealism infested Christian faith, distorting it and in fact contradicting it. Plato in the *Republic* was quite prepared to sideline the central human and bodily desires to form families and own property in favor of the higher spiritual life. For example, Christians influenced by Platonic idealism have sometimes taught that married sex should be without sexual joy. This jars against our increased affirmation of ordinary human life and work, which modernity emphasizes, and leads some to a secularist reaction against Christianity when it is thus entangled with Platonic idealism.[22] I contend that incarnational discipleship can meet this challenge of secularism by restoring a sense of realistic deliverance as expressed concretely in Jesus' Sermon on the Mount.

7. *War.* The wars of religion combined with Christendom's murderous oppression of Anabaptists and their free-church heirs and other nonconforming faiths caused a reaction against religion and in favor of generic, allegedly universal and rational language, especially in the public sphere.[23] This reaction was a major cause of secularism. Can incarnational discipleship point toward a public ethic more faithful to the way of Jesus with its call to peacemaking?

First we will take up the understanding of the origin of democracy and human rights.[24]

PART 2
MEETING THE SEVEN
CHALLENGES OF
A SECULAR AGE

Chapter 5

Democracy
And the Tradition of Human Rights

As we have seen, Charles Taylor knows that any complex historical outcome has multiple causes. He interprets democracy and human rights as originating in a faith-based English Puritan movement against church-state hierarchy and Platonic philosophy in the sixteenth and early seventeenth centuries. The origin of democracy was not secularism; it was a Puritan movement, based on biblical understandings of covenant justice.[1]

Then, in the eighteenth century, this origin was intensified in an Enlightenment-based reaction against church-state collusion. Enlightenment secularism arose in the eighteenth century for several reasons: first, reaction against clerical authoritarianism and what Taylor calls the "rage for order" by many Puritans; second, the search for civil consensus, which Enlightenment thinkers believed they could achieve based on reason rather than on church teachings; and third, reaction against the violence of wars of religion, especially on the continent but also threatening in England (see chap. 11).

I want to show that England came close, perhaps halfway, to an incarnational discipleship solution for these three problems by combining Puritan sovereignty of God through all of life with a free-church advocacy of following Jesus. The *free-church version* of Puritanism advocated religious liberty based on teaching and persuasion rather than coercion, wanted to develop policy by free discussion and mutual respect within constitutional limits, and would end the wars of religion, since everyone would have religious liberty. Admittedly, the version of Puritanism that dominated at first was not this free-church version; it was more authoritarian. But the free-church version was steadily attracting more members. Both kinds of Puritanism advocated church covenants, and this eventually influenced the development of democracy. As Taylor says, "The first puritan churches formed around the idea of a 'Covenant,'" and this caused "mutations in the social imaginary" to form the sense of society as based in constitutions, natural law, and human rights.[2]

But Taylor writes that a "rage for order" characterized the initially dominant kind of Puritanism. Furthermore, after several years of experimenting with democracy, the "Restoration" reestablished monarchy and a single official state church. The Enlightenment was, in turn, a reaction against this authoritarianism. It based democracy on humanly constructed social norms, without needing a basis in God. So the Enlightenment contributed to secularism. But the origins of democracy included covenant traditions from Puritanism, including religious liberty from free-church Puritanism, as well as the later secularism of the Enlightenment.

To test this understanding of the origins of democracy in Puritanism, we turn to a number of key thinkers. First let us contrast the ideas of Stanley Hauerwas and Jeffery Stout on the general question of democracy. How does democracy arise? What are its traditions—if indeed such traditions exist? I agree with Hauerwas in arguing against a purely traditionless democracy and ask for more than Stout's helpful but thin tradition of the practice of entering respectfully into each other's arguments. Searching for a third way, I probe contributions from Michael Walzer and others about where we actually got our democracy—the Puritans—and then some of the successors who implemented key practices from that tradition. The shape of this argument is a historical drama, since it is a historical question. I will then call a string of historical witnesses—one at a time, because it is helpful to get a sense of where each is coming from—including theorists such as John Howard Yoder, Ernst Troeltsch, James Bradley, Gunnar Myrdal, and leaders Abraham Lincoln and Martin Luther King. I have four objectives in juxtaposing these witnesses:

1. to demonstrate that there is such a democratic tradition
2. to identify some of its key ethical ingredients
3. to ask whether this tradition's kind of liberty with covenant responsibility helps avoid a reactionary kind of secularism, and
4. to see some particular Christian, incarnational discipleship contributions to the democratic strand of U.S. identity (without the idolatrous claim that U.S. identity equals Christianity).

STANLEY HAUERWAS AND JEFFREY STOUT
ON DEMOCRATIC TRADITION

Stanley Hauerwas interprets present civic culture in the United States by retelling a story about talking rabbits from Richard Adams's novel *Watership Down*.[3] Some rabbits represent Enlightenment liberalism: they despise tradition, and so they lack meaning. Another group is authoritarian, reacting against the Enlightenment. Hauerwas intends the rabbits to reveal the character of our culture. Even though I raised rabbits when I was a teenager, the *Watership Down* analogy lacks a group of rabbits I can identify with. My own interpretation of U.S. culture is more pluralistic, with several different traditions contending with each other. Our U.S. civic culture surely has a strain of individualistic liberalism that rejects history and tradition and advocates individual autonomy and self-advancement. But that is not all. Actual historical, sociological, or political analysis—*historical drama*—which discerns the tensions and contending traditions in U.S. political culture, reveals greater diversity. Hauerwas is moving toward greater diversity in his more recent writing.[4]

For example, the fourth chapter of *A Community of Character*, on "liberal democracy," reveals the key to much in Hauerwas's ethics. It is a devastating criticism of Enlightenment individualism, or what C. B. McPherson calls possessive individualism, combined with the Enlightenment's eroding and excluding of faith language from public discourse. I could not agree more with this criticism of possessive individualism, seen in the ideologies of laissez-faire or trickle-down justifications for greed and opposition to government regulation.

I agree so strongly with Hauerwas's criticism of Enlightenment individualism, as evidenced even in textbooks of Christian ethics that discuss general principles but never get around to exegeting the way of Jesus, that I defend his ethics as a much-needed corrective. His protests have created room for many of us to work in and sensitized many to what is wrong with Enlightenment individualism. He has called for focusing on church renewal, which we badly need, and which I deeply hope this book can foster.

Hauerwas quotes a perceptive analysis of Richard Nixon's Machiavellian lack of moral framework:

> He honestly did not know of any other moral framework by which to judge himself, truthful in that no other armature of principle was available to him on which to mold an understanding of his character. One searched for a hint of something in his character, some shred of belief or awareness, that might have given him the strength and the foothold—a motive—to act differently; but, save for the misgiving that his strategy might backfire, no such motive was there.[5]

It was my father who sought to warn the nation in 1956 and 1960, well ahead of what the nation finally learned during Nixon's impeachment in 1973–74, about what, in private conversation with me, Dad called Nixon's "moral blank where other people have their morality." I asked him what Nixon was saying in those meetings. "He always seemed to advocate not what would be just, or what would be good policy, but what would benefit our wealthy donors." Dad sacrificed his own promising political career when he tried to persuade President Eisenhower and the Republican Party to avoid the disaster he saw coming if Nixon became leader of the party.[6]

I find Hauerwas's quotation exactly right about Nixon. But I find it strange to think Nixon represents the broad diversity of U.S. political culture. The quotation calls for "principles that can be pointed to as the mainstays of the culture, principles of which . . . the society is the custodian . . . reinforced by the society."[7] A pluralistic interpretation of U.S. political culture can identify such principles contending against Nixon's Machiavellianism. John Howard Yoder and I both find such principles in my own father.[8] This book's dedication expresses some of my gratitude for him. But based on his interpretation of U.S. political culture as Nixon-like, Hauerwas says Christians must develop ethical skills of interpreting civic issues by being "uninvolved in the politics of our society and involved in the polity that is the church."[9] Yet he also writes, "This does not involve . . . a withdrawal from the world; rather . . . the church must serve the world on her own terms."[10] I suggest many of us need to be involved in the politics of our society to help it develop principles that are the mainstays of the culture. My own father learned his ethical integrity in his deep involvement in church and family, but also in many political struggles, which he always saw as moral and theological struggles as well. So did I, though I am a churchman engaged in caring for ethics in church renewal and in society, not a politician. I believe most of us learn from both church and society's struggles. The question is not, How do we be "uninvolved in the politics of our society"? But, How do we relate those two areas of moral learning and struggle? How do we develop an understanding of political struggles that is more faithful to Christian ethics and is not the reflection of neoliberal, trickle-down ideologies of greed that Hauerwas rightly diagnoses? How do we relate a thicker Jesus to the sovereignty of God through all of life?

DEMOCRACY AND PRAGMATIC TRADITION

Jeffrey Stout has published a major challenge to Hauerwas's argument. Stout begins his groundbreaking book *Democracy and Tradition* by acknowledging the challenge Stanley Hauerwas, Alasdair MacIntyre, and John Milbank raise— that liberal democracy systematically rejects or dissolves traditions. They are criticizing "liberal democracy" of the sort that John Rawls and Richard Rorty have advocated—which argues that appeals to faith are inappropriate in public discourse in a democracy because not everyone shares in the same faith. I have studied under John Rawls and dialogued with him and found him gracious, conscientious, and willing to adjust when cogently challenged. But his version of liberal democracy is not what I advocate. I join Stout in welcoming various faith languages to bring what insights they can to public discussion, and to seek to persuade others by making clear the insights that their faith can contribute. Stout says democracy is a tradition that asks us to work to understand others from their perspectives as much as we can.

Stout acknowledges that democracy should affirm traditions and be concerned for its own tradition of discussion. Democracy as a tradition is "anything but empty," he says. "The Preamble of the United States Constitution expresses our commitment as a people to 'establish justice, insure domestic tranquility, provide for the common defense, promote the general welfare, and secure the blessings of liberty to ourselves and our posterity.'"[11]

He defines the core of democracy as a tradition of public deliberation, open to all. We reason with one another about the ethical issues that divide us, especially on the justice or decency of political arrangements. The key is "the democratic practice of giving and asking for ethical reasons."[12] And he identifies this with the tradition of philosophical pragmatism, saying that traditionalists are correct in arguing that ethical and political reasoning spring from tradition. "They are wrong, however, when they imagine modern democracy as the antithesis of tradition, as an inherently destructive, atomizing social force." He concludes: "To put the point aphoristically and paradoxically, *pragmatism is democratic traditionalism.*"[13]

This association—that democracy is the tradition of pragmatism—is important because it forms the cornerstone of Stout's argument that religion also has a voice in public discussion. He envisions a free exchange in which "respective parties express their premises in as much detail as they see fit and, in whatever idiom they wish, try to make sense of each other's perspectives, and expose their own commitments to the possibility of criticism."[14] For this, for his commitment to justice, and for other reasons, I appreciate Stout's contributions.

But I think the tradition is much thicker. Democracy did not originate with the pragmatism of John Dewey, Walt Whitman, or Ralph Waldo Emerson; it stemmed from Puritanism in seventeenth-century England. Stout mentions this in two or three sentences in his book, noting, for example, that "the first modern revolutionaries were not 'secular liberals'; they were radical Calvinists."[15] But he never develops this tradition or what we might learn from it.

Notice the irony: Hauerwas criticizes liberal democracy for lacking tradition, but he identifies democracy monolithically with a *liberal* democracy that he tells us is opposed to tradition. All there is, he says, is traditionless liberalism. So he trains us to be blind to what traditions might actually be present in the democracy we have. He thus opposes democracy.[16] In contrast, Stout argues there *is* a democratic tradition, but reduces that tradition to the practice of discussion in philosophical pragmatism. He teaches us to see only a thin version of what tradition might be available. In a metaphor familiar to football players, there is a hole wide enough between these two positions to drive a tank through. Cornel

West does better, crediting the prophetic tradition of the Hebrew prophets and the prophetic strand in the Puritan Revolution, the Socratic and pragmatic tradition, and the African American tradition in blues and jazz, James Baldwin, Martin Luther King, and others.[17] For a lucid explication of the Calvinist Puritans' contributions to the development of democracy in the United States, see David Little, "Calvinism, Constitutionalism, and Religious Freedom: An American Dilemma," in *Calvin's Theology and Its Reception: Disputes, Developments, and New Possibilities,* ed. J. Todd Billings and I. John Hesselink (Louisville, KY: Westminster John Knox, 2012). This is an incisive essay that shows exactly how it was Calvinist Puritans and not secular liberals who first developed the documents foundational to U.S democracy. Esther Reed, Christopher Marshall, Nicholas Wolterstorff, and David Hollenbach give incisive help on human rights in Christian ethics, with their Christian theological grounding.[18]

THE PURITAN REVOLUTION

To close the gap between traditionless liberalism on one extreme and a tradition of pragmatism on the other, we focus first on the origins of democracy in the Puritan tradition, not only because that is where our democracy began, but also because incarnational discipleship asks us to look at that part of the tradition where the three themes of incarnational discipleship come together. We will therefore pay special attention to the free-church type of Puritanism, where the three themes of incarnational discipleship integrate most clearly. But I also recommend attention to Cornel West, *Democracy Matters,* for the right corrections and the broader vision.

Michael Walzer: Puritanism as the Source of Democratic Tradition

We begin our search for a deeper understanding of democratic tradition with political philosopher Michael Walzer's study *The Revolution of the Saints,* because it starkly raises the issue that Charles Taylor calls the Puritan "rage for order" and the subsequent secular reaction by the Enlightenment. In an intriguing way, Walzer also raises the question of combining the Reformed emphasis on the sovereignty of God with the free-church emphasis on following Jesus. Furthermore, he comes at the question as a political scientist who is Jewish, so his affirming the importance of Reformed Christianity and congregational life is striking.

Walzer is well aware of many scholars' biases against Puritanism, but he also sees something worth learning from in Puritanism as the source of our democratic tradition. He writes, "My only object is to make Puritan radicalism, so unattractive to my contemporaries, humanly comprehensible."[19]

Walzer argues that the Puritans' main contribution was their formation of "saints"—disciplined Christians committed to work for God's purposes in their own lives as well as in society. "The saint's personality was his own most radical innovation. . . . The saints saw themselves as divine *instruments* and theirs was the politics of wreckers, architects, and builders—hard at work upon the political world." Walzer claims that discipline, not liberty, forms the root of Puritanism:[20]

> What Calvinists said of the saint, other men would later say of the citizen: the same sense of civic virtue, of discipline and duty, lies behind the two names. Saint and citizen together suggest a new integration of private men (or rather, of *chosen* groups of private men, of proven holiness and virtue) into the political order, an integration based upon a novel view of politics as a kind of conscientious and continuous labor.[21]

This ethical integration reflects Calvinist teaching of the sovereignty of God through all of life, both personal and political. The Puritans followed Thomas Aquinas in rejecting the organic analogy of the state that requires us, the body, to obey what the king, our head, directs. Instead, the state is like a ship. The pilot's duty is to see that the ship reaches its telos, its destination—peace, justice, and cooperation between churches and commonwealth. If the ship's captain fails this duty, then we need to replace the captain with another pilot.[22]

The Puritan understanding of covenant also formed a basis for the saints' calling to work for constitutional democracy. People join the band of those who are seeking a new order and a personal discipline "by subscribing to a covenant which testifies to their faith. Their new commitment is formal . . . it requires that they abandon older loyalties. . . . This commitment is voluntary, based upon an act of the will for which men can be trained, but not born." This produces a new kind of politics, which Walzer describes as "purposive, programmatic, and progressive in the sense that it continually approaches or seeks to approach its goals." It is disciplined, methodical, and systematic—to transform their own character, and to transform the disorderly civil society so that it is more obedient to the will of God.[23]

Walzer concludes that in order for the liberalism of Locke and the Enlightenment to work, it requires character formation, voluntary subjection and self-control, which Puritanism provided. But liberalism lacked the realism about sin that the Puritans had. It was overly naive about human nature. "The result was that liberalism did not create the self-control it required." Walzer writes, "The Lockeian state was not a disciplinary institution as was the Calvinist holy commonwealth, but rather rested on the assumed political virtue of its citizens. . . . It can only be said that the Puritans *knew about* human sinfulness and that Locke did not need to know," because Locke's society could assume the commitment to character and to working for justice. Liberalism failed to develop the character in succeeding generations that it had inherited from Puritanism and that was necessary to make its society work.[24]

Liberalism rejected Puritanism because it was repressive, demanding overly strict discipline out of fear of disorder. Walzer is asking the question Charles Taylor raises—of secularism as revolt against "the rage for order" that authoritarian versions of Christianity provoke. Taylor writes that clerically driven reform and moralism was "extremely rigid on sexual matters," especially in the Catholic Reformation. But the peak came "in Calvinist societies, and was at its most marked among the Puritans of late sixteenth- and seventeenth-century England and America," focused not so much on sexual repression as on attempts to reorder whole societies. This then led to the secular Enlightenment reaction against Puritanism.[25]

Yet Puritanism had an antidote within itself against the coercion of forced repression. It was the free-church tradition, in which one could join a congregation freely or leave to find a more compatible congregation. Walzer gives us a clue: "Congregational life was surely a training for self-government and democratic participation." Congregations had a practice of mutual "watchfulness," through which fellow church members encouraged and admonished each other to live in obedience to God's will and battle against sin. And they engaged in democratic discussion to decide together what discipline they were willing to commit to. Walzer sees far-reaching consequences of such mutuality: "The radically democratic Levellers probably had their beginning in the Puritan congregations, in the debates . . . that preceded the elections of ministers."[26]

Walzer's mention of the influence of the Levellers on the development of democracy, and the congregations that practiced mutual admonition, alerts us to an important omission in his study that incarnational discipleship suggests we correct: "I have by and large ignored those tiny sects on the left-wing, so to speak, of English Protestantism, whose members have so often been treated if not as the counterparts then at least as the ancestors of modern democrats." He says he is ignoring the free-church sects and the Levellers because the Puritan mainstream of Presbyterians and Calvinists had far more power.[27]

This omits the Baptists, as well as the Quakers and the Anabaptists, who together were the originators of the widespread movement of the many different free-church or believers' church denominations. Their theology and ethics are analyzed and advocated by James McClendon's trilogy of *Ethics, Doctrine,* and *Witness.*[28] It was the Baptists and Anabaptists who baptized believers *into Christ* at an age when they could decide for themselves and when that experience of being baptized into a life in Christ would be intensely remembered and formative. Accordingly, their confessions were more Christ-centered than the confessions of contemporary Puritans.[29]

The Baptists had committed themselves to following a thicker Jesus. They insisted that the way Jesus made disciples was by teaching and persuasion, not by coercion. They held that the government has no competence in religion, and when it seeks to enforce faith it creates wars of religion and hypocrites who claim a belief they do not actually hold.[30] Here the first defining characteristic of incarnational discipleship, following a thicker Jesus, rules out coercion and so contributes to religious liberty. The sovereignty of God through all of life requires Christian responsibility in every area and thus bestows democracy to society. One result of religious liberty is a decreased need to react against religious domination, which weakens a major cause of secularism and strengthens gratitude to free-church traditions that support religious liberty.

The numbers of Baptists and free churches grew steadily, and they thrived in the Thirteen Colonies. Judged by their political power in the early seventeenth century, they were not terribly important. Judged by their influence on the kind of democracy that emerged from Puritanism, however, they were enormously important. It was their advocacy of religious liberty and independence of churches from the state that became the First Amendment to the U.S. Constitution.[31]

Where religious liberty spread, there was less need to react against state-imposed religion or church-imposed rage for order, since an angry member could join a different church. Where religious liberty spread, as in the United States, secularism has been less extensive; where two or more denominations were supported by the government, as in England and Germany, secularism was more extensive; where one church, in league with the government, dominated, as in France, secularism has been yet more extensive. Taylor comments, "The great enigma of secularization theory remains the United States. Why does this society so flagrantly stand out from other Atlantic countries?"[32]

Had England adopted religious liberty and independence of churches from the state when free churches advocated them in the seventeenth century, it could have decreased the resentment that caused secularism. Because the Anglican Church was established and financed by the government, it drew anticlerical resentment. But because dissenting churches expressed that resentment in the name of the gospel and their churches, the secularism was less than in Czechoslovakia or France, where the Roman Catholic Church dominated and dissenting Protestant leaders like Jan Hus or John Calvin were either executed or had to flee to another country. The secularism is still less in the United States, where free churches existed from the start, led by such as Roger Williams and William Penn, and where free churches eventually won the debate and governmental establishment of a church was prohibited by the First Amendment to the Constitution. The free churches, with their advocacy of Jesus' way of making disciples by teaching and persuasion, not by coercion, and their letting the heretical weeds grow along with the orthodox wheat, showed the way to reduce resentment-based secular reaction. That early, in the 1600s, these "free churches" were claiming that churches should be free from state support, and were advocating religious liberty not only for Protestants and Catholics, but also for Jews and Muslims—a hugely important witness against the genocide of the twentieth century and against the Islamophobia of the early twenty-first. For that witness, we turn to Richard Overton and his advocacy of human rights for all.

Richard Overton's Development of the Human Rights of Liberty, Life, and Dignity in Community

Walzer mentioned the Levellers as pioneers of democracy. Their most articulate leader was Richard Overton (1599–1664), a Baptist who lived in England during the contentious days of the English Civil War. He strongly advocated the human right of religious liberty on the biblical basis of following Jesus. His biblical study and his experience of religious persecution led him to extend the right to religious liberty step by step until in 1647 he published the first comprehensive doctrine of human rights.[33]

Overton shows an extensive knowledge of the New Testament, and the passages on which he focuses fit with his own confession of faith in 1615, when he joined the Waterlander Mennonite Church in Holland. He argued for human rights on biblical grounds, beginning with the free-church arguments for religious liberty that we have seen above. He also built his case from natural law as articulated by churches for centuries prior to the Puritan period, as well as from historical experience seen from the perspective of his faith: persecution causes wars, divisions, bloodshed, and hypocrisy; most wars, and especially the Thirty Years' War that killed one-third of the people of Germany, were fought over which religion would dominate and exclude the other. He viewed the right to religious liberty as a dramatic peacemaking initiative: there would be no need to fight a war to get "our" faith to control the government. His friend in Rhode Island, Roger Williams, argued similarly in *The Bloudy Tenent of Persecution* that religious persecution causes many wars over religion. Overton was also motivated by biblical concern for justice for the poor, which intensified when he got to know the poor who were jailed for their debts, as he was jailed for his faith.

His comprehensive doctrine of human rights as belonging to all persons, including Protestants, Catholics, Jews, and Muslims, in *An Appeal . . . to the Free People* (1647), included three major categories of rights:

1. *Liberty, with both religious liberty and civil liberty.* This included freedom from coercion in religion, from governmental establishment of religion, and from taxation for religion; freedom of the press; the right of prisoners not to be tortured, starved, or extorted; the right not to be arbitrarily arrested or forced to incriminate oneself; the right to a speedy trial; the right to understand the law in one's own language; and equality before the law. This is religious and civil liberty, not laissez-faire opposition to covenant accountability and to checks and balances against concentrated power.

2. *Life, including basic needs of life.* Overton championed economic rights, such as a free education for everyone; housing and care for poor orphans, the widowed, the aged, and the disabled; the right of the poor to maintain their portion of land and not be imprisoned for debt; the right to trade internationally without restrictions by monopolies. This is a consistent life ethic with justice that delivers people from what kills them or deprives them of life's requirements.[34]

3. *Dignity in community, with rights of participation for all* in a church of their free choice and in voting and participating in government regardless of one's beliefs; and the right to petition Parliament. Overton saw this as universal human dignity.

It is remarkable how Overton's initial three sets of rights have echoed through most church teachings on human rights to this day. On the civic level, we can even hear a thin echo in the American Pledge of Allegiance: One nation, under God, with (1) *liberty* (2) and *justice*, (3) *for all*. Democracy alone could descend to the rule of the majority, domineering over minorities, without respect for their human rights. But the United States has a *constitutional democracy*, with a Bill of Rights defending minorities.

Human rights have particular sources, but universal intent. For example, Overton had a particular source in Jesus' teaching and the Puritan struggle for religious liberty, with the universal intent that religious liberty applies to Muslims and Jews as well as Christians. His advocacy had a sense of covenant with God to come to the aid of all persons whose human rights are being violated. To distinguish this from the later, individualistic Enlightenment understanding that lacked the particular basis in Puritan faith, I call it *covenant-based human rights.*

We need to avoid the fallacy of confusing source with intent, as if *intending* religious liberty for all persons meant one was claiming a universal rationalistic *source*, as the Enlightenment later did. That is the fallacy many Germans committed in the nineteenth century, weakening their ability decades later to support democracy and oppose Hitler.

In our experience today, human rights come not only from the Puritans, or from the thinner adaptation of human rights by the Enlightenment, but from twentieth-century revulsion against gross violations of human rights by the Third Reich, Stalin's dictatorship, colonialism, and patriarchy. Fascists, communist dictators, colonialists, and segregationists opposed human rights, and we have learned that we need a tradition with strength and widespread support to oppose those movements of injustice. For example, Nicholas Wolterstorff begins his advocacy of human rights by describing how actual engagement in the struggle of oppressed people woke him up.[35] I have a similar witness of engagement in workcamps in Philadelphia slums, and then in the civil rights movement in North Carolina and Kentucky, and in The Revolution of the Candles in East Germany—which deeply moved me on the importance of a tradition of human rights that gives voice to the oppressed. Overton was personally affected by experiencing the injustice of imprisonment of the poor when he was jailed for his unauthorized printing. I ask anyone who opposes human rights whether he or she has engaged in any particular, concrete struggle for someone else's human rights. If they oppose human rights that direct our attention to the relatively powerless whose human rights are being violated by the powerful, what tradition of justice do they advocate that is strong enough in our pluralistic society to persuade people to defend relatively powerless people? If not human rights, what other U.S. tradition guards against concentrations of power that victimize the weak? Or are they subconsciously defending a status quo that works to deprive others less privileged?

To enable politics in this diverse nation to produce better justice, we deeply need a tradition and a narrative that many people can see as important for the national identity. It needs to be able to connect with a faith base so it is not merely secular and disconnected from what many faithful believers care about. But it needs to be able to persuade in civic discussion so persons of diverse faiths and persons of no faith can affirm it. In other words, it must be multilingual so it can make tactical alliances.

TACTICAL ALLIANCES: JOHN HOWARD YODER AND ERNST TROELTSCH

John Howard Yoder, the leading Mennonite theological ethicist, and Ernst Troeltsch, the influential Lutheran philosopher who struggled with historical relativism, have very different theologies and are not likely allies. But they both recognized the creative alliance between free-church Calvinism and democracy.

Yoder wrote that, like Jesus, we live and bear witness in a particular culture. We have no choice: We speak the language of pluralism and relativism as the New Testament writers spoke Greek. "Reality was always pluralistic and relativistic, that is historical." Pluralism/relativism is not foreign territory; it is the product of the Hebrew/Christian invasion. The question is how to say "Jesus is Messiah and Lord" in this language. So when we communicate that Jesus is Lord to people in our culture, we may make tactical alliances with the kinds of language used in our culture, including relativism, liberation, the Enlightenment, or the Gandhian vision.[36]

Yoder has been a mentor for me, and I have enormous gratitude for his friendship. He criticized a monolithic interpretation of culture that he found in H. Richard Niebuhr's *Christ and Culture*, and advocated a pluralistic interpretation.[37] He studied and dialogued with varieties of ethicists in Christian history and in his own time. He even learned German, French, Dutch, and Spanish in order to engage in dialogue with different perspectives. If incarnational discipleship is to develop a public ethic so that its ethic can guide us through all of life, Yoder says we need to interpret culture pluralistically so that we can find some strands with which to form tactical alliances.[38] Otherwise, we can find no toehold in the culture and thus cannot develop a public ethic. He argues that we need clear norms from Jesus so that we can evaluate the different strands of the culture, decide which can be used, which must first be transformed, and which must be flatly rejected.

In his "Christian Case for Democracy,"[39] Yoder begins with Jesus' realism in Luke 22:25–26: "The rulers of the nations lord it over them. Those who exercise authority let themselves be called benefactors. But it shall not be so among you; you shall be servants because I am a servant" (Yoder's translation). Jesus realistically names the domination that governments exercise. We need a form of government that builds in checks and balances against domination by concentrations of power. "Of all the forms of oligarchy, democracy is the least oppressive, since it provides the strongest language of . . . critique which the subjects may use to mitigate its oppressiveness." But it isn't justice; it only mitigates the injustice.

Yoder also argues for democracy and for religious liberty on the basis of 1 Corinthians 14:26–33, which advocates respectful discussion in Christian congregations, with every member being encouraged to contribute, and with the others weighing the various inputs and seeking an agreement—which Michael Walzer also advocated. This is "a theologically necessary vesting of the right of dissent." Democracy is based in respect for the dignity of the minority, the dissenter, the adversary. It is different from the Enlightenment's idea that the majority is the voice of God. It has more realism about the drive to dominate, and it builds in constitutional defenses of minority rights. "From this base, elements of the Enlightenment critique of authoritarianism can be recovered, accountably, because they can be authenticated as transpositions of original Christian testimony."[40]

Yoder also says we can use rulers' claims to legitimacy and beneficence for our critical and constructive communication. We can use rulers' and corporations' secular language, claiming they act for our good, to press them to do what they claim to do and thus prod them toward what we understand, in our Christian language, is closer to biblical justice. He argues for the toleration of diversity and of minorities that is present in democracies with human rights:

> A soft pluralism, when consistent, provides the most livable cultural space for Jews and Anabaptists, as well as for Jehovah's Witnesses and followers of Rev. Moon. As a *civil* arrangement, pluralism is better than any of the hitherto known alternatives. As an ecclesiastical arrangement, it is better than the monarchical episcopate. As a marketplace of ideas, it is better than a politically correct campus or a media empire homogenized by salesmanship. For such reasons, Stanley Hauerwas's characterization of English-speaking justice as a set of "bad ideas" (1991) strikes me as too simple.[41]

Ernst Troeltsch, the nineteenth-century German advocate of historical relativism, but with transcendent truth within the limits of historical relativism, also saw the free-church connection with democracy as a historical high point. Troeltsch studied nineteen centuries of Christian advocacy in his *Social Teaching of the Christian Churches*.[42] He found three periods in that history when the witness of churches made a major transformative impact on the surrounding culture: Augustine's tactical alliance with Platonism, Aquinas's tactical alliance with Aristotelianism, and free-church Puritanism's tactical alliance with democracy in early seventeenth-century England.[43]

What is striking is that in those nineteen centuries, the free-church Puritan period earned Troeltsch's top grade. Free-church Puritanism identified and helped form democratic themes and human rights themes in the culture of their time that they could use to communicate their message in a way that was not so isolated from the culture that they would not be heard. In this, they were like the Augustinian and Thomist periods, communicating effectively by connecting with cultural themes of their time. And in each case, as Yoder wrote, dangers lurked that the cultural communication could be used to set Jesus aside.

I have written criticisms of Troeltsch for the Kantian residue that he failed to get free from, and I do not accept him as an impartial judge of what is right. Neither would Yoder. What is striking is that both Yoder and Troeltsch advocate the free-church Puritan origin of the tradition of democracy with human rights as a historic breakthrough.

CONSTITUTIONAL DEMOCRACY, COVENANT, AND LIVING FAITH

But what are the specific qualities of that part of Puritan society that advocated religious liberty and which we can uphold as exemplary? What aspects of the Puritan approach to life might enable a culture to encourage democracy, navigate the complexities of soft pluralism, and practice incarnational discipleship? Here we look to three different historians touting three imperative values: constitutional democracy, covenant, and a living, independent faith.

Constitutional Democracy

Church historian James Hastings Nichols wrote *Democracy and the Churches* as if he were supporting our three themes of incarnational discipleship. He says that Puritan Protestantism historically represents "a fusion of Calvinism, Spiritualism, and the Baptist sect movement"—that is, the sovereignty of God through all of life, the presence of the Holy Spirit, and living in Christ. He also says it may be called "'neo-Calvinism' in contrast to the aristocratic and authoritarian Calvinism of the sixteenth century."[44] Max Stackhouse writes similarly of free-church Calvinism that is more Christ-centered and supports democracy with human rights by distinction from authoritarian types of Calvinism.[45]

The most important point is the Reformed contribution to *constitutionalism*, with its limitations on absolutism.[46] Accordingly I propose to speak of "*constitutional* democracy," to distinguish it from liberal democracy of the sort that Hauerwas rightly criticizes. Constitutional democracy includes realism that establishes checks and balances against concentrations of power and defends minority rights. Covenant-based Puritan churches with their practices of democracy contributed to constitution-based government with its practices of democracy.

Nichols sees the Reformed theme of the sovereignty of God as related to a rejection of the sovereignty of any one individual:

> The tradition of limited government is intrinsically more compatible with
> the theology and churchmanship of the Calvinists than . . . any of the other

major religious bodies of the period. . . . In the Reformed Church no one
. . . was sovereign. Christ as the sole head of the Church, and Christ as
presented in Scripture, was the law to which all Church officers and government must yield obedience.

In the state, as in the church, the Puritans opposed the concentration of
power in anyone, since we are all fallible. They believed any layperson had
the ability to participate in rule. "In the Church, the Holy Spirit might speak
through a humble layman; in the State, all men had access to the natural law
engraven in their consciences by God."[47] He admits, however, that sometimes
Calvin's practice lapsed into authoritarianism.

Nichols also sees the importance of the 1640s and 1650s in England as the
origin of democracy for us. He writes that the Puritan Revolution of the 1640s
and 1650s in England was "the critical epoch" when the democratic form of
government was forged. The U.S. Constitution and constitutional democracy
were its expression, not something drastically new or creative.

Covenant

In addition to the Puritans' emphasis on constitutional democracy and the
sovereignty of God, their stress on the importance of mutual covenants set
the stage for Western democracy. Church historian David Weir has examined
all available church covenants and civic compacts, patents, or constitutions
in early New England. He concludes that both separating and nonseparat-
ing Puritan churches regularly developed a church covenant, because they
had been actively discussing and debating what they stood for, in their own
practice of democracy in the churches. However, the settlements, towns, and
states lacked models for founding themselves, so they adapted the well-known
practice of church covenanting to legitimize themselves. The constitutional
emphasis in American democracy thus has its roots in the covenanting practices of churches:

> The theme of covenant is found throughout the Old and New Testaments
> of the Bible, and it is well established that . . . the early New England-
> ers—including those in Rhode Island—worked to some degree within a
> covenantal vision that had as its source the Bible and Reformed Protestant
> theology. . . . In the New World, the covenant was an instrument of forma-
> tion; the foundational covenants of the civil realm and the church laid the
> basis for the community.[48]

But Puritans were not the only ones to use the sacred covenant for new
secular purposes. Weir also draws from Champlin Burrage's study of Anabaptists and Baptists, *The Church Covenant Idea: Its Origins and Its Development*.
According to Burrage, the year 1640 was a watershed moment in the prevalence
of covenants. At the start of the English Civil War, several groups jettisoned
the Church of England, concluding that "the congregational form of church

government was the form taught by Christ and the Apostles." Baptist and Congregational churches continued the practice of church covenants into the following centuries and into the rest of what eventually became the United States. They made clear that Jesus Christ was the Lord and "our Head"—which meant that neither the king nor a bishop nor Canterbury was the head of the church.[49] Christ was the "only high priest & Prophet and King" over the church. But the covenants tended not to speak in similar terms of Christ as Lord or King over the civil realm. "That would have inflamed an already tense relationship with the monarchy in Old England."[50]

Independent Faith

Church historian James Bradley shows that the tradition of free-church advocacy of democracy and human rights extends beyond the seventeenth century. Despite the secular reputation of the eighteenth-century Enlightenment, the themes we have seen continue into that century in England—especially among free-church Dissenters who advocated political reform. Bradley is correcting secular historians who ignore the importance of living faith.

> The majority of the laity were orthodox in their theological convictions, yet the orthodox sources of radical political ideology have largely been neglected. . . . In the preaching of the orthodox pastors in particular, the authority of the Bible itself bulked large. . . . "The New Testament," said Dissenting pastor Murray, "is the Magna Charta of the Church, which is the kingdom of *Jesus Christ*; if once we make encroachments upon it, then the liberties of the *church* are at an end."[51]

The free churches were a major force supporting Whig policies of toleration, opposing the king's establishment of the Anglican Church and his warring against American independence. Bradley sees "remarkable coherence among Dissenting voters on behalf of Whig candidates,"[52] as ministers advocated religious liberty and civil liberty in tandem. Because Christ is Lord over the church of God,

> therefore the civil magistrate has no authority whatsoever in spiritual affairs. . . . Those who understand the New Testament "will reject all dominion over their consciences, but the Lordship of Jesus Christ . . ." The best method of expelling heresy is teaching the truth; people are properly convinced and moved by evidence and no other power is needed.[53]

Bradley writes that the practices of discussion and consent in their ecclesiastical polity became the basis for their advocating that the state is based on consent of the governed. This produces a different kind of politics than Max Weber's understanding of government as based on the monopoly of force. Recently, consent of the governed and nonviolent, direct action have been transforming countries from dictatorships to democracies with human rights in Latin America, the former East Germany, the Philippines, Tunisia, perhaps Egypt, and others.

Furthermore, the Dissenters were zealous for God's sovereignty and rule, and for the kingdom of God, so they understood politics in moral terms. Their living faith urged them to preach against the sin of neglecting "the rights of human nature, . . . and thus the rejection of civil liberty. . . . The implications of natural rights theory were far reaching, and the Dissenting ministers explicitly drew out these implications for the Dissenting laymen."[54] They taught what Abraham Lincoln later called government of the people, by the people, and for the people.

Free-church pastors were preaching against the same lust for power they perceived in the collusion of church and the local governments.[55]

> Wherever there was an alliance of Church and state, clergymen assumed the prerogative of magistrates, and magistrates in turn enforced the dignity of ministers for the end of riches and preferment. . . . This mixture of religious and secular authority was particularly offensive to Dissenters and led them to outspoken opposition to the secular power of the Anglican Church, the union of Church and State, . . . and "Popery," in all its forms. . . . Unlike continental anti-clericalism, however, there was little hint of rationalism or heresy in the Dissenting ministers' critique of the clergy. . . .[56]

But separation of church and state by these Dissenters and their Baptist predecessors like Overton means *independence* of churches from the state, not silencing the voices of churches on ethical matters with civic implications. When churches were under the authority of the state, and ministers owed their positions and salaries to officials of the government, they were muzzled. Criticizing state authorities or policies meant ministers would lose their positions and laypersons would be jailed. When churches opted out of that system and paid their pastors themselves, they were freed to teach what they understood the gospel to mandate, including when it disagreed with the government. Separation removed their restraints. Many did speak out for civil liberties, fair taxes that were not biased against the working class, democratic elections, and other human rights. They were championing independence of churches from the state, freeing them to address gospel ethics where they disagreed with the establishment.

Enlightenment forces turned this upside down, as if it meant churches should have no voice on the implications of the Lordship of Christ for opposing oppressive governments. But Dissenting pastors preached that Christians had "an 'unalienable right,' in the fear of God and with a due veneration for the king, 'to deliver their thought freely on the state of public affairs. The meanest subject of this empire claims this as his BIRTHRIGHT.' "[57]

Emboldened by their living faith, they also spoke for justice. Dissenting pastors focused on encouraging the ordinary people to understand their own natural rights and have confidence in their own judgment rather than passively deferring to upper classes. They used basic human rights to strengthen people's confidence in speaking out against injustice, in discussing issues, and in voting. They advocated "the consent of the governed" and "human dignity."[58]

Bradley writes of "a sensitivity to the oppressed, lower orders" shared by a number of the Dissenting pastors. One pastor preached a sermon urging local magistrates to "have no respect of persons, nor regard the rich more than the poor, but do justice to everyone." They criticized the requirement that "the 'honest poor' were obliged to support the voracious lusts and appetites of courtiers and placemen. To support a swarm of these impure locusts, the virtuous labourer and honest tradesman must be burdened with taxes beyond all reasonable bounds by which the rich prevent the poor" from the basic activities of life that the rich enjoy.[59]

The relevance of the Dissenters' example is not only that we can speak political ethics based on our faith; the question is whether what we speak is faithful to Jesus Christ or to some deceitful ideology. As Ephesians 4 states, "We must no longer be children, tossed to and fro and blown about by every wind of [ideological] doctrine, by people's trickery, by their craftiness in deceitful scheming. But speaking the truth in love, we must grow up in every way into him who is the head, into Christ" (Eph. 4:14–15). Today's church members are being blown about by well-funded ideological trickery on their televisions. Churches that avoid controversial issues leave their members ill-equipped for faithfulness to Jesus Christ. Churches need to equip their members not with vague sermons but teaching sermons, and with group discussions and small groups with a mission that engages discussion, discernment, and action.

In sum, Nichols identifies three distinctive themes in left-wing Puritans: [60]

1. The church was seen as "gathered" by a "covenant" that persons could join only by their freely committing themselves to the covenant. According to Nichols, "Church life was, in fact, democratic," and this influenced a public ethic of constitutional democracy.
2. They emphasized "the continuing role of the Holy Spirit in illuminating the mind of the Church." This meant that churches must be governed by mutual discussion, seeking the guidance of the Holy Spirit, and deciding democratically or by consensus.
3. The Levellers and Roger Williams advocated the independence of the civil authority from all theocratic domination by an established church, and instead the religious liberty and independence of churches from the state, based on Jesus' teachings.

These themes of incarnational discipleship, in the sense of public ethics, the Holy Spirit, and Jesus' teachings, contributed mightily to the tradition of constitutional democracy with human rights. And, as we shall see, that tradition has become crucial for American identity, along with other traditions that conflict with it.

DEMOCRACY IN PRACTICE

But does the tradition still have power in the United States? It has been threatened by traditions of racism and greed, of individualistic "me-ism," of opposition to constitutional responsibilities of the government, and of imperialism. Does the tradition still have the strength to battle against well-funded advocates of special privilege and injustice for others?

Gunnar Myrdal, An American Dilemma

One test is the famous study of American identity in the 1940s, faced by the dilemma of racial segregation and discrimination, by the Swedish sociologist Gunnar Myrdal. He wrote that despite the bewildering impression of chaotic unrest, "Still there is evidently a strong unity in this nation and a basic homogeneity and stability in its valuations. Americans of all national origins, classes, regions, creeds, and colors" have a social *ethos*, a political creed, in common. Myrdal concluded, "It is difficult to avoid the judgment that this 'American Creed' is the cement in the structure of this great and disparate nation." [61]

> These ideals of the *essential dignity* of the individual human being, of the fundamental *equality of all* men, and of certain inalienable rights to *freedom, justice, and a fair opportunity* represent to the American people the essential meaning of the nation's early struggle for independence. . . . These were written into the Declaration of Independence, the Preamble of the Constitution, the Bill of Rights and into the constitutions of the several states. . . . [They include] confidence in the value of the *consent of the governed* expressed in institutions, understandings and practices as a basis of *order, liberty, justice.*[62]

Notice the close resemblance between the threefold set of human rights that Overton laid out in 1647 and the "ideals" in the "American Creed" that Myrdal named and that I have italicized for emphasis. Myrdal says that the American Creed came in part from the Enlightenment, but more from Christianity of the "various lower class Protestant sects, split off from the Anglican Church. . . . Democracy was envisaged in religious terms long before it assumed a political terminology." He points out that much of the Bible is composed of narratives of oppression and deliverance in both the Old and New Testaments. In the Bible, "The rich and mighty are most often the wrongdoers, while the poor and lowly are the followers of God and Christ." And the third source is English law, with its respect for "the democratic concept of law and order." America, he says, has an "almost fetishist cult of the Constitution."[63]

But the American dilemma was the painful contradictions between the American Creed and the deep racial injustices and inequalities that the nation was stuck in (and to a lesser extent still is entangled in). Much of Myrdal's book studies and analyzes how deeply entrenched the segregation, discrimination, and racist beliefs and practices were.

Based on what they had learned of the "American Creed," Gunnar Myrdal and his assistants went way out on a limb, contrary to what most sociologists were saying at the time. Myrdal's team predicted that despite all the entrenched interests, loyalties and historical inertia supporting racist practices, the tradition of human dignity—of the fundamental equality of all, and of the inalienable rights to freedom, justice, and fair opportunity—would work to bring major change. It would happen soon.

In 1944, when there had been a half century of little evidence that change was coming for the relative status of African Americans, Myrdal's study of the American commitment to democracy and human rights led him to a bold prediction:

> Ten years from now this (past) period in the history of interracial relations in America may come to look as a temporary interregnum. The compromise was not a stable power equilibrium. . . . Not since Reconstruction has there been more reason to anticipate fundamental changes in American race relations, changes which will involve a development towards American ideals.[64]

The change that did come with the civil rights movement is a dramatic historical demonstration of the power of the tradition that Myrdal identified. And Myrdal recognized that a significant part of its strength came from its Christian roots. Myrdal's assistant, Arnold Rose of the University of Minnesota, wrote in the foreword to the book's second edition,

> To the student of social change, who must have historical perspective and be aware of continuities and rigidities in the social structure, the changes in American race relations from 1940 to 1962 appear to be among the most rapid and dramatic in world history without violent revolution. . . . But of particular significance for our analysis is the fact that Negroes *still* experience discrimination, insult, segregation, and the threat of violence, and in a sense have become more sensitive and less "adjusted" to these things.[65]

But neither Myrdal and Rose nor I are claiming that American identity is monolithic. Their study described extensive practices of racism that the American Creed would have to struggle against. And we are now threatened with huge economic injustices in a rapidly widening gap between the very wealthy and the broad swath of consumers, as well as the large numbers living in poverty, justified for many by a tradition of possessive individualism. That tradition of greed, backed by billions of dollars, is now fighting to obscure the American tradition of human rights for all and replace it with a definition of freedom to do whatever the powerful please, without checks and balances. We observe the earth's climate being changed, with devastating droughts, fires, hurricanes, and tornadoes, caused by increased carbon dioxide in the atmosphere from the burning of fossil fuels.[66] Entrenched interests oppose energy conservation but lead people to pray for rain. And, as Taylor shows, there is a tradition of secularism that also undermines the faith-basis for democracy and human rights. Each tradition has real force. We need to articulate what is right and wrong with each tradition, and with which tradition we will make a tactical alliance in our advocacy—or whether we will be silent about them.

In our work against torture as government policy during the Iraq and Afghanistan wars, David Gushee and I found that many people were driven one way or the other by passions about American identity. In my own involvement in the civil rights struggle, I found that some people who could not be persuaded by Christian faith were persuaded by their sense of American identity, much as Myrdal describes it. Gushee and I are deeply committed to Christian ethics as following Jesus, strongly to be distinguished from a partisan political loyalty or a secular ideology. Partisan political entanglement has been ruining Christian witness and distorting Christian faithfulness, especially since around 1980, and causing an increase in secularism and atheism out of reaction against authoritarian versions of ideology-entangled Christianity.[67] I am convinced that enormous injustice is being fostered by crafty manipulation of a badly distorted ideological reinterpretation of American tradition and that Christians who care about God's compassion and delivering justice need to become active in correcting those ideological distortions. We need to find a tradition, or at least a strand, in American identity that can motivate Americans to make their civic contributions. The tradition of constitutional democracy and covenant-based human rights as religious and civil liberty, life and justice, and human dignity in community, is the helpful tradition in American identity in our struggle with racism, segregation, discrimination, and greed. And we need to be clear that Jesus Christ is Lord over all those civic traditions.

Abraham Lincoln and Martin Luther King Jr.

I am urging people to notice that we have a great tradition that empowers our best selves as a people—working together in community. To help us all see that tradition, before partisan ideologies cover it over, I want to point to two individuals who connected with that tradition and thus achieved greatness: Abraham Lincoln and Martin Luther King Jr.

Our theologically greatest president, the guide for a major turning point for our nation, was Abraham Lincoln. His two best-known addresses are his Gettysburg Address and his Second Inaugural Address. Notice how he speaks of the three themes of Overton that have echoed through the tradition we have only begun to explore: liberty, equality (or the right to life and basic justice for all), and the human dignity for all the people of participating in government of the people, by the people, and for the people—under God.

> Four score and seven years ago, our fathers brought forth upon this continent a new nation: conceived in liberty, and dedicated to the proposition that all men are created equal. It is for us the living . . . to be here dedicated to the great task remaining before us: that from these honored dead we take increased devotion to that cause for which they gave the last full measure

of devotion; that we here highly resolve that these dead shall not have died
in vain; that this nation, under God, shall have a new birth of freedom;
and that government of the people, by the people, for the people, shall not
perish from the earth.

William J. Wolf has written a classic on Lincoln's sense of God's ways as
being higher than our ways, God's ways not being identifiable with any of our
causes, God's judgment falling on both sides, and the importance of praying for
God's mercy on all.[68] Such equanimity is present in Lincoln's Second Inaugural,
when the president said,

> Both read the same Bible and pray to the same God, and each invokes His
> aid against the other. It may seem strange that any men should dare to ask a
> just God's assistance in wringing their bread from the sweat of other men's
> faces, but let us judge not, that we be not judged. The prayers of both could
> not be answered. That of neither has been answered fully. The Almighty
> has His own purposes. . . .
>   With malice toward none, with charity for all, with firmness in the right
> as God gives us to see the right, let us strive on to finish the work we are in,
> to bind up the nation's wounds, to care for him who shall have borne the
> battle and for his widow and his orphan, to do all which may achieve and
> cherish a just and lasting peace among ourselves and with all nations.[69]

Lincoln was deeply committed to God and God's will, and to human rights
for African Americans, but was also deeply realistic about the limits to how far
and how fast he could lead the nation with the consent of the governed. *Douglass and Lincoln*, by Kendrick and Kendrick,[70] is especially insightful about his
struggle with the American dilemma. It tells of Frederick Douglass's prodding
Lincoln to declare emancipation of the slaves and to let blacks fight in the army.
Douglass was frustrated with Lincoln's slowness, but he was solidly persuaded
that Lincoln was sincere and agreed with him. That conclusion turned out to
be correct. Lincoln eventually did what Douglass was urging. Lincoln opposed
slavery in principle from the start, despite the claims of some skeptics, making
his opposition to extending slavery west via the Missouri Compromise the central theme of his 1858 campaign for the Senate and of that campaign's debates
against proslavery Senator Stephen Douglas. Stephen Douglas accused him of
believing that blacks and whites were equal, in Illinois where a large majority
sided with Douglas on that question. On the one hand, Lincoln denied the
charge, but then he argued, "There is no reason in the world why the negro is
not entitled to all the natural rights enumerated in the Declaration of Independence, the right to life, liberty and the pursuit of happiness. . . . In the right to
eat the bread, without the leave of anybody else, which his own hand earns, *he is
my equal and the equal of Judge Douglas, and the equal of every living man.*"[71] In
April 1863, during the war, Lincoln wrote to fellow Kentuckians that if slavery
was not wrong, "nothing is wrong. . . . I cannot remember when I did not so
think and feel." Lincoln "declared at Independence Hall in Philadelphia that he
'never had a political feeling that did not spring from the sentiments embodied

in the Declaration of Independence." He said that national commitment and those human rights were what give us the promise that soon the weights of slavery will be lifted from all, and that *all* would have an equal chance.[72]

Yet until well into the Civil War Lincoln did not think he had the power to act on that belief. He ended up accomplishing what he did not think he could accomplish, but what Frederick Douglass was enormously persuasive in pushing for. Lincoln believed God does more than and differently from what we expect, and he was right.[73] Lincoln was led to do what we now see was God's will by his commitment to the American tradition of human rights enumerated in the Declaration of Independence, and to the right to eat the bread that a person's own work earns. And he worked within the limits—sometimes frustratingly slowly—of the American tradition of the consent of the governed, insofar as that was possible in the nation's most polarized time. Frederick Douglass eventually declared, "the hour and the man of our redemption have somehow met in the person of Abraham Lincoln."[74]

The other guide for a major turning point for our nation, whom we have already met in an earlier chapter, is Martin Luther King Jr. His two best-known statements are his "I Have a Dream" and his "Letter from Birmingham Jail." These and Lincoln's two addresses are defining texts in our tradition.

King begins "I Have a Dream" by identifying with the tradition of Abraham Lincoln:

> Fivescore years ago, a great American . . . signed the Emancipation Proc-lamation. . . . But one hundred years later, the Negro still is *not free*; . . . the life of the Negro is still sadly crippled by the manacles of segregation and the chains of *discrimination*; . . . the Negro lives on a lonely island of *poverty* in the midst of a vast ocean of material prosperity; the Negro . . . finds himself in *exile in his own land*.[75]

Here are the three dimensions of human rights that Richard Overton originally articulated and that have stood since, but in their violation: unfreedom, injustice, and exile from *dignity in community*. King next sounds the theme of covenant in the form of "a promissory note to which every American was to fall heir," and connects it with "the Constitution, the Declaration of Independence," and "the promises of democracy."

We all know that his address focused on freedom and justice, but I want to draw attention also to its theme of dignity in community:[76]

> the solid rock of brotherhood . . . the high plane of dignity and discipline . . . we can never be satisfied as long as our children are stripped of their selfhood and robbed of their dignity by signs stating "for whites only". . . . Many of our white brothers, as evidenced by their presence here today, have come to realize that their destiny is tied up with our destiny and they have come to realize that their freedom is inextricably bound to our free-dom. . . . We cannot walk alone. . . . I have a dream that one day . . . little black boys and black girls will be able to join hands with little white boys and white girls as sisters and brothers. I have a dream today!

King's "Letter from Birmingham Jail"[77] reaches out to moderate white pastors who had criticized him instead of speaking for justice, and calls them to community together. For a writer sitting in his jail cell without research resources, King wrote a letter that is amazingly rich in references and quotes from civic tradition: Socrates, Thomas Aquinas, Martin Luther, John Bunyan, the Pilgrims at Plymouth, Thomas Jefferson, Abraham Lincoln, and T. S. Eliot—along with many citations from the Bible. King is connecting his readers with the democratic tradition, which is in his head and his heart even while he is locked up in a cell.

> One day the South will know that when these disinherited children of God sat down at lunch counters they were in reality standing up for the best in the American dream and the most sacred values in our Judeo-Christian heritage, and thusly, carrying our whole nation back to those great wells of democracy which were dug deep by the Founding Fathers in the formulation of the Constitution and the Declaration of Independence.

This is the tradition, the American identity, that we all need to keep holding up before our nation as we confront questions of torture of defenseless prisoners, the religious liberty to build a Muslim mosque, funding education for our children and the children of immigrants, health care for the millions who do not presently have it, and caring for people struggling for freedom, life with justice, and dignity in community in other countries as well. This is the tradition that does not alienate and create secularism because of its authoritarian exclusion of outcasts, but invites all into community. It has specifically Christian roots, and it welcomes the support it receives from other religious traditions and from secular sources as well. We are a pluralistic democracy, with human rights for all. And that is our strength—*e pluribus unum*. United we stand; divided we fall.

Chapter 6

Science

The Interactive Nucleus

When I was a boy in South St. Paul, Minnesota, some evenings in the early summer, Johnnie and Kitty Kelly, Ron and Jerry Erickson, and I would gather on the slope in front of the Kellys' house so we could lie on our backs and wonder at the amazing displays of the northern lights (which we later learned to call the aurora borealis). The displays were phenomenal. Beyond words! They were like huge blue or green curtains covering almost the whole night sky, slowly undulating as if being wafted by a cosmic wind. Only people who live in Alaska, Minnesota, northern Michigan, Norway, and so forth are likely to have seen them, and to know how truly awe-inspiring they are. But you can search the Internet for aurora borealis and see numerous images.

Recently I was reading on the second floor of Fuller Theological Seminary's library. Something I read led me to think of the Big Bang origin of the universe. I paused and tried to envision the whole universe, with all its galaxies, about fourteen billion years ago, jammed together in one unbelievably intense concentration of matter and energy, with gravitational forces, strong forces of the nuclei, enormous energy and compression—literally the mother of all black holes. Nothing would survive in that unfathomable concentration of energy and force and compression. Nothing would even escape. Only hydrogen, helium, and maybe some lithium nuclei could have survived; bigger nuclei would have been torn apart. If any nuclei had electrons, the electrons would have been stripped off by the indescribable forces. Nothing was alive except incomprehensible energy. And then suddenly this energy burst forth—pure chaos and heat—and began spreading across the universe.

I looked around to see students studying from many nations and many ethnic groups, thinking diverse and complex thoughts about their varieties of disciplines. And I marveled that somehow that chaotic energy of the Big Bang had been nudged to form into more complex nuclei, and then into stars and galaxies, and planets, and then into plants and animals, and into human beings of remarkable complexity like the students sitting there reading and thinking thoughts beyond my knowing. How in the world (how in the universe!) did we get from there to here?

I paused to marvel.

In this chapter I invite you to pause to marvel at the truly remarkable and awe-inspiring wonders of this universe. These wonders increasingly reveal an interactive universe rather than the Enlightenment's machine-like closed system operating according to fixed laws. Charles Taylor writes that the influence of Enlightenment Deism, seeing the universe as a machine closed to new breakthroughs, contributed to a secular view that God no longer does anything new. This was a major cause of secularism that new knowledge of quantum physics now enables us to lay to rest. We now see *indeterminacy* and *interaction* at the most basic level of the atom—with profound implications about the world in which we live and interact as human beings.

PROBING THE BINDING FORCES IN THE NUCLEI

I want to tell a bit of my own experience in probing the binding forces that hold nuclei together—the basic elements that make up our whole world—in order for us to sense the interactive nature of the most basic building blocks of our universe, from the bottom up. I began in nuclear physics, and James W. Butler offered me the plum job in research at the Naval Research Laboratory near Washington, DC. He invited me to assist him in his highly skilled and pioneering research with a two-million-electron-volt Van de Graaff accelerator, directing protons at various nuclear isotopes to probe their inner binding forces. The key was Jim Butler's refinement of this kind of research with remarkably accurate energy levels and with scrupulous attention to the kinds of errors that intrude in such research.

The Van de Graaff accelerator, two floors above our experiments, was set to produce protons at the exact energy level that we wanted to direct at the isotope. It sent the protons down a vertical beam tube from two floors above. When they got down to our level, an energy-defining magnet was set to the right strength so that protons at the intended energy would turn exactly ninety degrees and travel horizontally about thirty feet inside our beam tube to the target. Any protons whose energy was a little too strong would not be turned sharply enough by the magnet, and any whose energy was a bit too weak would be turned too sharply. They would miss the slit in the beam port in front of the isotope. A cylindrical copper tube 1½ inches wide pointing toward the beam of protons was placed around the isotope to be bombarded. It had a quarter-inch horizontal slit at its entry point, so only protons of the right energy could enter it.

We would bombard the nuclei with protons at a precise energy level, thus stimulating some of the atoms to decide to split into smaller particles and send positrons or gamma rays at different energy levels into our Geiger counters. Because Jim Butler so skillfully corrected for likely sources of error, he could aim the protons from the Van de Graaff accelerator at our target isotopes at more exact energy levels than anyone ever had achieved before. We were able to investigate binding forces in the nuclei of isotopes that no one previously had ever investigated. For example, previous to this research, there were no known excited states of copper^{59} or copper^{61}. We identified eighty-four states, thirteen bound and seventy-one resonant states.

There were three of us researchers. J. W. Butler and C. R. Gossett were highly skilled, and I was a novice assistant.[1] The accelerator had to work twenty-four hours a day, so each of us worked eight hours a day, alone, while the other two rested. So for eight hours a day, I was putting questions to the inside of these nuclei that no one before, in all the billions of years, had ever been able to ask. When the nuclei answered, and I recorded the answers in our twenty-channel analyzer and calculated a correction factor and graphed the results, it became strikingly clear that the nuclei had answered with zero-order and second-order Legendre polynomials—straight lines, diagonals, and almost perfect Legendre polynomials. (You can see what Legendre polynomials look like at Wikipedia; they are beautiful!) This meant that some of the nuclei had each captured one proton and were then splitting or decaying with several specific energy levels that we were measuring, and the resulting compound had a spin either of 3/2 or 1/2 depending on which Legendre variable they were showing.

They were telling us specific messages about their binding forces and their spins. And they were doing this as if alive, as if they were deciding when to split. The outcome was a somewhat irregular series of counts in our twenty-channel analyzer, with spontaneous clusters of clicks in our Geiger counter adding up to a statistical result. They were not monotonously regular as if automatic and immediate, the way a billiard ball immediately recoils when hit. The nuclei were responding to our questions, speaking our mathematical language, completely understandable, telling us the nature of their binding forces. It was as if they were saying to me, "Finally, someone has asked us. We have waited so many eons. We will answer you in language that you can understand!" For me, it was an experience of God's presence—or openness to God's presence—in the very foundations of physical reality. When I was finished with a day of research, I would go outdoors and just run as fast and as long as I could in exultation and gratitude.[2]

For a person of faith, this means God is doing new things every moment. Our universe is not a stationary machine; it is dynamic and alive at its very base. The nuclei of the atoms, the very building blocks of all nature, are each "deciding" every moment whether to stay the same or to split up and go different ways. They are alive, and responding to God's will. Nature is alive and interacting all the way down to the nuclei of the atoms. As a talmudic prayer puts it,

> Blessed art thou, O Lord our God, King of the universe, who formest light and createst darkness, who makest peace and createst all things. . . . In mercy thou givest light to the earth and to those who dwell on it, and in thy goodness renewest the works of [processes of] creation every day continually, a King who alone was exalted from aforetime, praised, glorified, and extolled from days of old.[3]

CHARLES TAYLOR: DEISM AS A CAUSE OF SECULARISM VERSUS QUANTUM PHYSICS

But Western science has not always celebrated an open, alive universe as I did in our nuclear physics lab. Charles Taylor identifies the challenge we are facing in this chapter concerning the incarnational discipleship dimension of the sovereignty of God throughout all of life: The eighteenth-century Enlightenment assumed that the world is a closed system, a machine that operates by fixed laws without any personal direction. It is closed to God's intervention and to our communal relations with one another. The result is a "shift towards the primacy of impersonal order. God relates to us primarily by establishing a certain order of things."[4] This is "a drift away from orthodox Christian conceptions of God as an agent interacting with humans and intervening in human history; and towards God as architect of a universe operating by unchanging laws, which humans have to conform to or suffer the consequences."[5] We then end up living in "an indifferent universe, with God either indifferent or non-existent."[6] Nancey Murphy has stated the problem particularly clearly: "It is an ironic bit of history: the laws that once served as an account of God's universal governance of nature have become a competing force, constraining the action of their very creator."[7]

Isaac Newton set out to explain nature "from mechanical principles."[8] On the basis of his laws of motion for a falling apple, he was also able to explain the motions of the planets. That then was expanded to seeing an atom as a sun-like nucleus with planet-like electrons orbiting around it, also obeying Newton's laws of motion. It was all very orderly, very precise, very law-abiding, very machine-like. Based on the theory that all particles obey Newton's laws of motion, mathematician Pierre-Simon Laplace (1749–1827) wrote,

> We may regard the present state of the universe as the effect of its past and the cause of its future. An intellect which at a certain moment would know all forces that set nature in motion, and all positions of all items of which

nature is composed, if this intellect were also vast enough to submit these data to analysis, it would embrace in a single formula the movements of the greatest bodies of the universe and those of the tiniest atom; for such an intellect nothing would be uncertain and the future just like the past would be present before its eyes.[9]

Nuclear physics has now progressed far beyond that machine-like, closed-system determinacy to an open and interactive view of basic reality. But this knowledge hasn't sunk in deeply enough. Let me outline three of the insights from the exploration of how the basic building blocks of the universe *interact* as indeterminate probabilities.

First, Louis de Broglie (1892–1987) and Erwin Schrödinger (1887–1961) developed the understanding that all the particles in an atom are *waves*, like the vibrations on a violin string. The equations describing those waves are probabilities for where the particles are likely to be—they have no definite location. Think of electrons not as planets circling around the sun, but as probability waves of vibration traveling back and forth on a violin string. Each of these waves has a "spin," like a spinning top, and since they have an electric charge, the spin creates a magnetic force, sometimes pointing up (plus) and sometimes pointing down (minus). And how they interact or do not interact depends on whether the probability waves overlap or not and on other probability functions. Particles in an atom are characterized by probability and indeterminacy, not definiteness and determinedness.

Physicists can predict "the *probability* of a given atom breaking up in a particular time interval." They speak of the half-life of plutonium, which means the time it will take, *on the average*, for half of a quantity of plutonium to split into smaller atoms. But they do not know when a particular atom will split; nor can they find a force that would tell them when it will happen. This knowledge only of the probable values of certain variables gives us "a looser form of causal coupling at this micro-level than had been taken for granted in classical physics."[10]

Second, we must realize that the atom is mostly space with *large relative distances* between the atom's particles, so interaction is only a probability. If a nucleus were the size of a bowling ball on the floor in front of you, its electrons would be like grains of sand scattered all over the county. Locating that nucleus is like flying overhead in a satellite and aiming at a county with a BB gun, hoping to hit the bowling ball without being able to see where in the county it is. But as my son, David, has said, if you keep aiming at your target with a steady stream of particles, eventually you are bound to get some hits. And that's exactly the point: when you aim protons at an isotope, each proton has only a probability of interacting with a nucleus, with no fixed exactitude.

The Heisenberg uncertainty principle says that the more precisely we determine an electron's position, the more indeterminate is its momentum; and the more exactly we measure its momentum, the less we can specify its location. Each is a probability curve with a standard deviation. James Kakalos has noted that "as we need both positions and momenta to employ a traditional Newton's law description of a system," Newton's law simply does not apply at the quantum level.[11]

And third, *string theory* is the new set of principles for nuclear physics, describing all the particles as vibrating strings. It is highly developed mathematically but not yet much tested by experimental physics, because it requires super high energies. It also says that there are huge uncertainties at the quantum level. Princeton University physicist Steven S. Gubser writes that when they interact only weakly, "strings travel a long way, or last a long time, before splitting or joining." And when they interact strongly, it "is chaotic and messy. Strings fly all over the place, but they're hardly strings anymore because they're splitting and joining so fast. . . . I expect it is hard to keep track of all the different branes and dualities. But . . . spatial dimensions in string theory are mutable. They come, they go, they shrink and grow."[12]

Except for string theory, these three findings are not mere theories without empirical verification. They make sense of many kinds of experimental results that older, deterministic theories do not explain.

In sum, the Enlightenment idea of a deterministic universe obeying fixed laws with no room for God to do new things simply does not cohere with the data. At the quantum level, existence, splitting, motion, are open to many possibilities. We live in an open universe, not a closed world system.

NANCEY MURPHY: INDETERMINACY AS AN ANSWER TO DEISM

Nancey Murphy is a highly respected philosopher of faith and science and of moral philosophy. In *Chaos and Complexity: Scientific Perspectives on Divine Action*, fourteen scholars assembled by the Vatican Observatory and the Center for Theology and the Natural Sciences refer favorably to her essay "Divine Action in the Natural Order." As the introductory essay concludes, "Nancey Murphy directs our attention away from chaos and complexity to the arena of quantum physics."[13] The book's authors decided to follow her lead and devote their future conference to the theological and philosophical implications of quantum physics.

Murphy describes the historical shift during the middle of the seventeenth century from the outdated Aristotelian view of God's action in the world to the Newtonian view that everything obeys "laws of nature." Those who have wanted "a more robust view of God's continued participation in the created order have been forced to think in terms of *intervention*,"[14] meaning that God breaks the laws of physics and intervenes miraculously. But this creates tensions with scientific knowledge—if scientific knowledge is about fixed laws that are always obeyed.

William Stoeger's essay in *Chaos and Complexity* affirms God's continuous providential involvement, as does Murphy. He, too, argues against a God of the gaps, who acts only in those gaps where science does not apply, or does not explain, what is happening. Both argue for God's continuous involvement as a necessary but not sufficient cause. However, he appears to consider this a criticism of Murphy's argument. But Murphy is arguing in tandem with scientific discovery, not arguing that God acts only where physical laws are suspended.[15]

She begins her essay by setting forth criteria of adequacy for what she will advocate:

> its primary confirmation should come from its consistency with both science and theology, and especially from the fact that it solves problems that have arisen at the interface between these two sorts of disciplines. . . . An adequate account of divine action must also be consistent with the sciences. . . . We are setting out to explain how God and natural causes conspire to bring about the world *as we know it*.[16]

She is not arguing for a gap in scientific knowledge where God or theology can rush in to fill the hole; she is arguing that philosophy should be consistent with what the sciences learn as well as what theology learns.

This fits the emphasis of incarnational discipleship on the sovereignty of God or Lordship of Christ through all of life. Bonhoeffer and incarnational discipleship oppose a two-realms or compartmentalizing or sectarian approach that limits the Lordship of Christ to only gaps in science, or to only individual personal relations, or to only a "religious" compartment of life, or to only relationships inside churches, while avoiding public ethics or scientific discovery. In previous chapters I have argued against Platonic dualism, and here we have another example: Bonhoeffer's rejection of dualism between faith and science. *Christ reveals God as reality—at the center of life, not merely in the gaps that scientific knowledge cannot explain.*

Dietrich Bonhoeffer identified the tension incisively when he was reading Carl Friedrich von Weizsäcker's book, *Worldview of Physics*. Bonhoeffer wrote that Christians should not eagerly search for gaps in present knowledge where science cannot explain what happens so that they can claim that this is where we need God to provide the answers that science lacks. That is the "God of the gaps" approach, eagerly looking for some anomaly, some gap in knowledge, that science cannot explain, and pouncing on it as the place where God can do something. When science then makes further discoveries, and pushes back the boundaries of knowledge ever further, "God too is pushed further away and thus is ever on retreat. We should find God in what we know, not in what we don't know; God wants to be grasped by us not in unsolved questions but in those that have been solved." Bonhoeffer says this is true not only of the relation between God and scientific knowledge; but also true of human questions about death, suffering, and guilt.[17] Again, Christ reveals God as reality—at the center of life, not merely in the gaps that scientific knowledge cannot explain.

Murphy is arguing for indeterminacy, which is supported by our understanding of nuclear physics. Is indeterminacy a gap in our knowledge where we don't yet know but some day may fill it in? Or is indeterminacy scientific knowledge that tells us that the universe is interacting on many levels and therefore is open to multiple causal inputs that are not rigidly determined?

Murphy points out that scientists have concluded that Newton's laws are no longer adequate. Post-Newtonian quantum physics, chaos theory, and top-down or whole-part causation have emerged. Science is increasingly pointing to multiple causation, with indeterminacy built in. Most physicists affirm this as knowledge of how the universe works, not a gap in knowledge to be filled in later. However, "since the demise of the Newtonian worldview, philosophical accounts of causation have not kept pace with science."[18]

Several issues need clarifying. One is that most philosophers have abandoned Platonic metaphysics that located the laws of nature in a realm of ideals, which they no longer saw as real.[19] Those of us who are not fans of Plato's long reach through Western history and the debilitating effect on Christian ethics of its two-realms dualism, or of the concept of fixed laws that militate against God's doing new things in our lives, celebrate this abandonment.

Second, contemporary understanding of nature requires differentiation into a hierarchy of levels of analysis, from quantum physics at the base up through biology, psychology, social science, ethics, and so forth. This is the answer I was driven to as a budding physicist who was also studying behavioristic psychology. I began wondering, is what we perceive as human selfhood merely the outcome of deterministic laws that govern the electrons that drive our brains? And where is the room for God? I daydreamed about myself as a brain in a vat of chemicals, with no body, sending electronic signals to mechanical arms that would reach out for what I wanted. But how is the mind, which depends on material flesh and electronic circuits, related to the brain, and how does the brain communicate its wishes to the "arms"? I concluded that nuclear physics must be right about electrons at its level of analysis, and behavioristic psychology must see some truth at its level of analysis, but to understand selfhood and ethical freedom and responsibility requires a higher, more complex level. Each level sees truth that transcends what is seen by the other levels. More recently, Nancey Murphy and neurologist Warren Brown are making important contributions similar to but far more sophisticated than what I was thinking then.[20]

In *Chaos and Complexity*, Thomas Tracy considers levels-of-analysis approaches, and rightly argues that the levels need to be seen as interacting. The crucial insight for such approaches to work logically is that the lower level not be regarded as mono-causal so that the higher level would have to "obey its determinism" or else "override" it or "intervene." The self must not be seen as "a closed causal structure"—as Tracy's analysis seems to do.[21] Precisely here Murphy's argument for a degree of indeterminacy and multiple simultaneous causation rather than a closed causal structure provides the key. In other words, our chemical balance affects how we feel, but if we decide also to take some drugs, that affects our chemical balance. Bottom-up causality affects how we think, but also top-down causality of our deciding changes the bottom level of our chemical state.

A third set of issues comes from quantum physics. Here is where Murphy focuses her essay. Neutrons outside of their nucleus soon—after an average of about ten minutes—split into a proton, an electron, and a neutrino. Tritium lasts an average of twelve years before it decays. Plutonium lasts about 2,400 years. But these are half-lives; they are the average time, not the definite time. They are the time when half of the particles, on average, will have decayed. No outside events, no fixed laws, no observable anything tells us when one of them "decides" to split. "The peculiarity of entities at the quantum level is that while specific particles have their distinguishing characteristics and specific possibilities for acting, it is not possible to predict *exactly when* they will do whatever they do."[22] This is what physicists call "indeterminacy."

Murphy suggests five possible ways to characterize this "indeterminacy": It could be (1) completely random and undetermined, but this is hard for the scientific community to accept. There must be some reason. It could be (2) internally driven by the entity itself, or (3) externally driven by the entity's relations to something else in the physical system. But most physicists have rejected this possibility. Or indeterminacy could be (4) activated by God. Murphy, however, argues for a fifth option: divine governance in combination with the entity's previous state and innate powers. "My proposal is that God's governance at the quantum level consists in activating or actualizing one or another of the quantum entity's innate powers at particular instants, and that these events are not possible without God's action." Each event at the quantum level needs to be represented as having multiple causes, including "the prior state of the entity or system, and . . . an intentional act of God to actualize one of the possibilities inherent in" the prior state. "For any event there will be at least two, usually three, necessary conditions: the prior state of the system, God's influence, and often influences from the environment."[23]

Murphy bases her conclusion both on the ontological claim that physics discloses truth at the smallest quantum level and "on the theological claim that God works constantly in all creatures." Furthermore, it supports our need to speak meaningfully of human freedom rather than complete determinism: "Current theories in quantum physics do provide a valuable ingredient for this theory of divine action: the currently accepted supposition of indeterminacy at the quantum level provides a handy analogue for human freedom, and thus grounds for the claim that God's action is analogously *non-coercive* at the quantum level."[24]

I could imagine a different theology that would say God creates the quanta so they will be this alive, this indeterminate, and always open to God's action when God intends to act, even if God is not always acting in each. In fact, Thomas Tracy's essay in the same book, based on a somewhat different theology, argues that "God freely constrains the uses of divine power out of regard for the integrity of creatures and the intelligibility of their world." God usually leaves quantum events undetermined.[25]

Both Murphy and Tracy, and the other authors as well, agree that quantum physics shows an openness to God's action at the very base of nature. Their slightly different theologies guide them as they interpret how often, how regularly, God is actively involved. The universe is open to the active sovereignty of God through all of reality, as incarnational discipleship says.

GOD'S ACTION: MORE LIKE INTERACTIVE PERSUASION THAN TOTAL DOMINATION

This understanding of God's continuous, living interaction with the basic building blocks of creation suggests something more like God's interactive persuasion than total domination. Philosopher William Stoeger writes that God's particular revelation happens in terms of

> personal relationships involving generous, self-sacrificing love and forgiveness. And our principal way of responding to God's revelation is in those same terms. So we experience revelation as personal and social, God among us—as creator and source of life, yes, but also as a personal presence and force who loves, invites love, gives and invites giving, forgives and reconciles, and invites forgiveness and reconciliation. The created, inanimate, and non-personal levels of reality, though they exist in their own right and reveal God and God's goodness, power, and love in their own way, and give glory to God in their own way . . . , exist also to enable the development and maintenance of persons to whom God can reveal him/herself and with whom God can maintain a personal relationship leading to the full and harmonious union of the divine with created reality. The degree to which this is desired by God is expressed in creation itself, in the Incarnation and all that follows from it, and in the sending of the Spirit. . . . The ultimate manifestation of this is in the Incarnation, and in the life, death, resurrection of Jesus, and sending of the Spirit of the Incarnate One, who is Wisdom, Word, Child of God.[26]

This summation of God's revelation corresponds perfectly with the three dimensions of incarnational discipleship. God is sovereign through everything in creation; is revealed in God's incarnation in the life, death, and resurrection of Jesus; and is present dynamically, interactively, as Holy Spirit.

Similarly, Murphy asks, How could we ever know of God's action, since there is ambiguity in distinguishing God's action from natural events? The answer is that we recognize God's acts "by the way particular events fit into a longer narrative, and ultimately into the great narrative from creation to the eschaton, from Genesis to Revelation." Murphy's solution takes God's revelation in Christ as normative in a way that fits scientific knowledge. She interprets the love of God revealed in Jesus Christ as sacrificial and noncoercive rather than totalistic and dominating. It depends at least partly on human response. God's action is interactive. She writes: "I shall claim that the relevant feature of God's action in Christ, displayed analogously throughout the whole, is its non-coercive character." God respects created entities. God does not create an electron that attracts another electron. Electrons repel other electrons, and God respects that.

God works with binding forces that hold atoms, with their electrons, together—most of the time. Murphy finds that God's respect for the integrity of creation is analogous to respect for human rights in the human realm. God's governance is "cooperation, not domination."[27] Again we glimpse the integrative approach of incarnational discipleship, seeing implications of God's revelation in Christ for the whole of life, not merely one compartmentalized sphere.

Murphy's point yields important resources for interpreting individual tragedies like having a wife dying of cancer, as Frank Tupper did,[28] or a son like our David legally blind and brain damaged from birth, caused by rubella virus. Even more, it can grapple with massive evil like the Holocaust, caused by the evil of Nazism, the punitiveness of the Versailles Treaty after World War I, and a long history of anti-Semitism. It can wrestle with the devastating drought and starvation in Somalia caused by greedy pollution in the West and authoritarian violence by terrorist warlords. Do not blame it all on God. There were other causes. Isaiah 53 sees the suffering of "the righteous one," who "had done no violence, and there was no deceit in his mouth," as caused "by a perversion of justice," by "they [who] made his grave with the wicked," they who made "his life an offering for sin." That was caused by unjust persons. Yet at the same time, Isaiah says in startling language, God was acting in the midst of that injustice, which grossly violated God's will for compassion, to bring us healing, to make us whole, to bear the sin of many, and to "allot him a portion with the great." God works in all things, even in evil things, seeking to bring some good in the midst of the evil (Rom. 8:28).

SEEING ACROSS LEVELS OF ANALYSIS, DIVERSE TRADITIONS, AND MULTIPLE CENTURIES

As a philosopher, Nancey Murphy sees across diverse traditions. She was raised Catholic and is influenced by Catholic piety. Then in her shift from Enlightenment thinness to more dynamic spirituality, she joined a charismatic community for a time. And now, strongly influenced by John Howard Yoder, she identifies with Anabaptist tradition. But in addition, as a philosopher who has wrestled with the challenges of natural science, Murphy sees the implications of the twentieth-century shift in nuclear physics away from Enlightenment Deism to a more dynamic understanding of the basic elements of the universe. She sees how this suggests that we can cure the closed-world-system virus and shift toward a dynamic, living, interacting God. She invites us to connect the shift in quantum physics with a recovery of a much more dynamic theology.

Various Christian traditions have somewhat different pieties—pieties of the sovereignty of God the Father, of the living Christ, or of the presence of the Holy Spirit. Each tradition gives evidence of recovering a more dynamic theology of the presence of the living God. H. Richard Niebuhr identified with Reformed tradition, which emphasized the sovereignty of God the Father. Seeing the thinness of the Enlightenment tradition handicapping his mentor Ernst

Troeltsch, and having his own tower experience of the sovereignty of God,[29] he wrote often of *God as the living God*, dynamically involved in forming our self-hood. He wrote *The Kingdom of God in America*, focusing on those times when American churches experienced a lava flow of awareness of the dynamic character of God: in the early Puritan period, in the Great Awakenings, and in the emergence of the social gospel. (He would surely have included the civil rights movement had he written the book thirty years later.)

Karl Barth likewise worked in the Reformed tradition, with its emphasis on the sovereignty of God the Father, but in seeing the poverty of Kantian Enlightenment-influenced German Protestantism, he developed a dramatically strong *theology of the living Christ*. Dietrich Bonhoeffer identified with a more Christ-centered Lutheran tradition, and influenced by a Christ-centered Baptist tradition in Harlem in 1930–31,[30] he wrote often of *the living Christ at the center of our lives*. In the Pentecostal movement that had forerunners in the spiritualists of the Reformation, including the Radical Reformation, and that burst forth at Azusa Street, we see the clearest emphasis on the dynamic presence of the living God in the midst of our lives—*as Holy Spirit*. The astounding growth of Pentecostal and charismatic movements in the twentieth century is testimony to the way people resonate with spiritualities that overcome the closed universe of Enlightenment Deism and sense God's dynamic action in the midst of our lives.[31]

Each of us identifies more with one or another tradition. And in our pluralistic and interactive culture, each has a foot in some other tradition—or several. Few of us are totally monolithic. Some will speak of the living God, some of Christ the center, and some of the Holy Spirit—doing new things in the midst of our lives. I invite us to affirm each other in that process of healing, deepening, and enlivening.

WHY DID MODERN SCIENCE ARISE DURING THE PURITAN REVOLUTION IN ENGLAND?

Answering the challenge of secularism that Charles Taylor raises, particularly in relation to natural science, points us to a second question: How do we understand the origin of natural science? Modern science originated, or was developed, in the Puritan period in England, at the same place and the same time that democracy, religious liberty, independence of churches from the state, and constitutional democracy developed. This is truly striking. There were so many other intellectually advanced countries and so many other times when all or some of these could have developed. Why did all this happen at the same time and among the same people? Something must have been happening there. And indeed, something much related to the three themes of incarnational discipleship.

Philosopher of science Ian Barbour asks, "Why was scientific development in the Middle Ages relatively meager?" There were advanced civilizations in China,

India, Greece, and Rome, and Arab scholarship in the Middle Ages, but none of them produced natural science.

> The scientific revolution happened only once in [human] history. Seventeenth-century England was the turning point in the history of science, and . . . the Puritans were its chief agents. Seven out of ten members of the Royal Society were Puritans—a ratio far out of proportion to the population as a whole; most of the virtuosi were active churchmen, and many of the clergy encouraged or themselves took part in scientific pursuits.[32]

Throughout the Middle Ages, people thought the way to understand nature was to debate the thought of classical Greek philosophers. It was a question of deducing logically what must be the case from the Greek philosophers, especially Aristotle, with Plato standing behind him. The Scholastics trusted Aristotle because he had a logically coherent system. Their method for achieving knowledge of how nature works was endless debate about what Aristotle meant, "unrelieved by recurrence to direct observation" of nature itself. Unfortunately, Aristotle's logic ignored "the quantitative relations examined in mathematics, and the complex possibilities of multiple relationships within a system."[33]

What changed in the Puritan period? By comparison with the Thomists, influenced by Aristotle, the Augustinians and Lutherans, influenced by Plato, and the Anabaptists, focused on the New Testament, it was the Puritans who recovered attention to the Old Testament.

The presuppositions of the leaders of scientific development, who were all living during the Puritan recovery of Hebraic realism, focused on *God the Creator, who was a lawgiver.* Nature could be expected to obey laws, which we might learn to understand.[34] So the order did not come from the teleological drives or tendencies *within* individual items, as it had for Greeks; it came from the ways items interacted with each other. Apples didn't fall because it was their purpose-oriented nature to want to return to their place on the earth, as Aristotle thought. They fell because of the law of gravity, which governs *interaction* between two masses—apples and the earth. Planets didn't circle around the sun because they had an internal drive or teleological purpose to want to move in perfect circles, or because there were invisible spheres in space causing them to move in circles. They circled because of the *law of gravity*, which describes the *interaction* between the mass of the sun and the mass of the planet, divided by the square of the distance between them. We are living in the Age of Interaction.

Eugene Kaaren's contextual analysis of the guiding theological presuppositions of Newton, Bacon, Boyle, and Helmont concludes that Newton's "view of God was basically similar to Boyle's in its stress upon will and law." The close analogy "to the seventeenth-century confidence (even delight) in God's law is Old Testament Judaism. . . . In fact, the scholarly recovery of the Old Testament in Hebrew may have contributed to the general confidence in divine law." Both Boyle and Newton learned Hebrew in order to understand the Hebrew Scriptures more accurately. Newton wrote: "We are to have recourse to the Old

Testament, and to beware of vain [Greek] Philosophy, for Christ sent his apostles not to teach Philosophy to the common people . . . but to teach what he had
taken out of Moses and the Prophets and Psalms concerning Christ."[35] Here are
the two incarnational discipleship themes of attention to Jesus' teaching combined with the sovereignty of God through all of life, interacting together as one
belief—even to the point of scientists learning Hebrew!

Second, and most importantly in the development of natural science, the
Puritans believed that *God has freedom that cannot be reduced to deductive thinking.* This meant that we need the humility to examine God's creation respectfully, carefully, inductively, to discover how in fact God has organized things.[36]
In other words, science needs to do experimental research, not simply do exegesis of what Aristotle thought. This is the process of self-correction, analogous
to the Hebraic practice of biblical realism and repentance from being stuck in
the hegemony of idolatrous ideologies—the third dimension of incarnational
discipleship.

In our time, scientists led by Heisenberg, Einstein, Schrödinger and others
have found by their observations that the laws governing quanta are expressed in
probabilities and are relative to contexts in space and time, not fixed Newtonian
laws. This is a tribute to the learned humility of scientists, willing to adjust their
thinking according to what they discover inductively, and according to mutual
corroboration in community checks and balances.

Kaaren concludes that Newton "did not honor the thought of Plato and Plo-
tinus as the greatest wisdom," but "Hebrew sources." He saw God as "the transcendent Lord of the universe." This was "much closer to Israel's God as Lord
of history than any Platonic or Cambridge Platonists' affirmations of divine
Spirit. . . . In sum, it is clear that Boyle, Bacon, and Newton presuppose a
sharp distinction between Creator and creation, and that this is no idle piety."
Accordingly, Kaaren writes, Bacon opened his *Refutation of Philosophies* with
the exhortation that God "did not give you reliable and trustworthy sense in
order that you might study the writings of a few men. Study the Heaven and
the Earth, the works of God himself, and do so while celebrating His praises
and singing hymns to your Creator." Kaaren says this liberation from traditional
philosophies was "deeply theological in Bacon's proclamations, Boyle's practice,
and the purposes of the Royal Society.[37] Similarly, the spiritualist and chem-
ist Johan Baptist van Helmont emphasizes "the necessities of humility before
God and charity toward man, if the prideful and idolatrous ways of Aristotelian
speculation . . . are to be overcome."[38]

When we read the writings of Puritans in the late sixteenth and early seventeenth centuries we are impressed with their empirical approach to the
moral and spiritual life as well. They kept diaries recording the temptations
of each day and the deliverance God gave them—and what they learned from
these observations. Many had a sense of the Holy Spirit present in their daily
lives, and so paid empirical attention to what they experienced God doing
in their lives. Many exulted that they could now read the Scriptures in their

own language and check whether interpretations by church authorities were accurate or corrupt—and they did this energetically. They could measure the claims, practices, and religious persecution by the official churches against their own reading of the New Testament, and they did so actively. They formed new church groups as they also formed the scientific group, the Royal Society, and checked their own interpretations against those of others in their communities or societies.

From a feminist perspective, Sandra Harding makes a strong case for the socially interactive nature of science, as well as for social interests shaping research.[39] She alerts us to the influence of social interests on what scientists see or pay attention to, and she argues for identifying what we have repressed, rather than closing ourselves into a set tradition.[40] This looks like the incarnational discipleship practice of repentance from closed-minded ideologies, and mutual, communal correction by shared discernment. Harding shows that the scientists also worked for correction of societal injustices until the Restoration in 1660, which stifled their practice of reform.[41]

These examples should clarify that by "continuous repentance" in incarnational discipleship, I do not mean merely emotional self-recrimination or merely feeling remorse, but actively seeking to identify possible sources of error and taking sensible measures to correct them, to build in checks and balances against error, and to seek correction by others in the community. This is a process of growth in clarity and accuracy, insight and learning. It was a key practice that enabled modern science to burst forth in mid-seventeenth-century England, the same time when the Puritan Revolution brought forth democracy and human rights. So this is my third cause—community correction—to add to others' analyses of why natural science emerged when it did: (1) God is Lord over creation, so expect some order; (2) God is beyond our deductive knowledge, so do inductive research, looking for the data, rather than merely exegeting a Greek philosopher; and (3) we make errors and our perceptions are influenced by our social interests, *so practice continuous repentance in community*.

I am suggesting that we learn from the scientists to see repentance as a life practice of identifying sources of error and building in regular practices of self-correction and community correction. Life is continuous learning, including learning from our mistakes.

SOURCES OF ERROR, CONTINUOUS REPENTANCE, AND THE HOLY SPIRIT

I commended nuclear physicist James Butler for paying careful attention to likely sources of error in our research with the Van de Graaff accelerator. Ethics has much to learn from Butler, himself a faithful Baptist. (I am not saying only Christians know to pay attention to possible sources of error; this is now built into the practice of science, as it was not in the Middle Ages.)

One source of error was the background radiation in the room, naturally occurring from our place on the planet, and differing somewhat from day to day. Each time I began my research, I first measured that background radiation at the different energy levels in our twenty-channel analyzer, recorded it, and then subtracted the background radiation from the results of our own bombarding the isotopes. (Some days the military's nuclear bomb testing in the atmosphere in Nevada produced so much radiation drifting over Washington, DC, that we could not do our research. The atmospheric test ban treaty of 1963 has put a stop to that source of radiation over our nation, thank God.)

Another source of possible error was fluorine atoms that could sneak into the beam tube, despite very careful cleaning of the tube by the only person in our large research building who had small enough hands to wipe them clean, and despite the almost perfect vacuum in the tube. Fluorine is highly chemically interactive and can interact with the bombarding protons and produce some confounding outputs. Butler describes elaborate methods both to minimize that source of error and to correct for it in interpreting the data.

Coulomb interaction with the silver backing on the nickel could have been confounded with the resonance we were measuring, causing it to be interpreted as several times stronger than it truly was. So James Butler arranged an innovative way to correct for that.[42]

Half of the long research report was devoted to identifying these and other likely sources of error, describing procedures taken to minimize them, to measure what could not be eliminated, and to take them into account in the results.

In addition, several sections of the research report compare our results with results others had obtained. Where they disagreed, we named and analyzed it to discern what could have caused the differences. We thanked other researchers and offered our results with an explicitness and openness that was fully subject to checking, verifying, or disconfirming by others in the scientific community. Much of the point was to be helpful to others so that they could adopt similar refinements in their own research. This kind of science proceeds not only by seeking to identify our own possible sources of error, but also by honesty, trust, and openness *in community with others* who may see something we do not see. It is interactive on the human level as well as the nuclear level. This is a key dimension of scientific method, a shared practice, from the beginning of modern science among the Puritans. Philosophers don't emphasize it very often, but I contend that it is crucial.

Thus we see that attention to the interactive nucleus points us to the practice of joy and gratitude for God's active presence, for God's doing new things in our lives, and continuous repentance and empowerment through learning. Faith in God gives us someone to be grateful to. And since God's thoughts are higher than our thoughts, it should give us the humility to practice a life of new learning and continuous repentance.

This is the theological point: Good science does not practice denial, ignoring the likely sources of error in our perceptions. It requires practicing continuous correction in a community of checks and balances. When you read the history of the developments of quantum physics, you are impressed with the scientists' sharing what they are learning and then waiting with anticipation for confirmation or disconfirmation from others. Continuous correction in one's own practice and in a community of mutual checks and balances—this is what theological ethicist H. Richard Niebuhr advocated as continuous metanoia, ongoing repentance.

This is a biblically realistic understanding of repentance, with realism about the fact that we live with many sources of errors, known and unknown; wisdom seeks to identify them and correct them and works in a community that will check and balance the errors.

Not everyone who thinks of the Holy Spirit thinks of the call we receive now and then to practice self-correction—of our thinking, our loyalties and interests, our emotions, or our actions. But in incarnational discipleship, we say the Holy Spirit or the living Christ is dynamic and alive and not able to be captured by any of our doctrines, ideologies, classes, races, or national interests. I want to call our attention to the connection between the Holy Spirit and the call to repentance for ideological closed-mindedness by a brief examination of the New Testament book that explores the Holy Spirit most fully, the book of Acts.

Acts speaks often of the Holy Spirit calling people to repent for their closed-mindedness, especially for their resistance against accepting Gentiles into their community. At Pentecost in Acts 2:1–12, "All of them were filled with the Holy Spirit and began to speak in other languages, as the Spirit gave them ability," persons from fifteen different nations—including Medes, Egyptians, Libyans, Romans, and Arabs. Acts 2:38 says the promise is for everyone, in all nations: "'Repent, and be baptized, *every one of you, in the name of Jesus Christ so that your sins may be forgiven;* and you will receive the gift of the Holy Spirit. For the promise is for you, for your children, and for all who are far away—*everyone* whom the Lord our God calls to him" (italics added). In Acts 6, when the Hellenists among the church members complained that their widows were being excluded from the daily distribution of food, the disciples decided they needed to appoint deacons who were Hellenists "full of the Spirit and wisdom" to lead them in overcoming this discrimination. In Acts 8:5–24, the apostles prayed that the Samaritans might receive the Holy Spirit—and they did. When the Ethiopian eunuch had been baptized, the Holy Spirit carried Philip away, clearly signaling his affirmation of baptizing the Ethiopian eunuch (Acts 8:29, 39).

When Saul (Paul) was converted from persecuting Christians to taking up his mission to Gentiles, Ananias laid hands on him so he would recover his sight "and be filled with the Holy Spirit" (9:17). His sight was healed, he was baptized, and he began his mission to the Gentiles. In chapters 10 and 11, the Holy Spirit tells Peter to welcome Cornelius, the Centurion: "What God made clean, you must not call profane" (Acts 10:15). In 10:37–48, the Holy Spirit was poured out on the Gentiles, astounding the Jews; so they asked, how can we prevent them from being baptized? "God has given even to the Gentiles the repentance that leads to life" (11:18). Since God gave the Holy Spirit to the Gentiles just as to the Jews, it seemed good to the Jerusalem Council and the Holy Spirit to give their blessing to the Gentile Christians without their having to be circumcised or to keep the law of Moses (15:3–8, 12, 28). The apostle Paul said, "I testified to both Jews and Greeks about repentance toward God and faith toward our Lord Jesus. And now, as a captive to the Spirit, I am on my way . . ." (20:21–22).

We see clearly that in the book of Acts the Holy Spirit successfully calls Christians to a practice of repentance for being too closed to accepting and admitting Gentiles. This is the third theme of incarnational discipleship—repentance for being stuck in idolatrous or hypocritical ideologies. We see it in Acts, and we see it in the practice of science, learned from Puritans who wanted to be faithful to God whose "thoughts are higher than your thoughts" (Isa. 55:9).

The clearest message from scientists calling for repentance today is that the glaciers are melting, the seas are rising, large areas are suffering from the worst droughts in history, and storms are getting more destructive as carbon dioxide is increasing in the stratosphere. Millions of people are suffering, and ever-larger numbers will suffer in the next generations. Furthermore, the earth has a finite quantity of oil, natural gas, and nonrenewable minerals. We are using them up at ever-increasing rates, so they will be mostly all depleted early in this century. They will not grow back. Because of our greed and ignorance, future generations will have almost no resources. We cannot find a nearby planet to migrate to. Mars will not do. Will the Big Bang end with the Big Chill?

Some ideologies advocate that the solution is to pump it up faster and thus use it up faster in this generation. We do not need scientists to tell us that this is astounding greed, ignoring the needs of all future generations. As Larry Rasmussen writes in his Grawemeyer Award–winning book, *Earth Community, Earth Ethics*, the biggest destructive force attacking the earth is humans with our machines.[43] He spells out the repentance we need, and connects it with Dietrich Bonhoeffer's theological ethics.

What a gift this earth is! And what greed to destroy it in the present generation without thinking of the next generations. Jesus teaches that God is presently active, caring for the birds, the flowers, and us people. He calls on us not to focus on hoarding goods for ourselves and on our own desires for consumption, but on God's reign and God's justice (Matt. 6:19–33). To pay attention to how we are destroying what God and future generations care for deeply is to be called to repentance expressed in major change in our lifestyles and major change in national and international policies.

Chapter 7

Individualism

The Buffered Self versus the Age of Interaction

We saw in chapter 6 that the closed-machine view of nature is being corrected by the current understanding of nature as alive and open to new events. Nature calls for humility and learning, and for human repentance because we are threatening it by our consumption. But science is not the only challenge of the secular age; another is the triumph of "the buffered self." The buffered self is detached individualism, withdrawn from modes of intimacy, from feeling interconnectedness and covenant with cosmos or community or bodily emotions.[1] The "buffered self" is our focus in this chapter.

If I believe I am entirely self-sufficient, that I am disconnected from others and should focus only on advancing my own cause, and that my self is inside me and is not intrinsically connected with others, then I am much less likely to be open to experiencing God's presence in my life. I am like a pinball, bouncing off others, but aiming toward getting to my own goal.

The buffered self was not our original tradition. As Charles Taylor writes, "The mistake of moderns is to take this understanding of the individual so much for granted, that it is taken to be our first-off self-understanding 'naturally.'" In truth, however, "our first understanding was *deeply embedded in society*. Our essential identity was as father, son, etc., and member of this tribe. Only later did we come

101

to conceive ourselves as free individuals first."[2] On the one hand, we understand ourselves to be living in a democratic age that imagines us—the public sphere and the self-ruling people—as collective agencies. But the idea that we are self-contained selves, pursuing self-interests, basically closed off from deep relations with others, removes littler narratives of God's breakthroughs in our lives, transformative experiences, moments of experienced joy and fulfillment, and epiphanies.[3] The result is secularism. Understanding selfhood as "buffered" has resulted in "a sense of malaise, emptiness, a need for meaning. . . . Everyone understands the complaint that our disenchanted world lacks meaning, that in this world, particularly youth suffer from a lack of strong purposes in their lives. . . . This ontic doubt about meaning itself is integral to the modern malaise."[4]

ALBERT CAMUS'S WAY OF OVERCOMING THE BUFFERED SELF

The lonely "hero" of Albert Camus's novel *The Stranger* exemplifies Taylor's buffered self to such a dramatic extent that I want to ask if we can learn something important from him. Can Albert Camus, an existentialist atheist of a particular kind, teach us something about how to correct the detached individualism of the buffered self? He may surprise us.

The Stranger

The Stranger (1942) begins with a telegram telling "the stranger" that his mother died today. He expresses no emotion; he only wonders if "today" might mean yesterday.[5] The "stranger" is Meursault—a stranger to other people's concerns and emotions.

He then speaks of making an arrangement with his boss to take two days off work to go to the funeral. He comments that he has no feelings about his mother's death, but maybe the funeral will make some impact on him, or at least make her death official. He says that when they lived together, he and his mother almost never talked. He had rarely seen her in the last year, since it was too much trouble to get a ticket and spend two hours on the bus journey.

The director of the nursing home says he has arranged for her funeral to have the rites of the church. Meursault says to himself that his mother had never thought about religion. The novel offers some details, including descriptions about a few who came to the funeral, and then details about the next day, a Sunday, at home sitting watching others in the street. All without feeling, all perfunctory. The stranger congratulates himself for getting through the funeral, and muses that the next day he will go to work as usual. He simply does what seems less uncomfortable than the alternatives.

He goes on through a few days of work and of nicely developing a relationship with the attractive and friendly Marie, whom we readers grow to like. She wants to marry him and he agrees, but when she asks him if he loves her, he says no. He can develop an outwardly fairly normal relationship, but does not exhibit compassion and commitment. He is emotionally detached, very "buffered" from deep relationships. They take a trip to the beach with a couple of friends, but all without involvement, without real caring relationships with the friends.

He takes a walk on the beach, and sees an Arab man with whom his "friend" had had a fight. He had pocketed the friend's revolver, as a backup for the fight. When he sees that the Arab man has a knife, at about ten feet distance, but is not attacking him, he squeezes the trigger and shoots and kills the Arab man, basically without reason except that the stifling heat and his own sweat are bothering him greatly, and then fires an additional four shots into his lifeless body. He comments only that each shot was another step in his undoing, with no thought of the Arab man's undoing.

After his arrest, the court-appointed defense lawyer worries that witnesses have said he'd shown callousness at his mother's funeral. He replies that he has not been in the habit of paying attention to his feelings. They just come and go. The lawyer leaves, obviously bothered by his detached lack of any feeling of remorse.

The magistrate then interviews Meursault. He asks earnestly if he believes in God, shows him a silver crucifix, and gives him the opportunity to express some sorrow and repent. But the room is oppressively hot and Meursault, the stranger, bothered by flies buzzing around, does not see how his feelings have anything to do with the matter. He doesn't feel remorse but merely inconvenience. In the trial, the prosecutor focuses his case on the stranger's not showing compassion at his mother's funeral, not showing much concern for anyone, and claims Meursault is a despicable person. The sentence is the death penalty.

After more than a year in prison, during which Meursault refuses the prison chaplain's request to come talk with him, the chaplain comes into his cell to see him, unannounced. Just then the stranger is thinking Marie has not written for ages and might be tired of being his mistress since he is about to be executed. Or maybe she is dead herself. In that case, he could hardly be interested in her. Whichever. A person can get accustomed to anything with time.

The first time I read the novel, I was identifying with the stranger, and thought the chaplain's approach was somewhat gauche; but now I see the chaplain's genuine compassion. He seeks earnestly to persuade Meursault to admit he partly believes in God, or to admit he is feeling some despair as he faces death. To no avail. He sits by his side on the bed; he spends time in silence, trying to understand; he asks probing questions, coming from various possible concerns, trying for some feeling response; he looks him straight in the eye; he asks if he can kiss him; he lays his hand on the stranger's shoulder.

He asks the stranger what he thinks of life after death. Finally the stranger, frustrated, yells at the priest that he only hopes he can remember the life he had on earth (which we are thinking was not much of a life, so disconnected from others). The stranger gets more irritated and says the chaplain is on the others' side. The chaplain puts his hand on the stranger's shoulder, saying that he is on the stranger's side, even though Meursault doesn't realize it because his heart is hardened. The chaplain promises to pray for him.

Then something seems to break inside the stranger, who begins yelling insults at the chaplain. He grabs the chaplain and bursts forth with real emotion for the first time in the novel. The dam has finally broken.

What the stranger has lacked throughout was genuine emotion and authentic connection with others. In the concluding sentence of the book, however, the stranger expresses the wish "to feel less lonely." The chaplain's sincere expressions of compassion have helped break the dam.

I think it was also the stranger's sense of death coming inexorably toward him. When I first read the novel many years ago I did not realize what I finally noticed when I read it in the French—the mechanical image of time: he senses the guillotine coming steadily toward him as a mechanical progression, as if he were tied down on a plank with an electric saw steadily coming toward him from the future, machine-like, impersonal, an inhuman apparatus.

As he contemplates death, he is thinking of all of us being terminated in the same way, but it is not so much a solidarity in death as a separation, an alienation, a reduction of all compassion to nothingness. So the priest's expression of compassion connects directly with his sense of death coming like an unswerving machine.

But when he finally erupts with emotion, and the priest leaves, he feels calm and takes a long nap. When he wakes up, the sight, the sounds, the feeling of the cool night air, with its smells—of the beyondness of the universe—shine down on his face, fanning his cheeks. He not only sees beauty from a distance; it comes into him, connecting him with a universe that was previously beyond him. And he becomes connected empathetically with people starting out on a journey by ship whose siren he hears, to a world that he had lost concern for, and connected empathetically with his mother. And then he experiences a future, not of a mechanical death machine, but of a fresh start toward a new life.

I contend that Camus had an almost mystical affinity with the infinity of the universe, the stars, the ocean, the desert. He was a person raised lonely—with a mother who seldom talked and never hugged him, and with a grandmother who could not talk, and without a father, who had been killed in war. His kinship with the infinity of the universe gave him an experience of connectedness, not only with the universe, but with others.

So the climax of *The Stranger* reads, "It was as if that great rush of anger had washed me clean, emptied me of hope, and, gazing up at the dark sky spangled with its signs and stars, for the first time, the first, I laid my heart open to the benign indifference of the universe."[6] Notice the role played by bodily emotion that penetrates the shell (rush of anger), receptivity despite the shell, and compassion that interacts with others (by the priest for him, and then by him for the travelers and his mother). Bodily emotion; receptivity; compassion. Prior to this breakthrough, he was almost brought to genuine caring by Marie. She was the one person who came to visit him in prison and the one person besides his mother whom he thinks of just before the priest comes.

Many have interpreted "the benign indifference of the universe" (*la tendre indifférence du monde*) with emphasis on the "indifference," as saying the universe has no caring. But I suggest "benign" deserves more than equal emphasis: Camus experiences a connection with the universe as benign. (The French, *tendre*, means "tender," "soft," "fond," "affectionate.") The next sentence reads: "To feel it so like myself, indeed, so brotherly [French: *fraternel*], made me realize that I'd been happy and that I was happy still."

And then, so as not to drift off into sentimentality, Camus combines the stranger's wish to feel less lonely with a realism about the kind of solidarity he could hope for when he is executed: "For . . . me to feel less lonely, it only remained to hope that on the day of my execution there should be many spectators and they should greet me with howls of hate."[7]

I want to wrestle with one theme in Camus's writing at some length— detached selfhood becoming transformed by connection with the infinity of the universe. I will trace it briefly through most of his writings. I contend that we have something deep to learn from Camus that relates to Taylor's theme of the detached, buffered self—and to overcoming it.

I am interpreting Camus differently than Taylor does, with his emphasis on Camus's "Myth of Sisyphus" and atheism. Camus was an atheist (of sorts), and I am a Christian (of sorts), and I love him. I identify with Camus's wrestle with loneliness, and I invite you to also. My own father was away in the war at the crucial time in my growing-up years, and my painfully shy mother did not know what to do with a boy who had too much drive. And there are other reasons for my loneliness. I identify with Camus's affinity with the universe—maybe partly because of my physics background, but more because of my faith. So my interpretation of Camus is sympathetic. In relating to Camus, I am not a "buffered self," but an "identifying self," and I want to explain that classification further. It is important for healing the buffered self.

The Plague

Camus's *The Plague* (1947) seems to articulate Camus's own commitments. "The plague" in the novel is the bubonic plague that is killing people in the city of Oran in Algeria, but surely it symbolizes what Camus named in his address upon receiving the Nobel Prize for Literature as "the death instinct at loose among us," including I think the killing of World War II, the genocide of Jews, the atomic bomb, and the slaughter of Arab Algerians by French colonialist policies and the reciprocal slaughter of Frenchmen by Algerian rebels.

The Plague describes the heroic efforts by Dr. Rieux, Tarrou, and others to combat the plague, and to take care of people dying from it. As the plague is finally lifting and fewer people are dying, Tarrou and Rieux go up to the top of a building to talk. The presence of night, sea, "sky swept crystal-clear by the night wind," stars, and breezes over the warm stone, prompt Tarrou to ask Rieux if they could be deeper friends, and let Tarrou tell the narrative of his life. Rieux agrees. Tarrou's life is a story of opposition to the death penalty, and against ideologies that justify killing. The plague-stricken are those who justify murder by the state.[8]

And so, to celebrate their new friendship, they decide to go for a swim in the Mediterranean. "The moon had risen and a milk-white radiance, dappled with shadows, lay around them. . . . They saw the sea spread out before them, a gently heaving expanse of deep-piled velvet, supple and sleek as a creature of the wild. . . . Before them the darkness stretched out into infinity." A strange happiness possesses them as they stare at the starry sky. Then they swim together, side by side. Upon returning, neither man speaks, "but they were conscious of being perfectly at one," and they knew they would cherish this night's memory.[9]

Again we encounter the infinity of the universe, the feeling of participation, the bodily experience of empathy and community. This, I think, is the emotional climax of *The Plague*. Before this, the narrative is about desperate weariness of tending to thousands and thousands of people dying. After this, the plague gradually lifts, although Tarrou dies from it.

"The Adulterous Woman"

Camus also published an intriguing short story called "The Adulterous Woman" (1956), surely titled after Jesus' compassionate defense of the adulterous woman from judgment and stoning (John 8:3). In the tale, Janine accompanies her husband, Marcel, on a business trip to Algeria for the first time. They have not had children, but she likes being loved by him. Although he once showered her with attention, their emotional relationship has faded and Marcel seems interested only in his business. Janine has realized that his true passion is money.[10] While feeling that her sexual desires are not being fulfilled, she is aware of an Arab man on the bus showing definite interest in her. She accepts his offer of a lozenge.

That night she wakes after having slept some. She reaches out to touch Marcel, but then is seized by anguish about her own eventual death. So she turns away from Marcel and senses that she will end up dying without ever experiencing fulfillment.

She hears a call that seems very close but without any sound reaching her ears. It seems to be coming from where desert and night mingle under the sky. She gets up and sneaks out of the room without waking her husband. She runs the length of the balcony, toward the parapet they had visited, and up the stairs. The cold air burns her lungs, but nevertheless she senses it as connecting her with the sky. She focuses on the infinitude of the night above her.

> It seemed to her that the sky above her was moving in a sort of slow gyration. In the vast reaches of the dry, cold night, thousands of stars were constantly appearing. . . . Her whole belly pressed against the parapet as she

strained toward the moving sky. . . . Then, with unbearable gentleness, the water of night began to fill Janine . . . , rising up even to her mouth full of moans. The next moment, the whole sky stretched out over her, fallen on her back on the cold earth.[11]

Her "adultery" is committed with the infinity of the universe, the sky, the night, the thousands of stars. She comes quietly back to bed with her husband, weeping copiously. She does not tell him, but I think Camus is letting us know that she found the liberation from fear she had been looking for in her bodily relationship with the slowly gyrating sky.

I am not asking us to believe that Janine, and Rieux and Tarrou, and the stranger, and Camus himself in his own presence to the infinity of the universe, had found God, exactly. The picture of God painted by Father Paneloux's sermon in *The Plague* as the flail that is striking down people with the plague as on a threshing floor is hardly what Camus could affirm.[12] The theme of connectedness and communion with the benign, brotherly infinity of the universe was a real experience for Camus. Camus was not a closed, buffered self, disconnected from the world beyond himself. We need a category like "*connected* atheist," or better, connected pantheist, or better yet, existential mystic. He was not quite *alone* in the universe.

I am not arguing that Camus was a "secret Christian." He was an atheist—of an unusual sort. But I am suggesting that Camus's theme of communion with the infinity of the universe is a shadow version of the incarnational discipleship characteristic of the sovereignty of God through all of life. His theme of *the benign nature* of the infinity of the universe, of bodily and emotional connectedness with others, and of entering empathetically into the sufferings and joys of others and acting in solidarity with human need, is a shadow form, a *humanistic/mystical form*, of the revelation of the love of God in Jesus of Galilee. It is certainly thinner than the "thicker Jesus" of incarnational discipleship, but pointing partially toward it. His theme of realism about human sin, our "death instinct," and our "fall," along with emotional breakthrough and repentance or penitence, hint of the incarnational discipleship dimension of the presence of the Holy Spirit and our life as continuous repentance. This is what made him different from the individualistic atheism of Jean Paul Sartre, whose play *No Exit* says, "Hell is other people." I suggest it pointed Camus toward speaking and doing truth in the historical test times that he faced—as we shall see.

In his address upon receiving the Nobel Prize for Literature, Camus said that he needs his writing "because it cannot be separated from my fellow men, and it allows me to live, such as I am, on one level with them. It is a means of stirring the greatest number of people by offering them a privileged picture of common joys and sufferings. It obliges the artist not to keep himself apart; it subjects him to the most humble and the most universal truth. And often he who has chosen the fate of the artist because he felt himself to be different soon realizes that he can maintain neither his art nor his difference unless he admits that he is like the others. . . . My generation's task is preventing the world from destroying itself."[13]

The Rebel

In 1951, Camus published *The Rebel*. He argued that we rebel against injustice; therefore we are. He had experienced injustice against Arabs in Algeria—ruled by French colonialists. He himself grew up in great poverty in Algeria, and was lonely in his own family. Their small apartment had no toilet and no running water. Still he knew he, a Frenchman, had far more than most Arabs in their native land. He was rescued from a life with no future by a teacher who saw his potential and guided him toward the higher education that would not have been expected for a child so buried in poverty. That teacher also taught him deep loyalty to the French tradition of democracy and human rights. As a newspaper journalist, he wrote numerous articles describing the starvation of many Arabs in Algeria, deprived of sufficient food for survival, an education, and the basic needs of life, by French colonialist policies. As a journalist and then eventually a famous novelist and essayist, he wrote intensely that either France would treat Arab Algerians with the French tradition of democracy and human rights, or the Algerians would develop hatred and violent rebellion that would throw France out of Algeria. He was right. He also engaged actively in the French Resistance against German occupation and German anti-Semitic policies of imprisoning and killing Jews. Thus he passed the historical test as Bonhoeffer, Trocmé, and the other saints of the faith did. I am fascinated by him—not only because he saw and acted rightly in those historical tests, but also because of what I perceive as his underlying struggle with both personal and existential loneliness in an infinite universe.

The Rebel advocates rebellion on behalf of justice for real people, not for an abstract ideology. Injustice is evil not because it negates a Platonic ideal of justice, but because "it destroys what trust and understanding humans can have in this life."[14] As Bonhoeffer and Trocmé opposed Hitler for killing Jews in the name of fascist ideology, Camus opposed French colonialism for killing Arabs in the name of colonialist ideology, and communism for killing Russians in the name of its ideology. Camus based his opposition in the nature of rebellion on behalf of human beings, human rights of the violated, the mutual understanding of persons, and the transcendence of the universe above ideologies that kill. That transcendence of the universe is symbolized by the bright sun of the Mediterranean:

> Historic absolutism, despite its triumphs, has never ceased to come into collision with an irrepressible demand of human nature of which the Mediterranean, where intelligence is intimately related to the blinding light of the sun, guards the secret. Rebellious thought, that of the Commune or of revolutionary trade unionism, has never ceased to deny this demand in

the face of bourgeois nihilism as well as imperialistic socialism. . . . Europe
has never been free of this struggle between darkness and light. It has only
degraded itself by deserting the struggle and eclipsing day by night.[15]

The Rebel and Camus himself received harsh and angry attacks from Jean Paul
Sartre and his allies, who had committed themselves to communism. This was
deeply painful to Camus. Equally painful was his inability to persuade France
to do justice and support human rights for Arabs in Algeria and his inability to
convince Algerian terrorists to cease their strategy of killing French civilians in
Algeria. As Camus's biographer Robert Zaretsky explains,

> Finally, in 1957, he declared he would no longer speak about the [Algerian]
> war in public—a vow that, with two exceptions, he kept until his death
> three years later. . . . By the early 1950s, Camus felt stifled and emptied;
> he feared he had fallen silent because he no longer had anything to say as
> an artist. The violent public quarrel with Sartre over Camus's philosophi-
> cal essay *The Rebel* led not just to the end of their friendship but also to
> deepening doubts on Camus's part about his art. As he told one friend, "I
> feel like ink absorbed by a wad of paper."[16]

The Fall

Camus's subsequent publication of his novel *The Fall* in 1956 may be read as
his own confession of repentance, as the necessary prerequisite for criticizing
anyone else's ideology. *The Fall* is a monologue by a character who is strikingly
self-absorbed, "buffered" from concern for others, full of bragging on his many
accomplishments. But there is one occasion—only one—when he is somewhat
"stirred" by compassion and receptivity—in the presence of a river, rain, and the
universe. While walking over a bridge in Paris,

> I passed behind a figure leaning over the railing and seeming to stare at the
> river. On closer view, I made out a slim young woman dressed in black.
> The back of her neck, cool and damp between her dark hair and coat col-
> lar, stirred me. But I went on after a moment's hesitation. . . . I had already
> gone some fifty yards when I heard the sound . . . of a body striking the
> water. I stopped short, but without turning around. Almost at once I heard
> a cry, repeated several times, which was going downstream; then it sud-
> denly ceased.[17]

For the rest of his life he was haunted by quiet laughter, when he would cross
a bridge over a stream, or when he thought he saw the slim woman floating on
the ocean while he was traveling by ship. "The whole universe then began to
laugh at me."[18]

So he embarked on a career of telling the story of his life to others, with
his own penitence, so others would be brought first to judge him and then to
judge themselves, and thus to their own repentance. Here I believe Camus is

mirroring what incarnational discipleship calls repentance in his own narrative way, expressing penitence for his broken relationship with Sartre, and wishing for connectedness with others.

INDIVIDUALISTIC EXISTENTIALISM VERSUS SOCIAL EXISTENTIALISM'S INTERACTIVE SELF

Sartre was an individualistic and atheistic existentialist—a very buffered self—who excused massacres for an abstract communist ideology. He saw himself as a mere writer and viewed Camus as actually engaged in struggles for justice. And this was true: Camus, by contrast with Sartre, was a *social* existentialist, not an individualistic existentialist. He cared for real people, interacted with Arabs as well as French colonialists, and engaged in the struggle for justice for people, not only ideas.

Sartre and Camus were not the only study in contrasts. Similarly, Søren Kierkegaard was an individualistic existentialist and Martin Buber a social existentialist. Buber wrote. "Beside Augustine stood a mother and beside Pascal a sister, who maintained the organic connexion with the world as only a woman as the envoy of elemental life can; whereas the central event of Kierkegaard's life and the core of the crystallization of his thought was the renunciation of [marriage with] Regina Olsen as representing woman and the world."[19] He is saying that Kierkegaard was too disconnected from others.

Nietzsche, the atheistic existentialist, advocated the ethics of the individualistic superman, and he influenced the Nazis. By contrast, Gabriel Marcel, and Reinhold and H. Richard Niebuhr, had a more robust faith in God and were social existentialists, advocating an ethic of caring and justice for all humans. Reinhold Niebuhr, however, was somewhat influenced by Kierkegaard's individualistic understanding of human nature and by a nineteenth-century idealistic interpretation of Jesus too transcendent to actually guide our social life. Yet Niebuhr changed to a more social understanding of the self in his later writings.[20]

Not only does closed, individualistic, buffered selfhood lead to secularism, but the lack of a robustly present God tends to lead to the kind of privatistic individualism that cares little for justice for actual persons. Though some humanists care greatly for justice—as Camus did—the door is open for the extreme self-centeredness advocated by Ayn Rand and others.

AYN RAND'S DRASTICALLY BUFFERED SELF

Ayn Rand epitomizes the drastically buffered self, secularism, and bare atheism. She was an evangelistic atheist who regularly opposed any contribution of faith to ethics, calling it irrational. She sought to convert others to follow her atheism. She titled her book *The Virtue of Selfishness* (1964). She shared Nietzsche's belief that Christian ethics were destructive to selfhood: "Christianity 'is the best kindergarten of communism possible.' Christianity taught believers to put others before self, an ethical mandate that matched the collectivist emphasis on the group over the individual. Thus a new system of individualist, non-Christian ethics was needed to prevent the triumph of Communism."[21]

Rand wrote that "if a person speculates on what 'society' should do for the poor, he accepts thereby the collectivist premise that men's lives belong to society."[22] Then the person starts being concerned about fair distribution of goods so the poor have enough to eat and survive. That leads to collectivism. Rand was twelve years old when she experienced "Russian soldiers in boots, carrying guns, confiscating her father's chemistry shop." She was then Alisa Rosenbaum. (She later changed her name to Rand, as did Rand Paul and Nathan Brand, both of whom she greatly influenced.) She "burned with indignation. . . .The Rosenbaums were an elite and privileged family. . . . Alisa and her three sisters grew up with a cook, a governess, a nurse, and tutors."[23] But all this was taken away by the communists. Nietzsche, the philosopher of resentment and atheism, became her favorite philosopher.

I empathize with her resentment at the communists; I teach two weeks each year at International Baptist Theological Seminary in Prague, where many students come from the former Soviet Union, and tell of the residue of that oppressive experience. Before the fall of the Soviet Union, I traveled in East Germany, Kazakhstan, Moscow, and Leningrad. I talked with people who had lost their faith in God, and in communism, and in their work (where low morale and inefficiency ruled). They were literally hopeless. But when I was invited to a speaking tour of East Germany that began the very day the Berlin Wall was opened, as I explained earlier, I experienced the blossoming of surprise and hope after a dreary half-century of communist domination. I can understand why Ayn Rand "burned with indignation" and wrote in reaction against the former Soviet Union.

In *The Virtue of Selfishness*, the chapter "Collectivized Ethics" is loaded with terms of reaction and resentment: collectivist, dictatorial presumptuousness and moral cannibalism of the altruist-collectivist code, psycho-epistemological chaos, appalling recklessness, a dense patch of venomous fog, the enslavement and destruction of medical science, power to devastate an entire nation, prehistoric savagery, a caveman who can't conceive of any reason why the tribe may not bash in the skull of any individual if it so desires, the Soviet serfs who die of epidemics, filth, starvation, terror, and firing squads.

Her first novel, *We the Living*, is an angrily anti-communist autobiography. Her writings are a reaction against her experience as a secular Jewish child whose family was deprived of its business, home, and wealth. At times her mother "erupted into full-blown rage. In a fit of temperament she would lash out at her children, on one occasion breaking the legs of Alisa's favorite doll and on another ripping up a prized photo. . . . She declared openly that she had never wanted children, hated caring for them, and did so only because it was her duty."[24] Rand learned rage from her mother. Historian Jennifer Burns is right when she says that in *Atlas Shrugged*, her best-known novel, "Rand let loose all the bile that had accumulated in her over the years. Particularly when John Galt takes center stage Rand's text seethes with anger and frustration and yields to a conspiracy theory. . . . The aggrandizing state has run amok and collectivism has triumphed across the globe. Rand's decaying America resembles the Petrograd of her youth."[25]

But doing ethics as reaction is dangerous. It blocks us from understanding the cares others have—especially if they see things differently. It causes a dangerous either/or, with hate and anger against the opposing pole of the either/or dichotomy, and an idolatrous absolutizing of one's own extreme pole. It excludes sensitivities to truths and realities in between. Life isn't just two opposite things; life is complicated. As John Paul Lederach writes, from a wealth of experience working to help people imagine a better, more peaceful future in situations of great conflict, "The moral imagination is built on a quality of interaction with reality that respects complexity and refuses to fall into forced containers of dualism and either-or categories."[26]

Reactionary ethics blocks us from caring about other dimensions of life and needs besides the one dimension of the reactionary polarization. It creates an authoritarian ethic that accepts only true believers and rejects those who have other valid concerns. And it causes the emotion of resentment or hatred to conquer our good sense. The outstanding study by historian Fritz Stern, *The Politics of Cultural Despair*,[27] shows how philosophers of resentment and reaction against modernity and the Enlightenment prepared the way for fascism in Germany. In their reaction against the Enlightenment, they advocated a homogeneous community—an Aryan German race. Although I have been a critic of the Enlightenment my whole career, I take this as a serious warning against doing ethics mainly as reaction against the Enlightenment.

Rand thought compassion for others who have needs leads to collectivism. Therefore, compassion is the root of evil. She calls this altruism—serving others *with no concern for one's own interests*. Her fictional hero, John Galt, says altruism advocates that "Your only definition of the good is a negation: the good is the 'non-good for me.' If *you* wish it, it's evil; if others wish it, it's good."[28] The opposite pole is selfishness, which is the root of good. Here she is dichotomizing, distorting Christian ethics as the exact opposite of her own ethic. Jesus does not fit Rand's dualistic either/or; Jesus calls on us to love our neighbor *as we love ourselves*. Most Christian ethicists affirm a role for proper self-love. But Rand defines love as an extreme form of altruism that allows no place for loving yourself. She says altruism teaches that "any concern with self-interest is evil, regardless of what those interests may be." In her reaction, she advocates that "Concern with his own interests is the essence of a moral existence."[29]

Rand never advocates mutual love, community, relationality, sharing, or covenant faithfulness, which many of us believe constitute the essence of life; it is

always either my individual self-interest as the single concern or total acquiescence to whatever others want. It is always either/or. She called the biblical
teachings that we are our brothers' keepers and that we need to come to the aid
of the poor and disabled "the altruist-collectivist premise," and "the collectivist
premise." She opposed Medicare for the aged as "the regimentation and disinte-
gration . . . of the professional integrity, the freedom, the careers, the ambitions,
the achievements, the happiness, the *lives* of . . . the doctors."[30] But she said
nothing about people who can't afford health insurance.

This of course directly opposes Jesus' commandment that we are to love God
with all our heart, soul, strength, and mind and to love our neighbor as ourselves
(Matt. 22:37–39; Mark 30–31; Luke 10:27). It directly opposes Jesus' many
teachings about compassion and aid for the poor and disabled. It also opposes
the many commands of the Old Testament about justice for widows, orphans,
immigrants, and the poor. So it is not surprising that her writings consistently
argue for atheism and against God.

ATHEISTIC NATURAL LAW OF SELFISHNESS

Ayn Rand needed a basis for her argument that our chief moral purpose is selfishness. So she developed her atheistic, individualistic version of natural law. In
Christian ethics, natural law is an appeal to reason that is shared by reasonable
people, including nonbelievers. The apostle Paul writes that Gentiles do not
have the law, but when they do by nature what the law requires, they show that
the law is written on their hearts or consciences (Rom. 1:18–23 and 2:12–16).
By contrast, Rand's individualistic, "objectivist" natural law says individual survival is the law of nature. Animals survive by instinct; humans survive by seeking
their own self-interest—not by paying attention to the interest of others.

Christians teach that we humans are social creatures; we survive by working
together, defending each other and caring for our children. Primitive humans
survived the threats from predators by banding together. In today's more
complex world, we survive by taking care of our children rather than aban-
doning them and by building an economic and political order that we depend
on. Humans are peculiar in that children need parents until they are teenagers
or longer. The challenges of rubella that threatened the life of our son David,
of glaucoma that threatened him with blindness, of the Great Recession that
threatens the economic life of our nation, of Hitler that threatened world civili-
zation—none of these did we meet individually. It took working together. The
opportunities to get an education, to learn complexities, to worship as a church,
to form a place of work, to have a home and food—these are not things any of
us achieve singly. They all happen as a community enterprise.

But Ayn Rand says reason dictates that survival comes from seeking individual self-interest—not by paying attention to the interest of others. "One's

sole obligation toward others [in respect to 'poverty, ignorance, illness'] is to maintain a social system that leaves men free to achieve, to gain and to keep their values. . . . The moral purpose of a man's life is the achievement of his own happiness."[31] This she says is what objective reason tells us.

She names her ethic "objectivism"—what she contends is the truth dictated by objective reason. It is the opposite of paying attention to faith, which she calls "mysticism." None of the history of loyalty, compassion, and cooperation to defend each other is here; it is systematically excluded. Her ethics of objectivism also says only reason matters; it represses emotions. Yet the signs are rampant throughout her writing that her emotional reaction against the Soviet collectivism of her youth plays a powerful role in her ethics. The ethics of reaction blinds people to the complex realities that dwell between the two absolutized extremes.

In her reaction against collectivism, Rand also rejects government action that expresses compassion and justice for the poor. She writes: "When I say 'capitalism,' I mean a full, pure, uncontrolled, unregulated *laissez-faire* capitalism—with a separation of state and economics. A pure system of capitalism has never yet existed, not even in America."[32] Rand's ideal economy would be even more unregulated than the robber baron era before the Great Depression of 1929 or the largely unregulated days that led to the Great Recession of 2008. It involves total trust in big banks, credit-default traders, mortgage lenders, and corporations to do what is right.

Rand has no qualms about placing so much trust in the hands of business leaders. "Those who advocate *laissez-faire* capitalism are the only advocates of man's rights," she insists.[33] The government "has no right to violate the right of private property by forbidding discrimination in privately owned establishments. No man, neither Negro nor white, has any claim to the property of another man. A man's rights are not violated by a private individual's refusal to deal with him. . . . If that 'civil rights' bill is passed, it will be the worst breach of property rights in the sorry record of American history. . . ."[34]

There are forms of "balanced capitalism" in which most production is done by private corporations, but the power of corporations is checked and balanced by child labor laws, minimum wage laws, restrictions on pollution, prohibition of racial discrimination, and regulations for mine safety, worker safety, restaurant cleanliness, food inspection, bank capitalization, mortgage lending, etc. Government organizes some functions, including police, fire departments, state universities, public schools, public hospitals, unemployment insurance, aid for the disabled, Medicare, Medicaid, and Social Security. Rand's reactionary advocacy of laissez-faire capitalism opposes all these services to the common good and checks and balances against concentration of economic power: private corporations, oil companies, big banks, and mortgage lenders should be allowed to do whatever seems right to them.

Her hero, John Galt, embodies an ethic of resentment and reaction, calling on all his followers to remove themselves from American society and instead to hide out in a small self-made town in the West, Galt's Gulch. This secret town is self-made and isolated from all the rest of America. It symbolizes the isolated individualism, the lack of caring about others, that her ethics advocates. She is attacking American government as if it were the collectivism she experienced in communist Russia. But American government is not Russian government.

Ayn Rand's extremely "buffered self," her atheism and isolated individualism, led to her ideology of individualistic self-advancement. She opposed compassion for others who are left out. But in addition her objectivism, with its belief in the isolated individual as totally rational and not driven by emotion, also blinded her to the power of her resentment against the rage in her childhood family and in her reaction against Soviet communism. She projected this in an extreme form against the American system of a balanced economy, with antitrust laws, progressive taxation, and checks and balances against overly concentrated economic power. She had neither the benign universe, the sensitivity to emotion, the connectedness with other persons, nor the sense of repentance that Camus had. She was a buffered self to the extreme, and she advocated that we all be like her.

Her blindness to the power of resentment can be seen in her unusual sexual arrangement. Nathaniel Branden (renamed Nathan Brand) was her disciple, coauthor, and official stand-in and lecturer spreading her ideology. She developed a sexual passion for Nathan; so she explained to her husband, Frank, and Nathan's wife, Barbara, that it was rational for her to have Friday afternoons privately with Nathan for sexual purposes. This Friday practice continued for several years until she discovered that Nathan had developed an extramarital sexual relationship with yet a third woman. She reacted furiously, publicly cutting off all dealings with him and all his roles in advancing her ideology. In her resentment, she also destroyed all her other friendships one by one. She died of cancer, completely alone. Barbara Branden and Nathaniel Branden each published memoirs in 1986 with lurid details of her relationship with Nathan and her habitual use of amphetamines. "To the outside world Rand emerged a deeply unsavory figure, manipulative, controlling, self-deceived, and wildly emotional despite her professed rationality."[35]

WE ARE NEUROLOGICALLY INTERACTIVE SELVES

Neurological research is showing that we are not closed, buffered selves. It demonstrates that Ayn Rand's objectivism of closed, individualistic self-interest badly misses our reality as interactive beings. Nancey Murphy and Warren Brown, in *Did My Neurons Make Me Do It?*[36] show that we are not merely individual, rational pursuers of self-interest. We are in fact intrinsically connected with and driven by our emotions and by our relations with others far more than we realize.

Human brains are unique in having numerous "Von Economo neurons." These neurons have very long axons (transmitters) reaching through much of the brain. They receive information about the states of the body like heart rate, blood pressure, blood vessel dilation, muscle tone, etc., and transmit that information to other parts of the brain. They are important for comprehending emotion and signaling the social significance of action and perception. They are "highly active during experiences of empathy, shame, trust, regret, detecting the mental and emotional states of others, and making moral decisions."

The adult human brain has many of these neurons, but infants and apes have few of them, and lower primates have none. They are crucial for responsible and ethical human action. They give intuitive awareness ("gut feelings") to our thinking and acting. This means emotions are critical for rational and uniquely human behavior and ethics. Murphy and Brown quote the philosopher Ludwig Wittgenstein: "The idea of thinking as a process in the head, in a completely enclosed space, makes thinking something occult. . . . One of the most dangerous ideas for a philosopher is, oddly enough, that we think with our heads or in our heads." We think with our whole selves. There is not some central control room in the brain where all the outside information arrives and gets evaluated and understood. Rather, the evaluating and understanding gets done by the whole brain, in interaction with the body, including emotional signals, all of which are interacting with other persons or realities, including Albert Camus's stars, sky, night air, and ocean. We are connected. We are interactive. Murphy and Brown note that "Consciousness is not linked to the activity of a single brain area, but is a functionally integrated network of neuronal activity that extends across widely distributed areas of the cerebral cortex," and these are continuously interacting with signals from the body interacting with other persons and realities in the body's neighborhood. Similarly, Neurologist Drew Westen writes,

> The vision of mind that has captured the imagination of philosophers, cognitive scientists, economists, and political scientists since the eighteenth century—a *dispassionate mind* that makes decisions by weighing the evidence and reasoning to the most valid conclusions—bears no relation to how the mind and brain actually work.[37]

Westen provides extensive evidence confirming what Murphy and Brown argue, emphasizing how the emotions, the "gut reactions," guide our decisions far more than we realize. We regularly decide based on emotions and passions, and then devise rational reasons to justify what our emotions guided us to do. These emotions are not simply about our own internal wishes and interests; they are deeply connected with loyalties to others. This connectedness, this interactive loyalty, this covenant relationship, has proved essential for human survival. Westen puts it in evolutionary terms: "Natural selection . . . favors animals that care for close relatives, which evolutionary scientists call 'inclusive fitness' (because it includes the 'fitness' of others who share their genes)."[38] Our loyalties enable us to decide very quickly; there is no long delay for rational weighing of the evidence.[39]

HOLISTIC ETHICS NEEDS CRITICAL ATTENTION TO EMOTIONS AND LOYALTIES

Therefore, holistic character ethics needs critical attention to loyalties, interests, and passions.[40] This corrects rationalistic Enlightenment-influenced models that seek to eliminate attention to passions and emotions from ethics. It also fits Jesus' teaching that "where your treasure is, there will your heart be also"; and in the next verse he says that your heart shapes your perceptions, and these shape your body: "if your eye is generous, your whole body will be full of light; but if your eye is greedy, your whole body will be full of darkness."[41]

So we need to pay attention to the widespread resentment during the present Great Recession that began in 2008, and to how we direct that resentment. Rand advocated the laissez-faire ideology of Ludwig von Mises, Frederick Hayak, and others, and directed her anti-communist resentment against the American system of checks and balances against unrestrained concentration of power and greed. We are learning that former Chair of the Federal Reserve Bank Alan Greenspan was much more deeply involved in Rand's inner circle and her laissez-faire ideology than we had previously realized. Greenspan actually became a member of the inner circle of her collective. He gave lectures in the institute that spread her ideas and had her attend his swearing-in ceremony at the White House. She published a book with essays by Greenspan, and he cosigned her breakup letter with Nathaniel Branden.[42] The ideology of opposition to regulation of big banks and to progressive taxation of the very wealthy led to Greenspan's errors, which he confessed after the meltdown of the economy and the Great Recession. In 2008, when the Great Recession hit during the last year of the Bush presidency, Greenspan repented before Congress of the ideology that had led him astray: "Those of us who have looked to the self-interest of lending institutions to protect shareholders' equity, myself included, are in a state of shocked disbelief." He had put his trust in the big banks and mortgage lenders without checks and balances against greed.[43]

Greenspan was stunned when he realized that the Great Recession was not caused by a government that was too active in regulating the big banks, the Enrons, the Ponzi schemes, the mortgage lenders, or the credit-default traders, but just the reverse. He and government had been infected by the ideology variously named laissez-faire, trickle-down, and supply-side. They had backed far off from regulating or even from taxing the very wealthy and powerful. His confession tells us that resentment—or better, corrective action—needs to be directed not against a government overly active for justice, but against an ideology that led government to back off from its check-and-balance responsibilities. This ideology is still blocking it from requiring banks to renegotiate loans so that they can avoid foreclosing on millions of homeowners and from restoring previous tax rates on the very wealthy so the government can fund jobs to repair the nation's decaying roads and bridges and can cease giving pink slips to schoolteachers.

Something like Ayn Rand's individualistic natural law theory is advocated in Tea Party literature, based on an interpretation of the Constitution that opposes government activism for justice: it contends government has no right to "to take taxes from one group so it could spend on another" group that cannot fend for themselves—"as in programs like Medicare or Medicaid."[44] Nor does government have the right to establish checks and balances against the concentrated power of increasingly large multinational corporations and big banks. In fact, however, this is a distortion of the U.S. Constitution for purposes of advancing an ideology of greed. The Constitution explicitly gives Congress the authority to raise taxes and to regulate interstate commerce.

The best-known Tea Party senator is Rand Paul of Kentucky. "In high school I cut my teeth on philosopher-novelist Ayn Rand, probably still one of the most influential critics of government intervention and champions of individual free will." He shortened his name to "Rand," and advocates the same Austrian School laissez-faire ideologists that Ayn Rand champions. He proposes to end all foreign aid, including aid to the hungry and aid to combat HIV/AIDS. He advocates abolishing the Department of Education and the Department of Energy, thus basically eliminating federal aid for schools and for energy conservation and antipollution. "It should be the free market that decides what type of energy we use, not the government."[45] Thus this ideology devastates God's good earth, programs for the poor, the unemployed, the disabled, those who cannot afford health insurance, and those who need an education.

But Rand Paul is not merely partisan. He says that voters have one main grievance—the national debt—which is the fault of both parties. "Much of the debt liability was incurred when Republicans controlled all three branches of government," he concedes. When Ronald Reagan became president, the national indebtedness accumulated from the previous two hundred years had totaled one trillion dollars. After the presidencies of Reagan, George H. W. Bush, and George W. Bush, the national indebtedness had multiplied twelvefold to twelve trillion dollars.[46] The tax rate for the top bracket had been 91 percent during Eisenhower's presidency. President Reagan cut it to 28 percent; Clinton returned it to 39.6 percent and balanced the budget.[47] Rand Paul says George W. Bush greatly increased the debt and entitlements, and initiated two long, expensive wars. Bush cut the tax rate for the top four brackets, with the biggest cut for the wealthiest bracket. He cut the tax rate on dividends and capital gains to 15 percent, so owners of stock pay only the tax rate of the working poor. He eliminated inheritance taxes for gifts to heirs of over $1 million and made other tax cuts for the wealthy and the corporations. When he left office, the nation was mired in the greatest recession since the Great Depression.

Its economic results are a strong argument against the laissez-faire or trickledown ideology that Ayn Rand advocated. It rigs the rules so that the income is shifted to the very wealthy, while the 80 percent of the people who are the consumer base see their share of income and their purchasing power decrease. Consumer purchasing power is 70 percent of the economy, so the economy declines.

Wisconsin Representative Paul Ryan, who drafted the budget bill that makes drastic cuts, including in Medicare, requires staffers to read Ayn Rand's *Atlas Shrugged*. He describes Obama's economic policies as collectivism—"something right out of an Ayn Rand novel." Ryan invoked the central theme of Rand's binary extremism when he said: "Almost every fight we are involved in here on Capitol Hill . . . usually comes down to one conflict—individualism versus collectivism."[48]

The influence of Ayn Rand's resentment against Soviet collectivism and advocacy of laissez-faire ideology impelled those who removed checks and balances from the mortgage lenders, the big banks, the dishonest Enrons, and the Ponzi schemes. This ideology is not Jesus' care for the poor. Our emotional resentment should be pointed toward the cause of the Great Recession, not its victims.

RECOVERING AN INTERACTIVE UNDERSTANDING OF SELFHOOD

But it's not just the economy that suffers from the effects of extreme individualism. Sociologist John Brueggemann gives extensive data showing that understanding the economy as pure private interest leads to a withering of our neighborhoods, families, and community involvement. His book *Rich, Free, and Miserable* (originally titled *The Market Is Stealing our Neighborhood*) shows that how we understand the economy affects how we understand other dimensions of our lives. Not only are we too focused on economic competition to have the time needed for involvement in community, but the dominating image of life as self-advancement influences us to understand the rest of the world that way.[49] He brings the analysis of Robert Bellah et al. (*Habits of the Heart* and *The Broken Covenant*), Larry Rasmussen (*Moral Fragments and Moral Community*), Robert Putnam (*Bowling Alone*), and others to more recent experience. Of these, I especially commend Rasmussen, because he combines sociological analysis with ethical action and church organization, all with elegant prose. Rasmussen understands the world of interaction in which we are now living.

What he adds is that recovering a social understanding of selfhood requires recovering an understanding of churches as community, and of the economy as based on covenant obligations and human rights.[50] We began to see this in chapter 5, on the covenant tradition's understanding of democracy. Anyone who makes wealth in this society is benefiting from the education that the society gives to workers and consumers, from the society's justice supported both by the legal system and police and the character and consent of the governed, from the transportation systems provided in large part by people and government working together, and from the natural resources that are a gift of God—many of which will not grow back once they are consumed. Benefiting from all this creates a covenant obligation by the wealthy to the community.

This is the age of economic globalization and interaction. Every nation's economy is dependent on the global economy. In 2011, the threat of a Greek default on debt threatened to pull the world into a recession. The question was whether Europe could act in covenant cooperation to assist Greece sufficiently and whether Greece could act in covenant responsibility to its European partners as well as its own people. Multinational corporations have growing power over national governments and over the lives of most everyone. We depend on a peaceful world with a sense of responsibility to one another and to the actions that keep the world peaceful. We depend on one another to heal the looming climate crisis and the exhaustion of natural resources.

In chapter 5, we saw the American tradition of covenant responsibility and human rights of life, which includes basic needs of life, liberty (which includes religious liberty and citizenship rights to vote and peacefully assemble and run for office), and dignity in community. The Declaration of Independence based this on our all being created by God with unalienable human rights. This is what has guided America when it rose to the occasion and abolished slavery, built a social safety net of Social Security, Medicaid, and Medicare, abolished legal segregation during the civil rights struggle, and now does better on religious liberty for Muslims than many European nations. Ayn Rand and the laissez-faire ideology want to decapitate that American covenant at the neck and replace it with an ideology of laissez-faire freedom in which each individual should be left to fend on his or her own. We would then have sawed off the American guiding spirit. That is the extreme of the buffered self. Those of us who care about the American tradition of human rights need to work together to defend it against decapitation by an uncaring ideology of individualistic greed.

MARKERS OF GOD'S ACTION IN OUR LIVES

In sum, the human being is emotionally interactive, not an isolated, buffered self or purely a rational seeker of self-interest. And so is our globalizing world and its economy. The neurological, sociological, economic, and philosophical trend toward the interactive self can reverse the cause of secularism and atheism that we see in the buffered self. It can open our sense of selfhood emotionally and interactively to the presence of God in our lives. I began pointing the way of deliverance from the buffered self via Albert Camus's sensitivity to the benign universe, bodily emotion, connectedness with other persons, and penitence or repentance. Each of these themes is abundantly clear in Jesus' teachings. I thought it intriguing to see it in Camus, the sensitive rebel, and in neurology, sociology, and economics.

Camus has led us to wrestle with loneliness and with connectedness with the universe and others. Ayn Rand must have wrestled unhappily with loneliness in her life. We have seen that neurologically, psychologically, sociologically, and economically we are not merely self-contained selves, but are in interaction with each other. Ours is the age of globalization and the age of interaction. Awareness of our interactive nature can help overcome secularism: it can open us to connection with God's presence, with the small actions of God's presence in our lives, somewhat as Camus opens to connectedness with the infinity of the universe and with others. But what interactions in our lives can we experience as God's presence? Here is where the incarnational discipleship theme of the thicker Jesus comes in.

How shall people who have recovered a sense of the interactive self notice and give thanks for God's action in our lives? We saw in chapter 6 on the interactive nucleus that it is inadequate to perceive God's presence only in actions that we cannot explain. As Dietrich Bonhoeffer said, this "God of the gaps" gets driven outside the center of our lives. Instead we see God interacting in the center of our lives, not on the extremely rare occasions that break laws, but daily, in many smaller occasions. Jesus teaches that we have mustard seeds of the kingdom now. Jesus came at a time when people were not seeing God's action in their lives and there was nothing new under the sun. They thought that life was basically domination by a Roman Empire and by their own wealthy power holders and unjust authorities. In this context, Jesus said the reign of God is at hand, and this is being fulfilled now in our midst.

What we need are the markers, the characteristics of the mustard seeds of the reign of God that happen in our lives, so we can appreciate them and give thanks. Here there is not space to say all I would like to say. I have made the case elsewhere[51] and plan to make it yet more. The Aramaic scholar Bruce Chilton, who can sense the Aramaic behind the Greek translation we have of Jesus' teachings, concludes that every time Jesus proclaimed the reign of God, he quoted words from about twenty-five passages in the prophet Isaiah in Aramaic. He intended people to understand the reign of God in the context of the prophet Isaiah's proclamation of God's deliverance.

We can identify seventeen passages—many of which Jesus quoted from— where Isaiah proclaimed that God is bringing deliverance or salvation.[52] Various themes recur throughout those passages: *Deliverance* from various kinds of captivity or bondage; breakthroughs of *justice* and good news to the poor; practices of *peacemaking*, *healing* from illness or blindness; *joy* that comes from the sense of participation in God's compassion; *repentance or return to God*; and a sense of *God's presence*, including as Holy Spirit or as light in the midst of darkness. The very same themes in Isaiah recur throughout the message of Jesus.

We can experience breakthroughs of deliverance, justice, peacemaking, healing, joy of participation, repentance, and a sense of God's presence. These are seven kinds of mustard seeds—small breakthroughs—of God's present action, God's reign. As interactive selves rather than buffered selves, we can experience God's deliverance in our lives. We can notice them and give thanks to God for them. Many people, as they lie down to go to sleep at night, say a prayer of gratitude for little breakthroughs during the day. I hope that identifying these seven marks of God's gracious deliverance can help you notice breakthroughs to give thanks for.

Themes of deliverance are manifest in Jesus' teachings and in his ways of relating to people with compassion. Thus, from the perspective of incarnational discipleship, these are indicators of God's presence in our lives. Incarnational discipleship sees the teachings and deeds of Jesus the incarnate Galilean Jew as the revelation of the kinds of actions in which we experience God's presence. God's action is not experienced in the way that Paneloux in *The Plague* indicated, but in the way that Jesus indicated.

Jesus very often quoted passages from Isaiah—far more often than he quoted any other prophet or book of the Bible. But no one thinks Jesus carried a scroll of Isaiah around in his back pocket so he could look up quotations. He had memorized much of Isaiah. That means he had meditated deeply on Isaiah. And it means that we should pay attention to Isaiah as we seek to understand Jesus' teachings.

I recommend a regular practice of quietly meditating in God's presence, seeking to listen for God's will in our lives. For me it is best early in the morning, when my mind is more relaxed and open—less "buffered." I have been following something like the devotional method of Ignatius of Loyola—slowly meditating my way through Isaiah, four to six verses per morning, with the help of commentaries by Brevard Childs and John Goldingay, and trying to imagine what Jesus might have thought and felt as he meditated on these passages. And then I practice a listening prayer, listening for what God might be saying to me through this passage, through Jesus, and through the Holy Spirit. Then I write a little in my journal about what hits me. This has been very significant for me. I commend it for others.

Recognizing and celebrating these markers in our lives—God's mustard seeds of deliverance—can help us overcome the "buffered self" as advocated by Ayn Rand and others. But as we will discover in the following chapters, sometimes religion itself is a contributing cause of people's embrace of secularism. Theological misunderstandings and religious wars have contributed to suspicion and cynicism. In seeking to recover an interactive self and society, we need to examine carefully how Christian thought and action may have unwittingly catalyzed the cause of secularism.

Chapter 8

Sin

*A Realistic Understanding
of Sin and Selfhood*

We have seen that to think of ourselves as buffered or isolated, closed off from other persons, misses the reality of who we really are. We not only depend on others; we interact regularly with others and are shaped by them in ways deeper than we realize. When we become aware of the interactions that shape our self-hood, we can also be more aware that God is interacting with us. But to notice God's presence, we need clues about the kinds of things God does in our lives.

Incarnational discipleship points to Jesus as the giver of these clues. Jesus teaches us to give thanks for the mustard seeds of God's reign that happen all around us: little breakthroughs of deliverance, justice, peace, healing, repentance, joy of participating in God's compassion, a sense of God's presence. These are markers of God's action in our lives. Thank God for the mustard seeds of God's deliverance!

But there is a darker side of our lives—injustice, violence, uncaring, and sin. In *A Secular Age*, Charles Taylor writes that Deism and optimistic liberal Christianity leave out the dark side of creation—the threat of nuclear war, impending climate crisis, massive unjust suffering, the world and universe's degeneration.[1] Deism was too Panglossian in its rosy picture of humankind, and it reduced all human meaning to the search for pleasure. People react against this over-optimism. It is unrealistic. If Christianity is too naive about life's dark side, people sometimes react against that, which is another cause of secularism.

Sometimes an ethics of practices and character, which I advocate, also falls into a superficial understanding of the dark side of human nature, if it puts its emphasis on habitual engagement in practices and traditions as the needed antidote to sin without attention to repentance for the sin embedded within our own Christian traditions and without a public ethic that provides checks and balances against sin. A moralistic view that we just need to get people converted, give them some helpful sermons, or urge them to do ethical practices, and then they will be good and support what is right, fails to provide the necessary depth of analysis.

The Great Depression, the Holocaust, Hitler's Third Reich, World War II, and now the Great Recession and the domination of huge multinational corporations and the destruction of our earth, have raised profound questions about liberal optimism as well as about the secular humanist view of human nature as essentially malleable.[2] But if we seek a deeper, more realistic view of the dark side of human nature, we need to look elsewhere than in an authoritarian view that too consistently denigrates human initiative, human responsibility, and human reason.

Taylor argues that when either Christians or secularists lack a deep view of sin as something within us as well as in others, their high ideals can turn to angry hatred against others who oppose their ideals.[3] That can turn to scapegoating, domination, and exclusion. This tendency applies equally to self-righteous Christians as well as self-righteous humanists who lack theological faith. Both need a profound understanding that we ourselves participate in solidarity in sin beyond our own awareness.

In this chapter, we'll explore economic justice as a window into larger issues of sin and selfhood. Since the eighteenth century, the economy has come to be seen more and more as the dominant metaphor for understanding social and political interaction. How we interpret the economy has hugely influenced how we interpret the rest of life. After investigating economic sin and injustice in recent American history, we will explore what Reinhold Niebuhr and Dietrich Bonhoeffer have to say about sin, greed, and selfishness. We also look to three biblical dramas from the book of Genesis for wisdom about how to recognize and diagnose sin. What are needed, we will see, are realism and honesty—and an understanding of ourselves as standing in solidarity with sin rather than outside of it.

DECEPTIVE IDEOLOGIES IN THE ECONOMY AND IN FOREIGN POLICY

Incarnational discipleship calls us to continuous repentance for getting entangled in ideologies that work to defend some special interests and lead to hypocrisy and injustice. Repentance requires honest realism about our own conscious and unconscious self-defenses and their power over us. It also requires clear ethical norms that throw a light on the wrongs of the ideologies.

In the buildup to the Great Recession of 2008–2009, advocates of laissez-faire or trickle-down ideology had developed the policy of concentrating wealth in the hands of the few and trusting them to do right with that enormous economic power. We saw in the last chapter that this greatly increased the incentives for greed—for extravagant profit-seeking and extravagant pay for CEOs, since greedy profits were no longer significantly taxed. They also decreased enforcement of regulations by the government and by the Securities and Exchange Commission on corporations, banks, and the economically powerful. They appeared to believe that the powerful do not need checks and balances and restraints against greed.

Bill Clinton continued the policy of favoring deregulation, supporting the repeal of the Glass-Steagall Act that had barred banks from trading in stocks and bonds and claiming junk bonds as security for their loans.[4] With its repeal, the floodgates were opened for banks to take on billions of dollars of high-risk investments as their capital and thus become vulnerable for bankruptcy—which triggered the bank collapses and near collapses and the Great Recession of 2008.

George W. Bush removed checks and balances yet more, appointing Harvey Pitt, an advocate of loosening regulations, as Chairman of the SEC (Securities and Exchange Commission), whose job is to regulate the stock market. He came to office promising a "kinder, gentler" SEC—light on regulating. Economist Paul Krugman wrote, "The SEC is seriously underfinanced: staff lawyers and accountants are paid half what they could get in the private sector, usually find themselves heavily outnumbered by the legal departments of the companies they investigate, and often must do their own typing and copying."[5] The scandals of Enron, Arthur Andersen, WorldCom, and Tyco, finally led to severe criticism of the SEC's laxity.

The SEC had received six substantive complaints since 1992 that Bernard Madoff was running a Ponzi scheme, but it failed to investigate even to the extent of checking Madoff's account with Wall Street's central clearinghouse and his dealings with the firms that were supposedly handling his trades. "If you're looking at a Ponzi scheme, it's the first thing you do," Madoff said. Those simple steps, he added, could have revealed years earlier that he was running the largest Ponzi scheme ever—the worst scandal in SEC history.[6]

After Pitt, the SEC got a serious chair who did his job for three years, but he was succeeded in 2005 by Christopher Cox, a former Republican congressman from California. The SEC then spent less on enforcement and imposed less in fines on wrongdoers, according to the Government Accountability Office. During the 2008 presidential campaign, Republican John McCain called for Cox's resignation because Cox had failed to investigate the practices that led to the collapse of banks and mortgages.[7]

With credit-default swap trading escalating into incredible amounts, and virtually unregulated; with mortgage agents benefiting from huge incentives to make profits on each loan arranged regardless of how irresponsible the loan; with mortgage companies packaging the loans and selling them to other lenders who would take the risks for the mortgagers' irresponsibility; with all of them claiming these foreclosures-in-waiting as capital, again unregulated and unexamined; and with tax rates for capital gains and top incomes cut so low that the incentives for greed were greatly increased—the unsound financial transactions grew exponentially. With tax rates on the wealthy reduced drastically, the government's indebtedness (which had totaled $1 trillion at the beginning of Reagan's presidency) suddenly exploded to $12 trillion by the end of George W. Bush's presidency.[8] The laissez-faire defense is that such tax cuts grow the economy. But shifting the tax burdens away from the wealthiest actually caused the real income of middle-class and lower-class Americans to decline from 1980 to 2008.[9] The naive belief in the invisible hand working via laissez-faire ideology without checks and balances came crashing down in the Great Recession—the largest crash since the Great Depression—in the last year of the George W. Bush administration. How could policy makers be so naive about sin, about the need for checks and balances against greed?

The economy is not the only arena in which the powerful ran unchecked. U.S. policy-makers since 9/11 declared that the checks and balances of international law, the Geneva Convention, and the protections of the U.S. Constitution and Bill of Rights do not apply to prisoners of war in the "War on Terrorism."[10] Prisoners have been disarmed and are powerless and under the control of soldiers who have been revved up with hostility against enemies. When guards are encouraged by authorities to perform cruel and inhumane treatment against powerless prisoners and all legal protections are lifted, the result is likely to be abuse. Similarly, those not imprisoned in Abu Ghraib and other prisons in the Middle East were put in Guantanamo, which, although under control of a U.S. military base, is in Cuba and therefore not protected by U.S. law or the Constitution. As a British barrister said during a conference at Denver Seminary, Guantanamo was "a legal black hole."[11] It had no legal checks and balances against torture. This astounded experts in England, Europe, and the Middle East, who knew that powerless prisoners need the checks and balances of international law and the Constitution to protect them.

A Pew survey of world opinion in March 2004 (www.people-press.org) concluded that an important factor in world opinion about the United States was the perception that it acts unilaterally without taking account of the interests of other nations. Large majorities in every nation surveyed (except the U.S.) believed that the United States pays little or no attention to their nations' interests in making foreign policy decisions. This opinion was most prevalent in France (84 percent), Turkey (79 percent), and Jordan (77 percent), but even in Great Britain 61 percent said the United States pays little or no attention to British interests. It was a drastic worsening of world opinion about the United States by comparison with previous polls. Similarly, a Gallup poll of U.S. opinion taken June 9–11, 2006, asked U.S. citizens if six different values were better off, the same, or worse off because of the Iraq War. Strikingly, by far the worst result came when they asked about "the image of the U.S. around the world." Sixty percent believed the international image of the United States had deteriorated, and only 11 percent thought it had improved.[12]

A U.S. policy of go-it-alone unilateral domination rather than international cooperation not only alienated the United States from other nations but also eroded U.S. security. Making war on Iraq before the international inspections were finished, and against the advice of almost all other nations, while already making war against Afghanistan, caused international resentment—especially in Muslim nations. Closing out other nations from bids for Iraqi reconstruction intensified the international hostility. Ignoring warnings of the international inspectors that 350 tons of very high explosives stored in Al Qa Qaa needed guarding when the U.S. army invaded Iraq in 2003 allowed these high explosives to fall into the hands of terrorists for use against U.S. forces and Iraqi citizens.[13] In all these ways, ignoring the checks and balances of wisdom from other nations increased anger and recruitment of terrorists, especially in Muslim nations. In 2003, the year when the war against Iraq began, 208 international terrorist attacks killed 625 people. As anger against the United States grew, the number of terrorist attacks exploded each year. In 2006 it reached 14,371 attacks that caused 13,186 deaths.[14]

How could policy makers so ignore that the United States, with its enormous concentration of power, needs checks and balances from international wisdom and international law? The erosion of respect for the wisdom of other nations and international treaties indicates a self-flattering naiveté about sin and the need for checks against concentrated power. The absence of such checks has produced disaster.

Actually, quite a few church members identified the president who put these policies in place as "the Christian candidate" and voted for him—twice. It seems clear that we need a deep and realistic view of human nature that affirms both sides of our nature: We are created in the image of God, with an actual claim to human rights for all and a potential for much good. But at the same time a realistic view owns our solidarity in sin—in all of us, not only in those we stereotype and pillory—and that recognition requires transparency, mutual admonition, and checks and balances. Otherwise, fallen human beings do great injustice. Without realism about sin, churches are led into idealistic irrelevance on the one hand or authoritarianism on the other.

WE NEED NIEBUHRIAN REALISM

Reinhold Niebuhr was the best-known American theologian in the twentieth century—especially well known for his realistic understanding of sin, of greed for power and profit, and self-deception.[15] He advocated checks and balances against concentrated power, whether economic or governmental. When asking how government leaders could be so gullible as to believe that holders of enormous concentrated economic power would do the right thing without needing checks and balances on greed, we can turn to Niebuhr for important guidance.

But we haven't looked to him, not enough. Why not? The answer in part is that his theology lost favor because he had a weak Christology, ecclesiology, and eschatology, and an individualistic nineteenth-century Jesus.[16] Nevertheless, when I was a student, Reinhold Niebuhr's writings enabled me to face the realities of sin I saw in my own seminary's administration; so I transferred to Union Theological Seminary where he became my teacher. His writings helped me to recognize sin on my own country's part (not only the Soviets' part) in the unbelievably dangerous and astoundingly overbuilt nuclear arms buildup; in the systemic racism of the power of the privileged and the customs of the culture; in a patriarchal culture that not only held many women back but did enduring damage to me and many other men; in the laissez-faire economic ideology that serves to cover up domination by the concentrations of wealth; and in my own sometimes unwitting, naive participation in all those sins. The ethical analysis in his writings and his lectures allowed many of us to own up to the realities of sin without becoming total cynics. He was my teacher at a time when some of the hidden realities of sin came crashing in on my naive young adulthood, and he made it possible for me to cope.

DIETRICH BONHOEFFER, *CREATION AND FALL*

Can incarnational discipleship build a realistic and deep understanding of sin, based on the more christologically appropriate Dietrich Bonhoeffer, with his strong emphasis on the incarnation of God in Jesus Christ? Bonhoeffer built an incisive correction of the nineteenth-century idealistic view of Jesus that still hampered one side of Reinhold Niebuhr's dualism: Bonhoeffer had the strong Christology, ecclesiology, and eschatology that incarnational discipleship calls for. He also had a realistic understanding of sin that enabled him to face the sin of Hitler's Third Reich more insightfully, from the start, than any other theologian.

When Bonhoeffer returned from his sabbatical year at Union Theological Seminary and Harlem to the University of Berlin in 1932, the first course he offered was "Creation and Sin: A Theological Exposition of Genesis 1–3." It connected powerfully for his students:

> The course proved to be an immediate success among the students who crowded into his lecture room. It was a winter of profound discontent in Germany; it was also a time of confusion, anxiety, and, for many, false hope, as social and political upheavals led to the demise of the Weimar Republic and the birth of the Third Reich. In the midst of these events Bonhoeffer called his students to focus their attention on the word of God as the word of truth in a time of turmoil.[17]

When Bonhoeffer interpreted Genesis 1–3, the drama "of creation, of the beginning," he paid attention to "all the methods of philological and historical research." But he was also listening for the word of God, as revealed in Christ.[18] "It is only from Christ that we can know what the beginning is," he wrote in *Creation and Fall*. "The story of creation must be read in a way that begins with Christ and only then moves on toward him as its goal. Indeed one can read it as a book that moves toward Christ only when one knows that Christ is the beginning, the new, the end of our whole world."[19] Thus Bonhoeffer's understanding of sin fits the thicker Jesus dimension of incarnational discipleship as well as its emphasis on realistic repentance.

Bonhoeffer says that the world sometimes dismisses the creation story as "a myth, a childlike fanciful picture of the dim and distant past." But in this drama of Adam and Eve we hear "God's word; this is an event at the beginning of history, before history, beyond history, and yet in history. . . . *We ourselves* are the ones who are affected, are intended, are addressed, accused, condemned, expelled."[20] The drama brings to light our own deep subconscious awareness of the reality about us. Adam and Eve seek to flee from God's presence, because it will reveal their shame. "We have all had the dream in which we want to flee from something horrible and yet cannot flee from it."[21]

BONHOEFFER DIAGNOSES SIX DIMENSIONS OF SIN

Sin mars the world in which we act; weakens our moral reflection; and lurks in our hearts, cultures, and power structures. Bonhoeffer wisely does not reduce sin to one single dimension, but profoundly diagnoses its snake-like way of sneaking into different dimensions of our lives and relationships. I delineate his diagnosis in six dimensions.

1. *Replacing God as the source of our knowledge of God with our own knowledge, our own conscience, and our own claim to universal reason, is the first dimension of sin.* Our basic sin is our "reaching out to grasp the strength and glory of the Creator for oneself."[22] It is about trying to replace God with our own ego; it is about *snatching power*. The serpent's question, "Did God really say, 'You must not eat from any tree in the garden'?" (Gen. 3:1 NIV) suggests the idea of "going behind the word of God and providing it with a human basis—a human understanding of the essential nature of God. . . . The serpent claims to know more about God than the human being who depends on God's word alone."[23] Seeking to answer the serpent's question "requires humankind to sit in judgment on God's word instead of simply listening to it and doing it. And this is achieved by proposing that, on the basis of an idea, a principle, or some prior knowledge about God, humankind should now pass judgment on the concrete word of God. . . . At that point they have become God's master, they have left the path of obedience, they have withdrawn from being addressed by God."[24]

2. *Divided loyalties split us from God and others.* Bonhoeffer describes Adam and Eve before the fall as living "in the unity of obedience." They live trusting God and one another, and are at peace. They live "out of the life that comes from God." But once they doubt God's instruction not to eat of the tree of good and evil and seek to replace God by their own knowledge, they have an "ultimate split . . . . It means no longer being able to live before God, and yet having to live before God. It means receiving life from God no longer as grace coming from the center and the boundary of one's own existence but as a commandment that stands in one's way and that with a flaming sword denies one any way of retreat."[25] This dimension of sin fits Jesus' diagnoses of divided loyalties between God and mammon, between praying to God and praying to show off for others, between giving our trust to the God who knows how to give good gifts and giving our trust to the dogs and pigs (Jewish designations for the Gentile and Roman power structures).[26]

"Divided loyalties" means that when we move out of a trust relationship with God, we replace God with a force, a power, that takes over our selfhood, distorts our perceptions, and perverts our actions. Genesis 3 speaks of the serpent; Genesis 4 warns of the power of resentment, "lurking at our door"; the historical drama of the Bible points to the power of idolatry to drive us to unrealistic perception and to destructive action. So, likewise, the apostle Paul writes of sin as bondage, enslavement to a power that entraps us. For example, Alcoholics Anonymous begins by admitting powerlessness in relation to a force that distorts our thinking, our actions, and our relationships.

The drama alerts us to various idolatries, various loyalties that rival God, such as racism in the culture, greed and economic striving, nationalistic desires for revenge, lust for sex, and varieties of addictions. Sin is a power that enslaves even without our realizing it. Realism in diagnosing our situation as a society begins by confessing that we are in the power of economic ideologies and militaristic forces. Sin is not only about rational choices of an isolated self, but also about coming under the power of a force that leads to destruction.

3. *Sin involves the desire to make ourselves equal to God.* The serpent promises, "you will be as God." Bonhoeffer's diagnosis is profound because he focuses on *the drive to be as God.* The temptation offered by the serpent is first to question what God has said, to place ourselves as equals to God, judging God's veracity, even making ourselves masters of God's truth; and second, to tell us we will be *as God.* Bonhoeffer repeats this phrase "as God" (*sicut Deus* in Latin) twenty-four times in five pages. And he writes of shame, cover-up, and hiding or evasion in shame thirty times in eight pages—far more than guilt. His emphasis on shame points not only to disobedience but also to the embarrassment of having sought to be equal to God, having broken our trust relationship with God.[27] In shame we practice evasion, flight from God.[28] "The word *disobedience* fails to describe the situation adequately."[29] It is rather tearing ourselves loose from the relationship of creature to Creator, and instead seeking to be equal to the Creator, with ego[30] and power that rebel against the limits of our created relationship. In this

divided loyalty, we feel shame for having sought to elevate ourselves beyond our means. And this also *divides us from* each other because of our urge to dominate.[31] It causes a fundamental split in our reality. It functions like a Freudian pathological defense mechanism: evading honest analysis of the cause of a serious problem and blocking realistic paths toward deliverance.[32]

The serpent says we will be as God, "*knowing good and evil.*" This cannot mean achieving moral knowledge. Adam and Eve already had moral knowledge: they could eat of any other tree except this one tree; they should leave father and mother, cleave together, and be fruitful and multiply; they should name the animals; they are responsible for tending the garden and keeping it. Nor can it mean to have sex: they had already been told to cleave together and have babies, and that is very good. It means to be as God, *possessing all knowledge, as God does.* "The tree of knowledge is the means to universal or divine knowledge," Bonhoeffer says. "It is idiomatic in Hebrew to express a totality by using two extremes, 'downsitting and uprising' (Ps 139:2); 'neither good nor bad' (Gen 31:24)." In 2 Samuel 14:17, 20, discerning good and evil is described as knowing "all things that are on the earth." "Knowing good and evil is in some sense, to be like God," to know everything, as God does.[33] Succumbing to this temptation hardly gave them godlike knowledge; the only knowledge it gave them was shame that they were naked. So they made fig leaves and hid in the bushes.

4. Sin is the temptation of power and domination. When we try to seize equality with God, it also means claiming the power to dominate others. Sin involves "the desire to rule, . . . the will to be creator, a reaching out to grasp the strength and glory of the Creator for oneself—a raising to unconscious awareness of one's own ego, a begetting and giving birth by one's own power." Bonhoeffer says this is "the desire to rule in the semblance of service." We can see the desire for power in every realm of human life, from the economic and political to interpersonal relationships. It shows up in the claim in sexual relations to be entitled to possess the other, "a refusal to recognize any limit at all; . . . a boundless obsessive desire to be without any limits." Sexuality becomes "a passionate hatred of any limit."[34]

A friend commented that in the book *Blink* Malcolm Gladwell discusses a marriage expert who can listen to fifteen minutes of a married couple's conversation and determine with about 90 to 95 percent probability whether or not the marriage will make it. When Gladwell asked the expert how he can do this, the expert listed all the things that can be toxic in a relationship—anger, an unforgiving attitude, and others. The relationship can survive these. But what no relationship can survive is pride and contempt, even if it's only on one end. Pride and contempt set up permanent hierarchies where one is above another and consequently either the shame that results from being treated with contempt or the pride that says this person is not worthy of being with you dissolves the relationship.

5. Sin is self-deception, hiding from God, defensive denial, and refusing to face our own limits. When God comes into the garden, Adam and Eve hide themselves from God among the trees. When God asks, "Where are you?" Adam says, "I heard the sound of you in the garden, and I was afraid, because I was naked; and I hid myself." He was not afraid because he was naked; he was afraid because he had distrusted God, disobeyed God, and tried to make himself equal to God. In his shame, he was being defensive and deceiving himself. Bonhoeffer says we each live in a struggle between "God's truth pointing to my limit, and the serpent's truth pointing to my unlimitedness."[35]

6. *Sin leads us to abdicate responsibility and blame others.* God asks Adam, "Who told you that you were naked? Have you eaten from the tree of which I commanded you not to eat?" Adam evades responsibility, makes excuses and blames "this woman" and even tries to blame God for giving him this woman—for whom he had been so grateful a few verses previously.

The dream that we all have of trying to flee from something that we cannot escape "repeatedly rises up out of the subconscious as knowledge of this, the true situation of fallen humankind. Adam tries to excuse himself with something that accuses him. He tries to flee further and yet knows that he has already been apprehended." Human defense mechanisms and ideologies try to evade the real problem.[36]

We can learn from Adam that we need self-critical awareness; our claims to be on God's side are usually self-deception in the service of self-aggrandizement. They are defense mechanisms that divert us from realistic awareness of the problems that threaten us. They are strategies of evasion that block insight into destructive actions that break relationships. We all need a community of blunt friends who will tell us the truth about ourselves.[37]

CAIN AND ABEL

Bonhoeffer began to interpret the drama of Cain and Abel in the fourth chapter of Genesis, but lacked the time to finish. Old Testament scholar Claus Westermann has rightly argued that the drama of human sin in Genesis should not stop after the fall of Adam and Eve's sin in chapter 3, but should include the actions of Cain and Abel in chapter 4. Chapters 3 and 4 are tightly connected, meant to go together: Adam and Eve are in both; in both God is calling humans to responsible action; in both, the humans fail to follow God's call to responsible action and evade God; in both, the consequence is alienation between humans and alienation from the earth; in both, they are driven out of their garden; in both, God still gives them protection. Understanding the fall only in terms of Genesis 3 while ignoring chapter 4 often produces an individualistic understanding of sin without the social dimension of brother dominating brother, and it often produces blindness to dimensions of power, domination, and violence.[38] Let us go further than Bonhoeffer had time to do. We will find that sin especially involves the final point made above: *abdicating responsibility.*

Abel's farming was productive, but Cain's was not. In the prehistory when this drama was first composed, agricultural technology said that the way to make your crops grow was to sacrifice to the gods. Cain blames his crops' failure on God for not looking with favor on his sacrifice, rather than taking responsibility himself.

But God looks with compassion on Cain and his resentment. God says to Cain, "If you do well, will you not be accepted? And if you do not do well, sin is lurking at the door; its desire is for you, but you must master it."

How can he do well?

Jesus must be thinking of Cain and Abel in Matthew 5:21–26 in the Sermon on the Mount: Jesus begins, "Thou shall not murder." Cain's murdering Abel was the first murder. Jesus speaks of being angry with your brother: Cain was angry with his brother. Jesus says one of the brothers is offering his gift at the altar of worship: Cain and Abel had offered their gifts at the altar. Jesus warns that anger can lead to judgment and destruction: it certainly did for Cain and Abel. And Jesus urges the brother first to go and make peace with his brother; then come and offer his gift. This is how Jesus says we can do well when facing the passion of anger and resentment—first go and make peace.[39]

If we follow Jesus, we interpret the drama of Cain and Abel as a call to take a transforming initiative: God has compassion; God takes the initiative, coming to talk with Cain; God seeks peacemaking. God hopes urgently that Cain will feel compassion, will take an initiative of responsibility, will go and talk with Abel; will seek peace with his brother. (Had he done so, Abel surely would have suggested how to farm more effectively, and the drama could have climaxed with two happy, prosperous, and living brothers!) But Cain fails to take the initiative of peacemaking. He gives in to his impulsive passion of resentment and domination, and he murders his own brother.

A second time God speaks to Cain: "Where is Abel your brother?" It is a confrontation of sorrow and love—sorrow for the fallen Abel, sorrow for the defeated Cain. It is a confrontation of compassion and reconciliation that hopes against hope that finally Cain will respond to God's love, see his own responsibility for his brother with compassion, take an initiative, and begin to make peace with God. Cain is being offered a second chance to strive against the resentment in his heart.[40] But instead Cain replies, "I do not know; am I my brother's keeper?"

Again and again in the story of Cain and Abel, God addresses Cain with compassion, hoping Cain will likewise feel compassion and take a transforming initiative of responsibility. Again and again God takes an initiative of reconciliation toward Cain, hoping Cain will take an initiative of reconciliation toward Abel and toward God. However, Cain repeatedly spurns the offer, shirkingly going the way of self-isolation.

A third time God speaks to Cain, calling on him to care, to open his heart, to turn and repent and make peace: "What have you done? Listen; your brother's blood is crying out to me from the ground! And now you are cursed from the ground, which has opened its mouth to receive your brother's blood from your hand. When you till the ground, it will no longer yield to you its strength" (Gen. 4:10–12).

Cain replies, "My punishment is greater than I can bear!" Is this the beginning of taking responsibility for what he has done? Is Cain acknowledging that this is *his* punishment for *his* evil deed, and it is too much for him to bear? Or is it only the concern of the isolated self for himself?

A fourth time God comes to Cain, in compassion for him, with a peacemaking initiative: "And the LORD put a mark on Cain, so that no one who came upon him would kill him" (Gen. 4:15).

> God speaks, does not turn away. God talks with Cain, and gives him protection for life. The cold-blooded murderer remains God's creation, God's human child. God looks on Cain with compassion. Cain is still a fugitive, but God protects him so he will live on. In the sign that God has placed on Cain, God protects Cain's life from angry vengeance. God's punishment is different from human punishment. Life remains life, even the life of the murderer. God wants the life of a sinner, not his death. Does Cain recognize the opportunity he is being given? Without this chance Cain would already be finished. And so would I.[41]

Incredibly, Cain misses it one more time. Cain misses the suffering love in God's words and deed. We might imagine that by now Cain would prostrate himself before God in abject remorse for his terrible crime, but he does not. Having chosen not to struggle with the resentment in his heart, he removes himself from God's presence; there will be no seeing God face to face, no blessing and new name. "Then Cain went away from the presence of the Lord, and settled in the land of Nod, east of Eden."

THE TOWER OF BABEL

The drama of the Tower of Babel in Genesis 11 confirms Bonhoeffer's understanding of sin in ways not often enough noticed. I go beyond what Bonhoeffer had time to do in order to point out its confirmation of his insights. Like Adam and Eve, the "Babel-onians" want to build themselves up to God's level—in the heavens. "Then they said, 'Come, let us build ourselves a city, and a tower *with its top in the heavens*, and let us make a name for ourselves; otherwise we shall be scattered abroad upon the face of the whole earth" (v. 4). The Babylonian empire was known for its drive to dominate others and for its exaggerated claims to power. The huge Babylonian gate and walls connected to it, adorned with massive animal-symbols of power, can be seen today in the Pergamon Museum in Berlin. Its intention is overwhelmingly clear—to impress anyone who enters with the dominating power of this empire. And the Babylonian ziggurat—most likely the model for the Tower of Babel story—was built to imitate a mountain, topped by a temple where the priest was supposed to be high enough to be intimate with a god.

The drama is full of irony. Although they decided to build up to God's level, they begin not on the top of a mountain like Zion, but on the hot, low plain of

Shinar, showing blatant ignorance of human limits. More—they build not with solid stone, as anyone starting out on such a highly ambitious intention should know to do, but instead use the crumbly man-made bricks of the ancient Near East. And instead of holding the bricks firmly in place with cement, as any sensible person should know to do, they use tar. So we picture a tower high enough to reach up to the heavens, made of crumbly bricks held together with tar made slippery and liquid by the hot sun on a baking plain, and we expect the outcome: the tower wobbles and the bricks slither and crumble.

But no: "The LORD *came down* to see the city and the tower, which mortals had built." The builders did not reach God's level: God had to come down to theirs. In fact, it is like the two other stories of shame, Adam and Eve, and Cain and Abel: God comes into their presence, descending to their level. God speaks and acts redemptively, dividing the people of Babel into many language groups so they cannot communicate with each other and thereby unite into one large, dominating empire.

And the irony goes farther: As Adam and Eve ate the fruit in order to become wise like God and achieved "the wisdom" that they were naked and should hide in shame, so the Babylonians built the tower in order to "make a name for ourselves; otherwise we shall be scattered abroad upon the face of the whole earth." The name they got means babble, because they lost their ability to understand each other's speech. "And the LORD scattered them abroad from there over the face of all the earth." Can you imagine their embarrassment and shame—now scattered all over the earth in confusion? We ourselves look all around us at the thousands of languages, and we laugh embarrassedly at American monolingual inadequacy in the practices of listening to others—we and the "Babylonians."

In the three dramas of Adam and Eve, the Tower of Babel, and Cain and Abel, we notice the motif of being alienated, split from others and from the earth. The desire to build ourselves up to God's level and to dominate others results in alienation and loss of community with others and with the earth. In my own dreams that parallel these stories, I end up trying desperately to communicate with others, but either I cannot make words come out or the others ignore me.

The temptation has both theological and social-ethical dimensions. It lures us to try to obtain knowledge equal to God's, and thus to be able to rival God and to have the power to dominate others. The drama of the fall probably was composed when Israel was developing a powerful empire under King Solomon, who had seven hundred wives and three hundred concubines competing for his favor, tremendous territory and military power, and a reputation for wisdom almost like God's. With all this power he therefore lacked advisers who had the nerve to speak truth to his power. The Yahwist (composer of the second creation account, the stories of the fall and Cain and Abel, and of the parable of the Tower of Babel) probably had this historical context in view, the problem of hubris during the reign of Solomon.[42] In 1 Kings 12 the leaders advise Solomon's successor Rehoboam to lighten the hard work that Solomon had laid on them.

But Rehoboam reacted just as Pharaoh once had—making the forced labor yet harder.[43] Widespread resistance against Solomon's and then Rehoboam's forced labor, too much like Pharaoh's slave labor, ensued. The drama of the exodus from Pharaoh's forced labor became a criticism of Israel's monarchy with its forced labor. The Yahwist was ambivalent, supporting David's monarchy as part of God's deliverance, but reacting against concentration of imperial power.[44] The books of Kings and Chronicles are realistic about the sinful temptations of power; they echo with the refrain that one king after another "did what was evil in the sight of God," including injustice and foolhardy war-making—without first counting the cost, as Jesus later said.

In his study of the first three chapters of Genesis, Bonhoeffer surely gives us a more profound understanding of human sin than does a definition equating it with only selfishness, or missing the mark, or having sex, or having moral knowledge.

ABDICATING RESPONSIBILITY—VERSUS THE FREE RESPONSIBILITY OF A *STELLVERTRETER*

But how does the sin of *abdicating responsibility*—the temptation of the powerless—relate to the sins of *power and domination* and *not facing one's own limits*, the temptations of the privileged?

Lisa Dahill points out that Dietrich Bonhoeffer's family "was well off, with a staff of ten full-time servants, and moved in the foremost cultural and intellectual circles in Berlin."[45] Furthermore, Dietrich was clearly a genius. In 1932, after his conversion to following Jesus, he reflected on the event during his high-school studies when the teacher asked him what his vocational intention was. Dietrich "quietly answered, 'theology,' and flushed." It "gave him such conflicting feelings of vanity and humility [and] consternation." He "deeply enjoyed this, and, at the same time, felt ashamed. . . . Now he stood solemnly in the presence of his God, in the presence of his class, now he was the center of attention. . . . And again he felt ashamed. For he knew about his pitiful vanity. How often he had tried to master it. But it always crept back, and now it spoiled even the pleasure of this moment." The other students stared at him with mistrustful and mocking eyes. His pride and self-promotion turned to shame for having so exalted himself and for being so scorned by the other students. He concluded his own description of the event: "I am strong. God, I am with you. Do you hear me? Or do you not? To whom am I speaking? To myself? To you? To those others here? Who is it that is speaking? My faith or my vanity?"[46] Dahill observes,

> Yet by all accounts he was a warm, sensitive, and appealing human being. For instance in the 'Portrait' that opens his biography, Eberhard Bethge writes: "Dietrich's smile was very friendly and warm. . . . In conversation he was an attentive listener, asking questions in a manner that gave his partner

confidence. . . . Bonhoeffer was incapable of treating anyone in a cursory fashion. He preferred small gatherings to large parties, because he devoted himself entirely to the person he was with."[47]

My own reading of the autobiographical hints in Bonhoeffer's writings agrees with Dahill's interpretation: he wrestled with how to accept his awareness of his own social and natural gifts and with shame for feeling himself more ambitious and gifted than others.[48] That part of the temptation of Adam and Eve, and of the Babel-onians, to seek a place higher than others, almost equal to God, and then to feel shame about overreaching, spoke to Dietrich. Therefore, he criticized the temptations of ego and disconnected individuality in philosophical idealism,[49] and in his own spiritual struggle and discipline. So he sought self-correction in his "self-effacing christocentrism," his "unrestricted self-surrender," his "self-denial," and his lifelong insistence that the Christian, like Jesus, must be a "person for others" practicing self-sacrificial *Stellvertretung* in love for others.[50]

Clifford Green writes that in the early 1930s, Bonhoeffer had not yet clearly distinguished—theologically or personally—between the dominating, self-centered ego as *power*, and the *strength* of the strong, healthy, mature ego. The self-centered ego should, indeed, be renounced. But the healthy ego should be affirmed. Otherwise "weakness can be indiscriminately affirmed. . . . Bonhoeffer unwittingly tends to negate strength as well as self-serving power, and to affirm weakness in an indiscriminate and undialectical way."[51]

Green diagnoses Bonhoeffer's struggle with power in society, as well as his struggle with his own ego-strength, his own power and how to limit it, with brilliant insight.[52]

> Awareness of the autobiographical dimension of *Discipleship* helps to clarify these Christological and anthropological conflicts. . . . Viewed in the light of Bonhoeffer's own struggle with personal power, . . . he is over-reacting against his own past. . . . Since he has not distinguished between mature and healthy ego strengths and selfish, dominating power, he is involved in the attempt to suppress the strengths of his ego—strengths which theologically and psychologically should be affirmed. There is thus a power struggle within himself.[53]

Green criticizes Bonhoeffer's language in *Discipleship* that Christ *invades, attacks, and annihilates* the powers of Satan and the world, and *assaults and breaks* the will of the flesh.[54] Dahill cites Green's language here but could be misinterpreted as implying that Green is affirming this language.[55] Actually Green is showing where Bonhoeffer, in his internal struggle, uses violent language inappropriately.[56]

Green and Dahill are both criticizing Bonhoeffer's hermeneutic of renunciation and self-denial in *Discipleship*—Green for what it means for both genders, and Dahill for what it means for women. Green is saying Bonhoeffer's self-renunciation needs to be transformed into relational, sharing, mutually participating, communal language in which both men and women are not continually struggling between self-assertion and self-censorship, but mature into mutual responsiveness, responsibility, and initiative. Dahill argues that self-denial is not the right answer for a woman who has spent her life oppressed by males with excessive power. It can be dangerous for oppressed persons who have been told all their lives to sacrifice self for others. So Dahill begins her book with the account of Shirley, whose alcoholic and abusive husband one night pinned her against the wall and sought to strangle her to death. "Raised in a conservative Christian home and taught to obey the male authorities in her life," she was fortunate not to have obeyed that message of self-sacrificial love that night. "She summoned all her strength and was able to claw him off her and run for her life."[57]

The powerless are tempted to give up and give in to the sin of abdicating from responsibility. Dahill argues powerfully and rightly that feeding them the antidote of pure self-sacrifice, self-denial, living only for others, giving in to the needs of others, is not the right prescription. It can exacerbate the temptation to surrender responsibility and initiative. Dahill is giving us additional reasons for emphasizing Cain's sin of abdicating responsibility.[58]

Dahill writes that during the resistance activity, when Bonhoeffer is "no longer among the privileged but among the threatened and marginalized," he speaks positively of self-love in a supportive letter to Eberhard Bethge, who was under enormous strain.[59] In his *Ethics*, "he posits *two ways* the relation between self and other can go awry: 'by absolutizing either my own self or the other person.' . . . For the first time he is asserting the equal dangers that can result from absolutizing another person."[60] I add that Bonhoeffer's strong emphasis in *Ethics* on free responsibility in Christ is the antidote he prescribes for the sin of abdication of responsibility.[61]

I identify with and affirm Dahill—not only her diagnosis that women tend to be socialized into "soluble selves," but also that men tend to be socialized into "separate selves" or buffered selves.[62] She writes sensitively of the need of women for assertiveness, initiative, and seizing responsibility, and not merely for self-sacrifice. I urge that we write in a parallel way of men's need for connectedness, community partnership, and *participative* grace. I appreciate Bonhoeffer's definition of participative grace, his seeing grace in Jesus' call to disciples to come follow him as participants in his mission, his motifs of trust and intimacy with Jesus in *Discipleship*, his well-developed vocabulary of participation (*teilnehmen, teilhaben, teilen, eintreten, Menschwerdung, Stellvertretung* [conformation with Christ, Christ taking form in us]), and his words for community and life together—all words for participation and connection, seeking to heal our neediness—men and women—for community and partnership rather than disconnection.

I read the early Bonhoeffer, not only the Bonhoeffer of the time of resistance, as experiencing *a kind of underside* in his sense of aloneness and his thoughts of death. This was exacerbated by his Prussian culture's disdain for too much self-revelation, too much sharing of feelings, and his own sense of shame about his own ego-drive, which caused some sense of separation from others. I identify with Bonhoeffer's definition of sin as leading to being split from God and others.

But here is the point: In *Ethics*, Bonhoeffer's emphasis is on acting with free responsibility—the antidote to the sin of abdicating responsibility. He saw the ethics of his day as abdicating responsibility in the midst of a depth of evil beyond description that demanded dramatic action—action with free responsibility in relation with God and others in our historical context. Here his concept of *Stellvertretung* is crucial; I shall explain it in the next chapter.

ETHICS WITHOUT SOLIDARITY IN SIN MISSES THE REALITY

We have seen six dimensions of Bonhoeffer's diagnosis of sin, based on theological exegesis of the drama of Adam and Eve and Cain and Abel. He wrote *Creation and Fall* with its diagnosis of sin in 1932, just after his turning to Christ-centeredness in Harlem and Union Seminary and just before Hitler became *der Führer* of the Third Reich. This realistic understanding of sin must have helped Bonhoeffer see the evil of Hitler's rule from the very beginning, ahead of other theologians: his diagnosis of the nature of sin continues in his *Ethics*, written in 1940 to 1943 during Hitler's dictatorship:

> Today we have villains and saints again, in full public view. . . . Reality is laid bare. Shakespeare's characters are among us. The villain and the saint . . . arise from primeval depths, and with their appearance tear open the demonic and divine abyss out of which they come, allowing us brief glimpses into their suspected secrets. . . .
> Ethical theorists, on the other hand, are blinded by it. With their preconceived concepts they cannot grasp what is real, let alone seriously encounter something whose essence and power they don't even recognize.[63]

Bonhoeffer saw that the leading ethical theories of his day were based on a rationalistic idealism. They could not face the reality of the evil that undermines those very ideals.[64] Bonhoeffer delineated several kinds of ethics and their various failures in facing evil. Reasonable people, he said, could not "see either the abyss of evil or the abyss of holiness. With the best intentions, they believe that, with a little reason, they can pull back together a structure that has come apart at the joints. . . . They withdraw in resignation or fall helplessly captive to the stronger party." On the other hand, ethical fanatics, who "believe that they can face the power of evil with the purity of their will and their principles," lose sight of the totality of evil, and rush like a bull at the red cape rather than at the one holding it, and "finally tire and suffer defeat."

People whose ethics is based on nothing but their own conscience are torn to pieces by the dilemmas they face, so they become anxious and unsure, and "deceive their own conscience in order not to despair." Those with an ethics of duty obey what is commanded, until they finally fulfill their duty even to the devil. They "never venture a free action that rests solely on their own responsibility, the only sort of action that can meet evil at its heart and overcome it." Those who take their stand on their own freedom and are prepared to sacrifice a barren principle to a fruitful compromise easily consent to the bad in order to prevent the worse, which can end in tragedy. And finally, virtue ethicists "in voluntarily renouncing public life, . . . must close their eyes and their ears to the injustice around them. Only at the cost of self-deception can they keep their private blamelessness clean from the stains of responsible action in the world."

All these groups fail because they lack a robust understanding of sin. Bonhoeffer writes that we cannot understand the depth of sin unless we see it through God's self-revelation in the incarnate Jesus Christ, where God's love takes specific and concrete shape, christomorphically, in the struggles of real history: "The central message of the New Testament is that in Christ God has loved the world and reconciled it with himself. . . . The world needs reconciliation with God, but cannot achieve it by itself."[65]

In *Ethics*, he begins his diagnosis of the sin of the Third Reich with God's reconciliation with the world in Jesus Christ, incarnate in real history:

> Only because there is one place where God and the reality of the world are reconciled with each other, at which God and humanity have become one, is it possible there and there alone to fix one's eyes on God and the world together at the same time. This place does not lie somewhere beyond reality in the realm of ideas. It lies in the midst of history as a divine miracle. It lies in Jesus Christ the reconciler of the world. As an ideal, the unit of simplicity and wisdom is as much doomed to failure as are all other efforts to face reality; it is an impossible, highly contradictory ideal. Grounded, however, in the reality of the world reconciled with God in Jesus Christ, the command of Jesus gains meaning and reality.[66]

Thus Bonhoeffer's remedy is to base ethics on God's revelation in real history, in the incarnation, crucifixion, and resurrection of Jesus Christ, as incarnational discipleship advocates. On that basis he develops his diagnosis of the sin of the history in which he himself had been thrust. He carries forward the six dimensions of sin in *Creation and Fall*.

1. *Replacing God as the source of our knowledge of God with our own knowledge, our own conscience, and our own claim to universal reason.* The idealistic, semi-Platonic ethical theories locate the good in an ideal above history that we claim to know by our reason. This stance splits idealists from the real in the midst of which we live. Lacking that grounding, they cannot grasp the depth of sin in the present context. "No one can look at God and at the reality of the world with undivided gaze as long as God and the world are torn apart."[67] We have to keep our eyes focused where God is active within the real world—in the incarnation.

In the incarnation, "God loves real people without distinction. . . . God overrules every reproach of untruth, doubt, and uncertainty raised against God's love by entering as a human being into human life, by taking on and bearing bodily the nature, essence, guilt, and suffering of human beings."[68]

By contrast, Bonhoeffer writes that Hitler does not love real humanity, but despises it.[69] He cynically calls human weaknesses strengths. "He hides his secret profound distrust of all people behind the stolen words of true community. . . . He praises himself with repulsive vanity and despises the rights of every individual. . . . His conventional protestations of solicitude for people are bare-faced cynicism."[70]

Bonhoeffer is unique among German theologians of that time in applying an explicit doctrine of human rights to Hitler's most apparent victims—the Jews, the disabled, Poles, and homosexuals—and thus having a clear norm with which to reject the Nazis' practice of "euthanasia" on their victims.[71] And he develops his doctrine of human rights on the basis of God's having become human in bodily form in the incarnate Jesus Christ and on the fact that God created us in bodily form.[72] Because this is a gift of God the Creator, human rights are not merely a claim we make for ourselves, but a mandate, a duty, to act in ways that support the human rights of every human being whom God has created, including Jews.

2. Divided loyalties alienate us from God and others. Bonhoeffer's diagnosis of people's folly, their being taken in by Hitler's demagoguery, and their lack of responsible action to oppose Hitler's horrendous injustice, names their divided loyalties—claiming to be ethical and Christian while basing their ethics on their own virtues rather than Christ. So they fall for the demagogic flattering of their alleged virtues. They are split: they claim loyalty to God, but actually follow the Führer. Bonhoeffer appeals throughout *Ethics* for basing our ethics single-mindedly on God's revelation in Jesus Christ.

3 and 4. Sin involves the desire to make ourselves equal to God and the temptation of power and domination. Despite needing to use coded language lest the Nazis realize he is talking about Hitler, Bonhoeffer names Hitler as "the *tyrannical* despiser of humanity," and several times tags him as a *tyrant* who succumbs to the temptation of power and domination. "In his deep contempt for humanity, the more he seeks the favor of those he despises, the more certainly he arouses the masses to declare him a god."[73] He diagnoses the people's idolatry of Hitler's power and his temporary success, saying that such idolatry leads to an inability to tell right from wrong.[74] By contrast, "the form of the crucified disarms all thinking aimed at success. . . . To be conformed to the crucified—that means to be a human being judged by God."[75]

He specifically diagnoses Hitler's idolization of death, rousing the crowds to die for nationalistic causes. Resurrection "has overturned the idolization of death that rules among us," where life is worth nothing, and existing life is annihilated.[76] Christ's resurrection breaks the power of death.[77] Christ is risen; the living Christ is present to us, especially in the church, and takes form in our lives.

5. Sin is self-deception, hiding from God, defensive denial, and refusing to face our own limits. Bonhoeffer sees in Christ "a sincerely intended love for humanity," by contrast with idealistic self-deception that overlooks meanness, reinterprets evil as good, and excuses what is reprehensible. When a person loves "a self-made picture of human beings that has little similarity to reality," then that person ends up hating the flesh-and-blood human being whom God has loved.[78] In the incarnation, God loves the real being, in its actual reality in real history, rather than a fantasy that pretends we are better than we are. Refusing to face our limits and our wrongs realistically means rejecting the truth that God brings in the incarnation. It may be idealistically intended, but it has the consequence of not confronting what leads us into evil. "Only as judged by God can human beings live before God. . . . In the figure of the crucified, human beings recognize and find themselves. To be taken up by God, to be judged and reconciled by God on the cross—that is the reality of humanity."[79] Throughout the central section of "Ethics as Formation," Bonhoeffer argues for facing our limits and dealing with others and ourselves as we are, not as an ideal.

6. *Sin leads us to abdicate responsibility and blame others.* Bonhoeffer diagnoses good people, who see through all this, but nevertheless "who withdraw in disgust from people and leave them to themselves, and who would rather tend to their own gardens than debase themselves in public life. . . ."[80] He insists that formation must happen concretely, among us, in the here and now: "We are placed objectively by our history into a particular context of experience, responsibility, and decision, from which we cannot withdraw without ending up in abstraction. So we, as historical people, therefore stand already in the midst of Christ taking form in a segment of human history that Christ has chosen."[81] This reads like a theme of Reinhold Niebuhr's, but in Niebuhr it is pragmatic and in Bonhoeffer it is incarnationally christomorphic.[82]

The responsibility Bonhoeffer advocates is theologically and realistically grounded. It is Christ taking form in us in our concrete, specific, realistically understood history. It is responsible to God, our Creator, who is revealed tangibly in real history, in Christ, and who creates us to live only bodily, not in a disembodied immortal soul. This responsibility is for others; Christ is Lord, and Christ is for others. It is clear that we are sinners, that we need limits and checks and balances, and that we distort our perceiving and deceive ourselves and others and so need the checks and balances of mutual admonition by others in community. Furthermore, our responsibility involves us in solidarity in sin, requires confession, and must depend on him who took our sin on himself at the cross, out of love for real human beings like us.

WE NEED CHECKS AND BALANCES AGAINST CONCENTRATIONS OF POWER

As we saw in the opening section of this chapter, Bonhoeffer's diagnosis of sin applies to us in our time. A realistic understanding of the sin of all earthly powers means we need checks and balances against any monopoly of power, whether by political, economic, or pastoral authority. Therefore Bonhoeffer points to the American Revolution as profoundly different from the French Revolution. In the new United States, he says, the Constitution was "written by men who know about original sin and about evil in the human heart." It established boundaries to restrain those in power, not only because of the innate human hunger for power but also because the founders recognized that "power belongs to God alone. This idea, rooted in Calvinism, was combined with another one that was essentially opposite and came from the spiritualism of dissenters who had fled to America, the idea that the kingdom of God on earth cannot be built by state power, but only by the church-community of believers."[83]

We saw the American tradition of democracy and checks and balances against concentrated power that Bonhoeffer is here advocating in our chapter 5 on democratic tradition. We now see how intensely that tradition needs defending against the takeover by forces of power and domination in our time. In the twenty-first century, the most powerful concentration of power is economic power. According to *The Wall Street Journal,* CEO pay rocketed 480 percent from 1980 to 2003. In the next year, 2004, it increased another 14.4 percent. According to the research firm Equilar,[84] the median compensation for chief executives at two hundred large companies was $10.8 million in 2010. This was a 26 percent increase from the previous year. In 2010, the top twenty-five hedge fund managers averaged $40 million each. During the last thirty years, average salary for workers has stagnated at about $35,000, meaning that the ratio of the average income of corporate CEOs to workers is growing greater and greater. And the power of money to influence politicians has inflated with Supreme Court decisions blocking campaign finance reform. According to *The New York Times,* "those who can afford to buy influence are rewriting the rules so they can cut themselves progressively larger slices of the American pie while paying less of their fair share for it. . . . 400 people control more of the wealth than 150 million of their fellow Americans."[85] Lobbyists for corporations, insurance companies, and military-industrial corporations outnumber members of Congress by many dozens. The legislators are dependent on money for advertising in order to get reelected, and that money largely comes from wealthy interests. The legislators themselves are almost all millionaires. Multinational corporations can do their business in any nation; if one nation insists on regulation, the corporations can simply leave for another nation. So the challenge given us by Bonhoeffer and by the authors of the U.S. Constitution is how to limit the power of money over legislation and government and how to develop realistic checks and balances for greed.

BONHOEFFER'S CONFESSION OF SOLIDARITY IN SIN DURING THE THIRD REICH

Prior to Bonhoeffer's time, governments avoided acknowledging their own responsibility for conflict and injustice, claiming that to do so would show weakness. This made it far more difficult to heal bitter historical wounds and make peace between nations. Bonhoeffer led the nations to begin correcting this collective abdication from responsibility.

In a remarkable ten-page section of his *Ethics*, Bonhoeffer confessed his own sins, the churches' sins, and Germany's sins.[86] He thus led Germany in acknowledging solidarity in responsibility for the evils of the Third Reich, expressing repentance, and seeking forgiveness from other nations. The practice of acknowledging responsibility has now spread around the world, including the Truth and Reconciliation Commission in South Africa, and has become a significant practice of just peacemaking between nations.

Bonhoeffer's confession did not arise in a vacuum; he based it explicitly on the Ten Commandments. I have italicized his references to the Ten Commandments in the text that follows. His confession echoes themes that we have seen in his profound diagnosis of our solidarity in sin. He names the church's timidity, its deviations and concessions to Nazi beliefs, its withholding the compassion it owes to the despised and rejected (Jews), its silence when it should have cried out for those who were crying out to God, *as evidence of its godlessness and idolatrous loyalty to the Nazi ideology rather than to the one God.* It has made *wrongful use of the name of Christ* by not resisting the misuse of that name for evil ends. It has *not kept the Sabbath holy* "because its preaching of Jesus Christ has been so weak and its public worship so limp." It has not opposed *contempt for the dignity of parents* by the Nazi youth organization, thus destroying countless families and being guilty for the self-divinizing of youth. It has witnessed *murder and hatred* "without raising its voice for the victims and without finding ways of rushing to help them. It has become guilty of the lives of the weakest and most defenseless brothers and sisters of Jesus Christ," clearly meaning Jews, the brothers and sisters of Jesus.

> It has found no strong or authentic message to set against the *disdain for chastity and the proclamation of sexual licentiousness.* It has looked on silently as *the poor were exploited and stolen from,* while the strong were enriched and corrupted. It has not condemned *the false witness of those who destroyed the lives of countless people by slander, denunciation, and defamation.* . . . It *has coveted* security, tranquility, peace, property and honor to which it had no claim, and therefore has not bridled human covetousness, but promoted it.

Thus "the church confesses itself guilty of violating all of the Ten Commandments. It confesses thereby its apostasy from Christ."

Such self-scrutiny can be painful, but it became the essential step for Germans to move toward healing. Without hope for grace, Bonhoeffer says, we point out that someone else has been equally or more sinful, and so defend ourselves from honest self-awareness and honest confession. "An unfruitful self-righteous morality takes the place of confessing guilt face-to-face with the figure of Christ."[87]

We can only stand in awe before this remarkable confession by a German patriot, who intentionally returned from the United States, where he would have been safe, in order to participate with his own people in seeking to form a Germany different from Hitler's ignominy. And we can affirm his profound practice of solidarity in sin as a model for becoming less defensive and evasive ourselves, and more honest and realistic in our own practices of acknowledging our solidarity in sin.

The profundity of Bonhoeffer's analysis of sin, with its dimensions of replacing God, divided loyalties, power-drive and domination, and self-deception in ideologies that try to justify our greed, illuminate what we see corrupting the soul and the power structures of our nation. Bonhoeffer recognized that sin is not only what we do individually and intentionally, but also what we are sometimes seduced into unaware because of our participation in the political, economic, and media influences in our national culture.[88] Bonhoeffer's awareness of solidarity in the sin of his Nazi Germany helps us diagnose our different kind of solidarity in sin in our culture. He worked to strengthen antibodies and checks and balances, both ecclesiastical and secular. He left a witness. Will we do likewise?

Chapter 9

The Cross

*Compassionate Presence
and Confrontation*

Sin is not our whole story. We are still created in the image of God, "response-able" to God, caring for others, dependent on our community with others, and participants in the creativeness of creation. God still loves us, despite our rebelliousness. Yet we have a problem.

In the previous chapter, we saw a deeper and more realistic understanding of sin, based on incarnational discipleship's mandate for interpreting Jesus more thickly and concretely, as Bonhoeffer does. Incarnational discipleship's call for the Lordship of Christ or sovereignty of God through all of life and not only one part of it supports this understanding of sin as relating to both social and individual dimensions. Some may be uncomfortable with such a holistic understanding, but it is surely biblical. And it correlates with incarnational discipleship's demand for repentance and for independence from entanglement in ideologies.

In sin, we replace God with some other source, rather than living in the presence of God and basing our ethics on God's revealing of God's will. So we then have divided loyalties and are alienated from God and others. Seeking to be equal with God and to know as much as God does is also seeking to lord it over others with dominating power. The result is injustice—domination, violence, greed, and exclusion of others from our caring and community. Incarnational discipleship says sin corrupts all of life and goes deeper than we realize. We get stuck in pious self-deception, hiding from God, blaming others, refusing to face our own limits, and abdicating responsibility for what we do and what we fail to do. This results not only in guilt, but also in shame.

Shame is deeper than disobedience and guilt. It is about the pride of trying to replace God or be equal to God; or the sloth of abdicating responsibility before God. This idolatrous ambition, this God-rivaling pride, or this sinking into abdication of responsibility, alienates us from God and from others, building a barrier of pride and shame between us and God and between us and community. Instead of living with trust in God and others, we consciously and subconsciously build defensive barriers against God's presence and the presence of others.

Facing this deep problem and its corrupting influence on our whole lives, holistically, may be uncomfortable, but it may also be a step toward healing. So let us ask how the cross of Christ brings us healing. Let us face the challenge that Charles Taylor has put to us: the understanding of the meaning of the cross of Jesus Christ that most people have does not provide them an adequate answer for how the cross brings us healing. And this is a cause of secularism.

THE CROSS BRINGS HEALING, BUT HOW?

The question is how we understand the cross as dealing with sin, including our own defense mechanisms and resistance. Charles Taylor understands the cross, (profoundly, I think) as bringing healing to the split, the alienation, that human sin creates between us and God by *God's entering into* the heart of our resistance:

> God's initiative is to enter, in full vulnerability, the heart of the resistance, to be among humans, offering participation in the divine life. The nature of the resistance is that this offer arouses even more violent opposition. . . . Christ's reaction to the resistance was to. . . . continue loving and offering. This love can go to the very heart of things, and open a road even for the resisters.[1]

Notice that Taylor diagnoses the problem as our resistance, our building barriers against loving presence that wall us off from relationship. Genesis calls this our hiding in shame. Redemption requires somehow restoring relationship through, beyond, underneath, or despite those barriers of resistance. Taylor's key—entering into the heart of the resistance—gives the clue that we need.

Yet, Taylor writes, the hegemony of the judicial-penal model of the atonement "plays an important role in the later rise of unbelief, both in repelling people from the faith, and in modifying it in the direction of deism."[2] Taylor is right: many Christians lack adequate understanding of the meaning of the cross, and this is a cause of secularism.

When I was teaching a section of twenty freshmen at Berea College, the students were Christian, and they knew I was Christian, so they were not shy about expressing their Christian faith. We had just read a chapter discussing the crucifixion of Jesus. I asked them, "How did Jesus' death do something about our sin?" Long silence. Finally, Harry Keith, one of the most thoughtful and articulate students, said, "Well, you know, Jesus died for our sins." I replied, "Yes, I know, but *how* did Jesus' death do something about our sins?" Silence. No answer ever came. Not one of these bright Christian college students could give any explanation of *how* Jesus' death did something for our sins—even a bad explanation.

My purpose is not to criticize various theories of the meaning of the cross. Each theory serves a function for some Christians, and each claims some basis in experience and Scripture. I recommend that churches offer a series of teachings, or sermons, on the major theories, and on the incarnational theory I am about to propose, allowing affirmations and criticisms of their explanatory power, perhaps during Lent.[3] None of the theories has been given official standing by any Catholic or Protestant confessional statement. Orthodoxy does not lock us into one theory over against the others.[4] Lisa Cahill writes that theologians have developed several theories of the meaning of the cross: "sacrifice, ransom, redemption, penal substitution, expiation, atonement, scapegoat, and recapitulation. . . . It *should not* be interpreted as somehow . . . a punishment demanded by God for human sin. Nowhere does the New Testament say. . . . that God refuses to forgive unless paid by the death of sinners, much less the death of an innocent man!"[5]

N. T. Wright contends that the problem with leading theories of the meaning of the cross is that they are based on a framework of interpretation from a later cultural understanding rather than the biblical framework already in the Gospels. He says Anselm "cut the cross loose from its scriptural moorings and placed it within a feudal system of honour and shame." The *Christus Victor* theory of the Greek Fathers placed it "within the world of mythical satanic powers."[6]

As Wright is suggesting, many theories isolate the cross from Jesus' teachings and ministry. The result is cheap grace. People believe their sins are atoned for, but don't connect this with Jesus' way of life. Therefore, false ideologies worm their way in, replacing the point of Jesus' mission and message with their accommodation to interests of the world. I saw this in a student who objected when I said Isaiah prophesied that the suffering servant would come in peace, and Jesus taught peacemaking, so Jesus fulfilled Isaiah's prophecy. He said Jesus came to die for our sins, and it did not matter whether he fulfilled Isaiah on peacemaking. The student insisted on ruling out the relevance of Jesus' life and message in one fell swoop.

Incarnational discipleship may offer promising help. It grounds theological ethics in thick scriptural understanding of the incarnate Jesus in the Gospels, as rooted in the drama of the Old Testament, and especially the prophet Isaiah; so it does not replace the context of the cross in Jesus' teachings and life with another cultural framework. It insists that the real character of God is truly revealed in Jesus; so it does not split God's character from Jesus' love.

I want to suggest a new angle on the meaning of the cross based on what the cross means in the theology of Dietrich Bonhoeffer and in the Gospel of Mark. As Bonhoeffer suggested, I ask us to see the events "from below, from the perspective of the outcasts, the suspects, the maltreated, the powerless, the oppressed and reviled, in short from the perspective of the suffering."[7] Let us see the cross from the perspective of what Jesus is doing with the marginalized, and what he is doing with or to those who oppress the marginalized. Then let us ask what God is doing *in and through* Jesus, from below, not what God is doing *to* Jesus from above. The Scripture says that God was *in* Christ, reconciling the world to himself (2 Cor. 5:19), not that God was *above* Christ, becoming reconciled to the world.

PREVIEW: THE PARABLE OF THE SHAMEFUL SON

Jesus gives us a preview when he tells the parable of the atonement between the father and the lost son in Luke 15:11–32. The condition of the lost son is alienation and shame as well as guilt: he has taken his part of his father's estate as if his father had already died; he has squandered all the property in loose living; he has sunk into such need that he has hired himself out *to feed pigs*; "he would gladly have filled himself with the pods that the pigs were eating." Surely—especially for a Jew—this describes abject shame.

His father not only forgives his guilt from past sins, but also deals with his shame. When he sees his son, he is filled with compassion; he runs and puts his arms around him and kisses him. He tells his slaves to bring the best robe and put it on him; put a ring on his finger and sandals on his feet; get the fatted calf and celebrate! His father welcomes him into the family again.

I want to point to grace as *entering incarnationally into the midst of our lives*, we who are alienated from God and from our fellow human beings. Central to our fallen human condition is evasion of God and one another and recoiling either in flight or in violence if someone upsets our defense mechanisms. Our evasion is compulsive; we can't save ourselves. We need God to break through our evasion and enter into the midst of our hiding.

As in the parable of the Prodigal Son, the solution for our human alienation needs to be not only forgiveness of guilt, but also overcoming our shame that leads us to hide our real selves from God and others. Our problem is relational.[8] Guilt concerns a past deed that can be forgiven. Shame indicates a present sense of inadequate selfhood and therefore hiding and defensiveness. To be healed, the person with shame needs to be re-incorporated into community. The cross needs to bring not only forgiveness for past guilt, but also God's presence that enters through our barriers of defensiveness and restores our trusting and obedient relationship with God. Only God can restore this relationship.

When we encounter the human Jesus, we are also encountering God, because God's Holy Spirit is fully present in what the human Jesus does.[9] Jesus is the Son of God. Our sin and alienation are *alienation from God*, as well as from God's creatures—other humans and the creation itself. To be redeemed, we need God, Godself, to enter into the midst of our alienated lives, as the father of the prodigal son did, thereby overcoming our defensive alienation. This is what God does in Jesus Christ. God is in Christ, reconciling us and the world to Godself. The incarnation is not merely about a general truth, or only about a subjective experience. It is about God doing something new in Jesus Christ. In Jesus Christ, we are confronted by God, who enters into our place of evasion, deception, and shame and takes us with our sin into community. By this invasive work, God transforms us in Christ. The cross is God's demonstration of the injustice of authoritarians who dominate and crucify, disciples who betray and deny, and the ashamed who hide. It is God's taking all of us into God's compassion and deliverance, and inviting us into community with faith.[10] I want to show this in Dietrich Bonhoeffer's theology, and then in Mark's Gospel.

AN INCARNATIONAL THEORY OF THE CROSS IN DIETRICH BONHOEFFER

I am struck by how often Dietrich Bonhoeffer mentions shame as well as guilt—and also loneliness, isolation, hiding from God and from others. I think that rings true for many of us. It connects with Taylor's diagnosis of "the buffered self," the self disconnected and alienated from others, and from God. "Shame can be overcome only where the original unity is restored"[11] in the coming together of the world and God in the incarnation, and by seeing the depth of evil revealed in the crucifixion of Jesus. Look at *the incarnate* Jesus—"behold what a human being! . . . Only the consummate love of God can meet and overcome reality." In our shame we withdraw and hide compulsively; we are unable to face reality with full honesty, unable to gaze on it or to let it gaze on us. Only by God's coming to be present, entering incarnationally into the midst of our lives-in-hiding, giving us love where we are unlovable, can we be reconciled.

Bonhoeffer means more than viewing Jesus as a model or mentor. The incarnation involved an objective act by God, who reconciles alienated, estranged humanity to God and to each other as an ontological achievement of atonement, by God's entering fully into the life of the world and suffering with it.

Notice how clearly Bonhoeffer depicts the love of God incarnate in the man Jesus as entering into the midst of the reality of our shame. He often uses the word *eintreten*, entering in, stepping into the midst. God enters in, incarnationally, into the center where we are, whether we may be hiding in shame, doing injustice, or suffering from injustice. "The love of God embraces even the most abysmal godlessness of the world," Bonhoeffer writes in *Ethics*. "God treads [a form of *eintreten*—to enter into] the way of humble reconciliation and thereby sets the world free." God embraces human beings. . . . *God, in the conception and birth of Jesus Christ, has taken on humanity bodily.* God overrules every reproach of untruth, doubt, and uncertainty raised against God's love by *entering* as a human being *into* human life, by taking on and bearing bodily the nature, essence, guilt, and suffering of human beings. God becomes human out of love for humanity. God does not seek the most perfect human being with whom to be united, but takes on human nature as it is.

Look at *the crucified* Jesus. The cross is God's entering into our shame with costly love. In the cross Christ is pushed "into shame and death under God's judgment. Reconciliation with the world cost God dearly. . . . The secret, however, of this judgment, this suffering and this dying, is the love of God for the world, for human beings."[12]

Our culture's worship of success leads us into shame when we fail or fear failure, and into shameful contempt for those who fail. Jesus' concern "is neither success nor failure but willing acceptance of the judgment of God. . . . Over against the successful, God sanctifies pain, lowliness, failure, poverty, loneliness, and despair in the cross of Christ. . . . It is made holy by the love of God, who takes it all and bears it as judgment."

Look at *the resurrected* Jesus—"behold the human being, accepted by God, judged by God, awakened by God to a new life—see the Risen One!" What we see in the resurrection is "God's yes to this human being"; because Christ took on judgment and death, a new human being has been made. Henceforth I do not have to focus on my own shame, or on what has shamed me, or on my own efforts to rise above shame by some widely admired success; my new self is the self that is affirmed by God's affirming the self of Jesus.

> Within the risen Christ the new humanity is borne, the final sovereign Yes of God to the new human being. . . . The human being, accepted, judged, and awakened to new life by God—this is Jesus Christ, this is the whole of humanity in Christ, this is us. The form of Jesus Christ alone victoriously encounters the world. From this form proceeds all the formation of a world reconciled with God.

So now, risen with Christ, we are risen into formation by Christ. Grace is not formless, but christomorphic—it takes the shape that is revealed in the incarnate Jesus Christ. This does not mean formation by planning and programs, or that

> so-called Christian principles should be applied directly to the world to form the world according to them. Formation occurs only by being drawn into the form of Jesus Christ, by being conformed to the unique form of the one who became human, was crucified, and is risen. This does not happen as we strive "to become like Jesus," as we customarily say, but as the form of Jesus Christ himself so works on us that it molds us, conforming our form to Christ's own (Gal. 4:9).

Thus, Bonhoeffer offers an *incarnational* theory of the cross in the sense that God enters into the midst of our lives curved in upon themselves, and also in the sense that God reveals God's self, God's character, to us *in the particular actions and ministry of the incarnate Jesus Christ*.[13] Grace is christomorphic in an incarnational sense. Jesus was incarnate in a particular history, in the tradition of the prophets, above all Isaiah, and in the struggle of Israel under the double domination of the Roman Empire and the high priests in Jerusalem, and he did particular deeds and imparted particular teachings.

As *participants* in the risen Christ, we become participants in Christ's formation in the church and in the world. Several words translated "participation" echo throughout Bonhoeffer's writings; it is a central theme in his understanding of grace.[14] We no longer need to hide in shame; we are made participants in what Christ is doing in the world. This does not mean cheap grace, grace without change in our way of living, grace with no limits, no commitments, no covenants that guide us. Formation in Christ, participation in what Jesus Christ is doing in the world, is guided by what the incarnate Jesus did and taught and is doing now. It is guided and empowered by the Holy Spirit, who enters into the center of our lives, reminds us of what Jesus has taught, testifies on Jesus' behalf, takes what is Jesus' and declares it unto us (John 14:26; 15:26; 16:14). An incarnational theory of the cross places a strong emphasis on formation in the way of the incarnate Jesus Christ. This is *participative grace* as well as *christomorphic grace.*

As James McClendon urges, it also places a strong emphasis on the *presence* of God in Jesus Christ.[15] "To be conformed to the risen one—that means to be a new human being before God. . . . We live because Christ lives, and in Christ alone. 'Christ is my life.'" The understanding of the cross needs to include a strong emphasis on God's presence in Jesus Christ, "refusing the temptation to withdraw mentally and emotionally." Presence means "on occasion putting our own body's weight and shape alongside the neighbor, the friend, the lover in need."[16] *Presence* entails an interpersonal, pastoral component in one-to-one relationships and also a *public* dimension, where one's *presence* can call attention to a current injustice (e.g., the civil rights movement). We need greater attention to God's presence in Christ as Holy Spirit.[17] For these three reasons—emphasizing the way of the incarnate Jesus Christ, Christ's coming to be present in the midst of our lives, plus the call *to embody* the cross in our own discipleship—I call this an *incarnational* theory of the cross.

Bonhoeffer's term *Stellvertretung* is important for his understanding of the meaning of the cross. It is often translated as "representation," "deputyship," "action on behalf of," or better, "vicarious representative action." In Bonhoeffer's writings it has a deeper theological connotation—not only of representing others in a distant place where they are not present, but also of stepping into their shoes, entering empathetically into their place, and acting on their behalf with love. It contains the word, *Stelle*, "place," and *treten*, "to step," like *eintreten*, "to enter into another's place." So Bonhoeffer writes: "Christus . . . steht an ihrer Stelle [Christ stands in their place], stellvertretend für sie vor Gott [stepping into their place before God]." *Stellvertretung* is based in Bonhoeffer's christological emphasis on the incarnation as God's empathetically entering into human life in Jesus Christ, standing in the place of all humanity; and on the crucifixion as Christ's bearing guilt on our behalf. It connotes being-with-each-other and being-for-each-other, entering into the other's reality and even into the other's guilt. Over against the individualism of much of our culture, we need both the empathetic entering and the corporate solidarity of *Stellvertretung*. God's becoming human in Christ incorporates humanity as a whole and acts representatively on our behalf to do what we cannot do, and this changes our reality.

When Bonhoeffer acted courageously, truthfully, and sacrificially on behalf of his church and his nation, he was both identifying with them empathetically and acting on their behalf with corporate solidarity. He also identified with Jews and Hitler's other victims, acting with empathetic representation to defend their human right to bodily life. He did this as a vicarious representative—on behalf of people who could not defend themselves.

So I propose to translate *Stellvertretung* as "empathetic representative action" and "incarnational representation"—intending a depth of incarnational meaning that no translation can completely convey.[18]

MARK'S GOSPEL AS ENTERING INTO PRESENCE WITH COMPASSION AND CONFRONTATION

The Gospels give powerful testimony to this incarnational understanding of the cross. In Jesus Christ, God becomes present, entering incarnationally into the midst of our lives, taking our alienation, shame, injustice, and hostility into God's self. This theme is central for the Gospel of Mark.

Some scholars suggest that Mark wrote in order to explain how the Son of God and Messiah could have died the shocking, shameful death of crucifixion. Others contend he wrote to show that "the way" is not seeking power and glory but instead serving others with compassion. The Messiah would not be a Davidic king who brings national power to Israel, but a Suffering Servant who brings deliverance, healing, justice, and peace. In each case, *Mark shows how Jesus' enacted teaching leads to the cross*. Mark is misread when the Jesus of the first half is severed from the Jesus of the cross.[19]

So Mark performed the inspired work of bringing together a theology of the cross with a theology of the Son of God and Suffering Servant who has compassion on the outcasts and gives his life for them, and who offers concrete teachings of the way of following him in discipleship.

To Understand Jesus' Death We Need His Deeds *and* His Teachings

Mark's Gospel is not merely a passion story with an introduction; it is enacted teaching and healing, climaxing in the cross. The cross is anticipated in Mark

3:6; 11:1; and 12:12–13; and in Jesus' teachings in 2:20; 8:31; 9:31; 10:33–34, 45; and 14:24.[20] From the very beginning, Mark is teaching the meaning of the cross.

Matthew and Luke agreed that Mark was right. They incorporated Mark in their Gospels, and added yet more of Jesus' teaching, thus affirming that we need Jesus as teacher in order to understand Jesus as crucified. Their affirmation of Mark is one reason I chose to focus on Mark's Gospel here—since I cannot discuss all three in this space.

Like Christians in the first century, we too are in a time of a thinned-down, docetic or gnostic Jesus in which many praise Jesus for lifting us higher, but in which Jesus' way is glossed over. We have a Jesus thinned down to fit into the cracks in the reigning ideologies. We need a thicker Jesus, concretely teaching and embodying what the real Jesus taught and embodied. We need incarnational discipleship to understand the cross adequately.

The cross needs to be seen in the light of Jesus' healings and his deeds of compassion, of his proclamation and embodiment of the reign of God, of his confrontations of the authorities and their injustice, of his actual ministry as a prophet, suffering servant, and Son of God. We need more than a Jesus who was born and then was crucified. The cross needs to be understood in terms of the incarnate Jesus of Galilee as portrayed by Mark, Matthew, Luke, and John. We need the whole Jesus, historically incarnate.

Mark also speaks incarnationally in our three senses: affirming that we encounter God in what Jesus does; paying attention to what the incarnate Jesus says and does, not only to his birth and crucifixion; and calling our attention to how he enters into the midst of the lives of others with compassion that overcomes shame and defensive withdrawal.

"Son of God" is the key to who Jesus is throughout the Gospel of Mark.[21] *Mark begins in the very first verse* speaking incarnationally with a Son-of-God or a Spirit Christology: "the good news of Jesus Christ, the Son of God," on whom the Holy Spirit descends like a dove and about whom, in the words of Isaiah 42, a voice proclaims, "You are my Son, the Beloved; with you I am well pleased" (Mark 1:1, 10–11).

Immediately Mark places both John the Baptist and Jesus in the context of the announcement of the good news that the reign of God is at hand, as the prophet Isaiah had prophesied, and that God's Spirit is acting in Jesus, declaring—in the words of Isaiah and Malachi—that Jesus is God's Son.[22] Then John is arrested—foreshadowing Jesus' own arrest.

All this in only twenty verses. Then in verse 21, Jesus is engaged in teaching with authority and healing with compassion in Galilee. His whirlwind ministry around Capernaum involves nine episodes of healing and teaching. It ends with the Pharisees and the Herodians conspiring together to destroy Jesus (3:6), and an investigating party of scribes coming from Jerusalem and accusing him of being in league with Satan (3:20–30). He answers that his actions are empowered by God's Holy Spirit.

In three ways this beginning tour around Capernaum is already explaining Jesus' arrest and crucifixion—John the Baptist is arrested and we know he will be beheaded, the Pharisees and Herodians are conspiring to have Jesus destroyed, and members of the political-religious hierarchy in Jerusalem have already sent their accusers. And in three ways it is already explaining Jesus' motivation in later heading toward Jerusalem and his crucifixion—he is proclaiming the reign of God that Isaiah promised, the Holy Spirit is present, is acting, in what Jesus is doing, and Jesus is acting with compassion for those who need deliverance. Mark explains the cross by pointing to Jesus' teaching and compassion for those who need deliverance.

It is not simply that Jesus was healing; other prophets of that time were performing healings as well. It is that his healing was fulfilling Isaiah's prophecies that God is coming to deliver us, with joy over the presence of God's Spirit, with justice, healing, peace, and return to God.[23]

1. The Capernaum Section (1:21–3:12)

The Capernaum section begins, literally translated, "and they *enter into* Capernaum." The theme of *entering into* (like Bonhoeffer's *eintreten*) reverberates throughout the section in significant ways. God—in God's Spirit, in God's Son, in Jesus—is *entering into* the lives of people in dramatic ways—especially those who have been *closed out* by the domination system or by their own shame. In Greek, the verb *erchomai* (to enter in, to come into presence, to be present) appears eleven times in this section. (In the Gospel of John, this verb is used to point to the incarnation—God *comes to* the earth in Jesus, God *enters into* our midst in Jesus.[24]) Additionally, in these two chapters in Capernaum, the same verb with a prefix like *pros* (towards), *eis* (in), *ex* (out), and *ap* (away) occurs eighteen more times, for a total of twenty-nine occurrences of forms of the verb *erchomai*. This verb occurs in striking clusters in Mark, as markers for Jesus *entering into* the lives of people who need healing and forgiveness, *with compassion*. It's not that the verb is unusual in itself, but it comes in bursts, signaling an important incarnational theme.

The opening verse for the Capernaum section (1:21) announces the theme, but with a different verb that also means to enter into (*eisporeuomai*). In the first episode, we see the theme in verse 24, "have you *come* to destroy us? I know who you are, the Holy One of God." In the second episode, Jesus *enters into* the house of Simon and Andrew. There he heals Simon's mother-in-law by *coming to her* and taking her by the hand and lifting her up, touching her firmly, compassionately—a dramatic form of entering into the midst of her world with its illness. In the third episode they *bring* the sick *to* him (another verb indicating their coming into his presence), and he heals them. In the fourth scene, a leper *comes to him* begging, falls on his knees before him, and says. "If you choose, you can make me clean." Jesus is filled with compassion (1:41).

Later in the Gospel, Jesus is moved with compassion at people's hunger and their need of healing (6:34; 8:2; 9:22; 10:47–48; cf. 5:19). "Compassion" occurs twelve times in the Gospels, but less frequently in other parts of the New Testament. It seems to be a special theme of Jesus'. It comes from the word for "gut," and means a gut feeling of empathy and identification with someone in need. It is like God hearing the cries of the slaves in Egypt, seeing their need, and *coming to be present* to deliver them.[25] It is also a theme emphasized by the prophet Isaiah, Jesus' favorite prophet (Isa. 13:18; 14:1; 27:11; 30:18; 43:4; 49:10, 13, 15; 54:7, 8, 10; 55:7; 60:10; 63:7, 15). Jesus taught that God is the Compassionate One who comes to be present to us and delivers us, just as Isaiah did. Jesus *enters into* the midst of the lives of people *with compassion* despite the wrath of the powers and authorities against his actions; that is why he will be crucified.

Jesus touches the leper (1:41), just as he had taken the sick woman by the hand and lifted her up—dramatically entering into his life of exclusion and welcoming him into physical community. Jesus repeatedly acts to heal the shame of outcasts and make them members of the community.[26]

This pattern is also clear in Isaiah. The prophet Isaiah had felt excluded from God's presence by his own shame over his unclean lips, but God came to him in the form of the Seraphim and redeemed him by touching his lips (Isa. 6). Ever after, Isaiah spoke of God not as "the Holy One of Israel, too high for us to see or touch," but as "the Holy One of Israel, our Redeemer." God was holy not as the Excluder but as the Redeemer. And God welcomed Gentiles and eunuchs who observed the Sabbath into the temple (compare Isa. 6 and Isa. 56). In the New Testament, Jesus fulfills Isaiah's themes by entering into the lives of people—touching them, redeeming them, and confronting the injustice of the authorities who are oppressing them.

The fifth scene gives us one of the most memorable *entries into presence* in the New Testament: Four men bring a paralyzed man to Jesus, but the house is too crowded for them to gain entry. So they remove part of the roof and lower him down on a pallet in the presence of Jesus. Jesus addresses the paralytic as "son," symbolically making him a member of his family. And he pronounces him forgiven. The scribes say only God can forgive sins (and they want control over declaring anyone forgiven by God),[27] so they accuse Jesus of blasphemy. This is the same accusation for which Jesus will be condemned to death (Mark 14:64). Then Jesus demonstrates that "the Son of Man has authority on earth to forgive sins" (2:10): He heals the paralytic.

The sixth scene is equally dramatic in that social context of exclusion: Jesus sees Levi, the tax collector, an outcast in the eyes of the Pharisees. He invites Levi to be a follower, and goes into Levi's house to practice the intimate fellowship of eating together with other tax collectors and sinners. This is truly entry into the presence of outcasts. "I have *come* [*erchomai* again] to call not the righteous but sinners" (2:17).

In the seventh scene, some people ask him why his disciples are not fasting. Jesus' answer speaks about his presence: "As long as they have the bridegroom with them, they cannot fast. The days will come when the bridegroom is taken away" (2:19–20 RSV)—again, a foretelling of the crucifixion. The eighth scene shows Jesus and the disciples plucking grain and eating it on the Sabbath. When the Pharisees challenge them, Jesus answers that David met the need of his followers by *entering into* the House of God and eating the *bread of the Presence*. In the ninth scene, *he enters into* a synagogue, and heals a man with a withered hand.

By contrast, the scribes in 2:6 and 2:16, and the Pharisees in 2:24 and 3:6 do not *enter* or *come in*; they simply sit, observe, and discuss what Jesus is doing—from a detached distance—definitely not with compassion. Mark often describes a relation of hostility by spatial distancing, standing over against—the antithesis to *erchomai*.[28]

Four themes are clear in this first section of Mark: (1) Jesus is *entering into the presence* of outcasts, persons in need of healing, forgiveness, food, touch and welcome into community. (2) He is touching them, forgiving them, eating with them, and delivering them from their outcast status into community. (3) He is doing this out of compassion, out of sensitivity to need. And (4) in this compassion and deliverance, we see the character of the Son of God, God's Spirit, God's Son, bringing them into God's presence and overcoming separation and alienation. The section opens with the Holy Spirit declaring "You are the Holy One of God," and it climaxes with the spirits falling down before him and crying out, "You are the Son of God."

This compassion, entry into presence, and deliverance signal an incarnational theory of the cross. In all these actions to meet human need with compassion and deliverance, to move through defensive barriers and enter into the midst of people's lives, Jesus is refusing to stay within the domination-rules of the powers and authorities. As a result, "the Pharisees *went out*, and immediately conspired with the Herodians against him, how to destroy him" (3:6, italics added).

Mark opened his Gospel by telling us why Jesus was crucified: he entered with compassion into the presence of outcasts, delivered them and brought them into community with him and with others. In this compassionate delivering action he was the Son of God, the instrument of God's presence as Holy Spirit. He went against the domination of the powers and authorities who were unjustly treating all these people as unclean outcasts.

Precisely this is the theme of Willie Jennings' enormously insightful *Christian Imagination*. Jennings shows that colonialist Christianity first replaced Jesus' identification with particular Jewish embodiment and Jesus' entering compassionately into the actual historical life of indigenous people, with, instead, a Platonic and docetic claim to universal ideals. Then colonialist Christianity used this above-history and above-embodiment-in-a-land non-incarnational theology to position itself as above learning from the culture of colonial people. But Jennings also tells of one white missionary who learned to identify with the African who taught him how to translate. He was translating Hebrew Scriptures into African language, and thus also identified more deeply with Jesus as rooted in the particular history of Israel. He became convinced that the British colonialist structure in Africa was deeply unjust and dishonest, and gave his skills to the Africans, campaigning against the injustices. His historically incarnational work cracked open his perceptions so that "even colonized strangers began to seep inside and create cultural alienation for the translator and, even more, deep desire for those who speak native words. . . . That joining is a sharing in the pain, plight, and life of one another."[29]

2. Demonic Power, Jairus's Power, Jesus' Power (5:1–43)

Are the religious authorities always distant? Not in 5:22–43. One of the chiefs of the synagogue *comes* (*erchomai*) to Jesus and falls at his feet. He begs Jesus to heal his twelve-year-old daughter, who is at the point of death. He has faith in Jesus, recognizing him with honor and humility. He begs that Jesus *touch* his daughter: "Come and lay your hands on her, so that she may be made well, and live."[30] So Jesus heads for his home, "and a large crowd followed him and pressed in on him."

But here comes an interruption from a person of no social status and alienating shame. A woman who has had a hemorrhage for twelve years (as many years as Jairus's daughter has been alive) is ritually unclean and may also smell unclean. Her hemorrhage probably has caused her to be husbandless and powerless in a male-dominated society. She has spent whatever money she had on many physicians, who took her money but only made her worse. She is unclean, unmarried, penniless, a woman of painful shame in a male-dominated society, seeking help from Jesus who has more urgent things to do for an important man whose daughter is at the point of death.[31] Being unclean, she should not be coming into a crowd or be touching anyone. But she courageously *comes into* (*erchomai*) the crowd and touches Jesus' coat, a dramatic entry into presence. She believes that if she can only touch his garments, she will be made well. Will someone shame her for breaking the ritual rules? No, "immediately her hemorrhage stopped; and she felt in her body that she was healed of her disease."

So now Jesus can go on his way to see about Jairus's daughter. But no—it is important to Jesus to make contact with her, to enter empathetically into her situation. He asks, "'Who touched my clothes?' . . . The woman . . . came [*erchomai*] in fear and trembling, fell down before him, and told him the whole truth. He said to her, 'Daughter, your faith has made you well; go in peace, and be healed of your disease.'" He gives her a quadruple blessing: He addresses her as "daughter," thus treating her as a member of his family, very much included in community, and not as an outcast. He commends her faith—for which he was seldom able to commend his male disciples. He says "go in peace, and be healed."

Jesus has taken time to be present to the courageous woman. It is now too late; Jairus's daughter is probably already dead. Mark tells us three times that Jesus *enters* the house where the girl is lying—first using *erchomai* twice, and then using the word with which he began the Capernaum section in 1:21, *eisporeuontai*. And now touching is mentioned, for the fourth time in this section: Jesus *takes her by the hand* and calls on her to rise. And then comes another sign of compassion: Jesus senses that she must be hungry and tells them, "give her something to eat."

The verb *erchomai*—come in or enter into presence—is repeated seven times in this episode in the second half of Mark chapter 5. It is repeated three times in the first half of the chapter as Jesus enters into the life of the Gerasene demoniac. All of these encounters made Jesus ritually unclean—touching a leper, a woman with bloody issue, and a dead body—and entering into the presence of a demoniac. It is a very tangible entrance into community and relationship, literally taking on others' burden and sin. This is incarnational discipleship![32]

3. Entry into Jerusalem (11:1–33)

A third cluster of Jesus' entering into the midst of people's lives occurs in chapter 11, his "triumphal entry" into Jerusalem and the temple—the center of Jewish political and religious power. He rides in on a donkey, not a warhorse. Unfortunately what we celebrate as Palm Sunday is seldom taught for what it is—Jesus' entry into Jerusalem as the Messiah of peace, fulfilling Zechariah 9:9–10:

> Rejoice greatly, O daughter Zion!
>   Shout aloud, O daughter Jerusalem!
> Lo, your king comes to you;
>   triumphant and victorious is he,
> humble and riding on a donkey,
>   on a colt, the foal of a donkey.
> He will cut off the chariot from Ephraim
>   and the war-horse from Jerusalem;
> and the battle bow shall be cut off,
>   and he shall command peace to the nations. . . .

By riding a donkey, Jesus is declaring that he is *entering into* the presence of the powers and authorities in Jerusalem to confront them nonviolently, as Messiah of peace.

Once again the narrative begins with the word for "entering in" that began the Capernaum episodes and marked the healing of the courageous woman and Jairus's daughter (*eisporeuontai*). The people cried out: "Hosanna! Blessed is the one who *comes* in the name of the Lord! Blessed the *coming* kingdom of our father David," and Jesus "*entered into* Jerusalem *into* the temple" (author's literal translation). People's intuition is right when they call this Jesus' *entry* into Jerusalem. The word occurs seven times in the chapter, and forms of *erchomai* with a prefix occur an additional five times. Having entered into Jerusalem, immediately he *enters into* the center of power, the temple, and looks around at everything (Mark 11:11). It could hardly be clearer that he has entered into the heart of power, into Jerusalem, into the temple, to confront it and call it to repentance—as the following verses make explicit.

Then he *came* to Jerusalem and *entered into* (*erchomai* and *eisporeuomai*) the temple and began to drive out those who were selling, quoting Isaiah 56 and Jeremiah 7. Tae Ho Lee has carefully evaluated the seven leading interpretations of Jesus' prophetic symbolic action in clearing the temple of its greedy money-changers (11:15–19). He concludes,

Jesus engaged in a symbolic prophetic action against the Temple because of its breach of prophetic justice and its religious cover-up. The *Sitz im Leben* at that time was an oppressive and exploitive socio-economic system, over-burdening tax, tithe resulting in debt, corrupt high priests, and their unjust economic gain from the Temple operation; and therefore, in response, popular prophetic and messianic protest movements. Jesus' four actions in the Temple show his criticism against the injustices of the Temple system based upon his theme of prophetic justice. Jesus' citation of Isaiah 56:7 and Jeremiah 7:11 have a common theme of prophetic justice: *mishpat* and *tsedaqah*. . . . Justice was not a minor subtheme for Jesus; it was his action of confrontation that would lead either to repentance by the authorities or to their seeking his crucifixion.[33]

Justice is also at the heart of Mark 12:6, Jesus' parable of the tenants in the vineyard. The Gospel indicates that the tenants conspire to kill the son because of their greed for power and wealth, and "the chief priests, scribes and elders" (11:27) "realized that he had told this parable against them; they wanted to arrest him, but they feared the crowd" (12:12). Once again, Mark is telling us that the Jerusalem authorities conspired to have Jesus killed because he was confronting their injustice, their power and domination, and their divided loyal-ties—their greed for wealth. In telling this parable, he enters into the midst of what they are doing, naming the sin for which they need to repent. He is seeking to redeem the powers too—if they will repent.

4. The Anointing and the Garden (14:1–72)

One additional cluster of the verb to *enter in* occurs twelve times in chapter 14. A woman *comes into* the house of Simon the leper and anoints Jesus for burial. Jesus confronts a Pharisee for saying she should have been excluded. Jesus *comes* with the disciples *into* the room where they celebrate the Last Supper. He *comes* with them *into* Gethsemane, where he will be arrested and taken to be crucified. Three times he *comes to* the disciples whom he had asked to watch while he prayed and finds them sleeping. He chides them for abdicating their responsibil-ity as watchmen, and calls them to repent.

And who is the betrayer? Judas is identified not as a zealot, as some like to speculate, or as a money-grubber, as others like to suggest, but repeatedly as "one of the twelve" (vv. 20 and 43). Judas, the betrayer in this drama, represents us, the disciples. Jesus tells the chief disciple, Peter, that he will deny Jesus three times, and Peter refuses to believe it, failing to face his own limits. After Peter denies him three times (14:66–72), Peter "broke down and wept" with shame. Jesus knew the disciples would do this and told them so: their betraying and falling away does not lie outside the drama of the cross; it is taken up by Jesus into the meaning of the cross. As Myers suggests, "Mark's discourse stresses the complicity of each and every disciple—not just Peter or Judas—in the collapse of the community's loyalty to the way of Jesus."[34] Again we see that the cross is about God in Christ entering into our midst, confronting us and calling us to repent, and incorporating our betrayals and denials into his love. Mark shows that Jesus knows the disciples well. Jesus enters into their midst, including their misunderstanding, denials, even betrayal. He confronts them directly and honestly with their failures so they know he is not redeeming perfect disciples, but people with shame and guilt. He accepts their failure and takes it with him to the cross. He does not let it break the community, does not exclude them, but tells them twice he will go ahead of them to Galilee and still be in community with them (14:28 and 16:7).

I love the climactic scene in the Gospel of John where the disciples bring their catch of fish to the shore. The last episode with Peter was at the charcoal fire where he denied Jesus (John 18:18; 25–27). Now Jesus has prepared another charcoal fire on the shore where he greets Peter again (John 21:8). As Peter had denied him three times, he asks Peter three times, "Do you love me?" Peter has been painfully ashamed of having denied Jesus. Jesus enters into Peter's shame and restores Peter as a participant—and even a leader—in feeding his sheep.

Throughout the Gospel of Mark, Jesus brings outsiders into community. The minor characters do for Jesus what the disciples fail to do: The crowd flocks to him and receives his teaching eagerly; although in the end, stirred up by the chief priests, they clamor for his crucifixion. The father of the demon-possessed boy demonstrates faith, not the disciples. A woman outside of their circle, not those at the table, anoints Jesus for burial, and he says wherever the gospel is preached she will be remembered. Simon of Cyrene, a Gentile and not one of his disciples, takes up Jesus' cross. "It is a Gentile, a Roman centurion, not one of the twelve, who is the first human being to recognize and confess him to be the Son of God, and hence more than the Jewish Messiah. It is Joseph of Arimathea who obtains his body and buries him. . . . Finally, it is the women, not the disciples, who come to anoint him after his burial and who receive the message that he has risen."[35]

Jesus comes to Jerusalem and enters into the presence of the political-economic-religious authorities to confront them with their injustice, their power-domination, divided loyalties, theft of wealth, exclusion of outcasts, and violence. He comes to call them to repentance because that is God's will. This is the way of confrontational, delivering love.[36] It is the only way to bring the message of repentance to the powerful with real impact, and the only way to incorporate even their violence and injustice into the call for repentance and transformation. In his realism Jesus does not expect that they will repent, at least not all of them. But notice that when they ask him ensnaring questions about authority, or about paying taxes to Caesar, or about a woman whose husbands all went to heaven, he always answers them with a question whose answer would be to affirm the Holy Spirit, God's authority over all of life, or the authority of Moses (Mark 11:29–12:26). This puts them on the spot, inviting them to acknowledge loyalty to God. And when a sincere scribe asks him about the greatest commandment, and then praises Jesus' answer, Jesus responds: "You are not far from the kingdom of God."[37]

Shouldn't we interpret Jesus' entry into the presence of the authorities in Jerusalem, where they will crucify him, as his fulfilling God's will to call them to repentance? Jesus affirms to the high priest that he is the Messiah, the Son of God, and he also puts Pilate on the spot (Mark 14:61–62; 15:2–5). Crucifying the Son of God, this most powerful of all demonstrations of horrible injustice, is a call for repentance for all of us, whether we have a little bit of power or a lot. It is a call to repent for our support for violence against the violated, domination of the less powerful, exclusion of the marginalized, greedy deprivation of the poor, and failure in our responsibility as watchpersons. Jesus' death was *caused by* our sins, Jesus died *because of* our sins, Jesus died *for* our sins, *on account of* our sins—whether we are Jews, Romans, or disciples. Let us not shift the blame to someone else—God or the powerful or the disciples—thereby practicing self-deception. We all have a role in the drama—then and now.

Here I want to raise an important question for understanding the meaning of the cross. Throughout the previous "entry" passages, we have seen Jesus entering into people's lives *out of compassion* and often *confronting them* from within their lives, calling them to repent. Compassion and confrontation are not opposites but what is needed for healing. When a friend once asked me, "Glen, are you doing what I think you are doing?" it was the kind of confrontation I needed then, from one who was seeing inside my life with compassion. When Martin Luther King Jr. taught us to challenge segregating store owners with love, not hate, being clear the enemy was not whites but injustice, and hoping for their repentance so we could become one people, he was calling for confrontation from within the kind of compassion that enters into their midst. Was Jesus also confronting the powers and authorities, not only out of judgment but also out of love for enemies, calling for their repentance?

As Mark tells it, Jesus entered into Jerusalem, and into the presence of the powers and authorities there, knowing full well that they were plotting to have him crucified. He openly confronted them and called them to repent. Clearly the cross is judgment on the sin of all who oppress, exclude, are greedy, and do violence. Clearly Jesus' death is judgment on our sin. Is it also God's compassion even for the powers and authorities in Jerusalem, and for the Romans who crucify him, as well as for the disciples who betray, deny, and desert him? Jesus says from the cross, "Father, forgive them; for they do not know what they are doing" (Luke 23:34).

Tae Ho Lee calls Jesus' action of confrontation at the temple a "prophetic symbolic action."[38] The prophets performed dramatic actions not only as judgment, but also as calls for repentance. Jesus says to the disciples, "Whenever you stand praying, forgive, *if you have anything against anyone*; so that your Father in heaven may also forgive you your trespasses" (11:25). He says this in the context of his relating to "the chief priests, the scribes, and the elders." They *came to him* (*erchomai*) and asked who gave him authority to do these things. Jesus did not simply condemn them. He asked them a question—"Did the baptism of John come from heaven or was it of human origin?" The baptism of John was a baptism of repentance and of participation in God's forgiveness. Here was an opportunity for them to affirm God's call to repentance—for they knew that "all regarded John as truly a prophet." But they waffled: "We do not know." And then he told the parable of the vineyard and the tenants, which is clearly a confrontation, and also a call for repentance.

These challenges that Jesus threw down for the authorities are gauntlets for us as well. Chapter 15 tells of the Romans crucifying him, in a way that demonstrates and judges their and our sin. We all play a role in this judgment—Jewish authorities, Gentile crucifiers, disciples who betray, deny, and desert. But there are signs of repentance—Simon of Cyrene who carried his cross; the Roman centurion who said "Truly this man was God's Son"; Joseph of Arimathea, who went boldly to Pilate and asked for the body of Jesus; and the women who had looked on *from a distance, but then came (erchomai)* with spices to anoint him.

Surely the cross is confrontation and judgment of sin. But I suggest it is also compassionate blessing for repentance and for being close to the kingdom of God, even for a Roman centurion, a Jewish member of the council, a scribe, and disciple-women who had kept a distance but then came to him. Jesus died for *our* sins, whether we are male or female disciples, Roman crucifiers, or Jerusalem authorities. The question is, How do we respond?

This Is the Way of Confrontation for Injustice, Not Weakness

Some theologians glorify Jesus by praising his taking the way of weakness. William Hamilton so dwelt on this theme that it reduced his theology of God's action to near zero and led to his becoming a death-of-God theologian. Some have so emphasized "weakness" that it replaced careful, historically embedded exegesis of Jesus' way with its richness and thickness. Others have rightly objected against weakness as teaching victims of injustice simply to comply with injustice without complaint. A subtheme of my interpretation via compassion, presence, *and confrontation and call for repentance* is correction of that interpretation. Weakness is not what Jesus taught or glorified. The cross is both compassionate entry into shame, and confrontation of the injustice of domination-power. It was the most powerful call for repentance there can be—since the greed, injustice, and violence of the powerful was demonstrated in the most powerful way it could be, by their crucifying Jesus.

The cross is "the most fearful, painful, shameful form of execution practiced in late antiquity."[39] Morna Hooker writes,

> We need . . . to transfer ourselves from [our] culture in which the cross is an honoured symbol to one in which it signified utter degradation. . . .
> Nailing a man up naked—whether dead or alive—was the greatest possible indignity to which one could subject him. Crucifixion thus combined the death penalty with excruciating torture and with total humiliation. . . . In the Roman Empire it was used primarily to punish slaves: the threat of crucifixion was used to keep slaves subservient . . . [like lynching in the not-too-distant U. S. past; see James Cone, *The Cross and the Lynching Tree*]. Moreover, this barbaric death involved the display of his naked body in public—the final, utter degradation.[40]

Jesus surely does enter into shame. During the Last Supper, he declares: "Truly I tell you, I will never again drink of the fruit of the vine until that day when I drink it new in the kingdom of God" (14:25). As he was dying on the cross, a bystander ran and filled a sponge with vinegar wine and "gave it to him to drink. . . . And Jesus gave a loud cry, and breathed his last" (15:36–37). Can it be that Jesus' death on the cross, as compassionate entry into shame and suffering, and as confrontation of the powers that work injustice and of the disciples who betray and deny, is his entry into the kingdom of God? Mark's climax is not the resurrection, which is clearly promised but not described. Mark's climax is the cross.

What we have seen in Bonhoeffer we have also seen in Mark. Mark's drama of Jesus is a drama of redemption because it is God's compassionate coming in Christ into the midst of our lives as we hide in shame and with our defense mechanisms—we marginalized, we disciples, we powers and authorities. He overcomes our evasion and denial, our hostility and violence and domination-power, by confronting them and accepting them onto himself. He does not let them stay hidden and alienated. We all fear death, and especially do we fear dying alone, without companionship. Alienation, shame, violence, and fear of death can be healed only by entering into their midst, confronting them, and bringing us into community with God and with others. That is what God in Christ does on the cross.

AN INCARNATIONAL THEORY OF THE CROSS

N. T. Wright and Hans Boersma are right that we should not flinch from affirming that God judges sin. We need to clarify the meaning of judgment and who receives judgment in the cross. Isaiah 53 tells us that "he was despised and rejected *by others*." Those who despised and rejected him were the rulers and authorities of Israel and Rome, and the disciples, not God. "It was *our* infirmities that he bore . . . , yet we accounted him stricken, struck down by God." This "yet" is saying that our accounting him stricken *by God* was an error; it was *others* who struck him down. He accepted the suffering caused by our sin, violence, and unfaithfulness to God. "By a perversion of justice he was taken away." The perverters of justice in Mark are the human authorities and the disciples, not God. God does not do injustice. But "it was the will of the LORD to crush him with pain." I read this to say the authorities and disciples did the wrong, but God used this wrong to bring us redemption. The cross brought great suffering on Jesus and judgment on the injustice that crucified Jesus. Romans 8:28 says that in all things, which surely includes unjust things, God is working for good, which surely means God is not working for injustice but for good.

Let us be clear that in Mark, God is revealed in Jesus, in what Jesus does. It was the powers and authorities and the betrayer, not God, who plotted to crucify Jesus. It was judgment on their and our sin. And Jesus willingly suffered as a consequence of that sin, as the devastation of war often falls not on the leaders who make the war, but on the poor people who experience it, who tragically get in its way. The judgment is on those who caused the war. As Veli-Matti Kärkkäinen reminds us, René Girard argues that the cross transforms the practice of scapegoating, so that those who take out their wrath on a scapegoat are no longer seen as the righteous ones, but as the perpetrators of injustice. Now we see that God sides with the victim of scapegoating, not the perpetrators. Kärkkäinen explains, "Differently from the mythical concealing of violence, the biblical narrative exposes violence as violence and helps make an end of the cycle."[41]

"All we like sheep have gone astray . . . but the LORD has laid on him the iniquity of us all" (Isa. 53:6). The cross was judgment on the powers that crucified him as well as on us who despised him. "He disarmed the rulers and authorities and made a public example of them, triumphing over them" in the cross (Col. 2:15). The cross was an astounding revelation of the extent to which injustice and violence can go. And in Christ, God took even this on himself, opening the door to redemption for even the worst of us.

When I visited the Church of the Holy Sepulchre in Jerusalem and was meditating on two paintings of Jesus crucified, I was moved to believe that "Jesus died for our sins" means that Jesus died *because* of our sins; our sins caused his death. It also means that Jesus died as God's becoming present to us, offering forgiveness and calling us to repentance. It also means he died entering into our lives of shame, guilt, and alienation, breaking through defense mechanisms and denial with compassion. Jesus died for our sins.

Let me make this plain: The cross is Jesus Christ's act to enter into Jerusalem, as he had entered into the midst of the lives of people throughout the Gospel— the very perpetrators of injustice, violence, betrayal, and denial—to confront their wrong and to offer even them the opportunity to repent and be included in his mission, in community with him. Jesus does this amazing act of compassion and sacrifice because it is God's will to deliver them and us. In what Jesus does, God is acting because of God's judgment on the injustice, domination, violence, greed, denial, and exclusion, and because of God's compassion to redeem, to deliver from alienation.

If God in Christ does this painful act of compassion and confrontation for them and for the disciples, he also does it for me and for you, despite our alienation, sin, exclusion, denial, and fear of death. In the proclamation of the cross, God enters into our presence as Holy Spirit and invites us, despite everything, into saving community. Because of their and our resistance, there is a sacrificial price to be paid for this compassion and confrontation. God in Christ pays it, in order to enter into our hearts despite our resistance. They and we crucify him, but he continues to work to restore community. And he calls us to take up our crosses, to do likewise for others—to enter compassionately and sometimes confrontationally into their alienation.

In our sin, guilt, and shame, we distort and misperceive, deny and misunderstand. We practice greed, we exclude, we dominate and do injustice and violence; and then we hide and evade and pretend that we don't. Jesus does not pretend that we do not do this; he confronts it. He does not just give cheap forgiveness; he enters into the midst of our hiding and takes the destructiveness of our sin onto himself. He makes us participants in his own life. He does not make light of the depth of our wrongness; he pays the price for it because of his incarnational love and his calling us to repentance. Bonhoeffer is right:

> This is accomplished not by a general idea of love, but by the love of God really lived in Jesus Christ. This love of God for the world does not withdraw from reality into noble souls detached from the world, but experiences and suffers the reality of the world at its worst. The world exhausts its rage on the body of Jesus Christ. But the martyred one forgives the world its sins. Thus reconciliation takes place.[42]

The cross is the worst that we could do, crucifying the Son of God. It incorporates the violence, the hate, the exclusion, the domination, the greed for power or wealth, and the evasion in this one event. God takes all this into God's life and still enters into our lives with compassion to be present to us, making us participants in his community. This is how the atonement happens. The cross is God's presence in Jesus Christ to us even in our greed and violence. It is an action of forgiveness for us even in our worst, which often leads to the violence of killing and of rejecting God's compassion. The cross is a call to repentance and an offer of acceptance and participation in God's mission. The cross makes God's presence clear and invites us to participate in God's community. But we still fear that we will disobey and distrust and be hostile once again, and therefore will be rejected. We fear trusting in God. Therefore we need God to receive our hostility in the cross and show that it does not cancel the offer of presence and incorporation. "I will go before you to Galilee" (Mark 14:28): I will not abandon you.

If the incarnation is really about God entering into our lives, as Bonhoeffer insists, even though we are God's enemies (Rom. 5), then the theme of incarnationally entering into the lives of the excluded and restoring them to community must be central for the cross. Jesus' holiness is not seen in separation from outsiders, but in redemptive compassion that brings them into community. What Jesus did, he did for the deliverance of others—he said he was giving "his life as a ransom for many" (Mark 10:45) and pouring out his "blood of the covenant . . . for many" (14:24). Most discussions of these two teachings rightly emphasize the deliverance meaning of ransom and covenant; I urge us also to emphasize the compassion dimension of Jesus giving his life for many. As Jennifer McBride observes, "God in Christ draws human guilt into divine life, where it is then overcome. . . . Christ embraces the condition of human guilt in solidarity with real human beings in order to redeem."[43] Jesus' central teaching of "love your enemy" is not merely a feeling but an entering into the perspective of the other and bringing the other into community. Jesus' cross is the consequence of the anger of the authorities over his compassionate entry into the needs of outcasts and bringing them into community, and of the authorities' anger at his entering into their precincts and calling them to repentance.

DEEPER THAN ONE THEORY

The embodied drama of Jesus Christ's death on the cross is far deeper and more complex than any one theory of the cross can comprehend. I remember well when a group of us went to see Fellini's powerful film *La Strada*, in which the male character is offered the love and faithful presence he deeply needs by a humble woman who is all simplicity, caring, and goodness. As he begins to accept her love, they develop what she believes is a covenant relationship, but then he abandons her, riding off on his macho motorcycle, leaving her alone. That film hit me deeply. Normally I love to discuss the depths of meaning in a drama. But I was so overcome by its powerful portrayal of my own inner woundedness and capacity to wound that I could not say a word while my friends were engaged in discussing its meaning.

The crucifixion is like that. It is too deep, too complex, and involves too many facets of our inner human dramas for us to reduce it to only one theory about its meaning.[44] In the short space that follows, we can begin to examine how the incarnational discipleship understanding can add to each of the prevailing theories on the atonement. It may be received as enriching and articulating what is intended in other theories, or as the most persuasive theory in itself. I believe advocates of the other theories are groping toward the incarnational theory of the atonement.

In the classic **Christus Victor theory**, the cross disclosed the injustice of the rulers and authorities for all to see, making a public example of them, triumphing over them in the resurrection (Col. 2:15). This has great truth in it, and clear biblical basis. Hans Boersma concludes: "The main reason I have reserved my treatment of the Christus Victor theme until the end, however, is that I believe it is, in a real sense, the most significant model of the atonement."[45] But in the classical *Christus Victor* theory, God achieved this victory by deceiving the devil, offering Jesus as bait. The devil took the bait and swallowed the hook: getting the Son of God unjustly crucified exposed the devil's evil for all to see. This mechanism—God's trickery—makes little sense to many people and lacks biblical basis.[46]

Incarnational discipleship replaces this confusing metaphor: the mechanism for Christ's defeat of evil is not a hook in Jesus' bait, but God's compassionate entering into our lives, God's confronting the injustice of the rulers and ourselves. This is what the rulers and authorities reject and the disciples flee from. Jesus had predicted that rejection and brings it with him into the event of the cross. He discloses the injustice of the crucifiers and makes it part of the drama of reconciliation, so we know that he has redeemed not only our good side, but has explicitly included the very worst anyone could do in the crucifixion. The cross includes us with our sin. In the resurrection, Jesus becomes victor over the powers—and restores community.

An incarnational theory of the cross emphasizes compassion as well as confrontation, entering into the midst of the central concerns of others' lives with empathy and suffering. This is crucial if we are to understand Jesus' way of winning the victory. It pays close attention to what the incarnate Jesus actually did and said. It sees God doing a costly and dramatically new action in and through Jesus to enter into the midst of our compulsive evasion and alienation. It sees victory beginning already in the cross, as God acts in the cross with compassion even for evildoers while also revealing their horrible injustice.

The **moral influence theory** rightly sees the cross as influencing us to love others, but it emphasizes our moral reform rather than what God does uniquely and decisively in Christ's death. Hans Boersma's chapter on Abelard and Irenaeus concludes that moral influence should be part of the theory of the cross because it is "God's way of taking the human response seriously. He is not a God who harbors violence at the heart of his being and so forces us to enter into his kingdom. Rather, he is a God who welcomes us into his presence by means of persuasion" for transformed living. But moral influence lacks the objective action of God in Christ that incarnational discipleship sees in Bonhoeffer and the Gospels.[47]

Incarnational atonement says God moves bodily through our defensive barriers of shame, guilt, and alienation to bring us to reconciliation for our salvation, with forgiveness, inclusion, and redemption. What we see Jesus doing, God is doing objectively in Jesus toward us, compassionately entering in and confronting us. It is God's nature to suffer from our sin; here God not only *shows* it but *does* it. The historical drama of the cross as demonstrated in the Gospels in fact incorporates all the dimensions of sin into our relation with God: seeking to replace God, be equal to God, and dominate others with our greed; having divided loyalties and being split from God and others; practicing self-deception, defensive denial, refusing to face our own limits. All these occur in the event as Mark and the other Gospels narrate it. Furthermore, we all die and fear death. In incarnational atonement, God in Christ incorporates death into God's initiative and our relationship. Here God in Christ accepts all death and sin as part of the crucifixion and makes clear that it need not permanently separate us from God, thereby overcoming its alienation.

I affirm and identify with **Miroslav Volf's theme of *Exclusion and Embrace*** (named here after the title of his book) and want to go yet further. Volf's portrayal of Christ's embrace as an invitation that *waits for our initiative* to enter the embrace has less dynamic incarnational *entry through our barriers and creation of a new community* that Bonhoeffer and the Gospels portray God taking.[48] Volf believes that the most significant recent contributions on the meaning of the cross come from Jürgen Moltmann, and he is clearly influenced by Moltmann's deep insight in *Crucified God*, as I also am, with great appreciation. "A major thrust of Moltmann's thinking about the cross can be summed up in the notion of solidarity. . . . On the cross, Christ both identifies God with the victims of violence and identifies 'the victims with God, so that they are put under God's protection and with him are given the rights of which they have been deprived.'"[49] In *The Spirit of Life* Moltmann supplements the theme of solidarity with the victims by the theme of atonement for the perpetrators.[50] Volf emphasizes "the social significance of the theme of divine self-giving: as God does not abandon the godless to their evil but gives the divine self for them in order to receive them into divine communion through atonement, so also should we."[51] This fits the incarnational understanding well. Divine self-giving is what I mean by God's entering into our alienation in Christ. Embrace is what I mean by bringing into community.

The **nonviolent theory** as advocated by J. Denny Weaver rightly pays attention to Jesus' way of nonviolent obedience to God in the actual narrative in the Gospels.[52] Jesus rejects the strategy of violent rebellion chosen by the several false messiahs, and instead confronts the Jerusalem authorities and Pilate nonviolently. This is what I have been arguing for as well, although, with Steven Dintaman, I want greater emphasis on Jesus' compassion, with feeling, and the presence of the Holy Spirit, not only dutiful obedience.[53]

Morna Hooker, James McClendon, Joel Green, and Mark Baker conclude that we cannot find **the penal substitution view** in the New Testament— that Jesus pays the penalty to God that God requires, but that we cannot pay. Instead, they suggest we can find a participation view: Jesus enters into shame and disciples are called to participate in Jesus' cross, to take up our cross and follow him. Jesus has been vindicated and given authority; he has reconciled us to himself and made us members of a new community; we must share his shame, suffering, and death.[54] Making "participation" a central theme also moves in the incarnational direction.

Hans Boersma, representing Reformed tradition, argues for the governmental **theory of penal representation**, not penal substitution. He affirms the three traditional theories of the cross—*Christus Victor*, moral influence, and what he renames as penal representation—as well as Irenaeus's recapitulation theory and Girard's scapegoat theory. He criticizes and modifies parts of each, and then affirms a synthesis of all five with "hospitality of God" as a central metaphor, as Miroslav Volf employs "invitation to embrace" as his central metaphor.[55] Boersma's central theme of God's hospitality points in a direction similar to the theme of compassionate incarnational entry, confrontation, and community— which strikes me as more dynamic and more clearly based in the language of the Gospels than simple hospitality.

A misunderstood **retributive justice** understanding of the cross often moves people toward "justice means punishment," and influences our criminal justice system to throw too many people into prison for far too long and for unjust reasons.[56] We see in Boersma, McClendon, Volf, Weaver and many others a shift wholly or partially away from the feudal punitive theory. And we see each moving in the direction of the incarnational understanding: their themes of solidarity, participation, hospitality, presence, nonviolent obedience, and invitation to embrace are beginning to point in the direction that is made clearer and more articulate by the incarnational understanding of the cross, with compassionate entering into the life of the other, as well as honest confrontation and movement toward community.

Nevertheless, N. T. Wright and Hans Boersma argue that a theology that flinches at the judgment of God evades rightful judgment against injustice, violence, and alienation from God. Incarnational discipleship explicitly emphasizes judgment against all six of the dimensions of sin that Bonhoeffer diagnosed in the last chapter. This is the point of its theme of confrontation. Without that, sin is dealt with too lightly or not at all. A profound understanding of the meaning of the cross needs God's judgment against sin to be specifically biblically rooted, not floating freely for self-righteous application to a scapegoat whom we want an excuse to hate and to exact our vengeance against.[57]

Biblical theologian John Goldingay explains the meaning of **sacrifice** in the Old Testament, referring especially to Leviticus 4–5. He says in our guilt we feel uncleanness and shame, which cuts us off from community and puts us in debt. Sacrifices are offerings of restitution that deal with the stain, and payment of the indebtedness. He says we should see "Christ's death as a gift offered to God in the context of a person-to-person relationship of mutual commitment with its potential for love, favour, generosity, self-sacrifice, gratitude, and forgiveness" rather than "satisfaction of God's honour" or "intrinsically hierarchical and/or contractual webs of relationships." In what Jesus does, we see God acting to deal with humanity's stain and our being cut off from community. "In this connection sacrifice is not something human beings do to God (propitiation) but something which God does for humankind (expiation)."[58] This fits the incarnational understanding. Jesus enters sacrificially into the presence of the authorities to bring judgment on their injustice, to call for repentance by all who participate in injustice such as they portray, and to bring all of us, regardless of our violence and injustice, into the call to redemption. In what Jesus does sacrificially, we see God acting sacrificially in him.

Boersma, Volf, and McClendon affirm the main point in **René Girard's scapegoat understanding of the cross,** in which Jesus is an arbitrary victim. "*The cross lays bare the mechanism of scapegoating,*" Volf writes. "All the accounts of Jesus' death agree that he suffered *unjust* violence. . . . In *The Scapegoat*, Girard has rightly emphasized . . . that one of the functions of the Gospel accounts is to demask the mechanism of scapegoating. . . . Instead of taking the perspective of the persecutors, the Gospels take the perspective of the victim; they 'constantly reveal what the texts of historical persecutors . . . hide from us: the knowledge that their victim is a scapegoat,'" and that God identifies with the victim, not the victimizers. Girard says that God identifying with the scapegoat is new, and it begins a slow transformation of history.[59] The cross was God's judgment on those who did the crucifying, not judgment on Jesus; Jesus paid the price for their wrongness.

McClendon writes that societies often develop identity by selecting a scapegoat to stereotype and direct hate against. "Jews have frequently endured this victimization. Jesus was crucified . . . as a scapegoat. . . . Yet Jesus, whose life and teaching utterly opposed violence, brought an end to violence for all who would follow him. His death signals the end of the kingdom of violence and is thus ironically a sacrifice to end all sacrifice. . . . So Girard's theological message . . . is a summons to radical recovery of the original gospel."[60] In the climax of his argument, McClendon writes: "The resurrection was God's sign of self-identification with Jesus who had taken the nonviolent way of the cross. It was God's way, God's *only* way. . . . What Jesus does in our place is not merely what God requires but what God does, what God suffers."[61]

Shame, Empowerment, and Justice

Although many of these theories have intrinsic problems along with their great promise, in this final section let me point to some understandings of the meaning of the cross that are yet more similar to what I am suggesting. Feminist and womanist theology in particular provide rich sources for understanding an incarnational atonement; God enters into human pain just as we are called to enter into the suffering of others, and also confronts injustice.

From the perspective of pastoral care, Deborah Hunsinger's profound explanation of shame and its healing has great significance for the life of churches and the kind of community they need to develop. Left untreated, shame cultivates anger and withdrawal. "Rage, a natural reaction to the sense of exposure that accompanies shame, serves to protect the self from further exposure and to distance the person who activated the shame." [62] She advocates a "bilingual method,"[63] learning on one level from psychology and on another from theology. She interprets the gospel via Karl Barth's emphasis on the incarnation in a way similar to what I have been suggesting:

> In the Gospels' stories of Jesus' healing miracles, Barth notes, "God is not seen as standing over against human beings, judging them for their wrong-doing, but as *entering fully into* their suffering and need, taking on their burdens and pain. In the person of Jesus Christ, God shows compassion to sinners and is ready to heal them of their afflictions. When Jesus confronts the suffering human being, he is not directly concerned with sin as such, nor with identifying the sources of the suffering, but rather with delivering that person from affliction."[64]

She describes the reaction of shame in one of her clients: "Eva seems to see God as a punitive parent, reprimanding her for her sloth, while Barth sees God, on the basis of these stories, as essentially concerned with removing whatever might be causing the distress of one such as her. . . . Here God is seen as standing alongside people as healer and deliverer, not over against them as judge or punitive parent."[65] "Standing alongside" is close to incarnational atonement's theme of "entering into community with." The language of "entering fully into suffering and pain" is even closer, and Hunsinger's pastorally entering into Eva's shame is exactly what I am advocating.

I especially affirm the interpretations of some womanist theologians who combine the theme of compassionate suffering with those who suffer with a clear emphasis on confronting and resisting injustice and calling for repentance, which is crucial for the historical drama of the cross. For example, Karen Baker-Fletcher and M. Shawn Copeland emphasize Jesus' life, his suffering, and his empowering us to resist injustice and violence. "The task is not to focus on Jesus' life to the exclusion of his suffering but to examine both his life and his suffering in new ways that take into account women's understanding of evil, sin, and defilement." This means that we see Jesus' suffering as well as Black women's suffering and also Martin Luther King's suffering as the "persecution and violence suffered by those who resist evil and injustice."[66] And Cheryl Kirk-Duggan writes: "Incarnate love, as compassion, empowers a person or community to resist subjugation and violence. The pre–Civil War abolitionist movement and the civil-rights freedom-fighters' movement confronted and resisted the cruelty of U.S. apartheid."[67]

Much womanist theology strongly emphasizes the Jesus who suffers alongside humanity, not standing outside of it, and who resists domination and exclusion. Nekeisha Alexis-Baker writes that slaves experienced Jesus on the cross as trusted companion who understood their pain, sufferings, and sorrows. She cites John Howard Yoder in asserting that the cross is not about merely putting up with suffering fatalistically or passively; the cross involves resistance.[68] It also means God suffers for us vicariously, so we voluntarily take on others' suffering, including in resistance. Therefore, slaves also understood the cross as suffering for the sake of the larger community. It built deeply felt solidarity and mutual support.

Marie Fortune writes in a similar vein:

> Voluntary suffering is a painful experience which a person chooses in order to accomplish a greater good. . . . For example, the acts of civil disobedience by civil rights workers in the United States in the 1960s resulted in police brutality, imprisonment, and sometimes death for these activists. . . . Yet people knowingly chose to endure this suffering in order to change the circumstances of racism, which caused even greater daily suffering for many. Jesus' crucifixion was an act of unjustifiable yet voluntary suffering (1 Peter 2:21–23). . . . It is an example not of simply being a sacrificial doormat but of choosing, in the face of the violence of oppressive authority which threatened him, to suffer the consequences of his commitment. It was a witness to his love. . . .[69]

Here Fortune is describing what I call "delivering love," that enters into the experience of those in bondage, does the delivering deed, confronts injustice, and brings into community.[70] This is a thicker understanding of love than Nygren's unmotivated sacrifice that does not connect with justice. It's a thicker understanding of the cross, a thicker Jesus. And because it combines caring with justice, in action like that of the civil rights workers, it can guide a public ethic, through all of life. And it calls all of us to repentance if we do any less.

Jacquelyn Grant also calls attention to our need for justice, and avoids a theory of the cross with passive suffering. Confronting injustice is crucial for an incarnational understanding of why Jesus went to Jerusalem and why he was crucified. I love Grant's connection of compassion and confrontation, and I place her here in the climax for that reason. Grant writes,

> Chief among Black people's experiences of Jesus was that he was a divine co-sufferer, who empowered them in situations of oppression. . . . They were able to identify with Jesus, because they felt that Jesus identified with them in their sufferings. . . . Just like them, Jesus suffered and was perse-cuted undeservedly. . . . African American women's cross experiences were constant in their daily lives—the abuses, physical and verbal, the acts of dehumanization, the pains, the sufferings, the loss of families and friends and the disruption of communities. But because Jesus Christ was not a mere man, but God incarnate, they, in fact, connected with the Divine. . . . "Nobody knows the trouble I see . . . but Jesus. . . ." African American women experienced Jesus as a great equalizer not only in the White world, but in the Black world as well. Because Jesus died for all, all can preach, and all are made equal.[71]

Grant retains the strong emphasis on Jesus' compassionate suffering while rejecting a model of merely passive suffering. Jesus' suffering came because Jesus identified with our suffering. His suffering empowers us and confronts unjust causes of misery. This is exactly what I am saying with an incarnational theory of the cross. Grant writes of Christ *standing with us*, which parallels Christ *entering into our midst*:

God's power and glory are present in our human condition no matter what the dimension of our suffering, because in Christ's suffering God has chosen to stand with us. Yet when we look to see this power and glory in human life, it shines through most clearly in those whose lives are confronting the suffering by saying *no* to its dehumanizing power.[72]

IN SUM

What are the Gospels telling us? Jesus enters into the shame of the outcasts, the lepers, the prostitutes, the tax collectors, the lame, the women who were excluded. He touches them, heals them, and brings them into community. He dialogues with the authoritarians, calling them to repentance, but they respond by plotting his death. The meaning of the cross is consistent with the meaning of his teaching, healing, and acts of deliverance. The cross is the consequence of his compassion for the marginalized and of his confrontation of the injustice that the powers were committing against the marginalized. The consistency of Jesus' compassion throughout the Gospel, along with his confrontation, shows that he enters into Jerusalem to confront the powers because of his compassion, which is also a call to them to repent, as the prophets called the rulers of Israel to repent.

He goes to Jerusalem, where the powers and authorities are, and enters into their midst, riding a donkey as a Messiah of peace who will abolish the warhorse (Zechariah 9:9–10). He teaches in the temple, turns over the tables, and calls the powers and authorities to repentance for their injustice, knowing that it will surely lead to his death. To bring full redemption, he needs to enter into the experience of their injustice and violence, reveal it for the evil it is, and then overcome it by his contrasting justice, nonviolence, love, and presence. Because we have injustice and violence in ourselves, this too must be entered into by God in Christ, and turned into a part of the drama of redemption.

In the Synoptic Gospels Jesus confronts the injustice of the powers (high priests, Sadducees, Pharisees, scribes, and the wealthy) thirty-seven times for four kinds of injustice: exclusion of the marginalized, domination of the less powerful, oppression of the poor, and violence against enemies.[73] Many Christians think only of Rome as the governing power. But the rulers over daily life in Israel were the powers and authorities in Jerusalem. Jesus confronted them. He knew that if Jerusalem did not learn the practices that make for peace, if instead they practiced blame, projecting their troubles on Rome, it would foment violent rebellion against Rome and result in the destruction of Jerusalem and the temple—as he prophesied repeatedly. In a similar way, Jesus is calling us to turn from hating our enemy and heating up the fires of violence to confronting the log of shame and resentment in our own eyes, repenting for our part in injustice and practicing peace. Incarnational discipleship recovers Jesus' commitment to justice and his confrontations of the powers. Justice is crucial to our interpretation of the cross, as it is in the Gospels.

The cross is an offer of relationship, presence, and participation in community. The point is to accept the relationship, to be present to it, to participate in God's creative project, in community. An offer like this we either accept or reject; either we evade and ignore it or we let it transform us.

Chapter 10

Love

The Sermon on the Mount
as Realistic Deliverance

As we saw in chapter 2, many are so fascinated with the controversial questions concerning Bonhoeffer's eventual participation, after all else had failed, in the coup attempt against Hitler, that they do not notice what I contend is the far more important question: How do we explain Bonhoeffer's early perspicacity, clarity, and courage in speaking against Hitler's war spirit and injustice to Jews when most other theologians failed to speak, or even gave their support to Hitler?

Answering the question of Bonhoeffer's early perspicacity from the beginning of Hitler's rule in 1933 points us to what he was focusing on in those years, from 1931 through 1935—the Sermon on the Mount. So now we turn our attention to Bonhoeffer's way of interpreting those teachings. His interpretation initially gave him prophetic strength and clarity, but in his *Ethics* in 1940 to 1943, he indicated his intention to reinterpret it more realistically. One of the causes of secularism that Charles Taylor diagnoses is a "high ideals" interpretation of Christianity, including the Sermon on the Mount and love, as advocating *renouncing* everything, *versus affirming ordinary human life* and flourishing. Here I will demonstrate that the high ideals interpretation of the Sermon on the Mount that wormed its way into Christianity about fifteen centuries ago is based on a misperception of the structure of Jesus' Sermon as antitheses that contrast with the Hebrew Scriptures and is clearly wrong. Jesus is realistically diagnosing vicious cycles and pointing to ways of deliverance that put us in touch with God's presence in ordinary life and that affirm human flourishing.[1]

BONHOEFFER AND THE SERMON ON THE MOUNT

Why did Bonhoeffer see so clearly as early as 1933? Because he had strong and specific norms from his strikingly concrete interpretation of the incarnate Jesus. He testifies that the Sermon on the Mount had converted him from being an ambitious theologian to being an actual Christian. Reggie Williams has shown how this conversion took place during Bonhoeffer's year in Harlem and Union Theological Seminary (1931-32).[2] When Hitler came to power, Bonhoeffer was beginning to write his book *Discipleship*, or *The Cost of Discipleship*, about the Sermon on the Mount, and would soon be teaching the substance of that book in the underground seminary at Finkenwalde. It was while he was focusing on his concrete interpretation of the Sermon on the Mount that he made the crucial decision to oppose Hitler. He began *Discipleship*, "It is not ultimately important to us what this or that church leader wants. Rather, we want to know what Jesus wants."[3] This is the first dimension of incarnational discipleship. Bonhoeffer deeply wanted church renewal and church revitalization, and so do we; he believed this was the way to church renewal, and so do I.

But four years previously, in 1929, shortly after his graduate studies, we see a different Bonhoeffer. H. E. Tödt points out, with embarrassment, that "no doubt Bonhoeffer comes quite close [in 1929] to the approach of Althaus and Hirsch and many other nationalistic Protestants of that time. National struggle and economic struggle take place in a social-Darwinist sense as God's order of creation and of history. What is to be done ethically and concretely is finally decided only by considering how we are bound by these orders."[4] In other words, this view holds that when the state decides it is time to make war, then our response should be guided not by the Lordship of Christ, but by a nationalistic loyalty to the government and the nation in its need for greater territory (*Lebensraum*). Tödt quotes the 1929 Bonhoeffer:

> There are no actions that are bad in and of themselves. Even murder can be sanctified. There is only faithfulness to or deviation from God's will. There is no law with a specific content, but only the law of freedom, that is, bearing one's responsibility alone before God and oneself. . . . It is the most serious misunderstanding to turn the commandments of the Sermon on the Mount once again into a law by applying them literally to the present.[5]

That was 1929, when Bonhoeffer was twenty-three. But a year later, on his first trip to the United States and Union Theological Seminary—and Abyssinian

Baptist Church—Bonhoeffer experienced what he later called a conversion to real Christian faith:

> I know that at that time I turned the doctrine of Jesus Christ into something of personal advantage for myself. . . . For all my loneliness, I was quite pleased with myself. Then the Bible, *and in particular the Sermon on the Mount*, freed me from this. . . . I suddenly saw the Christian pacifism that I had recently passionately opposed as self-evident. . . . And so it went on, step by step. I no longer saw or thought anything else.[6]

And in a letter to his brother Karl-Friedrich, he wrote:

> When I first began, I imagined it quite otherwise—perhaps a mere academic matter. Now something very different has come of it. I now believe that I know at last that I am at least on the right track—for the first time in my life. And that often makes me very glad. . . . I believe I know that inwardly I shall be clear and honest with myself only if I truly begin *to take seriously the Sermon on the Mount*. That is the only source of power capable of blowing up the whole phantasmagoria [i.e., the Nazi illusion] once and for all. . . . There just happen to be things that are worth an uncompromising stand. And it seems to me that peace and social justice, of Christ himself, are such things.[7]

The leading Bonhoeffer scholar, Clifford Green, has called this a "personal liberation" and says that *Discipleship* emerged directly out of this new theological understanding.[8]

Eberhard Bethge shows that, already in 1932, Bonhoeffer was working on the Sermon on the Mount as soon as he had returned from New York to Berlin.[9] He lectured on the subject both in the university and then in Finkenwalde, and in 1937 published *Nachfolge* (*Discipleship*)[10] in which he recovers the Sermon on the Mount for living, obedience, and guidance in the church struggle. "Recovers" is the right word here: In the New Testament and the first two centuries of the church, the Sermon on the Mount was the most quoted and cited of Jesus' teachings.[11] It is the largest block of Jesus' teachings in the New Testament. As Bonhoeffer says, the church that bypasses the Sermon on the Mount is a church of cheap grace. In his day, the church was bypassing it.

In his interpretation of the Sermon, Bonhoeffer followed a concrete hermeneutic in which the teachings are meant for our regular practice. They are not mere ideals or general illustrations, and certainly not impossible teachings designed to convince us that we cannot do them so that we will then fall back in a kind of swoon into cheap grace. This was a shift from an ethic of the moment in a Germany that lacked the strength to resist the allure of nationalistic militarism.

I credit the concreteness of his hermeneutic and the centrality of Christ as Lord as significant factors in his being "the first, indeed almost the only one, who so centrally and energetically focused on and acted in the Jewish question."[12] Many clues in his interpretation of the Sermon on the Mount show how Bonhoeffer's standing up for oppressed Jews was guided by loyalty to the way of Jesus of Nazareth, even though he could not name them directly in the time of the Nazis. He writes in *Discipleship* of their need and debasement, of "those who are in misery, for those who are demeaned and abused, for those who suffer injustice and are rejected." [13] Here is one example from *Discipleship*:

> The protection of God's command [against murder] extends not only to brothers and sisters who belong to the church-community but beyond. This is clearly shown by the fact that the actions of a follower of Jesus do not depend on the other person's identity, but only on him whom the disciple follows in obedience. . . . Intentional words of derision rob sisters and brothers of their dignity in public. They intend to make other people despise them, as well. They aim in hatred to destroy another's internal and external existence. . . . That is murder.
>
> So the community of Jesus' disciples ought to examine itself as to whether it is here and there at fault toward sisters and brothers, and whether, for the sake of the world, it has participated in hating, despising, and humiliating others. To do these things is to be guilty of their murder. Jesus' community today ought to examine whether at the moment it enters God's presence for prayer and worship many accusing voices rise up between it and God and hinder its prayers. Jesus' community ought to examine whether it has given a sign of Jesus' love, which preserves, supports, and protects lives, to those whom the world has despised and dishonored. Otherwise the most correct form of worship, the most pious prayer, and the bravest confession will not help, but will give witness against it, because it has ceased following Jesus.[14]

Bonhoeffer had learned his commitment to the way of Jesus as commanded in the Sermon on the Mount in the context of his identifying with African Americans in Harlem. When he read the Sermon, he thought of "brothers and sisters who belong to the church-community [and] beyond"—oppressed African Americans—and then learned to see parallel oppression of Jews in Germany.[15]

BUT WHY IS THE SERMON ON THE MOUNT MISSING IN *ETHICS*?

Something strange occurs in Bonhoeffer's *Ethics*, written just a few years later. The concrete way of discipleship as seen in the Sermon on the Mount—that freed him from his unchristian use of theology, that was "the only source of power capable of blowing up the whole phantasmagoria once and for all," that simply was "worth an uncompromising stand," that he devoted years to writing and teaching—makes almost no appearance in his *Ethics*. If you are new to reading Bonhoeffer and you first read *Discipleship* and then read *Ethics*, you might shake your head and ask, where did the concrete guidance of the Sermon on the Mount go?

Only one of Bonhoeffer's references to the Sermon on the Mount gives tangible guidance in *Ethics*: a reference to justice in Matthew 5:10—to those who suffer for a just cause.[16] This supports the critical norm—justice—that guided Bonhoeffer's opposition against Hitler. The other references are all generally theological, without concrete guidance. Seven passages speak of "the knowledge of good and evil" as disunion with God and others, and they say Jesus' command of obedience undercuts this disunion and calls for union with God in Christ. One corrects Luther's contention in "Freedom of a Christian" that the tree first must be made good, and then the fruit will come naturally. Bonhoeffer rightly interprets Jesus in Matthew 7:17—"Its meaning is not that first the person is good and then the work, but that *only the two together*, only both as united in one, are to be understood as good or bad."[17]

A major question for scholars has been the extent of continuity and discontinuity in Bonhoeffer's theological ethics. I argue for continuity, especially his Christ-centered theological ethics, his holistic rather than dualistic Lordship of Christ in the center of life, and the sociality of human nature. Nevertheless, there is real development within the unity, as Clifford Green argues.[18] I suggest a shift at only one precise point: away from the *concrete guidance* of the Sermon on the Mount. *Ethics* has 358 references to New Testament passages, and only eighteen of them refer to the Sermon.[19] Only the one reference to justice gives any concrete guidance. In contrast, in *Discipleship* each section gives concrete guidance, often pertinent for opposing the Nazis.

We need to remember that Bonhoeffer wrote *Ethics* in spurts when he could find the freedom to write, and it is tragically incomplete because he was imprisoned and then executed before he could finish it. But the shift away from concrete guidance by the Sermon on the Mount is also a problem in the broad history of Christian ethics. When one surveys recent Christian ethics textbooks, one asks, how can all these purport to be textbooks in Christian ethics without learning anything from the largest block of Jesus' teaching in the New Testament—teachings about the way of life of followers of Jesus?[20] Bonhoeffer clearly saw that this rift needed to be healed, and his first draft of "History and the Good" in 1942 continued to work toward that healing. Although that rift was not fully healed even in the thoroughly christocentric and Sermon-on-the-Mount-converted Bonhoeffer, it symbolizes a much larger problem in the broad tradition. Pointing the way toward a more thorough healing in Bonhoeffer can bring reconciliation for the broader tradition.

REBELLION AGAINST IDEALISTIC PERFECTIONISM

In his last year of life, Bonhoeffer commented specifically on the danger of his own interpretation of the Sermon on the Mount:

> In the last few years I have come to know and understand more and more the profound this-worldliness of Christianity. . . .

> For a long time . . . I thought I myself could learn to have faith by try-
> ing to live something like a saintly life. I suppose I wrote *Discipleship* at the
> end of this path. Today I clearly see the dangers of that book, though I still
> stand by it. Later on I discovered, and am still discovering to this day, that
> one only learns to have faith by living in the full this-worldliness of life. If
> one has completely renounced making something of oneself—whether it
> be a saint or a converted sinner or a church leader . . . , a just or an unjust
> person, a sick or a healthy person—then one throws oneself completely
> into the arms of God, and this is what I call this-worldliness: living fully in
> the midst of life's tasks, questions, successes and failures, experiences, and
> perplexities—then one takes seriously no longer one's own sufferings but
> rather the suffering of God in the world. Then one stays awake with Christ
> in Gethsemane.[21]

This emphasis on "the sufferings of God in the world" resonates with Charles
Taylor's comment that after the year 1000, Christianity took much deeper
hold with new focus on christocentric faith and piety, focused on the suffering
humanity of Jesus. Prior to that, the cross did not often appear in Christian art.
But after that, Christian piety developed a stronger sense that Christ suffers with
us, and God's love for us is seen in Christ's compassionate entering into our
suffering.[22] Taylor concludes that whether one revolts against Christianity "will
depend, first, on how much one has already felt the inner point of our being
nevertheless in the love of God, that God suffered with us."[23]

But here is the challenge that Taylor identifies: At several times in its history
Christianity developed a demand for idealistic perfectionism that people found
oppressive. For example, he commends the appeal of the Anabaptist mode of
Christian faith, but contends that it requires everyone to be saints, which is
unreachable.[24] Similarly, Calvinist efforts to make all of society and life conform
to "rightness" caused reaction and anger against Christian faith.[25] Furthermore,
Taylor finds that in the eighteenth-century Enlightenment, preaching became
less concerned "with sin as a condition we need to be rescued from through
some transformation of our being, and more and more with sin as wrong behavior which we can be persuaded, trained or disciplined to turn our backs on. . . .
Religion is narrowed to moralism." It also lacks Christology and devotion.[26]
And, unfortunately, idealistic perfectionism and moralism lead to secularism, as
Taylor said.[27] Did Bonhoeffer find that his own interpretation of the Sermon on
the Mount had leaned too far toward idealistic perfectionism and renunciation,
and needed revising?

A HERMENEUTIC OF RENUNCIATION

In *Discipleship*, renunciation is the main theme of Bonhoeffer's interpretation of
the beatitudes.[28] The poor in spirit "live thoroughly in *renunciation and want*
for Jesus' sake." Those who mourn "are prepared to renounce and live without
everything the world calls *happiness and peace*."[29] The meek do not

claim any . . . rights, for they are the meek, who *renounce all rights of their own* for the sake of Jesus Christ. When they are berated, they are quiet. When violence is done to them, they endure it. When they are cast out, they yield. They do not sue for their rights; they do not make a scene when injustice is done them. They do not want rights of their own. They want to leave all justice to God.[30]

Bonhoeffer writes of *"renunciation of their own dignity,"* sharing in "other people's need, debasement, and guilt"—probably referring to the need of Jews. Those who are persecuted for righteousness' sake differ from the world "in renouncing property, happiness, rights, righteousness, honor, and violence."[31] The peacemakers *"renounce violence and strife.* . . . Jesus' disciples maintain peace by choosing to suffer instead of causing others to suffer. . . . They *renounce self-assertion* and are silent in the face of hatred and injustice. That is how they overcome evil with good."[32]

To have the courage to confront Nazi injustice, Bonhoeffer had to be ready to suffer at the hands of persecutors. Otherwise his fear could have stifled his readiness to risk. Renunciation proved an essential ingredient for his Christian peacemaking.

But giving up one's legal rights before Hitler's onslaught, renouncing all self-assertion, quietly suffering in the face of hatred and wrong, meeting the wicked (Nazis) in peace, and being ready to suffer at their hands sounds dangerously like an idealistic quietism without a strategy of initiative. The question is whether after the renunciation there is also a strategy of assertion—not so much self-assertion as the assertion of compassionate justice and firm determination and confrontation of injustice disciplined by faith in God's strategy of deliverance. To speak out early against Hitler and for justice for Jews in German society, to organize church leaders to refuse a loyalty oath to Hitler, and eventually to help plot a coup against Hitler, Bonhoeffer drew upon not only renunciation of his own personal security but also a great deal of assertiveness. Bonhoeffer stood out among all other Christian leaders in his early naming of Hitler's evil and his persistent organization of opposition against the injustice Hitler was doing to Jews in society as well as the injustice he was doing to the church. That required more than renunciation. It took a strategy of initiative.

Bonhoeffer asks if the faith-community that the beatitudes describe actually exists anywhere on earth. Clearly there is only one place, "the place where the poorest, the most tempted, the meekest of all may be found, at the cross on Golgatha. The faith-community of the blessed is the community of the Crucified."[33] But are not the beatitudes also promising the place of blessedness—participating in God's work to deliver? Is not the Christian life a double movement: dying to self *and* rising to delivering love?

Bonhoeffer was urging fellow Christians to overcome their passive acquiescence, finish their hesitant flinching, and take decisive action. I am asking whether his hermeneutic of renunciation was adequate for the action he pushed his community of resisters to take and adequate to the theme of deliverance and initiative in the Sermon on the Mount itself?

WE NEED AN ETHIC FOR CONFRONTING MASSIVE, CONCENTRATED POWER

When Bonhoeffer wrote *Discipleship*, the need he saw was to persuade churches to act in solidarity with Jews and be ready for persecution by the Nazis. So he emphasized an ethic of renunciation of racism and self-interest, and an affirmation of love for Jewish brothers and sisters. But by the time of *Ethics*, the context had shifted from needing to renounce self-interest to needing to confront a massive concentration of Fascist power. Where *Discipleship* failed to draw out the implications for Christians' public life and secular persons, in *Ethics* he had to develop them. "The whole of life, rather than almost wholly the Church, is the locus for discovering and exercising deputyship," and it is the responsibility of non-Christians as well as Christians.[34] Responsibility in Bonhoeffer's world required confronting massive, concentrated power.

The need to challenge vast concentrations of power is likewise a crucial dimension of our own context. Economic power, media power, and the political power that flows from economic and media power, are all becoming centralized. Laissez-faire ideology continues to be funded by giant concentrations of wealth, and it is defending ever more consolidation of wealth in the hands of the few while the large majority sinks. Consumption of large amounts of oil and coal is blanketing the earth with carbon dioxide and causing a massive climate crisis while depriving future generations of those sources of energy. Lobbyists and television ads that oppose policies for energy conservation produce ideologies that defend such special privilege while attacking God's earth and the people who depend on it for our lives. In such circumstances it is not enough for Christians to have an ethic of renunciation of our own power; we need an ethic of responsible action as we defy unholy fusions of power. We need an ethic like that of Martin Luther King Jr. and like the movement of "We are the people" that confronted the dictator Erich Honecker in East Germany and brought down the Wall. Bonhoeffer's resistance to massive concentration of power shows us the way in our context.

BONHOEFFER'S OWN REALISTIC GUIDELINES FOR REINTERPRETING THE SERMON ON THE MOUNT

Incarnational discipleship urges us first to do more careful exegesis of Jesus' way in its original context so that we can have a thicker and more accurate understanding of Jesus' teaching. Second, we must pay attention to how this can guide us in the whole of life, including in public ethics. And third, we have to be willing to repent, to learn and change. Bonhoeffer intended to do exactly these three things with his interpretation of the Sermon on the Mount.

In *Ethics*, Bonhoeffer writes that he intends "to answer the question of the validity of the Sermon on the Mount in human historical action." This will be "addressed at a later point," in "the domain of politics as particularly pertinent to historical action" (244).[35] He twice says he intends to write a chapter on "Politics and the Sermon on the Mount" (244, 298n191, and 236n68). He intended to, but he was executed before he could.

"History and the Good" is the only chapter in *Ethics* for which he wrote two drafts. Clearly he was wrestling with a problem, trying to solve it. The first draft rejects the idealistic split between the Sermon on the Mount as an ethic of renunciation, on the one hand, and Machiavellian realism as an ethic of unlimited "self-assertion, force, rebellion, and entanglement in guilt," on the other hand (236–45, 252). The solution, he argues, is to base interpretation of the Sermon on a realistic understanding of God's incarnation in Christ, in the midst of human sin. The action of the Christian "springs from the unity of God and world brought about in Jesus Christ. . . . This unity exists solely in the person of Jesus Christ, in whom God became human, acting *in stellvertretender Verantwortung* [which I translate as responsibility that enters into the place of the other incarnationally] and entering out of love for the real human being into the guilt of the world" (238). We can understand the Sermon on the Mount, Bonhoeffer insisted, only by realizing that Jesus' sayings reflect his existence as the one in whom God becomes human in actual history, "the one who lives in concrete responsibility for all human beings, really standing in their place and acting on their behalf (and not by confronting them with ideals that they cannot fulfill)." The Sermon on the Mount calls for self-denial not as a principle of renunciation, but as a call "to love one another, and thus to reject everything that hinders fulfilling this task." It rejects self-love in order to affirm that our neighbors, actual people living in the world, are individuals for whom we are responsible (235–36, 242–43).

So his norm now is no longer renunciation, but the kind of incarnational love that enters into the concerns of the neighbor and takes responsible action for the neighbor. Since God's love for the world also includes political action, Christian love can assume "the form of a person fighting for self-assertion, power, success, and security"—but only for responsibility to others. "Power is to serve responsibility," he insists (244–45). Bonhoeffer has shifted from *Nygren's idealistic definition of sacrificial love* that rejects calculation, confrontation, expectation of mutual response, or justice, to what David Gushee and I have argued is *delivering love* that includes these dimensions.[36]

Bonhoeffer now develops love, not renunciation, as the central theme in the Sermon on the Mount. Love is "a real belonging-together and being-together of people with other human beings and with the world, based on God's love that is extended to me and to them" (241). He rejects an idealistic and ungrounded interpretation of the Sermon on the Mount that is divorced from faith in the incarnation of God in Christ and in the reconciliation of the world with God through Christ. Such an interpretation that takes an ideal from above history and seeks to force it on historical reality produces either fanatical-revolutionary action or a retreat to a privatistic ethics that does not lead to concrete historical responsibility.

The second draft of "History and the Good" affirms the same guidelines on how to relate Jesus' way to concrete, historical responsibilities in the real world. Its conclusion adds some new material about free responsibility, use of force, conscience, social location, and willingness to become guilty rather than to deceive oneself about being pure. It affirms the human right to bodily life as grounded in the teaching of love of neighbor in the Sermon on the Mount, as well as in the Decalogue and in Paul, which Bonhoeffer developed further in "The Natural Life."

But it omits most—not all—of the specific statements on the Sermon on the Mount. I hypothesize that Bonhoeffer decided to postpone explicit reinterpretation until he could write the chapter he intended, and until he could work out his interpretation more specifically. That is now our task, following from a realistic understanding of sin (see chap. 8). The incarnation is where God and human reality, with its sin, come together:

> Only because there is one place where God and the reality of the world are reconciled with each other, at which God and humanity have become one, is it possible there and there alone to fix one's eyes on God and the world together at the same time. This place does not lie somewhere beyond reality in the realm of ideas. It lies in the midst of history . . . in Jesus Christ the reconciler of the world. (82)

In his last years of life, Bonhoeffer wrote similarly of the realism about sin and evil, mixed with power, in his interpretations of the incarnation and the cross.[37] That realism was expressed poignantly in the circular letters he wrote to his former students, most of whom had been forced to fight in Hitler's army. Each letter began by naming several more of his beloved students who had been killed in the war. "There are so many experiences and disappointments which make a way for nihilism and resignation for sensitive people," he wrote. "So it is good to learn early enough that suffering and God is not a contradiction but rather a necessary unity; for me the idea that God himself is suffering has always been one of the most convincing teachings of Christianity."[38]

Bonhoeffer interprets Jesus in the midst of the Third Reich, not with idealism, but with realism. And he continues to refer to the Sermon on the Mount as authoritative.[39] To continue his intention, interpreting the Sermon on the Mount for our guidance, we must look for the realism of sin and evil, mixed with power, in the Sermon on the Mount.

Larry Rasmussen suggests that Bonhoeffer, in *Letters and Papers from Prison*, "has begun a new and promising direction . . . a revived 'imitation of Christ' ethic, seen as the church's societal vocation. 'If we are to learn what God promises, and what he fulfills, we must persevere in quiet meditation on the life, sayings, deeds, sufferings, and death of Jesus.'"[40] He points to a few other examples, and then asks,

Is there not in Bonhoeffer increased attention to the concrete humanity of Jesus. . . ? Is there not now more attention to example, more talk of the way of Jesus and the being of Jesus. . . ? The point here is simply that in *Letters and Papers from Prison* the "imitation" ethic is present and is presented as a sharing or participating in the being of Jesus, seen in the human example of Jesus and his way.[41]

IS THE SERMON ON THE MOUNT PLATONIC IDEALISM OR PROPHETIC REALISM?

Rabbi Pinchas Lapide's *The Sermon on the Mount: Utopia or Program of Action?*[42] argues that Jesus is no Platonic idealist; Jesus is a Jewish realist, identifying with the realism of the prophetic tradition. Jesus saw rebellion against Rome as leading to disaster. Like the prophets, he diagnosed the problem realistically. He wept over Jerusalem because its people did not know the practices that make for peace, and were instead fomenting violent rebellion. He prophesied six times in the Gospels that the temple would be destroyed. That diagnosis was realistic: the subsequent rebellion led to the destruction of the temple in 70 CE and to exile for twenty centuries.

Reinhold Niebuhr, my teacher, also brought the correction of realism. But he never completed his realistic analysis; he never applied his realism to his Troeltschian and Weberian nineteenth-century idealistic interpretation of Jesus. He divided people into pragmatic realists whose ethic applies to the political side of life, and idealists faithful to the "high ideals" of the Sermon on the Mount who have almost nothing to say to the real world of politics.[43] This splits the solid rock of incarnational discipleship into sectarian idealism plus Jesus on one side and pragmatic realism plus secularism on the other side. So I have been working to repair that split, in the way that incarnational discipleship and Bonhoeffer's "History and the Good" suggest.

Two discoveries bring the repair. The first is Robert Guelich's realization that the beatitudes are largely patterned after chapter 61 of the prophet Isaiah—the chapter that Jesus selected for his inaugural sermon in Luke 4:18:

> "The Spirit of the Lord is upon me
>   because he has anointed me;
>   to bring good news to the poor,
> He has sent me to proclaim release to the captives
>   and recovery of sight to the blind;
>   to let the oppressed go free,
> to proclaim the year of the Lord's favor."

This is no passage about human effort to live up to high ideals. It is a prophetic passage of celebration because God is acting graciously to deliver us from our poverty and captivity, into God's reign of deliverance, justice, and joy.[44] Look how the Beatitudes echo this prophetic passage of deliverance:

Figure 10.1   The Beatitudes Are Largely Based on Isaiah 61

Isaiah 61	Matthew 5
61:1, 2 . . . good news to the oppressed . . . the year of the LORD's favor.	5:3 Blessed are the poor in spirit, for theirs is the kingdom of heaven.
61:1, 2 To bind up the brokenhearted . . . to comfort all who mourn.	5:4 Blessed are those who mourn, for they will be comforted.
61:7 They will inherit a double portion in their land [NIV].	5:5 Blessed are the humble, [45] for they will inherit the earth.
61:3 They will be called oaks of righteousness.	5:6 Blessed are those who hunger and thirst for righteousness . . . .
61:11 So the Lord GOD will cause righteousness and praise to spring up before all the nations.	5:10 Blessed are those who are persecuted for . . . righteousness, for theirs is the kingdom of heaven.

The second discovery is that the teachings in the central section of the Sermon on the Mount from Matthew 5:21 through 7:12 have been misinterpreted as dyadic antitheses, instead of the transforming initiatives that they actually are. I have published the implications of this finding elsewhere,[46] and only indicate the direction here. Corresponding to Bonhoeffer's unfilled intention to write on the Sermon on the Mount for political guidance, I will pay attention to the power dimensions of Jesus' diagnoses of vicious cycles in the Sermon as well as his emphasis on transforming initiatives. This will help us see the "thicker Jesus" of incarnational discipleship giving guidance for the Lordship of Christ in all of life, including the political struggle—which was Bonhoeffer's intention.

For example, 5:21–26 has been misinterpreted as an antithesis commanding us never to be angry, which would be an impossibly high ideal. This misinterpretation causes people to praise it as a noble aspiration, but then to do something else more realistic. Instead, the overwhelming evidence indicates that the central section, from Mathew 5:21 through 7:12, is fourteen *triads*—not dyads and not antitheses.[47] Each teaching begins with a traditional instruction from the Old Testament, such as "Do not kill." Then, second, each of the fourteen triads offers a realistic diagnosis of vicious cycles and power dynamics that cause injustice if we handle them inappropriately. It points our ethics toward naming the power dynamics that need confronting. Then, third, each triad concludes with a constructive alternative—with the interesting exception of the teaching on divorce—climaxing not in a renunciation, but in a transforming initiative that points the way of deliverance from being mired in powerlessness in the face of oppressive power. This interpretation recovers the original meaning more accurately, with its Hebraic realism.

DELIVERANCE FROM SEETHING IN POWERLESS ANGER

For example, Matthew 5:21–26 begins, "you have heard that it was said, 'you shall not kill . . .'" This is the *traditional teaching* from the Ten Commandments against murder. Second, Jesus *realistically diagnoses* ongoing anger and insulting as a power dynamic, a vicious cycle that causes alienation: "If you are *being angry* with a brother or sister, you will be liable to judgment." This is a participle in the Greek, as I have translated it—a diagnosis of a continuing action, not a command. The New Testament nowhere prohibits anger, an ideal so high it would be impossible to practice. Instead, The New Testament says Jesus "looked around in anger" in Mark 3:5.[48]

The climactic third member of the triad is the *transforming initiative*, or way of deliverance: "Leave your gift there in front of the altar. First go, and be reconciled to your brother. . . . Settle matters quickly with your adversary" (NIV). The climax is the way of deliverance taken by God in the incarnation, coming in Christ to make peace, and given to us as participants. It is a command to take initiatives to transform the relationship from one of anger to one of peacemaking. There are five imperatives in the Greek: Leave your gift, go, make peace, then give your gift, settle matters quickly with your adversary. Any married couple, any diplomat, knows the practicality of this practice.

As the idealistic tradition did, in his interpretation in *Discipleship*, Bonhoeffer puts the emphasis on the second item, the vicious cycle, and not on the third item, which is the climax. He spends two pages saying "the disciple must be entirely innocent of anger," which the Greek does not indicate, but only one paragraph saying we must be reconciled, which is where the Greek text puts the climax and the five imperatives.[49] There is nothing about the *way* Jesus practiced

Figure 10.2   The Triadic Structure of Matthew 5:21–26

Traditional Righteousness	*Vicious Cycle*	*Transforming Initiative*
5:21 You have heard that it was said to those of ancient times, "You shall not murder; and whoever murders shall be liable to judgment." (In the Greek, "shall not" and "shall be" are not imperatives, but futures; as translations of the Hebrew in the Ten Commandments, they do of course *imply* a command.)	5:22 But I say to you that if you are [being] angry with a brother or sister, you will be liable to judgment; and if you insult a brother or sister, you will be liable to the council, and if you say, "You fool," you will be liable to the hell of fire. (No imperatives in the Greek.)	5:23–26 So when you are offering your gift at the altar, if you remember that your brother or sister has something against you, *leave* your gift there . . . and *go*; first *be reconciled* to your brother or sister, and then come and *offer* your gift. *Come to terms* [*Make peace*] quickly with your accuser. . . . (Italics mark the Greek imperatives.)

reconciliation—with Samaritans, outcasts, Romans, tax collectors, zealots, and prostitutes. Jesus entered in the midst of people's lives, asked probing questions, confronted them, forgave them, healed them, touched them, brought them into community. Bonhoeffer here says nothing about the reign of God coming on earth, or the grace of incarnation and resurrection, or victory over alienation. By contrast, Jesus in Matthew devotes thirty-nine words in the Greek to diagnosing the vicious cycle, and eighty-four words to the transforming initiatives of making peace with the enemy (vv. 23–26)—in the third member, the climax of the teaching, where the imperatives are.

Let me be clear: I am not blaming Bonhoeffer. Bonhoeffer is my hero. He was following the standard pattern that had ruled interpretation for many centuries. Over time he became aware that he needed a more realistic interpretation. A transforming-initiative interpretation can help us follow Bonhoeffer's realistic understanding of Jesus in his later writings, and free him and us from the long historical influence of Platonic idealism. As we have seen, Jesus was no Platonic idealistic; he was a Hebraic, prophetic realist.

Furthermore, each of the fourteen teachings from 5:21–7:12 has this transforming-initiative structure (with one intriguing exception: 5:31–32).[50] In none of the fourteen teachings is the climax a prohibition or an effortful ideal; it is always a grace-based practical way of deliverance. It is a transforming initiative based on participative, christomorphic grace. It is the way Jesus Christ has pioneered the breakthrough of the kingdom of God, in which we can participate.[51]

REALISM ABOUT THE POWERLESSNESS OF ESCALATING RETALIATION

For a second example, consider Matthew 5:38–42, which begins with the traditional teaching about revengeful retaliation, "You have heard of old, eye for eye, and tooth for tooth." The diagnosis of the *vicious cycle* is not rightly translated as "Do not resist evil." That translation is influenced by the idealistic non-Hebraic tradition, and by predemocracy translators who supported monarchs, princes, and order, and opposed resistance movements. Martin Luther's translation as "do not resist evil" made the teaching seem impossible to him when he needed his prince to resist the pope's efforts to have Luther arrested. This led him to develop his two-realms ethic, limiting the Sermon on the Mount to individual relations.[52] Such a compartmentalized ethic had disastrous effects in history, particularly during the Third Reich, causing many Christians to think they should not resist Hitler. By contrast, Jesus taught in the tradition of the Hebrew prophets. He frequently resisted evil, including Pharisees and high authorities, Satan, and the apostle Peter when he urged Jesus not to go to Jerusalem where he would be crucified.

The Greek in verse 39 should be translated "not to retaliate by revengeful or evil means." *Mē antistēnai* is not a command; it is a Greek infinitive meaning "not to retaliate," with the connotation of violence or revenge. *Tō ponērō* means "by evil means." Clarence Jordan has shown that the dative case here can be either a dative of object or an instrumental dative; we decide based on context.[53] The context is that Jesus clearly resisted evil, but the means he used were not evil. Translating it "not to retaliate or seek revenge by evil means" is supported by New Testament scholars Clarence Jordan, Robert Ferguson, Walter Wink, Willard Swartley, and Luise Schottroff. The apostle Paul gives us the same teaching: "Never avenge yourselves. . . . Do not be overcome by evil, but overcome evil with good" (Rom. 12:19, 21). Teaching against retaliation and revenge reverberates through the New Testament (e.g., Luke 6:27–36; 1 Thess. 5:15, and 1 Pet. 2:21–23).

Drawing from this biblical tradition, the Catholic Mass includes realism about sin. In the main prayer, the priest invites us, "Let us recollect our sins." He pauses, giving enough time to meditate, enough for me to become aware of several of my sins. This particular Tuesday, as I write, is the Feast of St. Stephen, king of Hungary in the year 1,000. Father Richard Viladesau told of St. Stephen's sincere piety, his encouraging many missionaries to come to Hungary and organize churches, when Hungary was still mostly pagan, and his dedicating his crown and rule to Mary. Many Hungarians are named "Stephen," in its Hungarian form. But Father Richard told us that, as usually occurred in that time, King Stephen was also a warmonger, seeking expansion and wreaking revenge. The priest noted that each of us has part of our life open to the light, and other parts hiding in darkness (1 John 2:3–11). The homily about this significant saint was highly realistic, as is Catholic piety, usually, about recollecting our sins and the sins of even a saint like Stephen of Hungary—and as is also the Hebrew Bible, and Jesus of Galilee.

The *transforming initiatives* all command us not simply to comply with a power demand, but to invent a transforming initiative that moves the action onto our own turf: not only the first mile, but the second mile; not only the right cheek, but the cheek of equal dignity; not only the tunic, but also the cloak; not only giving to a beggar but also lending. The Roman soldier had the right to compel a Jew to carry his pack one mile. Jesus advocates carrying it a second mile, and I assume conversing on the way. Jewish law prohibited slapping someone with your left hand, so being slapped on the right cheek would be a backhanded slap of insult—"you dog, you slave, you good-for-nothing." Turning the *left* cheek was turning the cheek of equal dignity. Jewish law prohibited keeping someone's cloak overnight as a guarantee for a loan, so in Jesus' example the greedy creditor is suing you for the only other possession you have—your tunic. Giving him not only your tunic but also your cloak leaves you naked, thus revealing the greed of the creditor nakedly before the whole law court—a dramatic hyperbole. In the fourth case, Jesus says not only to give, but also to make a microloan. In each case, Jesus goes beyond merely complying and commands an empowering and creative initiative. And each initiative participates in God's gracious initiatives toward us.

BONHOEFFER AND JUSTICE: THE SERMON
ON THE MOUNT AND HUMAN RIGHTS

The realism of the more accurate interpretation of the Sermon on the Mount as realistic diagnoses of power dynamics and transforming initiatives that deliver us from those vicious cycles supports Bonhoeffer's struggle in Nazi Germany far better. Bonhoeffer was engaged in a life-and-death struggle for justice for Jews who were being unbelievably persecuted. He saw what was wrong with Hitler because, like the prophet Amos, he had a plumb line, a clear concept of justice, with which to measure Hitler's violations. Many German pastors and theologians, and their churches, failed to see the theme of justice in the New Testament. As Gerd Theissen shows, they were influenced by a politically conservative ideology that advocated supporting whatever authority was in power. In the first decades of the twentieth century, 80 percent of German pastors and most theologians opposed the democratic Weimar Republic and favored the conservative German Nationalistic Peoples' Party. Accordingly, they systematically neutralized Jesus' social criticisms, handing down to us an individualistic and otherworldly picture of Jesus that does violence to the evidence and to the scholarly methods they claimed to be following.[54] This distortion of Jesus undermined gospel-based opposition to the injustice of the Third Reich.

By contrast, in the section of *Ethics* on "The Natural," Bonhoeffer presents a concept of justice as an extensive outworking of human rights, and especially the rights of bodily life. "Since by God's will human life on earth exists only as bodily life, the body has a right to be preserved for the sake of the whole person."[55] His ethic of human rights guides his argument for the basic needs and joys of life of all humans, for opposing the Nazi "euthanasia" policies that were killing handicapped people, and for deliberating whether "the healthy could be saved only by the death of " Hitler.[56]

In his interpretation of the Sermon on the Mount in the earlier *Discipleship*, his only comment on justice concerns Matthew 5:10–12: "It is important that Jesus calls his disciples blessed, not only when they directly confess his name, but also when they suffer for a just cause."[57] In *Ethics*, he expands on this teaching, using the term "for a just cause" (*um einer gerechten Sache*) five times. He adds,

> With this beatitude Jesus thoroughly rejects the false timidity of those Christians who evade any kind of suffering for a just, good, and true cause because they supposedly could have a clear conscience only if they were to suffer for the explicit confession of faith in Christ; he rejects, in other words, the kind of narrow-mindedness that casts a cloud of suspicion on any suffering for the sake of a just cause and distances itself from it. Jesus cares for those who suffer for a just cause even if it is not exactly for the confession of his name; he brings them under his protection, takes responsibility for them, and addresses them with his claim. Thus the person persecuted for a just cause is led to Christ.[58]

Here Bonhoeffer is moving in the direction that I am suggesting, linking the Sermon on the Mount with *Ethics*.

A transforming-initiative interpretation of the Sermon on the Mount highlights the theme of justice in the Sermon,[59] thus strengthening the direction in which Bonhoeffer is moving, and in which we need to move in a time of massive concentration of power. The reign of God is central to Jesus' message and to the Sermon on the Mount. As we saw in chapter 6, one of the key characteristics of the reign of God is delivering, community-restorative justice based on God's compassion for those who suffer from injustice. In the Sermon on the Mount, Jesus advocates justice for the poor, inclusion of enemies, and peacemaking rather than violence, and he confronts the domination of the Pharisees. The same four dimensions of justice condemn the injustices of the Third Reich sharply and profoundly.

In the Sermon on the Mount, "Give to the one who begs" calls us to do justice to the poor. In the first century, as in ours, the poor had gotten poorer, while some rich had gotten much richer. The poor were in bondage to their poverty, and the rich to their wealth. Almsgiving was the welfare system then, so Jesus' teaching on almsgiving, both in Matthew 5:42 and in 6:2–4, was calling for justice for the poor and a turning by all from the worship of money. Almsgiving was the economic justice system.

In Matthew 6:19–34 Jesus gives two parallel diagnoses of the vicious cycle of hoarding greedily for oneself and trying to serve money as well as God. Instead we are to invest in the reign of God and God's delivering, community-restorative justice. First come the traditional teachings: "Do not hoard hoards[60] of wealth on earth," and "No one can serve two masters" (Matt 6:19 and 6:24). The vicious cycle is diagnosed: "where moth and rust consume, and where thieves break in and steal," and he will "either hate the one and love the other, or be devoted to the one and despise the other. You cannot serve God and wealth" (Matt. 6:19 and 6:24). Thus Jesus gives us two realistic diagnoses of the power of greed, which could not be more relevant to our time.

The transforming initiative is to store our treasures in heaven (Matt. 6:20—meaning in God and God's reign). And to "seek first God's reign and God's righteousness" (6:33). Thus again the Sermon on the Mount does not merely teach renouncing something or prohibiting something, but participating in the breakthrough of God's reign. Such participation is a more fulfilling alternative than living for greed. And it directly supports Bonhoeffer's argument for the justice of human rights in his *Ethics*, so long as we interpret human rights as he did—as sacredness of human life of all persons in community practice of both church and state, which opposes individualistic private rights that leave the needy to fend for themselves. The Sermon on the Mount is not about renunciation of rights, but about transforming initiatives to confront power and injustice nonviolently but forcefully.[61]

In *Discipleship*, Bonhoeffer's interpretation of these two teachings places all the emphasis on renunciation and not being anxious.[62] He takes the word

Gerechtigkeit to mean "the care and protection of Jesus Christ and his Father." The same is basically true of his interpretation of "Blessed are those who hunger and thirst for righteousness," as well as his interpretation of Jesus' teaching about giving alms to the poor in secret.[63] The Hebrew word that Jesus was referring to in these teachings means "delivering justice" or "restorative justice." If we can see the theme of delivering justice in the Sermon on the Mount, then Bonhoeffer's teaching on justice and human rights in *Ethics* can receive additional strong backing and enrichment, and be much more memorably taught. To heal the rift, we need to help people connect justice and Jesus.

We have examined only three of the fourteen triads of the Sermon on the Mount thus far, and will further the examination somewhat in the next chapter. But we have already seen the pattern:

- The traditional teachings from the Old Testament are affirmed and implemented. These are not *anti*theses in any sense that would oppose the Old Testament meaning. "Thou shalt not kill" or murder is implemented by the transforming initiative of going to make peace with your brother or adversary. "Eye for an eye" was intended to limit retaliation so it did not escalate to Lamech's sevenfold retaliation, or seventy-seven times (Gen. 4:24). Jesus went further, transforming it to nonviolent initiatives that confront the injustice and seek to move toward peacemaking rather than the vicious cycle of retaliation. Like the prophets, Jesus opposed hoarding money, and emphasized investing our money in God's causes and God's restorative justice.
- In each case, Jesus gives us a realistic diagnosis not only of an individual sinful deed, but of a vicious cycle of oppression by power and domination. This supports Bonhoeffer's diagnoses of the evil patterns of Hitler's cynical injustice and systematic violation of human rights, especially of Jews.
- Jesus regularly points us toward a transforming initiative, moving us toward the empowerment of participating in God's presence and God's breakthroughs of grace, peace, and justice. Precisely this kind of empowerment is what was needed for resistance against domination by the Nazis.

THE PATTERN IS CONSISTENT

We have seen the transforming-initiative pattern in three of the fourteen teachings. We lack space here to examine all the teachings, but can observe a consistency of pattern for all fourteen. The evidence is overwhelming that the Sermon on the Mount, the largest block of Jesus' teachings in the New Testament, does not impose dyadic ideals beyond our reach, but triadic transforming initiatives for deliverance from realistically diagnosed vicious cycles:

Figure 10.3   The Fourteen Triads of the Sermon on the Mount

Traditional Righteousness	Vicious Cycle	Transforming Initiative
1. You shall not kill	Being angry, or saying, "You fool!"	Go, be reconciled
2. You shall not commit adultery	Looking with lust is adultery in the heart	Remove the cause of temptation
3. If divorcing, give a certificate	Divorcing involves you in adultery	(Be reconciled: 1 Cor. 7:11)
4. You shall not swear falsely	Swearing by anything involves you in a false claim	Let your yes be yes, and your no be no
5. Eye for eye, tooth for tooth	Retaliating violently or revengefully, by evil means	Turn the other cheek Give tunic and cloak Go the second mile Give to beggar and borrower
6. Love neighbor and hate enemy	Hating enemies is the same vicious cycle that you see in what the Gentiles and tax collectors do	Love enemies, pray for your persecutors; be all-inclusive as your Father in heaven is
7. When you give alms . . .	Practicing righteousness for show	But give in secret; your Father will reward you
8. When you pray . . .	Practicing righteousness for show	But pray in secret; your Father will reward you
9. When you pray . . .	Practicing righteousness for show	Therefore pray like this: Our Father. . . .
10. When you fast . . .	Practicing righteousness for show	But dress with joy; your Father will reward you
11. Do not pile up treasures on earth	Moth and rust destroy, and thieves enter and steal	But pile up treasures in heaven
12. No one can serve two masters	Serving God and wealth, worrying about food and clothes	But seek first God's reign and God's justice/ righteousness
13. Do not judge, lest you be judged	Judging others means you'll be judged by the same measure	First take the log out of your own eye
14. Do not give holy things to dogs, or pearls to pigs	They will trample them and tear you to pieces	Give your trust in prayer to your Father in heaven

Some things call out to us about this illustration. First, the pattern is remarkably consistent throughout the fourteen triads from Matthew 5:21–7:12. Second, the grammatical forms Jesus uses confirm the triadic structure remarkably consistently. The verbs in the traditional teachings are futures and subjunctives. The verbs in the vicious cycles are continuous action verbs—participles, infinitives, and continuous-action indicatives—as fits diagnoses of ongoing vicious cycles. The verbs in the transforming initiatives are Greek imperatives—as fits the climaxes. Once we see the triadic pattern, the consistency leaps out before our eyes. It cannot be mere accident. Finally, it shifts the interpretation of the Sermon on the Mount from an impossible idealism, which would make no sense in the Jewish context, to a prophetic realism and grace-based empowerment and deliverance.

HEALING THE RIFT THROUGH PARTICIPATIVE GRACE

When we develop the hermeneutics of *Discipleship* further, so that it is not only renunciation but transforming initiatives, we can heal the rift between Bonhoeffer's interpretation of the Sermon on the Mount and his *Ethics*. The Sermon on the Mount becomes a grace-based way of deliverance from vicious cycles. The transforming initiatives take part in the presence of the reign of God, as revealed in the incarnate Jesus Christ. They represent the kind of grace that Bonhoeffer emphasizes: participative grace, not autonomous effort or cheap grace; christomorphic grace, not amorphous grace; conformation to Christ, not false purity. This grace-based, participative, christomorphic, transforming-initiatives interpretation fits Bonhoeffer's theology as he developed it in his *Ethics* significantly better than does a principle of renunciation.

In the first draft of "History and the Good," Bonhoeffer himself struggles to develop an interpretation of the Sermon on the Mount that moves in the direction I am suggesting. He explicitly rejects interpretations based on a principle of renunciation, which produce a two-kingdoms split that resigns Christian ethics to the domain of individual relations, and leaves historical-political relations mired in secular Machiavellian realism—an ethic of unlimited "self-assertion, force, rebellion, and entanglement in guilt."[64]

Instead, he suggests the Sermon on the Mount be interpreted as a call "to love one another, and thus to reject everything that hinders fulfilling this task" of love that enters into the worldly. The Sermon's teaching of self-denial is only for the sake of "clear recognition of reality, the neighbor, and the world; thus, and only thus, is one readied to perceive and undertake genuine responsibility. . . . Thus the Sermon on the Mount itself confronts a person with the necessity of responsible historical action."[65]

Here we see Bonhoeffer struggling to replace the hermeneutic of renunciation with incarnational love that enters into the place of the other (*Stellvertretung* as *treten an der Stelle*, stepping into the place of the other), and to do so with assertiveness and power. He is moving in the direction that becomes available when we see the Sermon on the Mount as transforming initiatives. But because love and responsibility alone do not give concrete enough guidance to guard against falling into the unlimited Machiavellian realism that he saw as the opposite danger, or into the occasionalism of 1929 that he had rejected, apparently he was not satisfied with this first draft. He intended to write a better interpretation of the Sermon on the Mount that would be helpful in a political ethics of the Lordship of Christ over the political authorities, as well as over family, church, and economics or culture.

We have followed the mandate of incarnational discipleship, doing concrete, thick exegesis of the Sermon on the Mount. We saw that the Sermon has been wrongly interpreted as Platonic ideals, which distorts Jesus' prophetic diagnosis of vicious cycles that trap us in self-defeating power dynamics, and which substitutes impossible ideals like "never be angry," which the New Testament nowhere teaches. Instead Jesus emphasizes transforming initiatives that empower us to overcome self-defeating and disempowering power dynamics. We see now how to fulfill Bonhoeffer's unfilled intention to write on the Sermon on the Mount for political guidance. That helps us see how the "thicker Jesus" of incarnational discipleship can give guidance for the Lordship of Christ in all of life, including the political struggle—which was Bonhoeffer's intention.

Furthermore, each of the transforming initiatives points us toward participation in the work of the Holy Spirit in our midst—the breakthrough of the reign of God, the presence of God. Going to make peace with your brother, adversary, or spouse is participation in what God does in Christ, coming to us to make peace with us, showing love to God's enemies. Praying, giving alms, and fasting not for show but in the presence of God, who knows our needs before we ask, is living in the presence of the Holy Spirit. When we serve God not mammon, and seek first God's reign and delivering justice, we participate in God's reign. Putting our trust not in power-interests, but in God who is trustworthy, is the third mandate of incarnational discipleship, trusting in the Holy Spirit, independent from the powers and authorities.

A transforming-initiatives hermeneutic knits Bonhoeffer's *Discipleship* and his *Ethics* together. It brings healing to the rift that he was working to heal. That rift causes "two grave errors . . . throughout the history of the church up to the present," as he himself said.[66] Working with him to heal this rift can enable us to recover the way of Jesus for Christian ethics for personal formation and for political ethics, and to let that ethics become regular practice. It can point to the way of deliverance in a time of dangerous concentration of power. Only with a realistic interpretation of the Sermon on the Mount do we have a thicker Jesus that coheres with the Lordship of Christ through all of life. That is crucial for the ethics of incarnational discipleship. It is what Bonhoeffer was striving for in his *Ethics*.

Chapter 11

War

*Jesus' Transforming Initiatives
and Just Peacemaking's Initiatives*

We have begun to see how accurate interpretation of Jesus' Sermon on the Mount can overcome the idealistic interpretation that blocks people from seeing its guidance holistically—for public ethics as well as private ethics. When I realized that the Sermon on the Mount is structured as transforming initiatives, that epiphany led to the new paradigm for the ethics of what we now call "just peacemaking."

Many people have been influenced so long by the Platonic idealism that Bonhoeffer was working to correct that they do not see how Jesus' teaching in the Sermon on the Mount could give realistic guidance for tough questions like war and peace. They put the Sermon in one compartment labeled "idealism" and questions about relating to other nations in another compartment called "realism." That two-realm split did terrible damage in weakening church resistance against the Nazis during the Third Reich in Germany and church resistance against segregation during the civil rights movement. Healing came from those who did not marginalize Jesus, who did not block Jesus from guiding their actions. Incarnational discipleship contends that if we desist from that imagination-blocking compartmentalization and focus on how Jesus Christ can be Lord through all of life, we may be surprised by the healing and faithfulness that result.

196

My own father was a member of the generation that fought in World War II, which killed fifty million or more people and caused unimaginable misery. They came back from the war determined to develop some different realities that would prevent wars like that. They developed a number of practices like the spread of democracy and human rights, the Marshall Plan for rebuilding Europe economically, the unification of Europe, the United Nations and other international organizations—and practices of conflict resolution and nonviolent direct action.

Partly as a result, the number and extent of international wars is decreasing dramatically. Milton Leitenberg of the University of Maryland's School for International and Security Studies has estimated that war and state-sponsored genocide in the first half of the twentieth century caused an average of 3.8 million deaths per year. But in the second half of the twentieth century wars and genocide killed fewer than one-quarter of that total—800,000 per year.[1] This has not only saved 150 million lives; it has lessened the misery of bereavement, loneliness, and poverty for many more persons. This effectiveness in preventing wars is not merely hoping for "ideals"; it is deep reality for millions.

It seems clear to me and a steadily increasing number of others that we should all learn the practices that are preventing many wars, teach them to our friends, and together prod churches, politicians, and governments to support them. This is why thirty Christian ethicists got together to develop a new paradigm for the ethics of peace and war called "just peacemaking." Just peacemaking does not debate whether war is justified or not. Maybe sometimes it is. Maybe it is not. We do not agree on that. But all thirty agreed that we need a new ethic that names and describes ten practices that are working to prevent wars, and that calls on people, churches, and governments to support those practices. People need to know the ten practices that are saving so many lives and preventing so much destruction in order that they can give them their articulate support and prod governments to do them. The new ethic is now a book called *Just Peacemaking: The New Paradigm for the Ethics of Peace and War*.[2] And now Jewish and Muslim scholars have joined Christian scholars in affirming the same ten practices, based on their scriptures. That book is called *Interfaith Just Peacemaking*.[3]

The ten practices of just peacemaking are displayed in Figure 11.

The thirty Christian scholars who wrote *Just Peacemaking: The New Paradigm* wanted to appeal to persons of various faiths or no faith who see the need to prevent or decrease wars, so we emphasized the political and historical evidence that the ten practices actually are working to reduce wars, without appealing explicitly to Christian theology and ethics or to the way of Jesus except in the book's introduction.[4] Our attention to what is actually effective in preventing wars fits the second theme of incarnational discipleship—an ethic that can offer guidance throughout all of life, here including tough issues between nations.

But because of our interest in appealing beyond our explicitly Christian grounding, the basis of just peacemaking in the first theme of incarnational discipleship—God's revelation in Jesus of Nazareth—is not much demonstrated in *Just Peacemaking*.[5] Accordingly, here I show how a thicker interpretation of

Figure 11.1   Just Peacemaking Correlated with the Sermon on the Mount

Initiatives

1. Support nonviolent direct action. (Matt. 5:38–43)

2. Take independent initiatives. (Matt. 5:38–43)

3. Use cooperative conflict resolution. (Matt. 5:21–26)

4. Acknowledge responsibility for conflict and injustice and seek repentance and forgiveness. (Matt. 7:1–5)

Justice (Matt. 6:19–33)

5. Advance human rights, religious liberty, and democracy.

6. Support economic development that is sustainable and just.

Include Enemies in the Community of Neighbors. (Matt. 5:38–43)

7. Work with emerging cooperative networks in the international system.

8. Strengthen the United Nations and international efforts for human rights.

9. Reduce offensive weapons and weapons trade. (Matt. 26:52)

10. Participate in grassroots peacemaking groups (as Jesus and the disciples formed groups, and so spread the gospel).

Jesus' Sermon on the Mount was what actually led to the new paradigm of just peacemaking, thus bringing together the themes of incarnational discipleship. I show how just peacemaking translates concrete interpretation of Jesus' teaching, by analogy, into a public ethic that gives important guidance for preventing wars. A thicker and more realistic interpretation of the Sermon on the Mount can become a guide for tough issues of conflict well beyond individual relations.

So the pattern of each section in this chapter will be first to name one of the just peacemaking practices, then to explain how it is related to the Sermon on the Mount, and then to explain the just peacemaking practice very briefly. How each practice is actually working to reduce wars is explained in *Just Peacemaking: The New Paradigm*. The contribution of this chapter is to show how each practice is related to Jesus' teaching in the Sermon on the Mount—which that book does not show. Thus we will be seeing how the particular teaching of Jesus suggests, by analogy, a just peacemaking practice that works in a public ethic that persons of other faiths or no faith are growingly supporting.

RELIGIOUS WARS, RELIGIOUS PEACEMAKING

But first, let us briefly refer to Charles Taylor's accurate contention that the entanglement of religion and war has been one of the major causes of secularism.

Philosophers Stephen Toulmin, Jeffrey Stout, and Charles Taylor diagnose the Enlightenment's shift from faith to secular reason largely as a reaction against religious wars—especially the Thirty Years' War of 1618–1648.[6] The German History Museum in Berlin gives an account of that devastating war that moved me deeply when I visited there: one-third of Germans died in the Thirty Years' War, and others experienced widespread suffering. What began as a war between Protestants and Catholics in Germany expanded into a large-scale conflict among political dynasties for domination throughout Europe. Seeing the historical evidence of that astounding disaster increased my commitment to developing an ethic of just peacemaking.

The English Civil War activist Richard Overton, whom we met in chapter 5, apparently had experienced the Thirty Years' War. He responded by advocating religious liberty and other human rights, not only for Protestants and Catholics, but also for Jews and "Turks" (Muslims)—impressive for 1640s England. Most wars, he argued, are caused by religious persecution. If nations would establish the human right to religious liberty and thus eliminate religious persecution, there would be no reason to fight any more wars over religion. Regardless of the religion of the ruler of a nation, the people would retain their religious liberty. At the same time, in the Thirteen Colonies, Roger Williams titled his famous book *The Bloudy Tenent of Persecution*. The bloodshed of war, he argued, is largely caused by religious persecution. Relief from this bloodshed, and from the hypocrisy of people who merely pretend to embrace a faith because they fear persecution, will result from establishing religious liberty.

Richard Overton and Roger Williams were Baptists; they advocated religious liberty on the basis of faithfulness to Jesus Christ, who commanded us to make disciples by teaching and persuasion, not by coercion. They said Jesus commanded his disciples to let the wheat and the weeds grow together (Matt. 13:24–30). So religious liberty and human rights were and are a peacemaking initiative based on religious faithfulness—on the mandate of incarnational discipleship for following Jesus' way concretely. Had England adopted their free-church solution, instead of reestablishing official religion in the Restoration of 1660, religion could have been seen as a source of peace and mutual respect, faithful to Jesus' teachings on peacemaking. England's Enlightenment would likely have been less secular than it turned out to be. How do we now overcome that secular reaction and develop religion as a source of peace and peacemaking—faithful to the way of Jesus?

As a child I was deeply affected during World War II when the news reached us that my father's ship had been torpedoed and sunk in the war against Japan, and that my father had died. My mother and I wept uncontrollably, as many other family members have grieved from the death of their loved ones in far too many wars. Except for us it was temporary grief: we learned later that Dad had survived.

I was also deeply impacted by the atomic bombing of the two Japanese cities, Hiroshima and Nagasaki. These were nonmilitary targets, and approximately 300,000 citizens of those cities were suddenly incinerated—or slowly annihilated by the delayed effects of radiation. I envisioned nuclear weapons spreading worldwide and threatening to kill us all. What could be done to control them and prevent the outcome of a sudden, intense cataclysm like Hiroshima and Nagasaki, killing much of the world's population?

My father finally returned from the war, but like most veterans, he did not talk of the horror that he had experienced. It was too painful. He did bring home photos of the emaciated POWs whom he had liberated from Japanese POW camps, and said they had been starving to death. He mentioned what he called the fanatical resistance of Japanese soldiers in the murderous battles for the Pacific islands. But I had to read John Hersey's *Hiroshima* and later see the film *Prophecy* to get a description of the unbelievable suffering of Japanese in those cities destroyed by atomic bombs, dying from the burning and then from the slower effects of radiation. When he returned from the war, Dad told me, "Glen, war is so horrible that we have to do all we can to prevent World War III and atomic war."

So I asked myself, how do we develop an ethic that is effective in preventing wars like that? An ethic that shapes churches actually to follow Jesus' call for peacemaking witness?

In the climactic sections of *A Secular Age*, Charles Taylor wrestles with how to explain causes of war. We could try to understand "certain powerful desires, sometimes even to the point of frenzy: berserker rage, love of battle, slaughter, . . . attraction to militias, fighting organizations . . . in biological, evolutionary terms . . . in some ways 'wired into' us." [7] Taylor says this has truth in it, but is inadequate. The sociobiological interpretation leads to fatalism: war and killing are simply given with human nature, and to try to decrease the number of wars is unrealistic—a hopeless effort to stifle human nature.

By contrast, Taylor writes, the cultural explanation says nations create meaning-structures that either incite violence and justify it as courageous or, on the other hand, that encourage citizens to be peaceful. So some nations are less violent than others. And when young men are unemployed and have little hope for a viable future, they are more likely to become recruits for violence. Or, on the other hand, if they see their society focusing on economic development and producing jobs, they can develop hope and become more peaceful. For example, my students and I were impressed that Palestinians in the West Bank of Palestine were working to build their economy and emphasizing education and nonviolence, though this is not true in Gaza. So Taylor concludes that war has to be understood not merely as a biological drive, but as meta-biological, shaped extensively by the search for meaning, by religious ritual, by varieties in cultures.

On the other hand, to interpret the propensity to violence as wholly a matter of culture, and to try to prevent it by rational education that will teach us to be peaceful, is also unrealistic. It engenders unrealistic hope, seeks to stifle powerful human drives, and is bound to fail. An idealistic and transcendent explanation leads to overoptimistic hopes and fails to prepare for the real threats of actual history. (See chapter 8 on a realistic understanding of sin.)

Taylor argues that a Christian and holistic interpretation says we do indeed have violent bodily inclinations. We are born out of the animal kingdom, with lots of aggression and sex drive, but we can be guided to transform these drives—not just to repress them—to experience some conversion, so that the energy turns more constructive. This is agape, straining to bring things back to God, with the energy to combat evil. Yet it will not totally overcome the bodily drives.

He writes of the self-righteous anger of humanistic advocates of justice, and of the authoritarian anger of the religious right and president George W. Bush seeking self-righteous vengeance in costly wars against terrorism. By contrast, he praises Nelson Mandela, Archbishop Desmond Tutu, and the South African Truth and Reconciliation Commission for helping people acknowledge their own complicity in conflict and injustice and seek repentance and forgiveness.[8] Such acknowledgment implements the third practice of incarnational discipleship: repentance and checks and balances against sin.

Similarly, Charles Kimball, an expert in comparative religion, compares Judaism, Christianity, Islam, Buddhism, and Hinduism, when they get entangled in religious violence.[9] He argues that authoritarianism and closed-mindedness that refuse checks and balances from other perspectives are major causes of religious violence. He advocates two solutions: (1) faithfulness to the central traditions of the religions opposing such violence instead of authoritarian perversions of those traditions, and (2) the ten practices of just peacemaking that the thirty scholars identified in *Just Peacemaking*.

THE TRANSFORMING INITIATIVES OF MARTIN LUTHER KING, CHARLES OSGOOD, AND JESUS

In 1955, Martin Luther King Jr. experienced a life-changing and indeed world-changing synthesis of his own African American Baptist emphasis on Jesus' teaching of love with the nonviolent direct action strategies of Gandhi. He had already read Gandhi, whose appreciation for Jesus' Sermon on the Mount is well known, but when King experienced nonviolent direct action energizing people to achieve desegregation of public transportation in Montgomery, Alabama, Jesus' teaching plus Gandhi's strategy plus experiential engagement came together for him in a flash of revelation. Love as simply giving in to racist oppression would not solve the racism. But love as nonviolent confrontation, joined with justice as deliverance, could.[10]

Seven years later, Charles Osgood published his book *An Alternative to War or Surrender*.[11] He argued that continuing the nuclear arms race, trying to build more nuclear weapons than our rivals were building, was not solving the problem. It was increasing the danger. But on the other hand, unilateral disarmament could not succeed politically, and it would not remove the threat of the other side's nuclear weapons. Just saying no, or merely being opposed to nuclear weapons, would not solve anything.

Instead we needed *a strategy of independent initiatives.* Our side could take an initiative to reduce the threat to the other side, explaining clearly that increased security for both sides was our intention. The initiative should not leave us weak; we would still have far more than enough nuclear weapons to destroy any enemy. And it should be visible and verifiable—the other side would not trust mere words. We could announce that if the other side reciprocated with a similar reduction, then we would take still another step. These are independent initiatives—independent from the years-long process of slow negotiations that seemingly never reduce anything but only legitimate what has already been built. Eventually they could lead to negotiations ratifying the reductions.

The example was President Eisenhower's 1957 and 1959 announcements that the United States was halting nuclear bomb testing for one year. He announced that if the Soviet Union reciprocated, then the suspension of tests could be extended, one year at a time. Nuclear bomb testing would be easily discovered by each side's detection techniques, so it was not a matter of relying on the Soviets' word. Eisenhower was responding to pressure from a world-wide peace movement to stop blanketing the world with nuclear pollution from test explosions of nuclear weapons in the atmosphere in Nevada. For example, evidence analyzed by Ernest J. Sternglass indicated that in areas where fallout occurred from the nuclear tests, the death rate of fetuses and infants, which had been steadily declining as medical practices were improving, suddenly stopped their decline and in some regions actually increased. Significantly more babies died than would have been expected. "The estimated number of excess infant deaths since 1951 reached a total of 375,000 by 1966 in the United States alone. . . . By contrast California, which received less fallout from the Nevada test, maintained its steady decline, although a decrease in the rate of decline became evident beginning within two to three years after the onset of hydrogen bomb tests in the Pacific in 1954."[12]

The Soviet Union did reciprocate, and bomb testing was halted for two and a half years. Then France started testing, and the U.S. and U.S.S.R. also resumed testing. But President Kennedy initiated a new testing halt, and again the Soviet Union reciprocated. This led to the Atmospheric Test–Ban Treaty of 1963 that has halted nuclear testing above ground ever since.

During this time, I was deeply engaged in the civil rights movement, first in North Carolina and then in Kentucky, and much influenced by Martin Luther King—as I still am. I was also deeply concerned about the nuclear arms race: the United States and the Soviet Union were building ten times as many nuclear weapons as it would take to cause the mega-explosions, firestorms, and world-wide radiation that would kill most of the world's population if they were used in a major nuclear war. Because of my own work in nuclear physics, I could not ignore the steadily increasing nuclear threat as easily as many have. Furthermore, it was my own father who had initiated the proposal of a unilateral nuclear test ban and reciprocations during his exploratory negotiations with the Soviet Union—on behalf of the U.S. government but daringly exploring beyond his official mandate.[13] So I paid attention to Osgood's strategy of independent initiatives as well as to King's strategy of nonviolent direct action. At the same time, I was beginning to see the transforming initiatives structure of the Sermon on the Mount. I had my own flash of revelation: King's nonviolent direct action and Osgood's independent initiatives could be seen as implementing Jesus' transforming initiatives in the Sermon on the Mount! Osgood combined with King pointed me toward a synthesis of Jesus' teaching and just peacemaking strategy.

The question hit me: Why doesn't Christian ethics have an ethic of peacemaking as transforming initiatives? Why do we keep debating whether wars are justified, as in pacifism versus just war theory, but not whether specific practices of peacemaking initiatives should be taken? The gospel is about God's initiatives of grace, not merely about what we are not supposed to do. Jesus' central message is about breakthroughs of the reign of God, not merely about when we have permission to do more violence. Biblical realism is about diagnosing sin pragmatically and seeking deliverance, not simply affirming some high ideals. And so emerged the new ethic, just peacemaking.[14]

MAKING CONNECTIONS BETWEEN THE TRANSFORMING INITIATIVES OF THE SERMON ON THE MOUNT AND JUST PEACEMAKING

Jesus lived and taught at a time when Jewish anger against Roman domination was building. Every now and then someone would claim to be a messiah and lead a group to rebel against the Romans, who would then massacre the group. A major war of rebellion was brewing. Jesus prophesied six times in the Gospels (including once in the *Gospel of Thomas*) that the temple would be destroyed. It came true: the war of rebellion began in the year 66, and in 70 the Romans destroyed the temple and much of Jerusalem, killing many Jews and exiling many others. Matthew's Gospel was written shortly after that destruction, with that devastation in mind. Peacemaking between Jewish followers of Jesus and other Jews was also needed. So Jesus' teachings on peacemaking were not merely otherworldly ideals; they offered specific guidance for dealing constructively with the injustices and for taking initiatives to resolve some of the hostility. They also fulfilled God's will for peace revealed especially in the prophet Isaiah, Jesus' favorite prophet. The Sermon on the Mount should be read with that real-world hostility and violence—and God's will for peace—in mind.

To see the connection between Jesus' way in the Sermon on the Mount and realistic guidance in the complex world of war and peace, we need some work on hermeneutics—the discipline of interpreting the meaning of biblical teaching for guidance today. I will give a very brief hint here of the holistic hermeneutical method I advocate, and put a fuller explanation on the just peacemaking website.[15] It will guide the sections below that connect transforming initiatives of the Sermon on the Mount with the practices of just peacemaking.

The challenge is that Jesus taught in the social context of first-century Galilee and Jerusalem. Daily life was ruled by the authorities in Jerusalem, though under the overall domination of the Roman Empire. We, on the other hand, live in the social context of the twenty-first century's globalizing society, where not the Roman Empire but excessive concentrations of economic wealth rule much of our lives. If we interpret Jesus' command to carry the Roman soldier's pack a second mile only literally and unimaginatively, it will have no meaning for us, since we are hardly likely to be confronted by any Roman soldiers. Unimaginative and literalistic transposition from Jesus' social context to ours would be anachronistic. But on the other hand, as John Howard Yoder says, reducing Jesus' teaching to a general principle like "go beyond the requirement" or even "take a transforming initiative" loses the vividness and specificity of Jesus' teaching. And developing a Christian ethic that ignores the way of Jesus is hardly Christian.[16] Neither a hermeneutical procedure that derives unimaginative legalistic rules nor one that reduces Jesus' way to an abstract principle or doctrine is faithful to the richness of Jesus' guidance.

Yoder advocates studying the implications of Jesus' teaching in its original social context. Hostility between Jews and Roman soldiers was simmering, and Jesus prophesied that it would boil over into revolt in which the Romans would destroy the temple (and kill many Jews). We should not reduce it to a thin and abstract principle but should bring the whole teaching, with its vividness and particularity, its graphic memorability, and with awareness of the first-century context, into our social context. We should then study what practice in our context can be analogous to going the second mile in Jesus' original context. For example, after the terrorist attacks of 9/11, several churches sent groups of Christians to guard Muslim mosques so that hateful extremists would not do violence against Muslims who opposed such terrorism. In the 2011 Arab Spring in Egypt that toppled the dictator Mubarak, many Christians and Muslims joined together in mutual support, though others engaged in violence.

William Spohn argues similarly, calling his method "analogical imagination."[17] He asks us to immerse ourselves imaginatively into the narratives of Jesus in the Gospels, as Spohn had done in his own Jesuit training with Ignatius's *Spiritual Exercises*, and then to look for analogous implications now. I call this "analogical contextualization," because I want careful study of the meaning in the original context, and critical study of the present social context, so that the analogy is not only imaginative but also analogous in social meaning. For example, Spohn writes that the act of footwashing was normally carried out by "a Gentile slave, someone who would not be contaminated by the impurity that clung to bare feet." So an analogous imaginative act in our social context occurred when an Irish-American pastor in an inner-city parish in Baltimore, in a "footwashing" worship ceremony, shined the shoes of twelve elderly African-American men.

Shining other people's shoes resonated with the original example of Jesus. It is the work of the poor, traditionally of poor black men who still bear the effects of chattel slavery. It was a shocking reversal to see the well-educated white pastor shine their shoes. The message was . . . the last becoming first and the first becoming last, the kingdom of God's reparation of justice long delayed.[18]

Here Spohn pays accurate attention to the meaning of Jesus' practice of foot-washing in his context and to what had analogous meaning in the context of inner-city Baltimore. It is not merely an abstract principle, but a concrete, analogous practice, accompanied by a reading of the original New Testament passage and a comment on its meaning in Jesus' context.

1 and 2. Nonviolent Direct Action and Independent Initiatives to Reduce Threat

Matthew 5:38–43 has "an eye for an eye" as the traditional teaching, and "not to retaliate by revengeful or evil means" as the vicious cycle. The transforming initiatives all command us not simply to comply with an oppressor, but to invent a surprising initiative that confronts the enemy but is consistent with love for that enemy.[19] I understand Jesus' teaching on love as "delivering love," which includes a confrontational dimension. It is not the idealistic denial of self-love. "Delivering love" enters incarnationally into the midst of the concerns of the other, confronts where needed, and seeks to build community.[20] It confronts adversaries nonviolently, hoping for transformation in the adversary, in ourselves, and in our relationship. This is exactly what Jesus' transforming initiatives of going the second mile, turning the cheek of equal dignity, giving the tunic as well as the cloak, and lending as well as giving to the beggar all accomplish.

Nonviolent confrontation that seeks transformation and community has an analogous practice in our time: "nonviolent direct action," the first practice of just peacemaking. In fact, we do not need much analogical contextualization to suggest this as a crucial practice of just peacemaking, since the strategy of nonviolent resistance was practiced three times by Jews against Roman governors around Jesus' time.[21] Nonviolent direct action, as practiced by Martin Luther King and the U.S. civil rights movement, is now spreading throughout the world, transforming nations from dictatorships to democracies and achieving better justice while preventing revolutionary war. In the Arab Spring, nonviolent direct action has overthrown dictators in Tunisia and Egypt. My students and I have just returned from a peacemaking course in Palestine and Israel. On the West Bank, Palestinians all explained that they have learned that violence does not work, and nonviolent action offers far more hope.[22] On pragmatic grounds, based on historical experience, they have committed themselves to nonviolent action and turned their attention to education and to building their society, which give significantly more hope.

In Gaza, however, Hamas still supports occasional violence at this time of writing, and Israel retaliates with ten times more violence. Violence is not working. I hope for a Hamas that learns what others have learned. I hope for an Israel that recovers its calling of being God's people who practice restorative justice.[23] The Hebrew prophets teach that remaining in the land depends on doing justice. The Israel that other nations can look to for guidance, as in Isaiah 2:1–5, must recover this prophetic calling concerning their settlements on Palestinian land and the human right of Palestinians to their own state, as Israel has the human right to its own state. Nonviolent direct action emphasizes that governments are based not only on the monopoly of force, but on the consent of the governed. If a government responds to nonviolent direct action in a nonviolent way, it has a chance for reform, as occurred in South Africa and in the American South after repenting for previous violence. If, on the other hand, the government responds with extensive violence, as in Libya and Syria, it loses the consent of the governed.

Less widely known, but highly important, is the second practice of just peacemaking, the strategy of "independent initiatives" that Charles Osgood developed, as mentioned above.[24] It has been working to achieve the Partial Test-Ban Treaty, reduce nuclear weapons, and open up negotiations for the Oslo Accords between Israel and Palestine, though Prime Minister Netanyahu reneged on obeying the agreement. President George H. W. Bush and Mikhail Gorbachev cooperated through independent initiatives to reduce both sides' nuclear weapons by half in a short time, just as the Cold War was ending. At the time of this writing we need independent initiatives between Israel and the two Palestinian governments.

In *Just Peacemaking*, we write that these two strategies—nonviolent direct action and independent initiatives—share features that connect them with Jesus' teaching in Matthew 5:38–42, as well as with the basic conviction of a theology of grace and the reign of God in which God does not merely wait passively, but takes the initiative for reconciliation:

> These . . . practices embody the same seven essential ingredients of Christian peacemaking: (1) they are not simply passive withdrawal, but proactive ways of grace that empower us to take peacemaking initiatives; (2) they acknowledge the log in our own eye and take our own responsibility for peacemaking rather than simply judging the other; (3) they affirm the dignity and interests of the enemy, even while rejecting sinful or wrong practices; (4) they confront the other with an invitation to make peace and justice; (5) they invite into community in a way that includes, rather than excludes, former enemies and outcasts; (6) they are historically embodied or situated and are in fact happening in our history; (7) they are empirically validated—they are making a significant difference in international relations and domestic conflict.[25]

3. Cooperative Conflict Resolution with Your Adversary

In the previous chapter, we examined Matthew 5:21–26 in the Sermon on the Mount. First, Jesus points us to the *traditional teaching* of the Ten

Commandments against murder. Second he diagnoses ongoing anger and insult as a *vicious cycle* that leads to judgment (5:22). Jesus is paying attention to the passions and loyalties dimension of our context and saying we can't simply deny them. Instead, we need practices that deal with them.

The third member of the triad, vv. 23–26, is the *transforming initiative*—not merely a negative prohibition of murder or anger, but a way of deliverance. It is a command to take initiatives that transform the relationship from anger to peacemaking. We saw in the last chapter that to avoid ever being angry would be an impossible ideal, but to go and make peace with a brother or sister, or an adversary, is the way of deliverance from anger. It fits prophecies of the reign of God in which peace replaces war.

I am convinced that here Jesus is interpreting the first murder, when Cain murders Abel. Both passages are about murder. In that passage and this one, a brother is giving his offering to God at the altar. In both cases, there is anger between the brothers. In Genesis 4, God admonishes Cain to do right, and in Matthew 5 Jesus specifies that to do right is to obey five imperatives (as we saw in the previous chapter): *drop* your gift, *go* to the brother, *make peace*, then come back and *give* your gift of worship; quickly *make peace* with your adversary.[26]

On the rules level, this is a direct command: *go make peace quickly*. It is not a Platonic ideal, or a virtue; neither is it a prohibition or a hard teaching: we often talk things over with others to smooth relations and make peace. This is a *practice*—a rules-based normative action regularly implemented by a community of disciples, a church. They see it as God's will for them and for others; they advocate that others in the society do something analogous: *Go make peace*.

On the principle level, making peace with your adversary is of prior importance to worship. "Those who say 'I love God' and hate their brothers or sisters, are liars. For those who do not love a brother or sister whom they have seen, cannot love God whom they have not seen" (1 John 4:20; cf. Hos. 6:6, which is quoted in Matt. 9:13 and 12:7). By this principle, Cain's gift at the altar was unacceptable to God because he had anger against his brother and was unwilling to go make peace (and learn from his brother how to be a more successful and less envious farmer).

On the basic convictions level, this practice participates in the way of grace that God pursued in Jesus when there was enmity between God and humans: God came in Jesus to make peace with us. This is the basic Christian conviction of the incarnation—central to our ethic of incarnational discipleship. Jesus incarnates the way of going to make peace not only in his entering into the lives of many marginalized people, but also entering into the midst of the high priests and authorities in Jerusalem at certain threat to his own life. And peace is a characteristic of the breakthrough of the reign of God—the work of the Holy Spirit in our lives.

One aspect of Jesus' going to his adversaries to make peace has puzzled some people: Jesus doesn't only talk sweetness and light; conflict resolution as Jesus practices it often includes direct confrontation and a call for repentance, in direct line with the prophets of Israel. Attention to Jesus' practice of his own teaching redefines conflict resolution in a way that moves it out of the context of ideals for the "righteous" and into the realism of honest confrontation in pursuit of mutual peacemaking. Self-righteous politicians who refuse to talk with their adversaries because they see talking as a reward for the righteous are missing Jesus' point. Sometimes we need to talk straight about a real danger.

What is the social context for Jesus' teaching here? I do not think we can fence in this teaching so that it fits only one narrow context—anger at Roman occupiers, or anger between Jewish Christians in Antioch and synagogues from which they have recently split, or economic disputes in Galilean villages in Jesus' day,[27] or disagreements within Matthew's congregation about how to form their new identity. In its time, the text most likely had application to all of these; and in our context, it has application to all of life. Davies and Allison argue cogently that the mention of Sanhedrin, altar, adversary, and prison do not fit a narrow interpretation as only applying to a fellow Christian "brother."[28] Willard Swartley argues similarly with reference to "the mixed Jewish and Gentile crowds depicted in Matthew's Galilean narrative as well as Jesus' response to the centurion, and the larger New Testament canon."[29] It is grounded in a basic conviction about God's action in bringing the reign of God, which is more inclusive than only one set of relationships.

I suggest the analogous practice is cooperative conflict resolution—one of the ten practices of *Just Peacemaking*. The discipline of conflict resolution is extensively developed in our time as an academic discipline as well as a regular practice in labor relations, international cooperation, and other interactions. Of course people will differ about specific implications, as in any ethic. Our loyalties and our interpretation of the social context influence how we see the implications. The important point is to keep working at the implications, not fence Jesus into irrelevance or marginalize him within only an individualistic realm.

4. Acknowledge Responsibility for Injustice and Seek Forgiveness

Repentance and forgiveness are of course central to Jesus' message and to Christian theology. In the Sermon on the Mount, Matthew 7:1–5 calls for the practice of repentance, taking the log out of our own eye. This practice also connects with the petition in the Lord's Prayer for forgiveness of our sins as we forgive others. The analogous just peacemaking practice is to "acknowledge responsibility for conflict and injustice, and seek repentance and forgiveness."[30]

Dietrich Bonhoeffer deserves credit for initiating this practice among nations. As we saw in the chapter on a realistic understanding of sin, in a remarkable ten-page section of his *Ethics*, Bonhoeffer confessed his own sins, the churches' sins, and Germany's sins.[31] After 1945, some churches in Germany took up

Bonhoeffer's confession, making similar confessions of their own. *Aktion Sühe-nezeichen/Fridensdienste* (Action Reconciliation/Peace Service), a Christian orga-nization influenced by Bonhoeffer, for decades has been sending conscientious objectors to do volunteer service for peace and justice to the nations Germany fought against during World War II—as a sign of atonement. These church confessions and actions prepared the ground for Chancellor Willy Brandt and President Richard von Weizsäcker's dramatic public repentance on behalf of Germany. This was a major step in Germany's own moral and spiritual recov-ery. And the practice of acknowledging responsibility has now spread to other nations, as a significant practice of just peacemaking between nations.

Donald Shriver argues that nations cannot live together peacefully without some practice of national forgiveness.[32] He points to President George H. W. Bush signing reparations payments for Japanese Americans imprisoned during World War II, Bill Clinton apologizing for U.S. inaction to prevent the Rwanda massacre, and the prime minister of Japan apologizing to South Korea for war atrocities during World War II. Prior to Bonhoeffer and Germany's apologies, nations had avoided apologizing, as if it were a sign of weakness rather than the strength that it in fact demonstrates. The practice of acknowledging responsibil-ity is now lancing the boil of resentment between numerous nations and thus decreasing the likelihood that resentment will erupt into war.

All ten practices of just peacemaking constitute a call for a church and a nation to repent for not knowing the practices that make for peace and for not enacting those practices. This is the third vertex of the triangle of incarnational discipleship: *calling us to repentance from cooptation by ideologies*, here specifically ideologies that foment war. We need openness to change and self-correction, and humility to hear others' perspectives with respect. Arrogant peacemakers are seldom effective peacemakers.

5 and 6. Practices of Sustainable Economic Justice, Human Rights, and Democracy

The fifth just peacemaking practice is to "foster just and sustainable economic development." This is spelled out in the longest of the ten chapters in *Just Peace-making*. It makes implicit connections with Jesus' practices and the basic con-viction variable of Christlikeness and justice beyond what I can spell out here. Matthew 6:19–34 teaches practices of economic justice: not hoarding money for ourselves, but making God's justice and reign our priority.

In addition, the thirty interdenominational scholars who collaborate in just peacemaking theory advocate another analogous practice in our time that also implements the practice of justice in Matthew 6:19–34: "Advance democracy, human rights, and religious liberty." Subsequent to the publication of *Just Peacemaking*, New Testament scholar Christopher Marshall has written a theo-logically sophisticated and perceptive argument for grounding human rights in biblical ethics, influenced by Richard Hays's hermeneutical method.[33] Marshall demonstrates that "human rights categories have become an almost universal currency of moral debate."[34] He argues that "The notion of human rights is deeply, and uniquely, grounded in the biblical story and Christians therefore have something special to say about human rights."[35] Nicholas Wolterstorff has also developed an insightful historical, theological, and philosophical argument for human rights as theocentrically grounded.[36]

Just Peacemaking adds three points. First, the worldwide pressures for human rights, supported by many churches, human rights organizations, and President Carter's building human rights into U.S. economic aid decisions, have provided steady oversight of many governments. Almost all Latin American nations have moved from authoritarian or dictatorial governments toward democracy, and this is true of many Asian and East and Central European nations. Second, no democracy with human rights made a war against another democracy with human rights in the whole twentieth century. This invites a third observation, that advancing human rights and thus pressuring for democracy has had a dramatic influence in preventing war and moving toward justice.

Recruitment of terrorists depends on resentment for perceived injustice— both relative economic deprivation and support for dictators rather than support for human rights. Changing that perception is the key to combating terrorism. *Just Peacemaking* supports what was President George W. Bush's effort to spread democracy, but it explicitly opposes seeking to do that by making war to seek regime change. The multiple deaths, hatred, religious and ethnic conflict in Iraq after such a war are vivid demonstrations of the problems that arise from a war of imposition. They contrast vividly with the many countries that have recently made that transition by means of nonviolent direct action, a push for human rights, and pressures from cooperative forces in the international system. Just peacemaking also supports former President George W. Bush's commitment to increase assistance to Africa and to increase economic aid to overcome poverty in the Millennium Challenge by $5 billion, and would urge president Obama and his successors, and Congress, to carry this commitment forward.

7 and 8. International Cooperation

Jesus' teaching of love for the enemy is his interpretation of Leviticus 19:17–18 on loving your neighbor as yourself. The question was, "who is my neighbor?" Jesus based his answer on a *basic conviction* about God's nature: God gives sun and rain to the just and unjust alike. Therefore we are to include enemies as well as friends in the community of neighbors. Jesus' teaching concerns not only individual relations; it concerns inclusion in community, based on God as sovereign over relations with diverse adversaries.

What is the analogous just peacemaking practice in our time? Four trends are developing increased cooperative networks among nations in our time of globalization: (1) the decline in the utility of war; (2) the priority of trade and the economy over war; (3) the strength of international exchanges, communications, transactions, and networks; and (4) the gradual ascendancy of liberal representative democracy and a mixture of welfare-state and laissez-faire market economy. Therefore, the two just peacemaking practices for our time analogous to "include your enemy in the community of neighbors" are "work with emerging cooperative forces in the international system," and "strengthen the United Nations and International Efforts for Cooperation and Human Rights."

Terrorist networks are in approximately eighty nations, and they cannot be eradicated by one nation acting alone. International cooperation is needed to gather intelligence, cut off funding, arrest terrorists, and avoid unilateral domination that increases the anger that leads people to overcome their normal human opposition to suicide and to engage in the act of massacring noncombatants. Unilateral domination by military action in the first decade of this century led to either disdain or hatred for the United States in much of the world, as measured by the Pew Global Reports. The agreed assessment by sixteen U.S. intelligence agencies in 2006 said that U.S. actions against Arab Muslims and support for dictators were increasing anger and increasing recruitment for terrorism and terrorist incidents. The official report of the U.S. Department of State[37] shows an astounding increase in worldwide terrorist incidents since the Iraq War began in 2003 and the United States began torturing prisoners:

- 208 terrorist attacks caused 625 deaths in 2003.
- 3,168 attacks caused 1,907 deaths in 2004.
- 11,111 attacks caused 14,602 deaths in 2005.
- 14,500 attacks caused 20,745 deaths in 2006.
- 14,414 attacks caused 22,719 deaths in 2007.
- 11,662 attacks caused 15,708 deaths in 2008.
- 10,969 attacks caused 15,310 deaths in 2009.
- 11,604 attacks caused 13,186 deaths in 2010.

Andrew Sullivan writes that since president Obama's efforts to show respect for Muslim nations and act more in cooperation, "al Qaeda's popularity in the Muslim world has plummeted."[38] We can expect that future data will show a decline in international terrorist incidents. As illustrated by the authors of *Just Peacemaking: New Paradigm,* empirical data show that nations that engage in international cooperation make war and have war made against them less frequently. We wrote this well prior to the George W. Bush presidency, and not against that administration. But the administration then provided another empirical test. It ignored the evidence from the international inspectors in Iraq that weapons of mass destruction were not present there, initiated the Iraq War despite opposition in the U.N. Security Council, removed the protection of international law from prisoners, withdrew support from nine international treaties, and worked to weaken the authority of the United Nations. Just peacemaking theory predicts a greater likelihood of war as a result. This administration declared three wars (against terrorism, Afghanistan, and Iraq), while threatening three "axis of evil" nations—Iraq, Iran, and North Korea. I do not know a historical precedent for declaring three wars in one four-year presidential term. My own empirical research found that unilateralism versus internationalism is one of the two strongest variables for predicting actions by foreign policy decision-makers.[39]

9. Reduce Offensive Weapons and Weapons Trade

Jesus admonished his disciple to put up his sword, and said, "all who take the sword will perish by the sword" (Matt. 26:51–52).[40] The context in his time was that false messiahs, some called *sicarii* or sword-bearers were starting rebellions that always got themselves killed by the Roman soldiers, and Jesus rightly prophesied that eventually this would lead to the Romans destroying the temple (and Jerusalem). And the context in Isaiah was that God willed that the Suffering Servant come nonviolently. The analogous practice for just peacemaking is to reduce offensive weapons and the weapons trade.

Wars between nations have become less frequent in recent years partly because initiating war does not pay: weapons have become so powerful that the retaliation by other nations is too destructive. But a nation is sometimes tempted to initiate a war if it builds up so many offensive weapons that it believes the other side will not be able to retaliate extensively. For example, Serbia had overwhelming offensive capability by comparison with Bosnia, Croatia, and Kosovo, and succumbed to the temptation to initiate three wars against them. The United States had overwhelming offensive capability against Iraq and Afghanistan, and succumbed to a similar temptation. For neither did it work out as expected.

Therefore, the ninth just peacemaking practice is to reduce offensive weapons capability, including the weapons trade, and thus reduce the temptation to initiate war. This is not just an ideal: In the seven years from 1988 to 1995, the purchase of weapons by developing nations dropped to one-fourth of what it had been.[41] Now George Shultz, Sam Nunn, James Goodby, Henry Kissinger, and a dozen other conservative former National Security officials, urge steps toward abolishing nuclear weapons. They say the threat now is not the Cold War, but terrorists getting nuclear weapons. So we are more secure if we reduce and then abolish nuclear weapons worldwide.[42] Key steps are to

- Halt all production of nuclear fissile materials.
- Ratify the Comprehensive Test-Ban Treaty.
- Agree with Russia to cut numbers of nuclear weapons in half, and then with other nations to cut further.

10. Encourage Grassroots Peacemaking Groups

According to Matthew 5:1–2 and 7:28–29, Jesus taught the Sermon on the Mount to his group of disciples and to the crowds. Jesus taught not only scattered individuals here and there or only the higher authorities in Jerusalem—though he did do that. Rather, he gathered a grassroots group of disciples and taught them, and they became crucial for spreading his message. And he taught in synagogues and villages, where he formed groups, and gave instructions for groups to make peace among themselves.[43] Eventually this became *ecclesia*, groups of followers of Jesus gathered together in worship, instruction, and sharing to meet needs.

By analogy, this suggests the tenth and final practice of just peacemaking: encourage grassroots peacemaking groups. Just peacemaking needs to spread both by pastors and church leaders teaching and practicing the whole way of Jesus, including peacemaking, and also by groups within churches that worship, study, and engage in actions of peacemaking witness. Lone individuals feel powerless to affect their communities and churches or to influence governments that make war. But gathered in groups, and networked with peacemaking organizations that provide information and alerts for timely actions synchronized with other groups, they are far more effective. Bread for the World, Peace Action, Friends National Committee on Legislation, Sojourners, and denominational peace fellowships and organizations provide such networks.[44]

Lutheran ethicist Larry Rasmussen advocates a strategy of small groups with a peacemaking mission inside churches, and also participation in groups and movements beyond churches where we can learn and be strengthened by cooperation and make our witness to following Jesus.[45] Small groups with a mission are different from small groups that only study, pray, and share in discussion but are committed to no action. People in small groups with a mission engage in service and witness, as well as study and discussion. I believe small groups, each with a specific mission, are one key to developing a sense of mission of the church that is crucial for church renewal in our time.

For example, All Saints Church in Pasadena has about fifty-five small groups, each of which has a particular mission, like ministering to people who are divorced, or to families that include people with mental disabilities or people who are mentally ill. There are small groups for peacemaking, for Muslim-Jewish-Christian relations, for ministry with the homeless, and so on. These groups give the church a dynamism and aliveness, as well as numbers of active participants that surpass any other Episcopal congregation in their diocese.

Incarnational discipleship is about digging deeper into what it means to follow Jesus in our lives and our witness. Small groups with a mission study implications of the way of Jesus, including Jesus' Bible—the Old Testament or Hebrew Scriptures—for the kinds of mission that each group is working on. Small groups with a mission encourage each other in carrying out these implications in the church and the world. If the mission is peacemaking, the group will connect with peacemaking organizations such as those mentioned above, and the group will discuss together and act to support the implications of their Christian commitments for action in the world.

Incarnational discipleship is about repenting for ideologies that replace loyalty to the way of Christ. Recent research by psychologists says that people accept correction of their unconscious biases much more in discussion with trusted others than in their own private thoughts.[46] Small groups with a mission help us grow. And they help churches grow in faithfulness—and in vitality.

Chapter 12

Conclusion

Validating Incarnational Discipleship

In chapter 4, I accepted Nancey Murphy's four criteria in *Theology in an Age of Scientific Reasoning* for validating a theological ethic on solid ground: (1) Is it possible to show that a coherent series of theories in incarnational discipleship exist in agreement with the apostolic witness to Jesus Christ, and function as a research program, guiding further research? (2) Does incarnational discipleship generate new content, resolving some challenges within Christian faith or producing some hitherto unexpected discoveries—what Lakatos calls "novel facts"? (3) Can some of these discoveries be corroborated within the community? Finally, (4) does an ethic of incarnational discipleship produce Christlike character and actions?

We began this book by exploring the fruits of the Spirit demonstrated dramatically in difficult historic test times by Bonhoeffer, Barth, Trocmé, King, Jordan, Day, Lester, the rescuers in David Gushee's *Righteous Gentiles of the Holocaust*, the Bulgarian rescuers in Parush Parushev's forthcoming *Humble Churches Getting the Nation to Do Right*, and the leaders of the Revolution of the Candles in East Germany that ousted the dictator and brought down the Berlin Wall with disciplined nonviolent action. Incarnational discipleship passed this test of character in very tough times with impressive witness, when others failed.

We have seen that incarnational discipleship meets criterion 1: a coherent theological ethic exists in the writings of the heroes of the faith that we have named. These heroes' first distinctive is their deep and specific interpretation of the apostolic and biblical witness to Jesus Christ. We have seen in every chapter how the way of Jesus, interpreted with attention to Jesus' historical context, and to the holistic and repentance themes of incarnational discipleship, develops a research program that responds to the challenges that Charles Taylor has set for us in his masterful book *A Secular Age*. Lisa Sowle Cahill of Boston College has just written a strikingly parallel argument in her forthcoming *Global Justice, Christology and Christian Ethics* (Cambridge: Cambridge University Press, 2013). It may be seen as one corroboration of my argument—though written independently.

The main focus of this book has been Murphy's second criterion, showing how dimensions of incarnational discipleship generate new content, answers, or remedies for causes of secularism that Charles Taylor has identified. We have seen that it does exactly this, in chapters 5 through 11. In chapter 5, we saw that constitutional democracy with covenant-based religious liberty and human rights produces a society with significantly less secularism. Taylor observed that reaction against the Puritan rage for order, and then reaction against the Restoration with its hierarchy and state-church establishment, led to the secularism of the eighteenth-century Enlightenment, in which democracy was perceived as based on people subjectively constructing social norms, not needing a basis in God. The incarnational discipleship theme of deep loyalty to the way of Jesus led free-church Puritans to advocate religious liberty, since Jesus made disciples by teaching and persuasion rather than coercion, and Jesus taught that we should let the wheat and the weeds grow together until the final harvest. Where religious liberty has been adopted, it has freed us from much of the resentment that arises when churches seek to dominate in partnership with a government or a particular political party. This is an important lesson for the United States during recent decades, with its "culture wars."

We saw that historic church practices of democratic discussion to discern the guidance of the Holy Spirit, plus the free-church Puritan practice of basing churches on freely consented covenants, led to basing democracy on constitutions that guarded minority rights and provided checks and balances against domination by concentrated power. There is no questioning the truth that these apostolic teachings gave important guidance to early Baptists, from Thomas Helwys to John Murton, Richard Overton and Roger Williams, and their free-church sisters and brothers. Several church historians, political philosophers, and sociologists have corroborated the Puritan and free-church influence on the origin of democracy, religious liberty, and human rights. Their affirmation fits Murphy's third criterion, corroboration in community.

Attention to the role of specific teachings of Jesus, most emphasized by free churches among the Puritan mix, enabled us to notice free-church contributions that are important for overcoming secularism, but which are often bypassed by social scientists and church groups still yearning for a kind of Christendom or Constantinianism in which churches become apologists for a political power group. Some Christendom-yearning Christians have a negative bias against the lessons from the free churches. Incarnational discipleship leads us to pay attention to free-church contributions that have reduced secular reaction against churches that adopt an authoritarian Christendom-yearning stance, and helped develop a public tradition that supports justice for minorities. We thus "discover" what for too many are "novel facts," in Lakatos's terminology, or ignored facts.

We saw the origin of human rights with three sets of rights: religious and civil liberty, life and justice, and human dignity in community, based first on biblical teachings and translated into civic language for public ethics. Thus a tradition that emphasized the Lordship of Christ was translated into a civic tradition that has found powerful resonance in American democracy. This civic tradition seems much more helpful for justice and the common good than the possessive individualism or authoritarian domination that also appear in American political culture, and that can cause a backlash into secularism. In the present polarization between ideologists of the religious right and the left or middle, who tend not to be aware of the contributions of free-church Puritanism, it is highly important to recover awareness of the tradition that Gunnar Myrdal, Martin Luther King, and Cornel West have pointed out, but that many neglect.

In chapter 6, we saw that modern science also had its origin in geniuses with strong Puritan faith commitments. But it later led to a view of the universe as governed by efficient mechanistic causation rather than *telos*-oriented final causation. This mechanistic universe seemed closed to God's present involvement. The result was providential Deism, in which God once arranged the universe for human benefit, but is no longer actively involved.[1]

Now we see that our universe is not a stationary machine; it is dynamic and alive at its very base. The nuclei of the atoms, the very building blocks of all nature, are each "deciding" every moment whether to stay the same or whether to split up and go different ways. They seem as if they are alive and responding to God's will. We are led to notice this by the emphasis of incarnational discipleship on the sovereignty of God or Lordship of Christ through all of life, and its emphasis on the living God, the Holy Spirit, ever doing new things. It is symbolic that philosopher Nancey Murphy, who articulates this vitality most persuasively, has both a Catholic integration of nature and grace, and a period of charismatic involvement, in her formation, along with a present Anabaptist commitment to Yoderian discipleship. She thus combines the sovereignty of the Creator through all of nature with awareness of the Holy Spirit, and discipleship as following Jesus.

In chapter 6 we also saw the self-critical practice of continuous correction, the scientific equivalent of ongoing repentance, along with attention to corroboration and correction in community, by the impressive research of James Butler, my early mentor. And we saw this in the scientists who were members of the Royal Society and who led the development of natural science—with their

Puritan loyalty to recovering Hebraic tradition. They expected order from the Creator while also anticipating that their preconceived notions of that order needed adjustment by empirical examination of the data, since God's thoughts are higher than the thoughts of ancient Greek philosophers.

We saw Dietrich Bonhoeffer and incarnational discipleship criticizing a two-realms or compartmentalizing approach that limits the Lordship of Christ—to only gaps in science, or to only individual personal relations, or to only a "religious" compartment of life, or to only relationships inside churches—while avoiding public ethics or scientific discovery. We saw Bonhoeffer arguing against a dualism between faith and science. *Christ reveals God as reality—at the center of life, not merely in the gaps that scientific knowledge cannot explain.* Thus again the tradition of incarnational discipleship led us to important awareness for understanding our history and for combating secularism.

In chapter 7 on the interactive self, I argued, from the contrast between Albert Camus and Ayn Rand, that ours is the Age of Interaction—neurologically, scientifically, philosophically, economically, and environmentally. We need a sense of God's work among us for connection, compassion, covenant, and the common good. We need markers for God's presence—breakthroughs of deliverance, justice, peacemaking, healing, joy of participation, repentance, and sense of God's presence, as mustard seeds of God's present action, God's reign. This meets several of Nancey Murphy's criteria: it is faithful to the apostolic witness to Jesus' central theme of the reign of God, it leads to significant "novel facts," and it is being corroborated by other scholars.

Charles Taylor makes the case that Deism and optimistic liberal Christianity leave out the dark side of creation, nuclear war coming, the climate crisis, entropy, and massive unjust suffering. The neo-Nietzschean, tragic view attacks such religion as too optimistic. Freud, Foucault, Tocqueville, Sorel, Jünger, and in a way Bernard Williams and Isaiah Berlin attack this optimism as well.[2] The tradition of incarnational discipleship led us to inquire whether a more realistic understanding of human nature could be built on a christologically and ecclesiastically persuasive theological base. In chapter 8 we put this inquiry to Dietrich Bonhoeffer, who came through with impressive profundity, perceptively diagnosing Hitler's horrors from the start. His own statement of repentance led German churches, then German political leaders, and now political leaders in numerous other nations to develop the practice of acknowledging responsibility for conflict and injustice and seeking repentance and forgiveness between nations. Bonhoeffer's incarnational discipleship has given us here a deeply needed "novel fact." It has been corroborated in healing processes such as the Truth and Reconciliation Commission in South Africa. It is also being taken up by other nations in ways not as widely known, but highly significant.[3]

In chapter 9, we saw that Taylor identifies the crucial challenge that Christianity has failed to articulate how the suffering of the cross brings redemption in a way that is persuasive for many in our time.[4] Theologians and church leaders are widely aware that new work needs to be done on the meaning of the cross.

Our guiding tradition led us to search out the understanding of the cross in the epitome of incarnational discipleship, Dietrich Bonhoeffer. There we found an emphasis on shame as well as guilt, and an intriguing theme of *eintreten*, entering incarnationally into the lives of alienated and defensive persons to heal their isolation. We found that the well-known theme of *Stellvertretung*, which is usually translated as vicarious deputyship, actually carries not only the sense of acting on behalf of other people, but also stepping into their place, into their shoes empathetically.

We found this same theme in the Gospel of Mark: God in Christ enters incarnationally into the place of alienation and overcomes the shame of those sinfully estranged from God. When I told one theologian that I was putting this question to the Gospel of Mark, he commented, "there is no interpretation of the atonement there." Nor am I aware of studies of Bonhoeffer's understanding of the atonement. Incarnational discipleship's emphasis on the "thicker Jesus" led us into Bonhoeffer and the Gospel of Mark and to an incarnational theory of the atonement that we then found to be implicitly emerging in various forms in current writings on other theories of the atonement, such as hospitality, solidarity, presence, embrace, and nonviolent obedience to God's will. An incarnational theory of atonement, which we explored in chapter 9, helps these theories become more articulate and more clearly rooted in the Gospels.

Lakatos is looking for what he calls "novel facts," and here is a suggestive development in the theory of the cross. I am not aware of previous interpretations of Bonhoeffer and Mark that home in on the atonement in the way incarnational discipleship has led us to do. The remaining question is corroboration by readers—Murphy's third criterion. I expect some to see this as persuasive and suggestive for the understanding of the cross that they would like to affirm for themselves; some to agree but ask for further development; others to see it as an interesting or even important supplement to their own understanding of the cross; and others to be so wedded to a particular theory of the atonement that they are suspicious of any additional interpretations. If the book achieves a fertile mixture of these reactions, I will be very pleased. Charles Taylor and my Berea students (and others) have clearly indicated that we need to seek a new dimension of meaning. Kuhn's *Structure of Scientific Revolutions* indicates clearly that no new paradigm achieves immediate consensus. Corroboration may come slowly.

Taylor's historical study discovers that there has been a perennial tension between loving God even to the cross and *renouncing* everything, versus affirming ordinary human life and flourishing. Historically, Platonic idealism and dualism infested Christian faith, distorting and contradicting it. Plato in *The Republic* was quite prepared to sideline the central human and bodily desires to form families, in favor of the "higher" spiritual life: married sex should be without sexual joy. But increased affirmation of ordinary human life and work lead to reaction against Christianity when it is entangled with Platonic idealism.[5]

Chapter ten pointed to the mandate of incarnational discipleship, doing concrete, thick exegesis of the Sermon on the Mount, replacing idealism and dualism with a realistic and holistic interpretation. In interpreting the Sermon, Platonic idealism misses Jesus' prophetic diagnosis of vicious cycles that trap us in self-defeating power dynamics. It turns his diagnosis of vicious power dynamics into impossible prohibitions like "never be angry," which the New Testament nowhere teaches. Instead Jesus emphasizes transforming initiatives that embolden us to overcome self-defeating power dynamics. We see now how the transforming initiatives interpretation can fulfill Bonhoeffer's unfinished intention to write on the Sermon on the Mount for political guidance. And this helps us see how the "thicker Jesus" of incarnational discipleship can give wisdom for the Lordship of Christ in all of life, including political struggles—which was Bonhoeffer's intention. Furthermore, it nudges us into the presence of the Holy Spirit's breakthroughs of the reign of God in life—which happen where God wills, not only in our little inner circles of control.

The transforming initiatives interpretation of the Sermon on the Mount is receiving good corroboration from New Testament scholars. For example, at the annual meeting of the Society of Biblical Literature, November 19, 2006, in Washington, DC, the Matthew section held a panel on the Sermon on the Mount. At its conclusion, the moderator announced: "We have reached one consensus: the Sermon on the Mount is transforming initiatives." Additionally, it is receiving much appreciation as the agenda for a textbook in Christian ethics and as a study book for church groups and individuals.[6] These are now being translated into eight languages, with others in the offing.

A transforming-initiatives hermeneutic knits Bonhoeffer's *Discipleship* and his *Ethics* together. It brings healing to the rift that he wanted to heal. That rift has caused "two grave errors . . . throughout the history of the church up to the present": pragmatic rejection of the Sermon on the Mount and idealistic or sectarian withdrawal from public ethics, as he himself said.[7] Working with him to heal this rift can enable us to recover the way of Jesus for Christian ethics for political ethics as well as personal and community formation, and to let that ethics be rightly concrete. It can point to the way of deliverance in a time of dangerous concentration of power. Only with a realistic interpretation of the Sermon on the Mount do we have a thicker Jesus that coheres with the Lordship of Christ through all of life. That is crucial for the ethics of incarnational discipleship. It is what Bonhoeffer was striving for in his *Ethics*.

In the final chapter, we explored the counterintuitive role religion has played in the rise of secularism. Taylor indicates that the wars of religion, combined with Christendom's murderous oppression of Anabaptists and their free-church heirs and other nonconforming faiths, caused a backlash against religion and in favor of generic, allegedly universal and rational language, especially in the public sphere, in the Enlightenment and its heirs. Taylor wrestled with understanding causes of warring and sought an ethic that prevents or decreases wars.

We saw that Martin Luther King's own African American Baptist tradition gave him a strong commitment to following Jesus' teachings on the strength of love, which he then combined with the Gandhian strategy of *satyagraha* and

Rosa Parks's initiation of the Montgomery bus boycott to produce a deeply faith-based public ethic of nonviolent direct action. Analogously, thick and concrete exegesis of Jesus' Sermon on the Mount, combined with an incarnational discipleship commitment to Christ's Lordship through all of life, produced the new paradigm for the ethics of peace and war, just peacemaking, with ten specific practices that are in fact significantly reducing the number and devastation of wars. This new ethic is receiving extensive corroboration by the thirty scholars responsible for the just peacemaking paradigm, and now by Jewish and Muslim scholars as well. The ethic is steadily spreading.

Just peacemaking is one more "novel fact" that has arisen from the ethic of incarnational discipleship. And yet another "novel fact" is resulting at least in part from the practices that are identified by just peacemaking: the reduction of the average annual deaths in war during the first half of the twentieth century from 3.8 million to 0.8 million in the second half of the century. The aim of just peacemaking is to bring the ten just peacemaking practices to widespread attention and expression and to increase support for them. If that can be a result of the tradition of incarnational discipleship, all will have been far more than worthwhile. It will have been life-changing and life-rescuing for millions of people and their families. It will have been a source of enormous gratitude.

In sum, we have seen that Nancey Murphy's four criteria are met by incarnational discipleship, a tradition with faithfulness to the apostolic witness to Jesus Christ that is guiding heroes of the faith in historic times of testing. Incarnational discipleship is generating what Lakatos calls "novel facts" on all seven causes of secularism that Charles Taylor diagnoses, meeting the challenges of the twenty-first century. These findings are receiving corroboration by others, and incarnational discipleship is forming heroes of the faith with character most all of us affirm.

Now the one remaining question: Will you join in the apostolic witness to a thicker Jesus—in the tradition of incarnational discipleship?

Appendix

Incarnational Discipleship

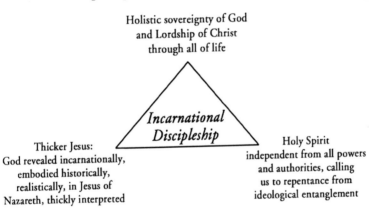

Figure 2.1 Incarnational Discipleship

Notes

Preface

1. Dietrich Bonhoeffer, *Discipleship*, ed. Geffrey B. Kelly and John D. Godsey, trans. Barbara Green and Reinhard Krauss, vol. 4 of *Dietrich Bonhoeffer Works* (DBWE 4) (Minneapolis: Fortress, 2001), 37.
2. Stephen R. Haynes and Lori Brandt Hale, *Bonhoeffer for Armchair Theologians* (Louisville, KY: Westminster John Knox, 2009), 5.
3. I had originally intended to begin the book with a simple, but moving, historical drama of Bonhoeffer's own witness. I wrote it as a readers' theater—a drama that a group of people can perform simply, reading their parts with some feeling, not needing to memorize them. We have performed it in a few seminaries and classes and churches, and it has proved to be deeply moving. If you want a brief introduction to Bonhoeffer and the themes of the book or want a readers' theater that you might consider performing, go to http://www.fuller.edu/academics/faculty/glen-stassen.aspx or www.fuller.edu/sot/faculty/stassen.

Chapter 1: Who Stands the Test of History?

1. Dietrich Bonhoeffer, *Letters and Papers from Prison*, ed. John W. de Gruchy, trans. Isabel Best, Lisa Dahill, Reinhard Krauss, and Nancy Lukens, DBWE 8 (Minneapolis: Fortress, 2010), 38–40, 50–52. Dietrich Bonhoeffer, *Barcelona, Berlin, New York*, ed. Clifford J. Green, trans. Douglas W. Stott, DBWE 10 (Minneapolis: Fortress, 2008), 326–27.
2. Philip Clayton, *Transforming Christian Theology* (Minneapolis: Fortress, 2010), 13–14, 44.
3. Bonhoeffer, *Letters and Papers from Prison*, DBWE 8, 38.
4. Alan J. Roxburgh and Fred Romanuk, *The Missional Leader: Equipping Your Church to Reach a Changing World* (San Francisco: Jossey-Bass, 2006), 66.
5. Charles Taylor, *A Secular Age* (Cambridge, MA: Harvard University Press, 2007), 594. See also Taylor, *Sources of the Self* (Cambridge, MA: Harvard University Press, 1989), 10, 16–19, 24, 26–28.
6. Fritz Stern, *The Politics of Cultural Despair: A Study in the Rise of the Germanic Ideology* (Berkeley: University of California Press, 1974).

7. Robert Bellah et al., *Habits of the Heart: Individualism and Commitment in American Life* (Berkeley: University of California Press, 1985, 2008).
8. John Brueggemann, *Rich, Free, and Miserable: The Failure of Success in America* (Lanham, MD: Rowman & Littlefield, 2010).
9. I have presented some evidence in Glen H. Stassen, D. M. Yeager, and John Howard Yoder, *Authentic Transformation: A New Vision of Christ and Culture* (Nashville: Abingdon, 1996). Since then, the evidence that points in the same direction has grown extensively. One example is the three studies of 80,000 members and two follow-up publications by the Willow Creek Association: Greg L. Hawkins and Cally Parkinson, *Reveal: Where Are You?*; *Follow Me: What's Next for You?*; *Focus: The Top Ten Things People Want and Need from You and Your Church* (Barrington, IL: Willow Creek Association, 2007, 2008, 2009).
10. Alasdair MacIntyre, *After Virtue*, 2d ed. (Notre Dame, IN: University of Notre Dame Press, 1984), 222.
11. Michael Walzer, *Thick and Thin: Moral Argument at Home and Abroad* (Notre Dame, IN: University of Notre Dame Press, 1994), chap. 5.
12. So Nancey Murphy writes, "My favorite books are all narrative accounts that help to place modern philosophy in historical perspective," in *Dialog* 46, no. 3 (Fall 2007): 306.
13. Glen Stassen and David Gushee, *Kingdom Ethics: Following Jesus in Contemporary Context* (Downers Grove, IL: InterVarsity, 2003), chap. 3, and the previous articles noted there.
14. Bruce McCormack, *Karl Barth's Critically Realistic Dialectical Theology* (Oxford: Clarendon, 1997), 111, 113, quoting Barth to Martin Rade, Aug. 31, 1914, *Offene Briefe*, 96.
15. Bonhoeffer, *Ethics* (Minneapolis: Fortress, 2005), 77–80.
16. H. Frankfort and H. A. Frankfort, *Before Philosophy* (Hammondsworth, Middlesex: Penguin, 1959), 237, cf. 247.
17. John Howard Yoder, *The War of the Lamb: The Ethics of Nonviolence and Peacemaking* (Grand Rapids: Brazos, 2009), 54–65 and section 3.
18. Frankfort and Frankfort, *Before Philosophy*, 245.
19. Ibid., 251.
20. James Wm. McClendon Jr., *Biography as Theology: How Life Stories Can Remake Today's Theology* (1974; repr., Philadelphia: Trinity Press International, 1990); "Three Strands of Christian Ethics," in *Journal of Religious Ethics* 6 (Spring 1978): 54–80; *Ethics: Systematic Theology 1* (1986; repr., Nashville: Abingdon, 2002).
21. *Biography as Theology*, 63–64.
22. Ibid., 65.
23. Ibid., 15. I prefer to call character ethics the ethics of character-in-community. McClendon sought to write accurate and realistic history, not narrative as fiction or autobiography as self-deception: "Autobiography runs an extreme risk of self-deception. . . . Augustine would teach us, if Freud did not, how many and how 'scientific' are the devices by which we protect ourselves from unwelcome reality." Accuracy and realism matter: "This result could in principle be overturned by showing that the biographical studies I have undertaken are misconceived or misconducted—that they do not in fact fairly represent the lives examined. I have attempted to correct the interpretations others have offered of my chosen saints; still others may in turn correct mine; such ongoing hagiographic revision is a part of the ongoing task of biographic theology." Ibid., 67–68; cf. also p. vi.
24. Ibid., 87.

25. Ibid., 159.

26. I profoundly appreciate Frank Tupper's study of the meaning of God's providence, based not in theoretical speculation but in a historical drama approach to Jesus' own struggle with the powers and authorities of his time. Hence Tupper's title, *Scandalous Providence: The Jesus Story of the Compassion of God* (Macon, GA: Mercer University Press, 1995). He explains that he intends to write not only "story" but specifically "the genre of dramatic history" and cites the literary analysis of Roland Frye (pp. 22 and 88). He also includes moving historical accounts of events such as the bombing of Vietnam, Cambodia, Hiroshima, and Nagasaki (pp. 145–51). I would tell of that bombing somewhat differently, but that is the virtue of historical drama, or dramatic history, as McClendon also says: "others can attempt to correct the account for its accuracy and its portrayal of the context of meaning."

27. Let the reader be forewarned: Adopting the method of historical drama means that I do not usually write didactically, first announcing what I think is the right answer and then seeking to convince you of it. I am more likely to identify a problem or a challenge and then wrestle with finding an adequate response. If you the reader experience some suspense in the process, then that may invite you to participate actively in the wrestle, searching for your own way of answering it. Hence it may become more of a shared community effort, and it may be more open to your own creative contributions.

28. As George Lindbeck writes, "It is a communal phenomenon that shapes the subjectivities of individuals rather than being primarily a manifestation of those subjectivities." Lindbeck, *The Nature of Doctrine: Religion and Theology in a Postliberal Age* (Louisville, KY: Westminster John Knox Press, 1984), 33. I do not mean to suggest that the text creates only its own world, as Lindbeck might suggest; hence my reference to "basis in real history."

29. As J. Kameron Carter writes, quoting Albert Raboteau, "history locates the citizenry within 'the nation's history,' within 'the national drama.' . . . 'History functions as a form of self-definition. In its pages . . . we read ourselves *dramatically*, as participants in a drama.'" Carter, *Race: A Theological Account* (New York: Oxford, 2008), 145.

30. As Cornel West writes, "Toni Morrison revises and revises so the book can be aural, so that the audience can participate with a spoken story." West, *Democracy Matters* (New York: Penguin, 2004), 99.

31. Rollin Grams, "Three Rival Versions of Theological Inquiry: Modernist, Deconstructive, and Tradition," manuscript draft (July 13, 2004), 35.

32. Richard Bauckham, *Bible and Mission: Christian Witness in a Postmodern World* (Grand Rapids: Baker, 2004), as summarized in Grams, "Three Rival Versions," 40.

33. Richard B. Hays, *The Moral Vision of the New Testament* (San Francisco: HarperSanFrancisco, 1996), chap. 13.

34. In memorable personal conversation in Sjøoviks, Sweden, and Heidelberg, Germany, in the spring of 1982.

35. Allen Verhey, *Remembering Jesus: Christian Community, Scripture, and the Moral Life* (Grand Rapids: Eerdmans, 2002), 120. The apostle Paul has learned "that his story as minister of the gospel must be told and lived as a performance of the story of Jesus' suffering."

36. I am not focusing on the more controversial question of Bonhoeffer's late desperate participation in an attempted coup against Hitler, but rather on the rightness of what almost all of us by now are clear about—seeing Hitler's evil and speaking out publicly, from the start. I will say something about that other question in a later chapter.

37. Charles Marsh, *The Beloved Community: How Faith Shapes Social Justice, from the Civil Rights Movement to Today* (New York: Basic Books, 2005).
38. Bonhoeffer, *Ethics,* ed. Clifford J. Green, trans. Reinhard Krauss, Douglas W. Stott, and Charles C. West, DBWE 6 (Minneapolis: Fortress, 2005), 88–90.
39. Yoder, *War of the Lamb,* 7–8, and chaps. 3 and 13.
40. "A view which criticizes what has come into being in the course of history, on the grounds of criteria which themselves are also drawn from within the course of history, is thereby obliged to be concerned with historical data in a way different from those traditions which claim each in its own way to be the 'mainstream,'" thus claiming that whatever developed within the mainstream of (their own) history is ipso facto the truth. John Howard Yoder, *Priestly Kingdom: Social Ethics as Gospel* (Notre Dame, IN: University of Notre Dame Press: 1984), 127.
41. Charles Kimball, *When Religion Becomes Evil* (San Francisco: HarperSanFrancisco, 2002), and idem, *When Religion Becomes Lethal* (San Francisco: Jossey-Bass, 2011).
42. See Susan Thistlethwaite, ed., *Interfaith Just Peacemaking* (New York: Palgrave McMillan, 2012), which emerged from a several-year project between the Just Peacemaking Initiative of Fuller Theological Seminary and the Salaam Institute of American University, combined with Susan Thistlethwaite's leadership at Chicago Theological Seminary. I commend Veli-Matti Kärkkäinen, *Christ and Reconciliation: A Constructive Christian Theology for the Pluralistic World* (Grand Rapids: Eerdmans, 2012).

Chapter 2: The Three Dimensions of Incarnational Discipleship

1. The background of the Barmen Declaration, and the declaration itself, may be read in Arthur C. Cochrane, *The Church's Confession under Hitler* (Philadelphia: Westminster, 1962). Hereafter cited as Cochrane.
2. After being ousted from his teaching post, Barth moved to Basel to continue his teaching and writing, and from there he continued to lead opposition to Hitler's injustices, violence, war-making, and takeover of German churches. Like the Barmen Declaration itself, Barth's theology was absolutely Christ-centered. It could not be clearer that he advocated the Lordship of Christ over all of life rather than only over an inner realm. Furthermore, he led a dramatic revolt in Christian theology that repented for conforming theology to some extra-ecclesial source such as nationalism, economic ideology, or a particular philosophy. He surely fits the dimensions of incarnational discipleship. Questions have been raised about whether the Christ-centeredness of his theology paid sufficient attention to Jesus of Nazareth in Jesus' own historical context, whether he was "Christomonist," whether he reacted too strongly against use of philosophical contributions to theology. But there is no question about his leadership of resistance against Hitler, his Christ-centeredness, his opposition to a two-realms dualism that would limit the scope of Christ's Lordship, and his refusal to accommodate Christ to the culture. Barth deserves far more analysis and attention than I can provide here, but I hope to do more in a companion book that also studies the theological ethics of André Trocmé, Christopher Marshall, and their followers.
3. Barmen Declaration, article 1; Cochrane, 239.
4. Ernst Käsemann, "The Problem of the Historical Jesus," in *Essays on New Testament Themes,* Studies in Biblical Theology 41 (London: SCM, 1964), 15–47.

5. David Gushee, *The Sacredness of Human Life* (Grand Rapids: Eerdmans, 2013).
6. Barmen Declaration, article 2; Cochrane, 240.
7. W. A. Visser 't Hooft, *The Kingship of Christ: An Interpretation of Recent European Theology*, The Stone Lectures for 1947, Princeton Theological Seminary (New York: Harper & Brothers, 1948), 24–25.
8. Ibid., 45.
9. Ibid., 49–50, 53–59, 62.
10. Barmen Declaration, Introductory Appeal; Cochrane, 237.
11. Barmen, article 3; Cochrane, 240–41.
12. Roger Stronstad, *The Charismatic Theology of St. Luke* (Peabody, MA: Hendrickson, 2002), 26–27, 30–39. The Holy Spirit has far more extensive importance in Christian ethics beyond what I can spell out here. I commend a classic essay by my teacher and mentor, Henlee Barnette, "The Significance of the Holy Spirit for Christian Morality," *Review & Expositor* 51, no. 1 (January 1955): 5–20.
13. John Howard Yoder, *For the Nations: Essays Public and Evangelical* (Grand Rapids: Eerdmans, 1997), 2–5; idem, *Priestly Kingdom: Social Ethics as Gospel* (Notre Dame, IN: University of Notre Dame Press, 1984), 61–62.
14. Sabina Dramm, *Dietrich Bonhoeffer and the Resistance* (Minneapolis: Fortress, 2009), chap. 3.
15. H. E. Tödt, "Discrimination against Jews in 1933—The Real Test for Bonhoeffer's Ethics," chap. 6 in H. E. Tödt, *Authentic Faith: Bonhoeffer's Ethics in Context*, trans. David C. Stassen (Grand Rapids: Eerdmans, 2007), 73.
16. *Karl Barth: Letters 1961–1968*, ed. and trans. Geoffrey W. Bromiley (Grand Rapids: Eerdmans, 1981), 250–52.
17. Reggie Williams, "Christ-Centered Empathic Resistance: The Influence of Harlem Renaissance Theology on the Incarnational Ethics of Dietrich Bonhoeffer" (PhD dissertation, Fuller Theological Seminary, 2011).
18. Dietrich Bonhoeffer, *Discipleship*, DBWE 4.
19. Dietrich Bonhoeffer, *Ethics*, DBWE 6, 47–75, 388–93.
20. Robert P. Ericksen, *Theologians under Hitler: Gerhard Kittel, Paul Althaus, and Emanuel Hirsch* (New Haven, CT, and London: Yale University Press, 1985); Wolfgang Huber and Heinz Eduard Tödt, *Menschenrechte: Perspektiven einer Menschlichen Welt*, 3rd ed. (Munich: Kaiser, 1988), 45–54, 124–30.
21. Bonhoeffer, *Discipleship*, DBWE 4, 225–35.
22. Reggie Williams, *Christ-Centered Empathic Resistance: The Influence of Harlem Renaissance Theology on the Incarnational Ethics of Dietrich Bonhoeffer*, forthcoming.
23. David Gushee, *Righteous Gentiles of the Holocaust: Genocide and Moral Obligation*, 2nd ed. (St. Paul: Paragon House, 2003), 164.
24. J. Kameron Carter, *Race: A Theological Account* (New York: Oxford, 2008), 4.
25. Carter, *Race*, 108, 115, and 117.
26. An official offered Trocmé two thousand francs as an annual subvention if he would collaborate with the employers and not obey the communist party. He refused, red with anger. "My parishioners were not, however, communists. They were socialists, friends of the mayor of Sin-le-Noble, named Foucault, who was very popular." He and Foucault were friends during all his six years there. "In 1929, the economic crisis as a consequence of the American depression fell on the land of the coal miners, causing unemployment, starvation salaries, and very

severe strikes. I could do no other than to be in close solidarity with my parishioners." André-Pascal Trocmé, *Une Autobiographie* (n.p., n.d.), 184.

27. André-Pascal Trocmé, *Jesus and the Nonviolent Revolution* (Scottdale, PA: Herald, 1973). A revised and expanded edition has now been published by Orbis (2003).
28. Ibid., 158, and passim.
29. Ibid., 125–26, 131, and chap. 12.
30. Ibid., 139.
31. André-Pascal Trocmé, "Extraits des Souvenirs d'Enfance et de Guerre" (Trocmé archive, Swarthmore College, n.p., n.d.). This is my translation here and in Trocmé's other French documents.
32. Trocmé, *Autobiographie*, 58–60, 86. Trocmé, "Extraits des Souvenirs d'Enfance," 23–24.
33. Trocmé, "Does a Danger of Fascism Exist in France?" (Swarthmore archive: 1958), 4.
34. See Glen Stassen, *Living the Sermon on the Mount* (San Francisco: Jossey-Bass, 2006), 56–57, on the meaning of Jesus' beatitude, "joyful are those who seek God's will in all that they are and do," which is the holistic biblical meaning of "those who are pure in heart," as opposed to the Platonic dualism that splits inner self from outer action.
35. Trocmé, *Jesus and the Nonviolent Revolution*, 159; and see especially p. 152.
36. Ibid., 167.
37. André Trocmé, *The Politics of Repentance* (New York: Fellowship Publications, 1953).
38. Gushee, *Righteous Gentiles of the Holocaust*, 151, 172–85.
39. Ibid., 152.
40. Ibid., 152, 155–56.
41. Ibid., 152–53.
42. Ibid., 132–37.
43. Ibid., 139–42.
44. Ibid., 140–43.
45. Tödt and Huber, *Menschenrechte*, 45–54, 124–30; Esther D. Reed, *The Ethics of Human Rights: Contested Doctrinal and Moral Issues* (Waco, TX: Baylor University Press, 2007), 70–78; Bonhoeffer, *Ethics*, 125n, 171–218; Glen Stassen, "Human Rights," in *Global Dictionary of Theology* (Downers Grove, IL: InterVarsity, 2008), 405–14; and idem, "The Christian Origin of Human Rights," in *Just Peacemaking: Transforming Initiatives for Justice and Peace*, ed. Glen Stassen (Louisville, KY: Westminster/John Knox, 1992).
46. John Howard Yoder, *Priestly Kingdom*, 61–62.
47. Yoder, *For the Nations*, 2, 53, 71.
48. Gushee, *Righteous Gentiles of the Holocaust*, 143.
49. Martin Luther King Jr., "Pilgrimage to Nonviolence," in *Strength to Love* (1963; repr., Philadelphia: Fortress, 1983), 150–52.
50. Martin Luther King Jr. and Clayborne Carson, *The Autobiography of Martin Luther King, Jr.* (New York: Warner Books, 1998), 84.
51. Martin Luther King Jr., *Where Do We Go from Here?* (1967; repr., Boston: Beacon, 1968).
52. See the enormously insightful *The Great World House: Martin Luther King, Jr. and Global Ethics* by Hak Joon Lee (Cleveland: Pilgrim, 2011).
53. James Melvin Washington, ed., *A Testament of Hope: The Essential Writings and Speeches of Martin Luther King, Jr.* (New York: HarperSanFrancisco, 1986), 232–33.

54. Ibid., 234.
55. King, "A Testament of Hope," as quoted in Hak Joon Lee, *The Great World House*, 187.
56. G. McLeod Bryan, *Voices in the Wilderness: Twentieth-Century Prophets Speak to the New Millennium* (Macon, GA: Mercer University Press, 1999); Ann Louise Coble, *Cotton Patch for the Kingdom: Clarence Jordan's Demonstration Plot at Koinonia Farm* (Scottdale, PA: Herald, 2002); Dallas Lee, *Cotton Patch Evidence* (New York: Harper & Row, 1971); Charles Marsh, *The Beloved Community: How Faith Shapes Social Justice, from the Civil Rights Movement to Today* (New York: Basic Books, 2005); James Wm. McClendon Jr., *Biography as Theology: How Life Stories Can Remake Today's Theology* (1974; repr., Philadelphia: Trinity Press International, 1990); Glen Stassen, *Living the Sermon on the Mount*, 55–57, et passim; William Tillman, *Baptist Prophets: Their Lives and Contribution* (Brentwood, TN: Baptist History and Heritage Society, 2006).
57. Clarence Jordan, *Sermon on the Mount* (1952, 1970; repr., Valley Forge, PA: Judson, 1993), 5.
58. Jörg Swoboda, *Die Revolution der Kerzen: Christen in den Umwälzungen der DDR* (Wuppertal und Kassel: Oncken Verlag, 1990), 5; my translation.
59. John Burgess, *The East German Church and the End of Communism* (New York: Oxford University Press, 1997), vii. I wrote about the Revolution of the Candles in "A Visit to East German Churches: Schooling for Democracy," *The Christian Century*, December 20–27, 1989, and in my *Just Peacemaking: Transforming Initiatives for Justice and Peace* (Louisville, KY: Westminster/ John Knox, 1992). Burgess focuses especially on theologians Heino Falcke, Wolfgang Ullmann, Richard Schröder, Wolf Krötke, and the movement *Aktion Sühnezeichen*. My own experience and reading focused more on Volkmar Deile and Andreas Zumach of *Aktion Sühnezeichen*, some Free Church leaders, and Bishop Albrecht Schönherr and Johannes Hamel from the generation that made the space for the movement to happen.
60. Burgess, *East German Church*, 64–65.
61. Ibid., 65; my translation of *stellvertredendes Handeln*.
62. The German word for "preservation" of creation is "*Bewahrung*," which connotes "defense" or "preservation." The East German mining industry was destroying the rivers, the air, and the earth wherever coal could be mined, as well as destroying many workers who ingested the pollution—especially in Bitterfeld, in my experience. I think a stronger translation is needed than the words usually used in English, the passive "integrity of creation." The church movement was *defending* creation, working to *preserve* it.
63. Burgess, *East German Church*, 62.
64. Ibid., 27–28.
65. Ibid., 64.
66. Michael O. Garvey, in Dorothy Day, *On Pilgrimage* (Grand Rapids: Eerdmans; and Edinburgh: T. & T. Clark, 1999), 21–22.
67. Dorothy Day, *Selected Writings* (Maryknoll, NY: Orbis, 1992), 69, 254, 261–62, et passim; Garvey, in Day, *On Pilgrimage*, 48.
68. Garvey, in Day, *On Pilgrimage*, 34.
69. Day, *Selected Writings*, 87, 88, 97–98, 114, 131, 170–71, 197, 198, 200–201, 265, 273, 277. "But the final word is love," 363.
70. Ibid., 94–95.
71. Ibid., 91, 240–44, 250, 253–57, 264, 280–93, 300, et passim.
72. Ibid., 262.

73. Ibid., 93. Note that the $995 figure is in 1940 dollars.
74. Ibid., 157. This was 1942: $17 billion for a defensive war, widely supported. Today the military budget is not $17 billion, or even $100 billion, but approximately $1,000 billion, including the cost of two wars that were initiated by the U.S. government in Afghanistan and Iraq. And with the Great Recession that began in 2008 and is only slowly lifting as I write in 2011, those politicians under whose policies the Great Recession began are now clamoring against the deficit, but saying taxes cannot be restored to previous levels and the military budget cannot be cut. The mathematical result is advocacy of cutting money for schools and education and programs for the people; the military budget and restoring taxes to the Clinton levels are "off the table." Yet the military budget is now so large it is the majority of the part of the budget that is "discretionary," the part that could be cut, as opposed to "entitlements" like Social Security.

Mathematically it would require cutting many teachers; unemployment payments; job stimulus programs; Pell Grants and college loans; Food Stamps and programs for the poor; and none of this would come close to plugging the hole in the budget.

Furthermore, military spending produces far fewer jobs than education, environmental technology, and rebuilding bridges, because one soldier in Afghanistan costs about $1 million per year. One teacher costs only about $50,000 per year. Therefore, $1 billion pays for one thousand soldiers in Afghanistan, but would provide jobs for about 20,000 teachers or construction workers. See www.NationalPriorities.org. What would Dorothy Day say today? Might she be wearing a yellow wristband from Sojourners saying "What Would Jesus Cut"?
75. Ibid., 11–12.
76. Ibid., 181.
77. Ibid., 81.
78. Ibid.
79. We may read an insightful account of her work for the poor in England and her work for peacemaking and leadership of the International Fellowship of Reconciliation in Paul Dekar, For the Healing of the Nations: Baptist Peacemakers (Macon, GA: Smyth & Helwys, 1993). Richard Deats has published Ambassador of Reconciliation: A Muriel Lester Reader (Philadelphia: New Society, 1991).
80. Eileen Eagan, Foreword to Ambassador of Reconciliation: A Muriel Lester Reader, ed. Richard Deats (Philadelphia: New Society, 1991), vii.
81. Eagan, Ambassador of Reconciliation, 21.
82. Ibid., 22–24.
83. Ambassador of Reconciliation, 22–23.

Chapter 3: Incarnational Discipleship Needs to Resolve the Tension from Platonic Idealism

1. Plato, The Republic, book 7.
2. Neil Postman and Andrew Postman, Amusing Ourselves to Death (New York: Penguin, 2005).
3. Bonhoeffer, Ethics, DBWE 6, 259.
4. Ibid., 49; see 47–62.
5. Ibid., 253.
6. Ibid., 252; cf. 56–57, 230, and 251–53.

7. Ibid., 246–47 and 259; my modified translation. I argue that Bonhoeffer's key term, *Stellvertretung*, should be translated with this incarnational theme of entering incarnationally into the place (*an der Stelle treten*) of the other person, as well as standing up for or representing that person. So here the German says, "he lives only as the one who has taken on and bears the selfhood of all humans . . . only in the full devotion of one's own life to the other person. . . . Because he is life, through him all life is determined as for incarnational (or empathetic) responsibility" (ibid., 268).

8. Ibid., 83–84. This answers the criticism of Rainer Meier, *Christuswirklichkeit*, that Bonhoeffer's central focus on the incarnation establishes a monism that does not account for the evil in the world. The incarnation for Bonhoeffer is not a monism, but an event that incorporates good and evil, God and real history, in one reality. Meier's book has many important insights, but at this point seems still influenced by the long arm of Platonism, with its idealistic dualism between Christ and evil, or between God and the conflicts of life.

9. Bonhoeffer, *Ethics*, DBWE 6, 249–50 and 253. The reference to the poorest of our brothers and sisters refers to Matthew 25:40 and "is possibly an echo of the reference to the Jews in Bonhoeffer's confession of sin on behalf of the church" (editor's note by Clifford Green, *Ethics*, 253n).

10. Ibid., 259.

11. Dietrich Bonhoeffer, "Lectures on Christology," in *Berlin 1932–1933*, ed. Larry L. Rasmussen, trans. Isabel Best and David Higgins, DBWE 12 (Minneapolis: Fortress, 2009), 309.

12. Ibid., 104.

13. H. Frankfort and H. A. Frankfort, *Before Philosophy* (Hammondsworth, Middlesex: Penguin, 1959), 237–47 et passim.

14. Bonhoeffer, *Ethics*, 105; and see editor Clifford Green's note, 105n.

15. Bonhoeffer, *Ethics*, 106–7.

Chapter 4: Can Incarnational Discipleship Answer Secularism's Challenges to Christian Faith?

1. Charles Taylor, *A Secular Age* (Cambridge, MA: Harvard University Press, 2007).

2. Nancey Murphy, *Theology in the Age of Scientific Reasoning* (Ithaca, NY, and London: Cornell University Press, 1990). Parenthetical page numbers in this chapter's text refer to this book.

3. Nancey Murphy, "Using MacIntyre's Method in Christian Ethics," in Nancey Murphy, Brad Kallenberg, and Mark Thiessen Nation, eds., *Virtues and Practices in the Christian Tradition* (Harrisburg, PA: Trinity Press International, 1997), 31–32.

4. Ibid., 32–33.

5. Jeffrey Stout, *Democracy and Tradition* (Princeton: Princeton University Press, 2004), 123. Charles Taylor argues similarly in *Sources of the Self* (Cambridge, MA: Harvard University Press, 1989), 515.

6. For example, Jon P. Gunnemann, "Habermas and MacIntyre on Moral Learning," *Annual of the Society of Christian Ethics* (1994): 83–108.

7. Alasdair MacIntyre, *Whose Justice? Which Rationality?* (Notre Dame, IN: University of Notre Dame Press, 1988), 394–95.

8. Ibid., 398; and Alasdair MacIntyre, "Moral Relativism, Truth, and Justification," in *The MacIntyre Reader*, ed. Kelvin Knight (Notre Dame, IN: University of Notre Dame Press, 1998), 218.

9. MacIntyre, "Moral Relativism," 219–20.
10. Collin May, *Society* 64, no. 2 (March 2009): 199–203.
11. Taylor, *Secular Age*, 11.
12. Ibid., 2–3.
13. They interweave as part of Taylor's 800-page historical account, and are not numbered or singled out explicitly; others could identify them somewhat differently.
14. Taylor, *Secular Age*, 196 and 207.
15. Ibid., 208. Johannes Althusius (1557–1638) was an important transitional figure between the Reformation and modernity who, as a Reformed Christian, offered a secular basis of the sovereignty of people and democracy, and federalism.
16. Ibid., 126–27.
17. Ibid., 5, 137, 157, 181–83, 244, 300.
18. Ibid., 157, 183.
19. Ibid., 635, 639.
20. Ibid., 78–79.
21. Ibid., 378.
22. Ibid., 81, 275–80, 305, 640.
23. Ibid., 159, 214–18, 657–60, 707–10.
24. If I were not seeking to respond to the challenges as Taylor identifies them, but engaging his diagnoses critically, I would add three other challenges. First, Taylor subsumes the conservative wish for order under authoritarian "reform" and "rage for order." Is there an appropriate wish for order that does not degenerate into authoritarianism? Second, feminism challenges the Catholic hierarchy's and fundamentalist Protestantism's teaching against the role of women as priests, partly caused by the Platonic split between mind and body. This drives some women and their male advocates toward secularism if they do not find churches that affirm their gifts. And third, Taylor's limiting his scope to "Latin Christianity" is understandable since his book is already 800 pages long. But we should take into consideration the way that colonialism failed to learn from colonized people (See, for example, Willie Jennings, *Christian Imagination: Theology and the Origins of Race* (New Haven, CT: Yale University Press, 2010).

Chapter 5: Democracy

1. Charles Taylor, *A Secular Age* (Cambridge, MA: Harvard University Press, 2007), 196 and 207; Charles Taylor, *Sources of the Self* (Cambridge, MA: Harvard University Press, 1989), 11, 13. On a historical note, Civil War began in England in 1642, and in 1646 Oliver Cromwell rose to power and instituted democratic rule. However, the Restoration of 1660 restored the monarchy and a state church, and the Great Rejection of Puritan pastors from their parish charges came two years later. The Glorious Revolution in 1688 brought the establishment of the Anglican Church in league with the government—a monarchy combined with a parliament. Smaller groups of disestablished dissenting churches continued independently.
2. Taylor, *Secular Age*, 196 and 207.
3. Stanley Hauerwas, "A Story-Formed Community: Reflections on *Watership Down*," in *The Hauerwas Reader*, ed. John Berkman and Michael Cartwright (Durham, NC: Duke University Press, 2001), 171–99; originally in Stanley Hauerwas, *A Community of Character: Toward a Constructive Christian Social*

Ethic (Notre Dame, IN: University of Notre Dame Press, 1981), chap. 1. Richard Adams, *Watership Down*, (New York: Avon Books, 1972).

4. Stanley Hauerwas and Romand Coles, *Christianity, Democracy, and the Radical Ordinary* (Eugene, OR: Cascade, 2007).

5. Hauerwas, *Community of Character*, 76.

6. Alexander Kirby, John Rothmann, and David Dalin, *Harold E. Stassen: The Life and Perennial Candidacy of the Progressive Republican* (Jefferson, NC: MacFarland Press, 2012).

7. Hauerwas, *Community of Character*, 76.

8. John Howard Yoder, *The Priestly Kingdom: Social Ethics as Gospel* (Notre Dame, IN: University of Notre Dame Press, 1984), 181.

9. Hauerwas, *Community of Character*, 74. Hauerwas is developing a possible advocacy of engagement in local political struggles in his book with Romand Coles, *Christianity, Democracy, and the Radical Ordinary*. There he says he is "halfway persuaded." I simply add that local advocacy often requires a change in national policies. The civil rights movement, the Nuclear Weapons Freeze Campaign, and the Revolution of the Candles in East Germany took a little more organizing effort than "halfway." It also deepened church engagement for many of us, because we worked to help churches become faithful to God's will and experienced breakthroughs of God's grace.

10. Hauerwas, *Community of Character*, 85.

11. Jeffrey Stout, *Democracy and Tradition* (Princeton: Princeton University Press, 2004), 3.

12. Ibid., 4–6.

13. Ibid., 11 and 13. Italics in the original.

14. Ibid., 10–11.

15. Ibid., 19, 204–5, 300.

16. Stanley Hauerwas and William Willimon, *Resident Aliens* (Nashville: Abingdon, 1989), 30–36; and Hauerwas, *Against the Nations: War and Survival in a Liberal Society* (Minneapolis: Winston, 1985); *After Christendom? How the Church Is to Behave If Freedom, Justice, and a Christian Nation are Bad Ideas* (Nashville: Abingdon, 1999); *Dispatches from the Front: Theological Engagements with the Secular* (Durham: Duke University, 1994). We need to make allowance for rhetorical excess, but that would reduce the irony. Contrast John H. Yoder, *For the Nations: Essays Public and Evangelical* (Grand Rapids: Eerdmans, 1987), 3–8, where Yoder rejects Hauerwas's advocacy of sectarian dualism; and see Glen H. Stassen, "Introduction: Jesus Is No Sectarian: John H. Yoder's Christological Peacemaking Ethic," in John H. Yoder, *The War of the Lamb: The Ethics of Nonviolence and Peacemaking* (Grand Rapids: Brazos, 2009), 11–15. Churches deeply need Yoder's recovery of the way of Jesus. Those who rightly or wrongly oppose "sectarianism" in Hauerwas engage in irresponsible and self-destructive stereotyping if they then distort Yoder with the same prejudice. Yoder wrote a half dozen books distancing himself from this stereotype. My concern is to free Yoder from historical prejudice and being identified with and subsumed under Hauerwas, and to persuade people to learn from him, not to provide definitive interpretation of Hauerwas.

17. Cornel West, *Democracy Matters: Winning the Fight against Imperialism* (New York: Penguin, 2004), 16–23, 149–55, et passim.

18. Esther Reed, *The Ethics of Human Rights: Contested Doctrinal and Moral Issues* (Waco, TX: Baylor University, 2007); Christopher Marshall, *Crowned with Glory and Honor: Human Rights in the Biblical Tradition* (Scottdale, PA: Herald, 2011); David Hollenbach, *Claims in Conflict: Retrieving and Renewing the*

Catholic Human Rights Tradition (New York: Paulist, 1979); Nicholas Wolterstorff, *Justice: Rights and Wrongs* (Princeton: Princeton University Press, 2008).

19. Michael Walzer, *The Revolution of the Saints: A Study in the Origins of Radical Politics* (Cambridge, MA: Harvard University Press, 1965), viii–ix.

20. Ibid., 3, 12–13, and 147; on the right and obligation of *participation*, cf. 18 and 28.

21. Ibid., 2.

22. Ibid., 177 and 180.

23. Ibid., 317–18.

24. Ibid., 302.

25. Taylor, *Secular Age*, 106; cf. 81, 87, 104–7, 156, 242–43, 305.

26. Ibid., 301.

27. Walzer, *Revolution of the Saints*, vii–viii and 21.

28. Nashville: Abingdon, 2002, 1994, and 2000, respectively. (*Ethics* is in its second edition; hence the date is 2002.)

29. For just two examples, the two authoritative confessions of the Particular Baptists were the First and Second London Confessions; see William L. Lumpkin, *Baptist Confessions of Faith* (Valley Forge: Judson Press, 2011). The first was mostly a verbatim copy of the Calvinistic True Confession, and the second was mostly a verbatim copy of the Westminster Confession. A careful comparison of the changes shows the Baptists systematically making the confessions more Christ-centered and also rejecting any role for government in imposing beliefs on churches. They affirmed others' confessions so extensively because they recognized other churches as Christian churches, even with some important differences. They wrote in their preamble to the First London Confession, "we have no itch to clog religion with new words." Historian David Weir, *Early New England: A Covenanted Society* (Grand Rapids: Eerdmans, 2005), notes that the Swansea Covenant speaks of "Christ" eleven times, plus "God's Son," "our Lord," "Lord and Saviour," "Dear Redeemer," "his holy Name," an additional five times, and "Him" several times, in only forty-four lines. It is significantly more Christ-centered than other covenants, which fits the experience as a believer of being baptized by immersion into the death, burial, and resurrection of Jesus Christ (186–87).

30. Glen Stassen, "Revisioning Baptist Identity By Naming Our Origin and Character Rightly," *Baptist History and Heritage* 33, no. 2 (Spring 1998): 34–54.

31. William Lee Miller, *The First Liberty: Religion and the American Republic* (New York: Paragon, 1985).

32. Taylor, *Secular Age*, 425.

33. Overton, *An Appeal to the Free People* (London: July 17, 1647), reprinted in D. M. Wolfe, *Leveller Manifestoes of the Puritan Revolution* (New York: T. Nelson & Sons, 1944), 154ff. See Richard Tuck, *Natural Rights Theories: Their Origin and Development* (Cambridge: Cambridge University Press, 1981), 147–50; William Haller, *Tracts on Liberty in the Puritan Revolution, 1638–1647*, vol. 1 (New York: Columbia University Press, 1933), 111; Glen Stassen, "The Christian Origin of Human Rights," in Glen Stassen, *Just Peacemaking: Transforming Initiatives for Justice and Peace* (Louisville: Westminster/John Knox, 1992), 137–63; Michael Westmoreland White, "Setting the Record Straight: Christian Faith, Human Rights, and the Enlightenment," *Annual of the Society of Christian Ethics* (1995): 75–96. Nicholas Wolterstorff, *Justice: Rights and Wrongs*, chap. 2, traces the concept of natural rights to the medieval decretists in the twelfth century, and then back to John Chrysostom,

and behind him, to biblical teachings. I am writing of the *first comprehensive doctrine* of human rights. We are both saying human rights preceded the Enlightenment and developed on biblical and faithful Christian grounds. Our arguments work in tandem.

34. See David Gushee, *Sacredness of Human Life* (Grand Rapids: Eerdmans, 2013).

35. Wolterstorff, *Justice*, vii–ix.

36. John Howard Yoder, *Priestly Kingdom*, 56, 59–62.

37. John Howard Yoder, in Glen H. Stassen, D. M. Yeager, and John Howard Yoder, *Authentic Transformation: A New Vision of Christ and Culture* (Nashville: Abingdon, 1996), 54–57, 66–72, 86–89; John Howard Yoder, *For the Nations: Essays Public and Evangelical* (Grand Rapids: Eerdmans, 1997), 1–5.

38. Yoder, *Priestly Kingdom*, 61–62.

39. Ibid., chap. 9. The following quotations and comments come from pp. 158–60 and 166–68.

40. Ibid., 168.

41. John Howard Yoder, "Meaning after Babble: With Jeffrey Stout beyond Relativism," *Journal of Religious Ethics* 24, no. 1 (Spring 1996): 135n.

42. Ernst Troeltsch, *Social Teaching of the Christian Churches* (1931; repr., New York: Harper & Brothers, 1960). For a brief but incisive criticism of Troeltsch and H. Richard Niebuhr, see Duane Friesen, "A Discriminating Engagement of Culture: 'An Anabaptist Perspective,'" *Journal of Religious Ethics* 23, no. 1 (Spring/Summer 2003): 145–56.

43. Ernst Troeltsch, *The Social Teaching of the Christian Churches*, vol. 2 (New York: Harper Torchbooks, 1960), 656–90.

44. James Hastings Nichols, *Democracy and the Churches* (Philadelphia: Westminster, 1951), 10.

45. Stackhouse, *Creeds, Society, and Human Rights*, 56–58.

46. Ibid., 19.

47. Ibid., 23–24. Nichols points out that the Calvinists did not invent their system. Their fundamental ideas for representative church government came from the conciliar thinkers of the late Middle Ages.

48. David A. Weir, 221.

49. Ibid., 146–47, 151.

50. Ibid., 158–59, first quoting Burrage and then explaining the rationale.

51. James E. Bradley, *Religion, Revolution, and English Radicalism: Non-conformity in Eighteenth-Century Politics and Society* (Cambridge: Cambridge University Press, 1990), 134–35; cf. also 127, 129, 132. See also Bradley's "Religious Origins of Radical Politics in England, Scotland, and Ireland, 1662–1800," in *Religion and Politics in Enlightenment Europe*, ed. James E. Bradley and Dale K. Van Kley (Notre Dame, IN: University of Notre Dame Press, 2001), 187–253.

52. Bradley, *Religion, Revolution*, 28–29.

53. Ibid., 137–39.

54. Ibid., 140–45 and 150–52.

55. Ibid., 172.

56. Ibid., 169–70.

57. Ibid., 143.

58. Ibid., 182, 184, 186; cf. 136.

59. Ibid., 168, 175, 179.

60. Nichols, *Democracy and the Churches*, 31–35.

61. Gunnar Myrdal, *An American Dilemma: The Negro Problem and Modern Democracy* (1944; repr., New York: Harper & Row, 1962), 1.

62. Ibid., 4, 8.
63. Ibid., 9–10 and 12.
64. Ibid., xxii.
65. Ibid., xliv.
66. See, for example, the report of the National Oceanic and Atmospheric Administration as reported on Newshour.pbs, July 10, 2012. The previous report was available as of that date at http://www.ncdc.noaa.gov/oa/climate/globalwarming. The new report should be available soon.
67. David Kinnaman and Gabe Lyons, *Unchristian: What a New Generation Really Thinks about Christianity . . . and Why It Matters* (Grand Rapids: Baker, 2007); Mike Slaughter and Charles E. Gutenson, *Hijacked: Responding to the Partisan Church Divide* (Nashville: Abingdon, 2012).
68. William J. Wolf, *The Almost Chosen People* (Garden City, NY: Doubleday, 1959); or idem, *Lincoln's Religion* (Philadelphia: Pilgrim, 1970). See also Allen Guelzo, *Abraham Lincoln: Redeemer President* (Grand Rapids: Eerdmans, 1999).
69. http://showcase.netins.net/web/creative/lincoln/speeches/inaug2.htm (accessed December 17, 2011).
70. Paul Kendrick and Stephen Kendrick, *Douglass and Lincoln: How a Revolutionary Black Leader and a Reluctant Liberator Struggled to End Slavery and Save the Union* (New York: Walker, 2008).
71. Ibid., 18. Lincoln put those words in italics when he published his debate speech.
72. Ibid., 86.
73. Ibid., 181; cf. 3 and 246–47.
74. Ibid., 8.
75. James M. Washington, *A Testament of Hope: The Essential Writings and Speeches of Martin Luther King, Jr.* (San Francisco: HarperCollins, 1991), 217; italics added.
76. My colleague Hak Joon Lee has written profoundly of the theme of community in King's call for redeeming the soul of America, in his *We Will Get to the Promised Land: Martin Luther King, Jr.'s Communal-Political Spirituality* (Cleveland: Pilgrim Press, 2006), and his "To Save the Soul of America: Martin Luther King, Jr. and the Renewal of America," *Perspectives* 23, no. 3 (March 2008): 5–9.
77. Washington, *Testament of Hope*, 289–302.

Chapter 6: Science

1. The results are reported in the authoritative journal for physics research, in an unusually long and important article: J. W. Butler and C. R. Gossett, "Radiative Proton Capture by Ni^{58}, Ni^{60}, and Co^{59}, *Physical Review* 108, no. 6 (December 15, 1957), 1473–95. They were gracious enough to include a thank-you for my research. Subsequent articles reported on further results. You can probably sense my joy and gratitude—not merely about the thanks, but about the awe-giving experience.
2. Charles Taylor offers a fine exultation from Hofstadter, with a background in physics, on awe at the interaction in the smallest parts of matter. *Sources of the Self* (Cambridge, MA: Harvard University Press, 1989), 348.
3. This is an excerpt from the foundational and ancient talmudic prayer said every morning by religious Jews. Here is a link, with thanks to Rabbi Marc Gopin: http://cojs.org/cojswiki/The_Benedictions_Before_the_Morning_Shema:_Accepting_God_and_His_Commandments.

4. Charles Taylor, *A Secular Age* (Cambridge, MA: Harvard University Press, 2007), 98 and 221.

5. Ibid., 270.

6. Ibid.

7. Nancey Murphy, "Divine Action in the Natural Order: Buridan's Ass and Schrödinger's Cat," in *Chaos and Complexity: Scientific Perspectives on Divine Action*, ed. Robert John Russell, Nancey Murphy, and Arthur R. Peacocke (Notre Dame, IN: Notre Dame Press, 1995), 325.

8. Newton, *Principia Mathematica* (1687), as quoted in George Gamow, *The Great Physicists from Galileo to Einstein* (New York: Dover, 1961), 54.

9. Pierre-Simon de Laplace, *A Philosophical Essay on Probabilities*, translated from the 6th French edition by Frederick Wilson Truscott and Frederick Lincoln Emory (New York: Dover, 1951), 4.

10. Arthur R. Peacocke, "God's Interaction with the World: The Implications of Deterministic 'Chaos' and of Interconnected and Interdependent Complexity," in *Chaos and Complexity*, 266.

11. James Kakalos, *The Amazing Story of Quantum Mechanics* (London: Penguin, 2010), 95; cf. 79–82.

12. Steven S. Gubser, *The Little Book of String Theory* (Princeton: Princeton University Press, 2010), 103, 105, 109.

13. Robert John Russell, "Introduction," in *Chaos and Complexity*, 29.

14. Peter Hodgson, *Theology and Modern Physics* (Aldershot, England: Ashgate, 2005) argues for an intervention approach.

15. Murphy, "Divine Action in the Natural Order," 342n, 354–55, 356, 358, 360, 364–66.

16. Ibid., 333, 329.

17. Dietrich Bonhoeffer, *Letters and Papers from Prison*, DBWE 8, 405–6.

18. Peacocke, 279; see also Tracy, "Particular Providence and the God of the Gaps," in *Chaos and Complexity*, 292.

19. Murphy, "Divine Action in the Natural Order," 337.

20. Nancey Murphy and Warren S. Brown, *Did My Neurons Make Me Do It? Philosophical and Neurobiological Perspectives on Moral Responsibility and Free Will* (New York: Oxford, 2007); Murphy, *Bodies and Souls, or Spirited Bodies?* (New York: Cambridge, 2006).

21. Tracy, "Particular Providence," 304–10; esp. 304 and 310.

22. Murphy, "Divine Action in the Natural Order," 341.

23. Ibid., 341, 342, 343, and 354.

24. Ibid., 354.

25. Tracy, "Particular Providence," 319–20, 322n.

26. Stoeger, "Describing God's Action in the World in Light of Scientific Knowledge of Reality," in *Chaos and Complexity*, 245–46 and 258–59.

27. Murphy, "Divine Action in the Natural Order," 330, 342, and 352; cf. 345, 348, 349, 351, 355, 357. The same point is crucial in Nancey Murphy and George F. R. Ellis, *On the Moral Nature of the Universe* (Minneapolis: Fortress, 1996), 174–78, 212–14, et passim.

28. See Frank Tupper, *Scandalous Providence: The Jesus Story of the Compassion of God* (Macon, GA: Mercer University Press, 1995).

29. Glen H. Stassen, D. M. Yeager, and John Howard Yoder, *Authentic Transformation: A New Vision of Christ and Culture* (Nashville: Abingdon, 1996), 130–37.

30. Reggie Williams, "Christ-Centered Empathic Resistance: The Influence of Harlem Renaissance Theology on the Incarnational Ethics of Dietrich Bonhoeffer," (PhD diss., Fuller Theological Seminary, 2011).

31. Paul Alexander, *Signs and Wonders: Why Pentecostalism Is the World's Fastest-Growing Faith* (San Francisco: Jossey-Bass, 2009).
32. Ian Barbour, *Issues in Science and Religion* (Englewood Cliffs, NJ: Prentice-Hall, 1966), 47–48.
33. Alfred North Whitehead, *Adventures of Ideas* (Cambridge: Cambridge University Press, 1933), 129–30.
34. James S. Trefil, *Reading the Mind of God: In Search of the Principle of Universality* (New York: Scribner's, 1989), emphasizes the importance of expecting logical consistency for the development of science, but not the Hebraic influence or the freedom of God and therefore the need for empirical investigation. But he tells of reading thirteenth-century sources when he was studying at Oxford: "The real difference I saw in the old writings was the almost total lack of reference to observation or experiment. They followed the medieval Aristotelian ideal of using pure logic to arrive at conclusions . . . that were then held to be self-evident products of reason itself. Alternatively, they sought to solve problems by appeals to the authority contained within accepted writings and texts" (p. 33). He also makes a comment that fits my own experience: "Though it is hardly publicized, there is a streak of something close to mysticism in most theoretical physicists" (p. 108).
35. Eugene Kaaren, *Religious Origins of Modern Science* (Grand Rapids: Eerdmans, 1977), 138, 140, 144. Whitehead, *Adventures of Ideas*, 129–35, 154, 167–78, and Ian Barbour, chap. 4, write similarly. Whitehead: "The Platonic group of notions . . . are philosophic, and in the narrow sense are not scientific. They suggest no detailed observation. Indeed it has always been a reproach to Plato that he diverted interest from observation of the particular facts" (193). "This new tinge to modern minds is a vehement and passionate interest in the relation of general principles to irreducible and stubborn facts. . . . It is this union of passionate interest in the detailed facts with equal devotion to abstract generalization which forms the novelty in our present society," A. N. Whitehead, *Science and the Modern World* (New York: Macmillan, 1925), 3. This passionate interest in the detailed facts may remind some of the young Jonathan Edwards's painstaking examination and description of the spider. It was only after the closest scrutiny of the spider that he drew his corollary about the workings of God.
36. Charles Taylor, *Sources of the Self*, 213–16. Furthermore: "Baconian science . . . gains a pious purpose within the framework of Puritan spirituality: not only . . . that it is to be directed to the general benefit of mankind, the condition of any proper calling—but also in that it is the search for God's purposes."
37. Kaaren, *Religious Origins of Modern Science*, 93–94, 102–4.
38. Ibid., 75.
39. Sandra Harding, *The Science Question in Feminism* (Ithaca, NY: Cornell, 1986), 56–57, 76–77, 88, 106, 122, 145–49, 206.
40. Ibid., 25, 48–50, 66, 86–91, 102, 201–10, 238, 244.
41. Ibid., 219–25.
42. See ibid., figures 8 and 9 and table 4. In my initial draft, I described these correction processes in some detail, but friends advised me that humanities specialists would cloud over: "It will lose 98 percent of your readers." I hope that was an exaggeration! But in the spirit that I am arguing for, I listened to the community correction.
43. Larry Rasmussen, *Earth Community, Earth Ethics* (Maryknoll, NY: Orbis Books, 1996).

Chapter 7: Individualism

1. Charles Taylor, *A Secular Age* (Cambridge, MA: Harvard University Press, 2007), 146. Cf. 38, 42, 133–37, 141, 148–49, 300–304.
2. Ibid., 157.
3. Ibid., 5, 137, 157, 181–83, 244, 300.
4. Ibid., 302–3.
5. Albert Camus, *The Stranger*, trans. Stuart Gilbert (New York: Vintage, 1960).
6. Ibid., 154.
7. Slightly modified translation for accuracy.
8. Albert Camus, *The Plague* trans. Stuart Gilbert (New York: Modern Library, 1947), 220–21, 227.
9. Ibid., 232–23.
10. Albert Camus, *The Fall and Exile and the Kingdom*, trans. Justin O'Brien (New York: Modern Library, 1956), 156.
11. Ibid., 179–81.
12. *The Plague*, 84–92 and 97.
13. http://www.nobelprize.org/nobel_prizes/literature/laureates/1957/camus-speech.html (accessed January 18, 2012).
14. Albert Camus, *The Rebel*, trans. Anthony Bower (New York: Vintage, 1991), 250.
15. Ibid., 266–67; see also 161.
16. Robert Zaretsky, *Albert Camus* (Ithaca, NY: Cornell University Press, 2010), 4.
17. Albert Camus, *The Fall*, trans. Justin O'Brien (New York: Alfred A. Knopf, 1961), 70.
18. Ibid., 80, 108.
19. Martin Buber, "Question to the Single One," *Between Man and Man* (New York: MacMillan, 1947), 40.
20. Reinhold Niebuhr, *The Self and the Dramas of History* (London: Faber and Faber, 1956); *Man's Nature and His Communities* (New York: Scribner's, 1965).
21. Jennifer Burns, *Goddess of the Market: Ayn Rand and the American Right* (New York: Oxford, 2009), 42–43.
22. Ayn Rand, *The Virtue of Selfishness* (New York: New American Library, 1964), 104.
23. Burns, *Goddess of the Market*, 9–10.
24. Ibid., 11.
25. Ibid., 172.
26. John Paul Lederach, *The Moral Imagination: The Art and Soul of Building Peace* (New York: Oxford, 2005), 36.
27. Fritz Stern, *The Politics of Cultural Despair: A Study in the Rise of the Germanic Ideology* (1961; repr., Garden City, NY: Doubleday and Co., 1965).
28. Ayn Rand, *Atlas Shrugged* (New York: Signet, 1996), 943.
29. Rand, *Virtue of Selfishness*, x.
30. Ibid., 106.
31. Ibid., 53–54.
32. Ibid., 32.
33. Ibid., 134.
34. Ibid., 184.
35. Burns, *Goddess of the Market*, 280.
36. *Did My Neurons Make Me Do It? Philosophical and Neurobiological Perspectives on Moral Responsibility and Free Will* (Oxford: Oxford University Press,

2007). The following summary refers primarily to pages 26–31, but the analysis extends throughout the book.

37. Drew Westen, *The Political Brain: The Role of Emotion in Deciding the Fate of the Nation* (New York: Public Affairs, 2007), ix.

38. Ibid., 71.

39. Westen's *The Political Brain* is a highly readable explanation of how the brain works and how it relates to ethical and political decision making.

40. "A Social Theory Model for Religious Social Ethics," *Journal of Religious Ethics* (Spring, 1977); "Critical Variables in Christian Social Ethics," in *Issues in Christian Ethics*, Paul Simmons, ed. (Nashville: Broadman, 1980); "Holistic Character Ethics," chapter 3 in Stassen and Gushee, *Kingdom Ethics: Following Jesus in Contemporary Context* (Downers Grove, IL: InterVarsity, 2003).

41. Matt. 6:21–23. The words usually translated "healthy" and "unhealthy" have the connotations respectively "generous" and "greedy."

42. Burns, *Goddess of the Market*, 149–51, 215, 228, 235, 243, 245, 269–70, 283.

43. Edmund L. Andrews, "Greenspan Concedes Error on Regulation," *New York Times* (October 24, 2008), B1.

44. Kate Zernicke, *Boiling Mad: Inside Tea Party America* (New York: Henry Holt, 2010), 74; cf. 64–77.

45. Rand Paul, *The Tea Party Goes to Washington* (Nashville and New York: Center Street, 2011), 122.

46. Congressional Budget Office, www.cbo.gov.

47. www.taxfoundation.org, "Federal Individual Income Tax Rates History," http://taxfoundation.org/article/us-federal-individual-income-tax-rates-history-1913-2011-nominal-and-inflation-adjusted-brackets (accessed January 15, 2012). For a fuller explanation, see Jacob Hacker and Paul Person, *Winner-Take-All Politics: How Washington Made the Rich Richer—And Turned Its Back on the Middle Class*, (New York: Simon & Schuster, 2010).

48. Jonathan Chait, http://www.tnr.com/blog/jonathan-chait/80552/paul-ryan-and-ayn-rand (accessed May 19, 2011).

49. John Brueggemann, *Rich, Free, and Miserable: Understanding the Failure of Success in America* (Rowman & Littlefield: 2010).

50. Larry L. Rasmussen, *Moral Fragments and Moral Community* (Minneapolis: Augsburg Fortress, 1993), 111–66.

51. Glen Stassen, *Living the Sermon on the Mount: A Practical Hope for Grace and Deliverance* (San Francisco: Jossey Bass, 2006), chaps. 2 and 3. See also *Kingdom Ethics*, chaps. 1–2.

52. Martin Luther, "Secular Authority: To What Extent It Should Be Obeyed, 1523," in John Dillenberger, ed., *Martin Luther: Selections from His Writings* (Garden City, NY: Anchor Books, Doubleday, 1961), 363-402.

Chapter 8: Sin

1. Taylor, *A Secular Age* (Cambridge, MA: Harvard University Press, 2007), 319, 635; cf. 633–41.

2. Ibid., 633–34 and 639.

3. Ibid., 698–99; cf. 685–86, 693–98, 703.

4. Jacob S. Hacker and Paul Pierson, *Winner-Take-All Politics: How Washington Made the Rich Richer—And Turned Its Back on the Middle Class* (New York: Simon & Schuster, 2010), 71 and 197–98.

5. Paul Krugman, *The Great Unraveling: Losing Our Way in the New Century* (New York: W. W. Norton, 2004), 129.

6. Diana B. Henriques, "Lapses Kept Scheme Alive, Madoff Told Investigators," *New York Times*, October 31, 2009.

7. Mark Landler and Sheryl Gay Stolberg, "As Fingers Point in the Financial Crisis, Many of Them Are Aimed at Bush," *New York Times*, September 20, 2008; Joseph Nocera, "Donaldson: The Exit Interview," *New York Times*, July 23, 2005.

8. Rand Paul, *The Tea Party Goes to Washington* (Nashville and New York: Center Street, 2011), 218.

9. See http://motherjones.com/politics/2011/02/income-inequality-in-america-chart-graph (accessed November, 2011).

10. http://texscience.org/reform/torture/yoo-delahunty-9jan02.pdf; and http://georgewbush-whitehouse.archives.gov/news/releases/2002/01/20020128-13.html.

11. More information may be found in several chapters of *Religious Faith, Torture, and Our National Soul*, ed. David P. Gushee (Macon, GA: Mercer University Press, 2009).

12. http://www.gallup.com/poll/23332/Americans-Views-Impact-Iraq-War.aspx (accessed February 14, 2012).

13. James Glanz, William J. Broad, and David E. Sanger, "Huge Cache of Explosives Vanished from Site in Iraq," http://www.nytimes.com/2004/10/25/international/middleeast/25bomb.html (accessed February 14, 2012).

14. U.S. State Department Report on International Terrorism, http://www.state.gov/s/ct/rls/crt/2010/170266.htm (accessed August 29, 2011).

15. This section is a version of my article, "Where is Reinhold Niebuhr When We Need Him?" *Process & Faith* 18 (Spring 2009), used with permission.

16. The theological weaknesses are criticized by his brother, H. Richard Niebuhr, "Reinhold Niebuhr's Interpretation of History," in *Theology, History, and Culture*, ed. William Stacy Johnson (New Haven, CT, and London: Yale University Press, 1996), 91–101.

17. John De Gruchy, introduction to *Creation and Fall: A Theological Exposition of Genesis 1–3*, by Dietrich Bonhoeffer, ed. John W. DeGruchy, trans. Douglas Stephen Bax, DBWE 3 (Minneapolis: Fortress, 1997), 1.

18. Ibid., 22.

19. Ibid. This is the second page of Bonhoeffer's introduction; he makes this clear from the start.

20. Ibid., 81–82.

21. Ibid., 129.

22. Ibid., 101.

23. Ibid., 106.

24. Ibid., 108–9.

25. Ibid., 88, 90.

26. Glen Stassen, *Living the Sermon on the Mount* (San Francisco: Jossey-Bass, 2006), 166–72; Stassen, "The Fourteen Triads of the Sermon on the Mount: Matthew 5:21–7:12," *Journal of Biblical Literature* 122, no. 2 (Summer 2003): 267–308.

27. Bonhoeffer, *Creation and Fall*, DBWE 3, 101 and 123–29.

28. Ibid., 127–30.

29. Ibid., 120; for guilt, see 104–5.

30. Clifford Green, *Bonhoeffer: A Theology of Sociality* (Grand Rapids: Eerdmans, 1999), 71, 76–79, 92–93, 108, 279–80.

31. Bonhoeffer, *Creation and Fall*, DBWE 3, 101 et passim.

32. Louis S. Berger, *Averting Global Extinction: Our Irrational Society as Therapy Patient* (Lanham, MD: Jason Aronson, 2009), 95–97.

33. Brevard Childs, "Tree of Knowledge, Tree of Life," *Interpreter's Dictionary of the Bible*, vol. 4 (New York and Nashville: Abingdon, 1962), 695–97. Cf. Terence E. Fretheim, "Commentary," in *New Interpreter's Bible*, vol. 1 (Nashville: Abingdon, 1994), 351. Here I am interpreting the tree of the knowledge of good and evil somewhat differently than Bonhoeffer, because Childs and Fretheim bring additional research beyond what was available to him. In fact, their understanding is more consistent with the main themes of Bonhoeffer's interpretation on the other points, which I believe bring great profundity.

34. Bonhoeffer, *Creation and Fall*, DBWE 3, 101, 117, 123.

35. Ibid., 113; cf. 115.

36. Ibid., 129.

37. Ibid., 99, 122–23. Bonhoeffer repeatedly writes of "the other" as providing the limits that I need: in his first book, *Communio Sanctorum*, in *Act and Being*, and here in *Creation and Fall* when he writes of Eve providing reality-testing for Adam, in *Life Together* when he writes of the practice of confession, and in *Letters and Papers from Prison* as Eberhard Bethge becomes his reality-tester.

38. Claus Westermann, *Genesis 1–11* (Minneapolis: Augsburg, 1984), 205, 230, and 285–86.

39. I first developed the following interpretation of the drama of Cain and Abel for the *Friedensdekade* (Ten Days of Peace) in East Germany, November 1989, where I had been invited to teach and preach on the theme of Cain and Abel. It could not have been more dramatic: the morning we entered East Berlin at Friedrichstrasse was the morning the Wall was opened and the isolation of East from West came to a dramatic end. The East Germans had practiced transforming initiatives of peacemaking and nonviolent confrontation, learned from César Chávez and Martin Luther King Jr. via Andreas Zumach and volunteers of *Aktion Sühenezeichen Friedensdienste*. In their Revolution of the Candles, they had toppled the second-worst dictatorship in Eastern Europe. It was indeed a remarkable revolution, in which not one person was killed. My wife, my son, and I experienced the first weeks after the fall of the Wall—each day in a different city of East Germany—learning from the remarkable East Germans, and teaching and preaching on initiatives of nonviolent peacemaking confrontation via the drama of Cain and Abel. "Cain and Abel and What It Means to Be Human" was the theme of the ten days of preaching that I was invited to do, in what turned out to be the first two weeks of East German freedom, won by nonviolent transforming initiatives.

40. Elizabeth Barnes, *The Story of Discipleship: Christ, Humanity, and Church in Narrative Perspective* (Nashville: Abingdon, 1995), 90–92.

41. From the study book prepared by East German Christians for the *Friedensdekade*, November 1989, my translation.

42. Frank Crüsemann, *Der Widerstand gegen das Königtum: Die antiköniglichen Texte des Alten Testamentes und der Kampf um den frühen israelitischen Staat* (Neukirchen-Vluyn: Neukirchener, 1978), 167, 174.

43. Ibid., 174; 179–80.

44. Ibid., 217.

45. Lisa Dahill, *Reading from the Underside of Selfhood: Bonhoeffer and Spiritual Formation*, Princeton Theological Monograph Series (Eugene, OR: Pickwick, 2009), 61–62.

46. Eberhard Bethge, *Dietrich Bonhoeffer* (Minneapolis: Fortress, 2000), 39–41.

47. Dahill, *Reading from the Underside*, 69, referring to Bethge, xvii–xviii.
48. Green, *Bonhoeffer*, 71, 76–79, 92–93, 108, 122, 124, 137–38, 141n, 166–67, 279n.
49. Ibid., 214 et passim.
50. Dahill, *Reading from the Underside*, 56–57, 83, 145, 191.
51. Green, *Bonhoeffer*, 171 and 177.
52. Ibid., chap. 4 et passim.
53. Ibid., 175; cf. 171–79.
54. Ibid., 173 and 176.
55. Dahill, *Reading from the Underside*, 180, 183.
56. Dahill is right when she says that in *Discipleship* she "finds the motifs of trust and intimacy with Jesus to be at least of equal importance to Bonhoeffer as that of the commanding authority of Christ" (ibid., 183). I am sure Green agrees, as I do.
57. Ibid., 1–2.
58. Charles Taylor, *Secular Age*, 81, 305, also identifies a definition of love as pure self-sacrifice without any self-love or self-affirmation as a historic cause of secularism. I agree and am responding to that problem here and in chapter 9 below. David Gushee and I develop the criticism and advocate an incarnational discipleship understanding of "delivering love" in chapter 16 of *Kingdom Ethics*.
59. Dahill, *Reading from the Underside*, 49–50.
60. Ibid., 192; cf. 87.
61. Bonhoeffer, *Ethics*, DBWE 6, 257–89.
62. Dahill, *Reading from the Underside*, 12.
63. Ibid., 76–77.
64. Bonhoeffer diagnoses this and the following types of ethics in *Ethics*, DBWE 6, 77–80.
65. Ibid., 66.
66. Ibid., 82.
67. Ibid.
68. Ibid., 84; cf. 94.
69. Ibid., 85.
70. Ibid., 86–87.
71. Ibid.,171–218,
72. Ibid., 173–74, 179–80, 182, 184–95.
73. Ibid., 85–87.
74. Ibid., 88–89 and 89n.
75. Ibid., 90, 95.
76. Ibid., 91.
77. Ibid., 92.
78. Ibid., 87.
79. Ibid., 88.
80. Ibid., 87.
81. Ibid., 100–101.
82. Bonhoeffer develops this theme of free responsibility in Christ, which is the antidote to the sin of abdication of responsibility, in "The Structure of Responsible Life," *Ethics*, DBWE 6, 257–89 .
83. Ibid., 126.
84. Equilar, "The Leading Provider of Executive Compensation Data," www .equilar.com (accessed November 15, 2011).
85. Drew Westin, "What Happened to Obama?" *New York Times*, August 7, 2011, SR 9 and 10. See also "The Real Say on Pay," *New York Times*,

September 1, 2010, and Louise Story, "Executive Pay," *New York Times*, March 3, 2011, for data in this paragraph including the reference to the *Wall Street Journal* study. Also see Hacker and Pierson, *Winner-Take-All Politics*, for the analysis of the larger political context behind this explosion of the wealth of the few while others' wealth does not increase in the United States by contrast with other industrialized nations.

86. Bonhoeffer, *Ethics*, DBWE 6, 134–45.
87. Ibid., 135–36.
88. See Jennifer McBride, *The Church for the World: A Theology of Public Witness* (New York: Oxford University Press, 2012), for a profound advocacy of a nontriumphal public ethic based on Bonhoeffer's understanding of repentance, with a strong sense of social and structural solidarity in sin.

Chapter 9: The Cross

1. Charles Taylor, *A Secular Age* (Cambridge, MA: Harvard University Press, 2007), 654.
2. Ibid., 78–79. Also see 262–63.
3. An insightful summary is offered by chapter 5 of James William McClendon Jr., *Doctrine* (Nashville: Abingdon, 1994). A fuller assessment with strong biblical basis is Mark Baker and Joel Green, *Recovering the Scandal of the Cross: Atonement in New Testament and Contemporary Contexts*, 2nd ed. (Downers Grove, IL: InterVarsity, 2011). I am grateful to Joel Green for his affirmation and for nuances to my understanding of Mark's context.
4. This point is made clearly by Baker and Green, *Recovering the Scandal*, 41, 53, 87, 91, 110–11, 165, 239, and chapter 4.
5. Lisa Cahill, "A Theology for Peacebuilding," in *Peacebuilding: Catholic Theology, Ethics, and Praxis*, ed. R. Scott Appleby, Gerard F. Powers, and Robert J. Schreiter (Maryknoll, NY: Orbis, 2010), 312.
6. N. T. Wright, "The Cross and the Caricatures: A Response to Robert Jenson, Jeffrey John, and a New Volume Entitled *Pierced for Our Transgressions*," manuscript. See also Baker and Green, 27–31, et passim.
7. Bonhoeffer, *Letters and Papers from Prison*, DBWE 8, 52.
8. See Norman Kraus, *Jesus Christ Our Lord: Christology from a Disciple's Perspective* (Scottdale, PA: Herald, 1990), chapters 12–14. Kraus develops his understanding out of his experience as a missionary in Japan, and mine comes out of my experience in my own American tradition and my study of Dietrich Bonhoeffer. I intend to ground it not primarily in a diagnosis of the human condition, but much more in an appreciation for what God has done in Jesus Christ. Hence it is an *incarnational* theory, not a shame theory. Kraus would probably concur. See also the insightful assessment of Kraus's relational theory in Baker and Green, *Recovering the Scandal*, chap. 7.
9. Baker and Green, *Recovering the Scandal*, 68, 82–83.
10. I resonate with much in Athanasius, *On the Incarnation* (Crestwood, NY: St. Vladimir's Seminary Press, 1996), as well as Irenaeus; and Kathryn Tanner, *Christ the Key*, (Cambridge, MA: Cambridge University Press, 2010), although, unlike Bonhoeffer and my advocacy here, her "incarnational theory of the cross" focuses on the metaphysical fact of the incarnation, rather than who the incarnate Jesus was; Miroslav Volf, *Exclusion and Embrace: A Theological Exploration of Identity, Otherness, and Reconciliation* (Nashville: Abingdon, 1996); and Paul Fiddes, *Past Event and Present Salvation: The Christian Idea of Atonement* (Louisville, KY: Westminster/John Knox, 1989).

But I cannot develop this as I would like within present limits. I commend the insightful study of Bonhoeffer's concept of "accepting guilt" (*Schuldübernahme*) by Christine Schliesser: *Everyone Who Acts Responsibly Becomes Guilty: Bonhoeffer's Concept of Accepting* (Louisville, KY: Westminster John Knox, 2008). However, I believe Bonhoeffer's "accepting guilt" refers first to the social solidarity of national and ecclesiological guilt for the war and the Holocaust and guilt for not acting responsibly but instead looking away and sometimes being silent in the face of great injustice, prior to participation in the coup attempt.

11. Bonhoeffer, *Ethics*, DBWE 6, 306. The following quotes come from ibid., 82–84. The italics are mine.

12. Ibid., 88–95.

13. See the insight of Jürgen Moltmann about the Apostles' Creed, as quoted and explained in Glen Stassen and David Gushee, *Kingdom Ethics: Following Jesus in Contemporary Context* (Downers Grove, IL: InterVarsity, 2003), 130 et passim.

14. James A. Todd, "Participation: An Overlooked Clue; Bonhoeffer's Description of the Christian Life-Style," *Encounter* 34 (1973): 27–35.

15. James William McClendon Jr., *Ethics*, vol. 1 of *Systematic Theology*, rev. ed. (Nashville: Abingdon, 2002), 85, 89–90, 106, 115, 118, 195–97, 254; vol. 2: *Doctrine* (Nashville: Abingdon, 1994), 113–17, 214, 239–32, 377–81.

16. McClendon, *Ethics*, 106. The bulk of McClendon's explicit references to *presence* are found in part 1 of *Ethics*, which focuses on the body's intrinsic worth, and he notes the important role God's *presence* played in earliest incarnations of black Christianity in order to make sense of human suffering, particularly slavery. As creatures we are "bound to our environment"; we need a community of supportive presence (109).

17. McClendon, *Doctrine*, 240. The Spirit is at work today through four related practices: worship, kingdom work, disciple witness, and hearing the biblical word. McClendon's decidedly christocentric focus clearly informs his understanding of *presence*, and also shows Yoder's influence. For this and the previous note, I owe thanks to Justin Phillips.

18. See Christine Schliesser, *Everyone Who Acts Responsibly Becomes Guilty* (Louisville, KY: Westminster John Knox, 2008), 45–46, 90–91, 124–30. "Christ the *Stellvertreter* is the love of God for humanity." It is "personal self-giving." "'The preaching of God's love speaks of the community into which God has entered with each and every person....' Most concretely, the Spirit through the Word actualizes the divine love in human hearts." See Clifford J. Green, *Bonhoeffer: A Theology of Sociality* (Grand Rapids: Eerdmans, 1972, 1999), 56–58 and 225.

19. Ched Myers, *Binding the Strong Man*, 469–72.

20. Arland J. Hultgren, *Christ and His Benefits: Christology and Redemption in the New Testament* (Philadelphia: Fortress, 1987), 63. "What impressed his hearers . . . was . . . the note of compelling authority which characterized his teaching. . . . 'The deeds of Jesus were recounted by Mark from the point of view of their parabolic function.'" Ralph Martin, *Mark: Evangelist and Theologian* (Exeter: Paternoster, 1972), 113–14.

21. Mark progressively reveals what Jesus' identity as the Son of God means; this is the focus of Mark's Christology. Craig Evans, *Mark 8:27–16:20* (Nashville: Thomas Nelson, 2001), lxxi–lxxii. "It is the title 'Son of God' . . . which most scholars agree is the most important title for Jesus." W. R. Telford, *The Theology of the Gospel of Mark* (Cambridge: Cambridge University Press, 1999), 38.

22. For insightful discussion of the significance of Mark's beginning, see Rikki Watts, *Isaiah's New Exodus in Mark* (Grand Rapids: Baker Academic, 2000), chaps. 3 and 4.
23. See Stassen and Gushee, *Kingdom Ethics*, chap. 1.
24. The verb occurs 82 times in Mark. Matthew and Luke continue Mark's emphasis: 108 times for Matthew and 97 for Luke. The Gospel of John uses it 142 times. It is a special Gospel emphasis; Paul's letters and the other New Testament letters altogether use it 69 times.
25. The prophet Isaiah strongly emphasized the exodus, and the Gospel of Mark emphasizes Isaiah more than any other Old Testament book. Cf. Watts, *Isaiah's New Exodus in Mark*.
26. Watts, *Isaiah's New Exodus in Mark*, 323–24.
27. Ibid., 155.
28. Myers, *Binding the Strong Man*, 393.
29. Willie James Jennings, *The Christian Imagination: Theology and the Origins of Race* (New Haven, CT, and London: Yale University Press, 2010), 165.
30. Also in Mark, Jesus praises a scribe who affirmed his teaching the Great Commandment of love of God and love of neighbor: "You are not far from the kingdom of God" (12:34). Does Jesus die for the scribes and synagogue officials, also?
31. See Myers, *Binding the Strong Man*, 200–203. I owe thanks to Erin Dufault-Hunter for inspiration here.
32. Gratitude to Jana Riess for this insight.
33. Tae Ho Lee, "Jesus, Social Justice, and the Reform of Chaebols" (PhD dissertation, Fuller Theological Seminary, 2006).
34. Myers, *Binding the Strong Man*, 365.
35. Telford, *Theology of the Gospel of Mark*, 134.
36. I define Christian love as "confrontive," delivering love in *Kingdom Ethics*, chap. 16.
37. I have cited Ched Myers often because I find him insightful, because he sets the drama of the cross in its real history so effectively, and because he makes the theme of radical incarnational discipleship so central. Yet his conflict social theory and my more pluralistic theory—though also with conflict—see this point differently. See Myers, *Binding the Strong Man*, 317–18.
38. Tae Ho Lee, "Jesus, Social Justice, and the Reform of the Chaebols."
39. Evans, *Mark 8:27–16:20*, 511.
40. Morna Hooker, *Not Ashamed of the Gospel: New Testament Interpretations of the Death of Christ* (Carlisle, UK: Paternoster, 1994), 8–12, 15. Cf. Baker and Green, 192–209.
41. Veli-Matti Kärkkäinen, *Christ and Reconciliation* (Grand Rapids: Eerdmans, forthcoming).
42. Bonhoeffer, *Ethics*, DBWE 6, 83.
43. Jennifer McBride, *The Church for the World: A Theology of Public Witness* (New York: Oxford University Press, 2012), 58.
44. See Kärkkäinen, *Christ and Reconciliation*, chap. 11, on the mixing of metaphors in Paul's teaching on the meaning of the cross.
45. Hans Boersma, *Reappropriating the Atonement Tradition* (Grand Rapids: Baker Academic, 2004), 181. But see Baker and Green, *Recovering the Scandal*, chap. 8, where Darby Kathleen Ray's interpretation makes better sense.
46. McClendon, *Doctrine*, 202.
47. Boersma, *Reappropriating the Atonement Tradition*, 132, 187–89.

48. Miroslav Volf, *Exclusion and Embrace: A Theological Exploration of Identity, Otherness, and Reconciliation* (Nashville: Abingdon, 1996), 120; 125–29, 141–42, 176, 214.

49. Ibid., 22–23.

50. Ibid., 121–22.

51. Ibid., 23.

52. J. Denny Weaver, *The Nonviolent Atonement* (Grand Rapids: Eerdmans, 2001), and Weaver, *Anabaptist Theology in the Face of Postmodernity* (Telford, PA: Pandora, 2000). With Frank Tupper, I prefer to speak of "historical drama" rather than "narrative"—as Weaver writes, "the confrontation *in history*." See Frank Tupper, *Scandalous Providence: The Jesus Story of the Compassion of God* (Macon, GA: Mercer University Press, 1995), 21–22.

53. Cf. Stephen Dintaman, "The Spiritual Poverty of the Anabaptist Vision," *The Conrad Grebel Review* 10 (Spring 1992), 205–8.

54. Morna Hooker, *Not Ashamed of the Gospel*, 139–41; Baker and Green, *Recovering the Scandal*, chap. 4, and pp. 109, 131–36, 198; McClendon, *Doctrine*, 219.

55. Boersma, *Reappropriating the Atonement Tradition*, 170–79.

56. Christopher D. Marshall, *Beyond Retribution: A New Testament Vision for Justice, Crime, and Punishment* (Grand Rapids: Eerdmans, 2001). The United States has an astoundingly larger percentage of its population in prison than any other democracy—many for unjustly punitive and lengthy sentences destructive to them and to the U.S. and state budgets. The authoritarian strain in our culture is doing us enormous damage.

57. N. T. Wright, "The Cross and the Caricatures." Boersma, *Reappropriating the Atonement Tradition*, 243.

58. John Goldingay, "Old Testament Sacrifice and the Death of Christ," 6–8, and "Your Iniquities Have Made a Separation between You and Your God," 51, in Goldingay, ed., *Atonement Today* (London: SPCK Press, 1995).

59. Volf, *Exclusion and Embrace*, 292, 139. Italics are in the original.

60. McClendon, *Doctrine*, 233.

61. Ibid., 236–37.

62. Deborah van Deusen Hunsinger, *Theology and Pastoral Counseling: A New Interdisciplinary Approach* (Grand Rapids: Eerdmans, 1995), 179 et passim.

63. Ibid., 152 et passim.

64. Ibid., 189; italics mine.

65. Ibid., 190.

66. In Karen and Garth Baker-Fletcher, *My Sister, My Brother: Womanist and Xodus God Talk* (Eugene, OR: Wipf and Stock, 1997), 76; cf. 78–80. Cf. M. Shawn Copeland, "Wading through Many Sorrows," in *A Troubling in My Soul*, ed. Emilie M. Townes (Maryknoll, NY: Orbis, 1993), 124.

67. Cheryl A. Kirk-Duggan, "African-American Spirituals: Confronting and Exorcising Evil through Song," in *A Troubling in My Soul*, 161–62.

68. Nekeisha Alexis-Baker, "Freedom of the Cross: John Howard Yoder and Womanist Theologies in Conversation," in *Power and Practices: Engaging the Work of John Howard Yoder*, ed. Jeremy M. Bergen and Anthony G. Siegrist (Scottdale, PA: Herald, 2009), chap. 5.

69. Marie Fortune, "The Transformation of Suffering: A Biblical and Theological Perspective," in *Christianity, Patriarchy, and Abuse*, ed. Joanne Carlson Brown and Carole R. Bohn (New York: Pilgrim, 1989), 141–42.

70. Stassen and Gushee, *Kingdom Ethics*, chap. 16.

71. Jacquelyn Grant, "Womanist Jesus and the Mutual Struggle for Liberation," in *The Recovery of Black Presence: An Interdisciplinary Exploration; Essays in Honor of Dr. Charles B. Copher*, ed. Randall C. Bailey and Jacquelyn Grant (Nashville: Abingdon, 1995), 139. Cf. Jacquelyn Grant, *White Women's Christ and Black Women's Jesus* (Atlanta: Scholars Press, 1989), 212; and Jacquelyn Grant, "The Challenge of the Darker Sister," in *Feminism and Theology*, ed. Janet Martin Soskice and Diana Lipton (Oxford: Oxford University Press, 2003).
72. Jacquelyn Grant, "The Sin of Servanthood: And the Deliverance of Discipleship," in *A Troubling in My Soul*, 202.
73. Stassen and Gushee, *Kingdom Ethics*, chap. 17.

Chapter 10: Love

1. A parallel clarification distinguishes the Christian understanding of love as delivering love over against Anders Nygren's idealistic understanding of love as purely sacrificial without any motive to create justice and community. David Gushee and I have demonstrated that distinction in chap. 16 of our *Kingdom Ethics: Following Jesus in Contemporary Context* (Downers Grove, IL: InterVarsity, 2003).
2. Reggie Williams, "Christ-Centered Empathic Resistance: The Influence of Harlem Renaissance Theology on the Incarnational Ethics of Dietrich Bonhoeffer" (PhD dissertation, Fuller Theological Seminary, 2011).
3. Bonhoeffer, *Discipleship*, DBWE 4, 37. See also Bonhoeffer, *Ethics*, DBWE 6, 47–49: "The source of a Christian ethic is not . . . the reality of norms and values. It is the reality of God that is revealed in Jesus Christ."
4. H. E. Tödt, "Discrimination against Jews in 1933: The Real Test for Bonhoeffer's Ethics," in Tödt, *Authentic Faith: Bonhoeffer's Theological Ethics in Context* (Grand Rapids: Eerdmans, 2007), 81; cf. 78–82.
5. See Bonhoeffer, *Barcelona, Berlin, America, 1928–1931*, DBWE 10, 367.
6. Eberhard Bethge, *Dietrich Bonhoeffer: A Biography*, rev. ed. (Minneapolis: Fortress, 2000), 206, italics added.
7. Bethge, *Dietrich Bonhoeffer*, 206, italics added.
8. Clifford Green, *Bonhoeffer: A Theology of Sociality* (Grand Rapids: Eerdmans, 1999), 3; cf. 15 and chap. 4. Green shows that it had happened *by* 1932; I argue it happened *in* 1931, in New York, and showed publicly in 1932.
9. Bethge, *Bonhoeffer*, 208.
10. Bonhoeffer, *Discipleship*, DBWE 4, 4.
11. Warren S. Kissinger, *The Sermon on the Mount: A History of Interpretation* (New York: Scarecrow, 1975), 6.
12. Karl Barth, as quoted in H. E. Tödt, "Discrimination against Jews in 1933," 73.
13. Bonhoeffer, *Discipleship*, DBWE 4, 106.
14. Ibid., 121–23.
15. Ruth Zerner first made this clear in "Dietrich Bonhoeffer's American Experiences: People, Letters, and Papers from Union Seminary," *Union Seminary Quarter'ly Review* 31, no. 4 (Summer 1976): 268–71 et passim. Cf. Josiah Ulysses Young III, *No Difference in the Fare* (Grand Rapids: Eerdmans: 1998), 21–26; Hans Pfeifer, "Learning Faith and Ethical Commitment in the Context of Spiritual Training Groups: Consequences of Dietrich Bonhoeffer's Post Doctoral Year in New York City 1930/31," *Dietrich Bonhoeffer Yearbook* 3 (2008). Originally published as *Dietrich Bonhoeffer Jahrbuch* 3 in 2007. The fullest study is Reggie Williams, "Christ-Centered Empathic Resistance: The

Influence of Harlem Renaissance Theology on the Incarnational Ethics of Dietrich Bonhoeffer" (PhD dissertation, Fuller Theological Seminary, 2011).

16. Bonhoeffer, *Ethics*, DBWE 6, 346.
17. Bonhoeffer, *Discipleship*, DBWE 4, 51.
18. Green, *Bonhoeffer*, 13–17 et passim.
19. The index in Bonhoeffer's *Ethics* indicates twenty-four references, but three refer to editors' footnotes rather than to Bonhoeffer's text, two refer to the first draft of "History and the Good," and one is erroneous.
20. Richard Hays' fine *Moral Vision of the New Testament* (San Francisco: HarperSanFrancisco, 1996) is a New Testament ethics, and therefore does include the Sermon on the Mount, though not with the hermeneutic of transforming initiatives that I advocate (now with support from Hays). Happily, others recently have seen the need to repair this strange omission: recent Christian ethics textbooks by Dallas Willard, William Spohn, Allen Verhey, Lee Camp, Harvey Cox, Stanley Hauerwas, and Glen Stassen and David Gushee do give significant attention to the Sermon on the Mount.
21. Dietrich Bonhoeffer, *Letters and Papers from Prison*, DBWE 8, 486: cf. also 456.
22. Rita Nakashima Brock and Rebecca Ann Parker, *Saving Paradise : How Christianity Traded Love of This World for Crucifixion and Empire* (Boston: Beacon, 2008) demonstrate this truth extensively, but criticize it as coinciding with an otherworldly emphasis that decreased attention to justice and coincided with the violence of the crusades. This is why I contend it is so important to understand the cross as both compassion for those who suffer or have shame, and confrontation of injustice and call for repentance.
23. Charles Taylor, *A Secular Age* (Cambridge, MA: Harvard University Press, 2007), 64 and 307.
24. Ibid., 81–82.
25. Ibid., 86, 262, 278.
26. Ibid., 225–56.
27. Ibid., 81, 305, 623–24, 640.
28. Bonhoeffer, *Discipleship*, DBWE 4, 100–110.
29. Ibid., 103, italics added.
30. Ibid., 105, italics added.
31. Ibid., 106–9.
32. Ibid., 108, italics added.
33. Ibid., 109.
34. Larry Rasmussen, *Reality and Resistance* (Nashville: Abingdon, 1972), 40 and 90.
35. Bonhoeffer, *Ethics*, DBWE 6, 244. (Subsequent references to Bonhoeffer's *Ethics* in this section will use parenthetical references to cite the page number.)
36. Glen H. Stassen and David P. Gushee, *Kingdom Ethics: Following Jesus in Contemporary Context* (Downers Grove, IL: InterVarsity, 2003), chap. 16.
37. Dietrich Bonhoeffer, *Conspiracy and Imprisonment 1940–1945*, ed. Mark S. Brocker, trans. Lisa E. Dahill, DBWE 16 (Minneapolis: Fortress, 2006), 1, 46, 106–11, 207–8, 256–58, 284, 378, 501, 602–3, 607, 613.
38. Ibid., 284.
39. Ibid., 55, 66, 257, 529, 549, 559, 641.
40. Larry Rasmussen, *Dietrich Bonhoeffer: His Significance for North Americans* (Minneapolis: Fortress, 1990), quoting Bonhoeffer, *Letters and Papers from Prison*, Letter of August 21, 1944.
41. Rasmussen, *Dietrich Bonhoeffer*, 160–62.
42. Maryknoll, NY: Orbis, 1986.

43. Reinhold Niebuhr, "Why the Christian Church Is Not Pacifist," *Christianity and Power Politics* (New York: Scribner's, 1952), 4, 5, 8, 10.

44. For further explanation, see Gushee and Stassen *Kingdom Ethics*, chap. 2, and Glen Stassen, *Living the Sermon on the Mount: A Practical Hope for Grace and Deliverance* (New York: Jossey-Bass, 2006), chap. 3.

45. My translation as "humble," which I argue elsewhere, along with others, is more accurate than "meek."

46. Stassen, *Living the Sermon on the Mount*; or for the more technical, scholarly evidence, see Glen Stassen, "The Fourteen Triads of the Sermon on the Mount: Matthew 5:21–7:12, *Journal of Biblical Literature* 122, no. 2 (Summer, 2003), 267–308.

47. Glen Stassen, "The Fourteen Triads of the Sermon on the Mount."

48. Dale Allison, in *The Sermon on the Mount* (New York: Herder & Herder, 1989), 64 and 71, points out that early Christian tradition "did not know an injunction against all anger: Ephesians 4:26; Mark 1:41 (where the original text may have had Jesus 'moved with anger'); Mark 3:5; Matthew 21:12–17. . . . For the most part later Christian tradition followed Ephesians 4:26 and did not demand the elimination of all anger—only anger misdirected." Matthew 23 shows Jesus angry, and in 23:17 Jesus calls his opponents fools, against the reading of Matthew 5:22 as a command.

49. Bonhoeffer, *Discipleship*, 121–23.

50. See explanation in Glen Stassen, *Just Peacemaking: Transforming Initiatives for Justice and Peace* (Louisville, KY: Westminster/John Knox, 1992), 260–61 and n. 27.

51. The pattern of transforming initiatives is now increasingly being affirmed by New Testament scholars. For one example, Dale Allison, *Studies in Matthew* (Grand Rapids: Baker Academic, 2005), 183n and 193n writes, "I accept the correction of Glen H. Stassen, . . . *JBL* 122 (2003), pp. 267–308." "Stassen's scheme . . . does work remarkably well for much of the Sermon on the Mount and is a contribution to interpretation. . . ." Or see many references in Willard Swartley, *The Covenant of Peace: The Missing Peace in New Testament Theology and Ethics* (Grand Rapids: Eerdmans, 2006).

52. Martin Luther, "Secular Authority: To What Extent It Should Be Obeyed, 1523," in John Dillenberger, ed., *Martin Luther: Selections from His Writings* (Garden City, NY: Anchor Books, Doubleday, 1961), 363-402.

53. Clarence Jordan, *Substance of Faith*, ed. Dallas Lee (New York: Association Press, 1972), 67.

54. Gerd Theissen, *Social Reality and the Early Christians* (Minneapolis: Fortress, 1992), 10–13.

55. Bonhoeffer, *Ethics*, DBWE 6, 185.

56. Ibid., 195.

57. Bonhoeffer, *Discipleship*, DBWE 4, 109.

58. Bonhoeffer, *Ethics*, DBWE 6, 346–47.

59. See Stassen and Gushee, *Kingdom Ethics*, chaps. 1 and 17.

60. My translation; it is a play on words in the Greek.

61. Stassen, *Just Peacemaking*, 63–70. For a historical and theological argument, see my "Human Rights," in *Global Dictionary of Theology* (Downers Grove, IL: InterVarsity, 2008), 405–14.

62. Bonhoeffer, *Discipleship*, DBWE 4,162–68.

63. Ibid., 106, 146–52.

64. Bonhoeffer, *Ethics*, DBWE 6, 239; cf. 236–45. The second draft speaks similarly on 252.

65. Ibid., 242.
66. Ibid., 236.

Chapter 11: War

1. John Horgan, "Wars Are Decreasing," *Slate Magazine*, August 4, 2009, cites research results from the SIPRI Yearbook for 2009, anthropologist Lawrence Keeley, economist Samuel Bowles, as well as political scientist Leitenberg. The anthropological data compare percentages of the human population killed in wars for ancient history with recent times, as well as numbers in the twentieth century. All agree that percentages of deaths from war are dramatically decreasing, contrary to the pessimism or fatalism of our usual perceptions.

2. Glen Stassen, ed., *Just Peacemaking: The New Paradigm for the Ethics of Peace and War* (1998, 2003; repr., Cleveland: Pilgrim Press, 2008).

3. Susan Brooks Thistlethwaite, ed. *Interfaith Just Peacemaking* (New York: Palgrave McMillan, 2012).

4. On the Web site, www.justpeacemaking.org, we point to specific pragmatic and Christian implications of the just peacemaking practices for current conflicts.

5. I should clarify that among the Christian scholars who wrote *Just Peacemaking: The New Paradigm*, not all emphasize the Sermon on the Mount as much as I will here. Some focus on broader biblical and theological teachings of grace-based initiatives, justice as central in biblical narrative, biblical and church teaching on the importance of covenant and community, the common good, and human rights, the mission of the church to the world, the sovereignty of God, the way of the Lamb as doing the teachings of Jesus in the book of Revelation, natural law and natural rights, and the creation of all persons in the image of God with human dignity and human rights.

6. Stephen Toulmin, *Cosmopolis: The Hidden Agenda of Modernity* (New York: Free Press, 1990); Jeffrey Stout, *Flight from Authority* (Notre Dame, IN: University of Notre Dame Press, 1981).

7. Charles Taylor, *A Secular Age* (Cambridge, MA: Harvard University Press, 2007), 657–60.

8. Ibid., 706–10.

9. Charles Kimball, *When Religion Becomes Evil* (San Francisco: HarperSanFrancisco, 2002), and idem, *When Religion Becomes Lethal* (San Francisco: Jossey-Bass, 2011).

10. Glen Stassen, "Peacemaking," in *Bonhoeffer and King*, ed. Willis Jenkins and Jennifer McBride (Minneapolis: Fortress, 2010), 196–200.

11. Urbana, IL: University of Illinois Press, 1962.

12. Ernest J. Sternglass, "Infant Mortality and Nuclear Tests," *Bulletin of the Atomic Scientists* 25, no. 4 (April 1969): 18–20. Some debate complicated Sternglass's analysis, but I judge that his replies won the day: *Bulletin of the Atomic Scientists* 25, no. 8 (Oct. 1969): 24–32; and 25, no. 10 (Dec. 1969): 29–34.

13. Alexander Kirby, John Rothmann, and David Dalin, *Harold E. Stassen: The Life and Perennial Candidacy of the Progressive Republican* (Jefferson, NC: MacFarland Press, 2012).

14. Glen Stassen, *Just Peacemaking: Transforming Initiatives for Justice and Peace* (Louisville, KY: Westminster/John Knox, 1992); Stassen, *Just Peacemaking: New Paradigm*.

15. It goes further than I should try to fit into this chapter, and I will put it on the www.justpeacemaking.org for interested readers to examine under "holistic hermeneutical method for just peacemaking." Also on my own Web site, www.fuller.edu/sot/faculty/stassen. I have presented it to the New Testament scholars in the Matthew section of the Society of Biblical Literature, and a version of it is in chapter 3 of *Kingdom Ethics: Following Jesus in Contemporary Context* (Downers Grove, IL: InterVarsity, 2003).

16. John H. Yoder, "The Possibility of a Messianic Ethic," chap. 1 in *The Politics of Jesus* (1972; repr., Grand Rapids: Eerdmans, 1994).

17. William C. Spohn, *Go and Do Likewise: Jesus and Ethics* (New York: Continuum, 1999), chap. 3.

18. Ibid., 52–54.

19. In *Covenant of Peace: The Missing Peace in New Testament Theology and Ethics* (Grand Rapids: Eerdmans, 2006), 64–65 and 68–72, Willard M. Swartley argues that Walter Wink's interpretation of these initiatives in *The Love of Enemy and Nonretaliation in the New Testament*, ed. Willard M. Swartley (Louisville, KY: Westminster/John Knox, 1992) has much to commend in it but that Wink emphasizes the shock value of confrontation too aggravatingly. Instead, he suggests, Luise Schottroff's account is more persuasive, especially since she pays attention to the central teaching of love for the enemy, which precedes it in Luke and comes as climax in Matthew (Schottroff, "'Give to Caesar What Belongs to Caesar and to God What Belongs to God': A Theological Response of the Early Christian Church to Its Social and Political Environment," in *The Love of Enemy and Nonretaliation in the New Testament*, 223–57). In my essay "The Politics of Jesus in the Sermon on the Plain," in *The Wisdom of the Cross*, ed. Stanley Hauerwas, Chris Huebner, and Mark T. Nation (Grand Rapids: Eerdmans, 1999), 150–67, I have argued for a chiastic structure in the Sermon on the Plain, in which Luke 6:32–35— the teaching on love for enemies—is the pivotal core, thus also supporting Swartley and Schottroff.

20. *Kingdom Ethics*, chap. 16. "Delivering love" may be seen as basically identical with Swartley's understanding, and with our shared attention to Jesus' connection with the prophetic tradition and especially Isaiah, and as integrating Schottroff's and Wink's insights. Wink's argument is based on 5:38–42; Schottroff adds 5:43–48; I add the structure of the fourteen triads from 5:21– 7:12 as consistently climaxing in transforming initiatives. I argue that transformation of relationship is central, not Wink's causing the Roman soldier to violate Roman law.

21. Yoder, *Politics of Jesus*, chap. 5, "The Possibility of Nonviolent Resistance"; *Just Peacemaking: New Paradigm*, chap. 1.

22. Mohammed Abu-Nimer makes this argument incisively in his *Nonviolence and Peace Building in Islam: Theory and Practice* (Gainesville: University Press of Florida, 2003).

23. Marc Gopin, *Holy War, Holy Peace: How Religion Can Bring Peace to the Middle East* (New York: Oxford University Press, 2002), and Michael Goldberg, *Why Should Israel Survive?* (New York: Oxford University Press, 1995).

24. Stassen, ed., *Just Peacemaking: New Paradigm*, chap. 2.

25. Ibid., 19.

26. W. D. Davies and Dale Allison, *The Gospel according to St. Matthew*, vol. 1 (Edinburgh: T. & T. Clark, 1988), 510; Pinchas Lapide, *The Sermon on the Mount: Utopia or Program for Action?* (Maryknoll, NY: Orbis, 1986), 49; Dale Allison, *Studies in Matthew* (Grand Rapids: Baker Academic, 2005), 66–78;

Claus Westermann, *Genesis 1–11: A Commentary* (London: SPCK; Minneapolis: Augsburg, 1984).

27. I interpret Richard Horsley's limitation of Jesus' peacemaking to economic conflict in villages, with no reference to Rome, in his *Jesus and the Spiral of Violence: Popular Jewish Resistance in Roman Palestine* (San Francisco: Harper & Row, 1987), 262–69, as a reaction against Hengel's apparent advocacy of passivity as the alternative to Brandon's Jesus-as-a-zealot interpretation. A transforming initiatives interpretation may help cure this dualistic split between passivity and violent revolution. Horsley shifted to having Rome very much in mind in his *Jesus and Empire: The Kingdom of God and the New World Disorder* (Minneapolis: Fortress, 2003). Christopher Bryan's *Render to Caesar: Jesus, The Early Church, and the Roman Superpowers* (New York: Oxford University Press, 2005) is persuasive. See also Warren Carter's books on the same subject and Craig Evans's summary of Rome's claims for its emperors in his *Mark 8:27–16:20* (Nashville: Thomas Nelson, 2001), lxxxi–xciii.

28. Davies and Allison, *Matthew*, 512–13.

29. Swartley, *Covenant of Peace: The Missing Peace in New Testament Theology and Ethics* (Grand Rapids: Eerdmans, 2006), 58, 67.

30. *Just Peacemaking: New Paradigm*, chap. 4.

31. *Ethics*, DBWE 6, 134–45.

32. Donald W. Shriver, "Acknowledge Responsibility for Conflict and Injustice and Seek Repentance and Forgiveness," in *Just Peacemaking: New Paradigm*, 98–115; idem, *An Ethic for Enemies: Forgiveness in Politics* (New York: Oxford University Press, 1998, 1995); idem, *Honest Patriots: Loving a Country Enough to Remember Its Misdeeds* (Oxford: Oxford University Press: 2005).

33. Christopher D. Marshall, *Crowned with Glory and Honor: Human Rights in the Biblical Tradition* (Telford, PA: Pandora, 2001); see also idem, *Beyond Retribution: A New Testament Vision for Justice, Crime, and Punishment* (Grand Rapids: Eerdmans, 2001).

34. Marshall, *Crowned with Glory and Honor*, 17; cf. 26.

35. Ibid., 21.

36. Nicholas Wolterstorff, *Justice: Rights and Wrongs* (Princeton: Princeton University Press, 2010). For other sources and my own argument in brief, see my "Human Rights," in *Global Dictionary of Theology* (Downers Grove, IL: InterVarsity, 2008).

37. http://www.state.gov/s/ct/rls/crt/2010/170266.htm (accessed August 29, 2011). As of July, 2012, the reports are accessed at http://www.state.gov/j/ct/ rls/crt/, but I do not see where they now reach back to the total numbers for 2003 and 2004. The numbers for 2005 and subsequently are still there and are declining somewhat to approximately 11,000 per year; I predict steady decline if the United States discontinues warmaking in the region, and especially if it emphasizes working for justice and human rights in the region.

38. Andrew Sullivan, "The Long Game," *Newsweek* (January 23, 2012), 34.

39. "Individual Preferences and Role Constraints in Policy-Making; Senatorial Response to Secretaries Acheson and Dulles," *World Politics* (October 1972); reprinted in Chittick, *The Analysis of Foreign Policy Outputs* (Boston: Charles Merrill, 1975).

40. Swartley, *Covenant of Peace*, 76; Swartley supports this theme throughout the New Testament.

41. *Just Peacemaking: New Paradigm*, 186

42. See http://twofuturesproject.org.

43. N. T. Wright, *Jesus and the Victory of God* (Minneapolis: Fortress, 1996), 297–300; and Matthew 18:15–20.
44. See "How to Form a Church Peacemaker Group" at www.justpeacemaking .org.
45. Larry L. Rasmussen, *Moral Fragments and Moral Community* (Minneapolis: Augsburg Fortress, 1993), 128, 162, 166. See also Jeffrey Stout, *Blessed Are the Organized* (Princeton: Princeton University Press, 2010).
46. For example, Jonathan Haidt, "The Emotional Dog and Its Rational Tail: A Social Intuitionist Approach to Moral Judgment," *Psychological Review* 108, no. 4 (2001), 825 et passim.

Chapter 12: Conclusion

1. Charles Taylor, *A Secular Age* (Cambridge, MA: Harvard University Press, 2007), 126–27.
2. Ibid., 635, 639.
3. Walter Wink, *When the Powers Fall: Reconciliation in the Healing of Nations* (Minneapolis: Fortress, 1998).
4. Taylor, *Secular Age,* 78–79 and 378.
5. Ibid., 81, 275–80, 305, 640.
6. Glen Stassen and David Gushee, *Kingdom Ethics: Following Jesus in Contemporary Ethics* (Downers Grove, IL: InterVarsity, 2003); Glen Stassen, *Living the Sermon on the Mount: A Practical Hope for Grace and Deliverance* (San Francisco: Jossey-Bass, 2006).
7. Stassen and Gushee, *Kingdom Ethics*, 236.

Index